INDEPENDENT
BIMONTHLY
LITERARY
MAGAZINE

REVISTA
LITERÁRIA
INDEPENDENTE
BIMENSAL

ADELAIDE
Independent Bimonthly Literary Magazine
Revista Literária Independente Bimensal
Year III, Number 11, January 2018
Ano III, Número 11, janeiro de 2018

ISBN-13: 978-0-9996451-6-1
ISBN-10: 0-9996451-6-1

Adelaide Literary Magazine is an independent international bimonthly publication, based in New York and Lisbon. Founded by Stevan V. Nikolic and Adelaide Franco Nikolic in 2015, the magazine's aim is to publish quality poetry, fiction, nonfiction, artwork, and photography, as well as interviews, articles, and book reviews, written in English and Portuguese. We seek to publish outstanding literary fiction, nonfiction, and poetry, and to promote the writers we publish, helping both new, emerging, and established authors reach a wider literary audience. We publish print and digital editions of our magazine six times a year, in September, November, January, March, May, and July. Online edition is updated continuously. There are no charges for reading the magazine online.

A Revista Literária Adelaide é uma publicação bimensal internacional e independente, localizada em Nova Iorque e Lisboa. Fundada por Stevan V. Nikolic e Adelaide Franco Nikolic em 2015, o objectivo da revista é publicar poesia, ficção, não-ficção, arte e fotografia de qualidade assim como entrevistas, artigos e críticas literárias, escritas em inglês e português. Pretendemos publicar ficção, não-ficção e poesia excepcionais assim como promover os escritores que publicamos, ajudando os autores novos e emergentes a atingir uma audiência literária mais vasta. Publicamos edições impressas e digitais da nossa revista seis vezes por ano: em setembro, novembro, janeiro, março, maio e julho. A edição online é actualizada regularmente. Não há qualquer custo associado à leitura da revista online.

(http://adelaidemagazine.org)

Published by: Adelaide Books, New York
e-mail: info@adelaidebooks.org
phone: (917) 727 8907

FOUNDERS / FUNDADORES
Stevan V. Nikolic & Adelaide Franco Nikolic

EDITOR IN CHIEF / EDITOR-CHEFE
Stevan V. Nikolic
editor@adelaidemagazine.org

MANAGING DIRECTOR / DIRECTORA EXECUTIVA
Adelaide Franco Nikolic

GRAPHIC & WEB DESIGN
Istina Group DBA

PORTUGUESE LANGUAGE EDITOR / EDITORA PORTUGUESA
Adelaide Franco Nikolic

BOOK REVIEWS
Heena Rathore
Jack Messenger
Ana Sofia Pereira
Scott Morris

CONTRIBUTING AUTHORS IN THIS ISSUE

Kenneth Vanderbeek, L.S. Engler, Richard Dokey, Anthony Saunders, Laura Solomon, Ruth Moors-D'Eredita, Amada Matei, Kathryn Merriam, Jessica Ciosek, Sevasti Iyama, Souzi Gharib, Brooke Reynolds, Helen Grochmal, Dustin Pickering, Abigayle Thompson, Michael Malloy, Brett Kaplan, Alan Kulatti, Daniel White, Susannah Luthi, John McLaughlin, Maureen McCafferty, Dana Hart, Ben Rosenthal, J. David Liss, Jeff Richards, Jean E. Verthein, Sasha Chinnaya, Vincent Yu, Tim Urban, John Tavares, Heide Arbitter, Taylor Lovullo, Maryetta Ackenbom, Jack Coey, Wally Swist, A. M. Palmer, Kat Kiefer-Newman, Desiree Jung, Anita Gorman, Thomas Larsen, Bill Vernon, Kimberly McElreath, Jeff Bakkensen, Tony Whedon, Frannie Gilbertson, Allen Long, Antonio Wong, John Ballantine Jr., George Freek, Gloria Monaghan, Holly Day, John O'Connor, Patrick Mahoney, Annelise Mozzoni, Debbie Richard, Edward Bonner, Donovan James, Richard Dinges, Tomas Sanchez Hidalgo, David Matthews, Victoria Randall, Robert Beveridge, Thom Young, Martin Altman, Lenny Lewis, Patrick Hurley, Nolo Segundo, Colin Dodds, Matt Barker, Irene Mitchell, Abigail Van Kirk, Lana Bella, Mark Prebilic, Kathy Coman, Roger Singer, Hannah Kludy, Tamara Williams, Noah Slowik, Eduardo Escalante, Mitchel Montagna, Ian Smith, Don McLeod, Daniel Senser, Emily Butler, Henry Reneau

CONTENTS / CONTEÚDOS

Front cover photo:

Doors of the Convent of Christ in Tomar, Portugal— by A.F. Nikolic

Interior illustrations— From the series "Postcards from Portugal" by A.F. Nikolic

Editor's Notes

Stevan V. Nikolic

NEW YEAR'S RESOLUTIONS

A RESOLVE

For Every Morning of the New Year

I will this day try to live a simple, sincere and serene life, repelling promptly every thought of discontent, anxiety, discouragement, impurity and self-seeking, cultivating cheerfulness, magnanimity, charity, and the habit of holy silence, exercising economy in expenditure, carefulness in conversation, diligence in appointed service, fidelity to every trust and a child-like trust in God.

From a Calendar by Bishop John H. Vincent.

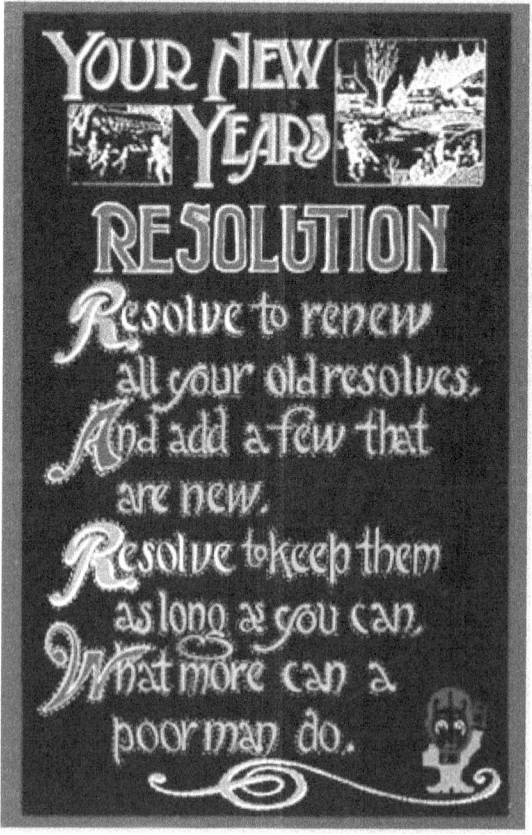

YOUR NEW YEARS RESOLUTION

Resolve to renew all your old resolves. And add a few that are new. Resolve to keep them as long as you can. What more can a poor man do.

THE SALVATION OF JOHN AMBERT
by Kenneth Vanderbeek

"We live in a challenged world, where the lion is devouring the lamb."

The Reverend John Ambert put his sermon down for a moment to reflect. Except for his candelabra, the parsonage was dark. However, a wash of red light outside was just beginning to expose the bedroom to a palpable clarity, as an image on film. He was straightening the alb sleeves and amice in his mirror when it came to him. Taking up his pen he crossed out the word challenged and substituted evil. Nodding with satisfaction he now attended to his face, an eyebrow pluck here, a bit more rouge there; and as he commenced reading the sermon in its entirety a third and final time, henceforth he paused only for sips of his chalice wine.

This holy man was quite fond of his attire, a reverence originating when he was a boy and his older sisters had often dressed him up as their minion; and this affection had only escalated into his fledgling adulthood. In the case of his vestments, although it was optional he wore the biretta (he liked how it contrasted with his blonde hair, making the latter seem to glow), and not until the height of summer would he dispense with the cappa, the 'black cape.' To his great pride he kept more than a dozen pectoral necklaces, the choice of which to wear on Sunday contingent on the sermon, the day's sacred significance, or his mood; and these hallowed crosses of the Trinity he augmented with gold collar buttons, cufflinks, and a large pearl broach. By sunrise his mirror reflected the image of a delicate though strikingly attractive man of God, the halo compliments of angels and the old candelabra — the crowning touch, as always, his great gem bracelets, which he shackled one each to a wrist and ankle.

The Reverend John Ambert was one of eight children (the sole male), the previous seven also products of a strenuous rhythm; and as the last (conceived just shy of his parents' decision of chastity), his vocation had naturally been prearranged. As soon as he'd reached an age at which his calling, of its most rudimentary earthly and spiritual duties, was understood, he'd accepted it in complete assent; indeed, with a burgeoning rigor. Gregarious from the start, in part due to the indulgence of his seven adoring siblings (they'd nicknamed him Card'nal for his innate abilities in leadership, organization, and devotion), as he grew, his gift for gab took increasingly the form of outspokenness in his repudiation of cliques, mediation of arguments, dispersal of bullies, and incessant pursuit of other Godly causes.

This distinguishing quality followed John Ambert into adulthood. And yet, though outwardly compassionate and affable, The Reverend John Ambert harbored an omnipresent fear that he might be perceived by some as unsuited to his calling, as if the sacred cloth gave the impression of its meek wearer rather as a pedestrian, or worse, a charlatan, his diminutive stature and high voice undermining his virtues in the public mind as untenable. To subvert impressions that he might be too fragile for his duties, or even reticent, he fashioned a conspicuous persona of spiritual strength and consummate moral conviction, both stemming from an intricate comprehension of the human condition in its historic and present implications (he was a student of religious history, current affairs, public opinion, and above all, knowledge), all the while maintaining a robust schedule — which he did his best to nudge in favor of community service over private penance. He was proud of his early record as a virtuous and enlightened Child of God, which he prayed manifested in his every gesture and word, especially during his Sunday sermons. Of the divine significance of the number three, he delivered his sermons three times, at seven, nine, and eleven o'clock. Lately his homilies, as that to which he had made the last edit, embraced a particular devotion to tolerance.

"It is lamentable to think," soon he would proclaim to the usual hundreds in attendance at his services, "that here and now, in this, the twenty-first century following the death and resurrection of our Lord and Savior — this awesome time of advanced reason and knowledge, hallmarks of mankind's greatness — it is lamentable to think that marriage is still universally proclaimed the sole privilege of a man and a woman, God's only 'sacred' union; further, that it is still universally believed heterosexuality is the one and only 'true' province of a legitimate soul and a legitimate body. Yet consider this: Once it was also a foregone conclusion that epileptics were possessed by the devil, that African Americans were perceived as nothing more than beasts of burden, and that women were denied the vote on the basis that men considered them inferior decision-makers. My people, know that it is but a matter of time before the misconceptions about homosexuals shall too be vanquished, that under man's laws they will enjoy the same privileges as heterosexuals, as they already do under God's...." The other reason The Reverend John Ambert held three services was because, with each, memory and chatter increased exponentially as his awakening parishioners began exporting his messages well beyond the confines of their one-hour seclusion, the net effect being that soon their passion (if not always aligned with The Reverend's) mimicked, if not surpassed, his own.

The Reverend John Ambert was a vigorously intelligent man; at university he had graduated in the top twenty-five of his class and been mentioned by many among the faculty as a bona fide

candidate for the Fulbright Scholarship to continue his religious studies abroad; at seminary he had graduated number one; and so far, during his three years behind the pulpit, he had not once wanted for a sermon topic. As a product of the new century, this time of recharged sexual promiscuity and intense political partisanship, he was especially mindful of the everyday concerns, stresses, and temptations of his flock, and strove to address these with language that was transparent, empathetic, and useful. Always straining for balance between instruction and enlightenment, he nevertheless believed that he had already proved an adeptness at distilling right from wrong on many subjects, traditional and modern, from the most basic calls to faith, hope, marriage, parenting, peace, soulful wellbeing, and wisdom, to humble directives on latter-day topics ranging from anger management to workplace harmony. He would intone: "Yea, though the righteous walk in light, the brightest light shines on the sinners." Above all he felt at ease navigating that most difficult of topics, sin — from the seven deadly sins, envy, gluttony, greed, lust, pride, sloth, and wrath, to those he deemed prevailing sins, foremost among them trespassing, violence, and intolerance. He loved his flock, whom he called his Folks. From his pastoral apex in the old cathedral he had already admonished them to supplement their faith with good works. Though, of course, this notion of salvation was controversial, he defended it steadfastly, his rationale being that good works are faith's "checks and balances"; that is, that good works (manifestation of the mind) must flow in tandem with faith (manifestation of the heart). "It is written that we who uphold Jesus Christ as our Savior are already forgiven of our sins through faith alone," he asserted. "Yet such absolution is given only for our original sin, that which is innate in all human beings since the time of the Garden. Mortal sin — adultery, murder, rape, and the like — because it can only be forgiven at Judgment, and because forgiveness then is not even guaranteed, must therefore be vanquished during our mortal lives. Thus good works, like faith, *naturally* stem from Christ's teachings, which commend moral exactitude."

Not surprisingly, this declaration caused a stir. The local, and also the regional and national, publications of the Church had immediately featured intensive commentary, the prevailing message being condemnatory, of course, with cries among clergy and lay alike for punishment and censure. Yet instead of calling a summary inquisition the hierarchy laid low, that the furor might get 'swept under the rug'; the elders chastised the young pastor by letter only, in the hope that it would make him come to his senses. Meanwhile, among The Reverend Ambert's parishioners reactions came in somewhat mixed, from whispered repudiation (and even acceptance), to underground debates in an ardent quest to imagine what influences or impulses had propelled him to such "heretical nonsense" (or "brilliant insight"), to vociferous rage (primarily among the most conservative), which ignited, in the least, confrontation and demands for full clarification. In one particularly chiding affront (an email), a parishioner may have spoken for all detractors: "Shame on you, Rev. Ambert, in your haughty attempt to pin salvation on 'good works!' That, sir, is a sin, your sin! For faith, as every true believer knows, is the holy legacy of our Savior's sacrifice — by His death on the cross He bore our sins and forgave them! On the contrary, sir, this is not our work to do; Christ did it for us, that we shall be saved through our faith in Him!" Even so, against a heightened rigorous scrutiny by his elders The Reverend John Ambert remained resolute in his conviction, and to reinforce it, in subsequent services cited examples of what, to his insistence, constituted a "litany" of good works toward salvation: "...in order to safeguard against adultery one must not only resist temptation but also minister to those who feel helpless in its clutches; in order to safeguard against greed one must demonstrate charity; in order to safeguard against intolerance one must purge the self and act for the welfare of others unconditionally...." That Monday, he'd received another letter.

In truth, John Ambert had come to these assertions from a longstanding melancholy in which burned a seemingly inextinguishable, and, he was certain, unpardonable guilt.

As has already been established, John Ambert was a gifted leader. Among all the boys in the neighborhood, it had been he who had typically headed up the school's social activities; he who had organized the summer baseball games at the park and the winter hockey matches at the frozen pond outside of town; it had been he, small in size yet great in stature, to whom the others had turned for advice in every kind of conflict, from minor squabbles to territorial disputes. Throughout his youth John Ambert had worked, with unshakable conviction, to shape his character such that it would be distinguished by an adherence to the purest constraints of objectivity, fellowship, and fairness; in a phrase, to project himself as an eminently reliable and honorable servant. Yet this effort had not been easy, given his home environment. His mother, Dot Ambert, was woefully demur and a consummate worrier; she especially worried about her tormented son, and had become so convinced that it was only a matter of time until she'd worried herself to death over him that, mid-marriage to her husband, on the basis that she felt she'd not the strength of will any longer to co-manage them, she'd relinquished all her rightful powers of parenting to him. Jack Ambert, a mill worker, had passed his perfectionism to his son, and was also prone to moods and provocation. Strapped in youth with a stutter he'd never been able to shake, throughout his life he'd forsaken many opportunities for fulfillment for fear of ridicule or reproach. In John, he'd hoped to behold a reflection of himself as he could have been: a pillar of his vocation. Instead, in his only son he beheld little more than a dreamer and weakling — "The Runt," he called John — and altogether dismissed the boy for his brooding, pensiveness, and, predominantly, what the father ultimately decried as an ardent femininity.

Naturally, young John Ambert had withdrawn. For solace he'd immersed himself in books: fantasies and classic novels at first, but soon also the works of the modern philosophers, particularly of the rationalists Immanuel Kant, for his belief that reason is the source of morality, and Arthur Schopenhauer, for his belief that individual morality arises from "collective consciousness"; and too, he devoured the works of the Christian philosophers, Reinhold Niebuhr and others. All this absorption of so much critical thinking, in addition to strengthening his intellect, also fortified his will; the pivotal consequences being the rise of an effusive love of self (born of a burgeoning pity of his stoic father) and resolute independence (born of pity in kind of his passive mother). One day, he was twelve, in response to a particularly upbraiding remark in which the father had essentially pegged the "dreamer" as an aimless good-for-nothing, John Ambert had retaliated by saying: "At least my life is whole, the result of a healthy philosophical foundation!" At the time, the father had been half-asleep in his favorite chair, the plush sofa kind, a hand-me-down from his mother, when slowly he'd stood up. "A healthy philosophical foundation, you say," he'd yawned. He'd continued, "Is this what you mean?", and slapped John Ambert so forcefully that the blow had knocked him to the floor. As usual, by the time the boy had been able to rise again, the father had disappeared.

These were the principal laws John Ambert had learned in youth: the law of wrongdoing and consequence; and the law of dominance, one over another.

Years before the comfort of books, whenever the father had chastised or clouted John Ambert he had afterward immediately run for sanctuary to one of his sisters' rooms, where the sweet voice of accordance and the color pink had salved his wounds. Yet a time had eventually come when, instead of scabbing and healing, those injuries had festered like rancid fruit, as bruised as his whole.

As the interests of his older sisters had transitioned to school events, sleepovers, and boys, John Ambert had redirected his interminable itch for solace to other male peers who were troubled. The core group numbered four: two brothers he'd met at the frozen pond when, happening by, they had invited themselves into the skate, the third befriended with a pack of cigarettes John Ambert had stolen from the pharmacy on a dare; the last a cousin, who was also a black sheep. One day, after the skate and a brief diversion to town to fetch jerky and pop, sauntering back to the woods in the common direction of their respective homes the five boys had encountered another. He was sitting against a tree, humped over a little, a cane at his side, his knees propped almost to the eyes, a large jar of something embraced by both arms like a favorite stuffed animal. They asked the sprite who he was. "Pea-nut But-ter," the boy grinned. The smoker leaned in. "What's your last name? And Jelly?" Hackles fogged the frozen air. The boy hadn't a chance to retreat; the four were upon him in a wisp and stretching him like canvas.

In the crystalline solstice grief gasped from him like smoke rings branding the frozen air. Until then an awful sense of wonder of the yearling's struggle had kept John Ambert locked in his tracks, for he understood not why the struggle felt empowering. "What are you doing, Card'nal? Get over here and help!" one of them cried. A dead ash leaf lilted then on the lad's forehead. Then another. And another. Upon each landing, a teardrop made its way down the peanut-butter mask the four were making of the face. When they'd finished, they grabbed John Ambert and threw him into the sauce, whereupon he tasted a mingled sweat of contempt and charity before being thrown back again. As he tumbled away, he made himself believe he could not see the abused as they tore away his pants, savages reeling in vile pleasure, their sticks already aimed.

Ostensibly, John Ambert's family was devastated by the brutal assault. To Jack Ambert especially, his son's despicable turn more than confirmed his aberrant sexuality. Often now, with his thoughts of the girly boy, the father would shudder: He'd look in a mirror and see his son. No longer could he golf with the guys that he'd not suddenly be consumed by a feeling of self-loathing, as though he were walking the course in a waddle and conversing in lisps; no longer could he go anywhere in the world that he did not sense a thousand condescending stares. Facing all his friends and acquaintances was an ominous labor. What could he now say about John Ambert: "Still, I am proud"? No. He hated his son.

The father's first reaction to the brutal attack, of course, had been to slap the boy and stomp away. But Jack Ambert gleaned no satisfaction from this act — though he knew that nothing about his son could provide hope of a full reconciliation: The boy's fall had opened a wound that neither time, nor mindfulness, nor God Himself could ever heal. Dot Ambert felt no less devastated. She, who'd always listened intently to her son's soliloquies on good versus evil, conviction versus doubt, fairness, egalitarianism, the Rights of Man..., now she could only hear, whenever she tried to recall the righteousness in him, the police report of his terrible wrong. For months she could not attend church: not just because of her lost faith, but also because of the judgment of peers. Often now she would rub her abdomen and weep, wondering how she could have delivered such an anomaly into the world. Now, of all her children, it was he who constituted the whole of her worries, this "lost sheep!" And as for John Ambert's sisters, his sanctuary, they had likewise been transformed: pink no more but coal-black; their faces pressed now in perpetual pouts and sneers, their tongues screwed in eternal silence. One of them (probably not coincidentally, the eldest) crystallized the feelings of all when she said, "Shame brother, for far have you strayed from the world you imagined!"

John Ambert was sent to a juvenile detention center for rehabilitation. Test results deemed him "cognizant of the difference between right and wrong," so drugs were dismissed in favor of counseling. His assigned advocate, Dr. Kurt Neuer, an ancient man with a white Socratic beard and pensive blue eyes, had studied under Carl Jung, and was thus well-versed in the Swiss psychiatrist's theories on individuation (the psychological process of integrating opposites, such as consciousness with unconsciousness), as well as the master's contention that, because God's Word instructs man how to live, all ideas about behavior must be examined within the context of religion. Jung wrote: "Religions are systems of healing for psychic illness. That is why patients force the psychotherapist

into the role of a priest, and expect and demand of him that he shall free them from their distress. That is why we psychotherapists must occupy ourselves with problems which, strictly speaking, belong to the theologian." Dr. Neuer knew much about religion, and also about angst and rebellion and light and lightness. He'd spent nearly the whole of World War II as a prisoner at the German concentration camp Ravensbrück, to which originally only his mother and both sisters had been herded of the contention they were gypsies, but to which he'd soon followed as their "abettor."

His first months (he never knew how many; he'd lost count after six hundred eighty seven days) he'd somehow managed to conquer death in a pit not much bigger than himself, under an iron cover in which was a hole for light no larger than a pfennig, and on rations consisting, in part, of his feces. In the whole, nearly four years (fall 1941 to liberation in April 1945), he'd tell you that he'd

survived from "love of the enemy," hope, and luck, in that order. Upon meeting John Ambert, the first thing he said was:

"Do zu know, in German Ambert means a bright, shining light?"

The boy nodded that he did not.

"Ja! And do zu know also, in German Neuer means new?"

Again the boy nodded that he did not.

"Well, together," said Dr. Neuer, placing an arm gently around his underling's shoulder, "'ve shall give to a certain bright, shining light a new beginning. Ja? Ja!"

In the beginning, Dr. Neuer met with the boy first thing each morning after breakfast (after, in order to advance the likelihood that his patient would be alert), then again before lunch, and finally at seven o'clock, two hours before compulsory time for the wards to retire. Each of the first two sessions convened one hour; the last, two hours, the second hour reserved for respite, casual conversation (or none, if the boy preferred), and a choice of milk or fruit smoothie plus a generous

slice of Bienenstich (yeast dough with Bavarian cream filling, topped with almonds and honey), a favorite of the doctor's from the old country. Except for when he was in the midst of creating a new poem (often he visited the facility's outlying woods for reflection and contemplation), John Ambert rarely chose silence over dialogue during the evening session, so taken had he been by Dr. Neuer's probity and approbation, that these qualities had all but instantly freed him of feelings of apathy and superiority. Nor would Kurt Neuer ever ask John Ambert why he had been an accessory to the rape of the disabled boy; the good doctor refused to juggle questions or assessments of "predispositions" — genetic and environmental factors that so far had shaped the boy and may thus have conspired in directing his fateful action. Rather, Dr. Neuer concentrated wholly on availing the boy to a world of acceptance and possibility, and poured his interest fully in John Ambert as he had been presented: possessed by shame and trepidation.

"Well, then," continued the doctor, "'ve ist here today because of vhat is confirmed by za report as a terrible act, an unfortunate act. Correct?"

"Yes, sir," said John Ambert.

"Please, my boy, dispense viz za zir!" waved the doctor. "Call me Dr. Neuer; ur better, Kurt!"

The boy shrugged.

"Ha, ist bashful! Vy — because I am za zo-called authority figure here?"

John Ambert nodded.

Dr. Neuer rose from his chair. "Listen my goot young acolyte, do not be trapped by impressions! Neither zu, nor I, ist more important — more zacred — zan za other. Oonderstand? Ve ist both human, ja? Made of za zame substances, flesh und blood. Am I correct, Mr. Ambert?"

"John," whispered the boy.

"Ha, ha, ha!" laughed the doctor, "zu ist learning. Ist goot!"

John Ambert did not acknowledge the praise; his eyes had filled like beakers to their rims: blue sapphires in acid. He had no idea, anyway, what the answer was to the doctor's question, "Ve ist both human, ja?": was not sure, comparing himself to this man of extraordinary courage and wisdom, whether his own substance, tainted as it was, had any remaining value.

Yet as the doctor's inquisitions formed a foundation, their meetings progressed.

Dr. Neuer's uppermost objective was to help his young acolyte "feel in deference to zo much thinking." Along with this call, he had the boy ultimately reciting in full the "Moral Alphabet" and putting to task its A to Z tenets in emotive daily exercises.

One day the good doctor asked John Ambert to say the first thing that came to mind. Not surprisingly the boy shrugged. "Don't think!" said Dr. Neuer. "Let it come." He snapped his fingers. "The world is flat," said John Ambert. "Goot! Now, go deeper!" Before the doctor had finished the boy sputtered, "How was Jesus like a tree?"

"Yes, now ve ist getting zumvhere!" said Dr. Neuer. Naturally he asked his young acolyte to elaborate.

John Ambert proceeded to describe how strong his Savior was, like an oak: how true, like the best hardwoods. How, in pathos tinged by conviction,

like the sagging yet sturdy branches of the willow, He had born all the sins of man. "And yet, how human He was," John Ambert added, "such that He, too, felt doubt, and abandonment. —How indignant He was toward the money-lenders in the Temple!"

"Ah, but remember," replied the good doctor, "that oon personalizing those emotions Jesus absorbed our sins, that upon His death und resurrection they would be vanquished in His name und through our enduring faith in Him."

"And yet," interjected the boy, "could it be that on account of His exclamation on the cross, 'My God, my God, why have you forsaken me?', that Jesus actually was no more human than we?"

"Consummate," corrected Dr. Neuer, "that by such searing separateness from His father, Jesus, in his last earthly moment, was able to finish His good works — and ours."

For the remainder of their time together, some three months, the mentor and the protégé would rekindle this dialogue often, and, indeed, afterward sustained it for many years....

Initially after his release from the detention center, the sunny days of the world seemed brighter to John Ambert and the overcast not so much. Humanity's social commerce seemed invigorated and the march of days quickened. He felt as he might if he were in love.

Within the month, as he celebrated his thirteenth birthday the wish he made was that he might embark on an extracurricular mission of aid to the hopeless, wayward, and misbegotten. As another three years must pass before he'd get his driver's permit, his approving parents served then as his principal means of transport to and from the mission destinations (and, of course, whenever those destinations happened to be removed enough from the greater traffic, he'd ride his bike).

At the start of his chosen work, in an effort to pace himself, as well as to abide the necessity of maintaining good grades at school, John Ambert served only the town's foster home. Yet as it seemed increasingly logical that this calling would not undermine the academic, starting the second quarter following his discharge from the juvenile detention center he further availed his Samaritan services at the food pantry and an elderly care center. By the end of his first year of rehabilitation, having hardly finished his first month in high school, he was also aiding the homeless in skid row and assisting in isolating the protest blockades at the abortion clinic.

He went on to serve the local chapters of Action Against Hunger and the Alzheimer's and AIDS Foundations, served with distinction at the American Red Cross, helped in fundraising for the Catholic Charities, comforted children at McDonald's House, marched with the Salvation Army and chanted with the mothers of MADD; and in his freshman summer volunteered at the Christian Care Foundation for Children with Disabilities, in his sophomore helped build houses for Habitat for Humanity, in his junior sat with the condemned at the maximum-security prison upstate, and in his senior year comforted PTSD vets of foreign wars. In college, he continued tirelessly to serve in these causes and added several more obligations, including as an assistant scout leader for the Boy Scouts, volunteer at the local Boys Club, and correspondent for Children of Peace International.

Still, the guilt of his youthful transgression felt unpardonable.

Now, with the arrival of the first Sunday of Lent, The Reverend John Ambert turned his attention again to the subject of tolerance, placing in the series of homilies he would deliver for the next six weeks especial focus on the sins of the high priests and Pharisees, principal among those sins, envy; culminating in a meditation on salvation. More than ever he poured himself into this work, the work of tolerance, which, nearly to the last, his Folks received in awe and with deep ardor, their passion more than ever aligning with, even surpassing, his. Then Easter arrived, and the culmination.

"My Folks, dear Folks," he said. "On this hallowed day of our Savior's death, His glorious resurrection, and the promise of death no more, let us continue to reflect on tolerance, which is our acceptance, nay, love, of all human beings. Love thy neighbor, as thyself." A mellifluous hush, like the Holy Spirit whispering, rose through the cathedral. "My Folks, the burdens of our earthly life are many. So many to conquer; too many perhaps to overcome." He paused. "O guilt. Remorse. O hope! Do you still spring eternal? Friends, bear

tolerance for your enemy, for he is also you; forgive the sins of the sinner, for he is also you." He turned to cough. "Excuse me, that was just the devil. He's had enough!" Tempered laughter made its way to the altar. He coughed again. "Where was I?" He

pulled a handkerchief from beneath the alb and patted his forehead. "Oh, yes, tolerance. Doubt not, nor chide, nor dismiss thyself," he said, "for to do so is doubly to forsake your brothers and sisters. Rather, love thyself — and the world — without bias or preconception. For just as a vase broken is not the end of the world, so also is it true with every mistake." This is what The Reverend John Ambert said on Easter. Afterward, as his parishioners filed out, he said goodbye, and wished each in turn everlasting wellness and contentment. Then, nonchalantly, he made his way back through the cathedral and out, into the garden....

First thing Monday morning he was standing at his mirror straightening the alb sleeves and amice, as he had just twenty-four hours before. Today, though, he also wore a sturdy belt. Next he applied a pectoral necklace, which he'd selected based on his early mood of tranquility, then the cappa, and finally his great gem bracelets, one each which he shackled to a wrist and ankle. Then, as always in culmination, he attended to his face, the usual dab of rouge here, an eyebrow pluck there. Extinguishing the flames of his candelabra, he entered the world. First stop was the Post Office, where he dropped off a bucket of letters to his family, his Folks, and to Dr. Neuer.

This morning he had forsaken the breaking of bread in favor of taking a walk to the old beloved woods of his youth. There, well beyond the pond, in the darkest part, at a dried-up creek bed at the foot of a sandstone precipice, he picked up a stick. For a moment he examined it closely, turning it over and over in his hands, once or twice even stabbing the air with it, and then suddenly dropped it for a more earnest pursuit of a section of ground that might be particularly barren of life, a small plot of dirt untouched by the light above. As soon as he'd found it he put his hands to work tracing two lines in the dirt, one perpendicular to and intersecting the other, and when he'd finished thus, reached into his belt for the hammer. Then he lay down, with his shoulders at the intersecting point.

He sat up, but only briefly. This for the purpose of removing his shoes and then driving the first of two spikes extracted from them into his stacked feet. Then he lay down again, and turning, as best he could repeated the procedure by driving the second spike into his left hand.

If it weren't for the fact that he hadn't the luxury of being able to hammer into the free hand, he would have packed a third spike. But for this he forgave himself.

About the Author:

Kenneth Vanderbeek studied at the Bennington Writers Workshop, Bennington College, Vermont. His literary work has most recently appeared in the Canadian journal, The Nashwaak Review (essay); and in the U.S. journals, Kudzu House Quarterly and The Bryant Literary Review (fiction). He is currently at work on a novel and short story collection. Vanderbeek writes, and resides, in St. Louis, Missouri.

GRAVEDIGGER

by L. S. Engler

Grayson Miller lived a quiet life, haunted by a single summer that lingered in his memory like a ghost. He never tried to escape it, exorcise it, or shove it away, finding a cold comfort that it was there. A reminder of when he could feel something other than the dull ache of longing. It was the summer he started digging graves for the church, exchanging his hard labor for a small place to stay, since he had nowhere else to go. It was the summer he fell in love for the first time, the only time. Rebecca, from English class, from Calculus, came to visit him while he worked, perched on a headstone as he cleaved into the soil, creating the little pockets where people would hide their loved ones, their memories, their secrets. He would dig to the rhythm of her voice as she told him stories of life, postulating on how it would all end there in the deep pits he dug with a single shovel. He liked having her company while sweat rolled down his back in the heat. He liked the way she laughed at her own jokes and the way dirt clung to his fingernails despite his gloves. The way the scent of earth clung to him like a shroud.

Sometimes, late at night, Rebecca would stay with him in the groundskeeper's cabin at the far end of the cemetery, where they would watch recorded tapes of old horror movies. More often than not, he'd fall asleep in her arms, too worn from work to keep his eyes open. She usually slipped away before morning, but the smell of her would linger in the small shack, lavender soap, deep cleaning shampoo, something different to sustain him before he returned to his world of grass and loam.

Autumn swept in with cool showers and burning leaves, nature beginning her slow march toward winter death, and Rebecca's thoughts turned more macabre. She asked how he could stand doing something so morbid, day in and day out, and he thought about it while shoveling out a resting place for another unknown corpse. Eventually, he gave a simple, sincere answer, the only one he could think of.

"It makes me feel alive," he said without a touch of irony.

Rebecca tilted her head, chestnut hair tumbling away from her shoulders.

"Would you feel so alive if you were digging that grave for me?" she asked.

He couldn't respond, unable to imagine it, but he found his answer once winter set in. The ground was frozen solid, his movements limited by layers of clothing for warmth, a different beast than digging in the summertime. He hadn't dug a grave for anyone he'd known before, much less someone he had loved as much as Rebecca. He didn't feel alive that day, and he wished he could have told her so. Maybe it would have made a difference. Maybe she'd still be sitting on top of the headstones, babbling, instead of lying six feet under them, silent.

The warmth of summer crept back into his soul when the soil thawed and began to smell of rich decay again. Just as life returned to the trees and the grass and the flowers planted by dutiful mourners, it returned to Grayson. He started his day with a visit to Rebecca's grave, picturing her perched on the headstones, chestnut hair tumbling away from her shoulders. He'd tell her about the movie he watched the night before, imagining himself in her arms as sleep overtook him. Then he'd hoist his shovel over his broad shoulders and get back to work, digging graves for the dead to help himself feel more alive, every day of his long, quiet life.

About the Author:

L.S. Engler writes from outside of Chicago, though she grew up chasing dragons in the woods of Michigan. She is the editor of the World Unknown Review, as well as the author of many short stories and a few novels, most recently the Slayer Saga, a trilogy about zombies. Her work has most recently appeared in To the Victor, Ghost Stories, and the Saturday Evening Post

HAVE YOU READ THE BROTHERS KARAMAZOV?

By Richard Dokey

Thunder boomed behind the blackened sky. Arthur Hollenbeck ducked into the tiny pastry shop. He shook his overcoat. A few drops of water ran down behind the collar of his shirt. The water traveled to a spot between his shoulder blades.

His cell phone rang.

"Mr. Hollenbeck," the voice of his secretary said, "the Feathercraft contract is complete and ready for your review."

"All right, Katherine," he said. "Thank you. I was looking at the Beckler property over here and got caught in the rain. It's really coming down. I'm in a small pastry shop on West 24th. I'll have a cup of coffee and wait it out a bit. I'll be in directly. How about the Crown offer? Any word?"

"I've scheduled an appointment for you with Mr. Crown for three o'clock."

"Good girl. What would I ever do without you?"

"Well, about that raise, then?"

He laughed. He enjoyed Katherine. She was a kidder. He actually did not know what he would do without her. She organized his entire day into an efficient schedule.

"I'll think about it. That is, when I get warm enough," he teased.

He sat under a window and turned his back to the rain.

He did not enjoy using the cell phone. There was something ephemeral about speaking into a flat, black box one could carry in a shirt pocket, talking anytime, anywhere with anyone who wanted to talk. He glanced about the shop.

It was a nondescript pastry shop like the shops he had known when he was young: cubby holes with wooden tables and chairs one sees for sale at the edge of sidewalks, a glass case with trays of doughnuts and sweet rolls. Someone in a soiled apron might make a toasted cheese or tuna sandwich. On top of the case were plates of pie and cake, covered by glass domes, in the center of which were round, black knobs. Always there was a dome of day-old pastry and a sign that read "two-for-one." The selections were not choreographed in polished metal frames against the back wall, but written on powdered chalk boards next to the case. Like this shop, the coffee table was always at the far side of the room. His shops used shiny aluminum urns to dispense coffee from beneath black spigots. A fruit jar held tips. This shop had a table with white porcelain mugs and a hot plate, upon which sat steaming Pyrex pots. One of the pots had orange print.

Arthur Hollenbeck was amused at this wave of nostalgia. He tipped the girl who brought him a mug of coffee.

The shop contained an odd assortment of patrons, nondescript people, a hodge-podge, quite unlike the people at Starbucks or Peets or Panera, where he took pleasure in seeing himself reflected. These people were from cramped apartments nearby, from kitchens and shops, men in coveralls, others in plaid shirts and baseball caps, women in print dresses or wrinkled pants, who looked as if they should be on the line in a cannery. Several students with backpacks thumbed messages, all the while managing to talk with anyone who managed to talk.

Next to the coffee table, a young woman sat alone reading. She was a student. That is, he assumed that she was a student, but in a kind of out-of-date way. A brown leather briefcase rested beside her on the floor. She was plain. Yet, when he looked more closely, he might say that she was pretty, in that vague way something is pretty when you first encounter it and before it becomes worn and common. His anxiety about escaping the storm was palliated by her odd intensity. It was pleasant to sit in a nondescript café sipping burnt coffee with people he would never see again and would not recognize if he did.

Perhaps it was the briefcase. It had a fat belly and a clasp beneath the handle. His father had been a real estate broker and had owned such a briefcase. Sometimes, when he wasn't in a hurry for work, his father permitted him to lift the briefcase. It was a heavy briefcase, filled, he had always believed, with important papers. He was proud to be able to lift it and to hear what his father would say because he had succeeded in taking it all the way to the front door. His father was dead. His mother was in a care facility on the other side of the city. He saw his mother when he could.

He remembered the old house. He lay under the great oak in the back yard, looking up through the ragged leaves at clouds building in a blue sky. It seemed a moment ago. It was millions of moments, but all the moments were now. Child hood was a moment, hidden beneath moments, when feeling came as the wind came, or the rain came against the cedar fence beyond the great oak, or the shadows of leaves at evening came, lingering upon his window pane.

He shook his head. The coffee mug was empty. He decided for a refill and made his way across the room. The young woman had the book up. He could not see her face. He saw the name on the book.

"Excuse me," he said, standing above her. "Isn't that Russian?"

She lowered the book. Her eyes were marvelous. They were a translucent green, very bright and large.

"Yes," she said. "It's not in Russian, of course. It's just Russian."

"Yes," he said. bending closer. "I recognize the name."

"Oh, have you read The Brothers Karamazov?"

"No, no," he said. "Not that one. I don't believe I ever did, I should say. When I was in school, there was something by that writer, though."

"Dostoevsky."

"Yes. Is that how you say it?"

"Feodor Dostoevsky."

"That's the one. It's difficult to pronounce those names. When you're not Russian, that is. Is it interesting?"

"Oh, yes," she said. "Very."

"What's it about?"

"Evil," she said. "And good."

"Well, I guess that about covers it all, wouldn't you say?" He laughed.

She looked at him out of the corner of those enormous green eyes.

"So, you're a student," he said. There could be no other reason to read such a book.

"Yes. The University."

"Ah," he said. "And what are you studying?"

"Nothing in particular," she said. "That's the problem. I'm interested in so many things. It's very hard for me to choose anything. I wish I didn't have to choose, but I know I have to, no matter what."

"That's true," he said. "It's hard to make up one's mind, when one is young. I remember trying to make up my mind."

"What did you choose?"

"Come to think about it, I believe it chose me. My father was a broker. I went in for business. I was a business major. I stayed on for the MBA."

"Oh, how nice," she said. "It must be good knowing what to choose when you start out."

"Yes. I always thought I was fortunate," he said. "And, wouldn't you know, I am busier now than ever I was in school. Perhaps that's just part of being an adult. You're right, though. There are more things these days, so many more for anyone to deal with. These new technologies. It makes one wonder, doesn't it?"

"About what?"

"About choosing anything properly. All these distractions. That's what I call them anyway." He nodded toward a nearby table, where other students thumbed their machines.

"Oh, yes," she said. "Yes. I don't know enough about anything to choose something wisely. Not really, I mean. I know I must choose. But, then, won't I have to go ahead and do that something? How can you choose something and be sure? That is, if you can't know what you're getting into until you've gotten into it. It is confusing. It's like my sister. She got married, and then she got unmarried. She chose someone because she thought she knew him, and then she didn't know him, and she got divorced because she said that then she knew him. It's all so mixed up. One is as good as the other, don't you see? And you don't know if what you've chosen is good until after you've chosen it. And there you are." She blushed. "Listen to me," she said. "I'm sorry."

"No, no," he replied. "That's fine. That's all perfectly natural. It's true about everyone, particularly when one is so young. We all start out confused."

She looked across the room. "I have no idea what to become," she said softly. "But everyone has to become something, I suppose, to live, I mean. But how can I make a commitment to something when I don't know if that something is good for me to commit myself to or not? Am I making any sense at all?"

"Perfect sense," he said. "When I was your age, I wasn't committed either."

"But you finished your MBA."

"Well, yes, of course I did, but then it never occurred to me about any commitment. I just wanted to stop wasting my time and get on with it."

"Well, anyway, you knew how to choose something."

"I didn't know."

"You chose business."

"It seemed the proper thing to do."

"And it was, then."

"Yes. Certainly it was."

"Then you were lucky. You chose something and didn't know if that something was right for you, but then it was. I can't imagine myself being lucky that way. I'm terrible with luck. If I don't know what I'm doing, it's always a mess."

"You'll find the right thing," he said. "For you, that is. That's what school is for."

"I suppose it is," she said, a bit downcast.

"Look here," he said. "You'll go off and be quite successful. I'm sure of it. You've got sense. And you'll have a fine family too." He smiled. "You seem too intelligent not to be successful."

She blushed again. "Oh, I don't know about any of that," she said. "I don't think of myself that way."

"But here you are in school," he said.

"Yes, certainly," she said. "But this something must be something that I truly must do. It has to be with people. I know at least that much."

"Isn't everything with people?"

"I suppose," she said. "But something truly with people, even if it's not important to anyone else and nobody knows anything about it but me. If it matters to me, if it truly matters, then that's what matters. I'll have chosen the right thing."

"I see," he said.

"Sounds silly, I suppose."

"No, not at all," he said. "There are many paths to success. If you do what matters to you, why wouldn't that be successful?"

"It would, then, wouldn't it?" she said.

"Of course it would. You're young. You have all of your life." He pointed at the book. "You like this, then?"

"Oh, yes," she brightened. "Very much. It's very deep and very complicated and emotional and thoroughly human. I'm lost in it. I don't think about anything else when I'm reading."

"And that's good?" he asked. "Being lost that way, I mean."

"Oh, yes," she said. "You have to be lost in it if you're going to understand anything. How else could someone read something?"

He nodded. "I don't know," he said. "I'm not much of a reader that way. I could never get into anything that wasn't real to me. To my life, I mean. Such things were required, of course, so I read them. They didn't seem to matter about anything that I had to do. Not really. They were so, well, Russian, and they went on forever, with lecture notes from the professor tacked on. And all you did at the end was to write a paper that nobody cared about anyway, most of all the professor. Then you forgot about it the next day."

"You sound like my roommate," she smiled. "She hates lit classes."

"I didn't hate them, of course," he said. "They just were so extraneous. If you know what I mean. I would think that would be even more so these days, when there's hardly enough time to turn around."

"It does feel like that sometimes," she sighed. "Maybe that's why I love books like this so much."

"I only meant, with so much one has to do and so many distractions, there's no time for being lost." He smiled.

"It must be nice, then, to be so successful," she said. "You've done exactly what you wanted to do."

He thought a moment.

"I think I am successful," he said, with some embarrassment. "I've met my goals, certainly."

"Oh, then there's that," she said. "How do I set goals when I'm not interested enough in anything to know where I'm going so I can set goals? I don't stay long enough with something to decide anything. I run around in all sorts of directions. Goals are like places on an itinerary to me. I can't get off anywhere because, well, where am I going? I don't want to be like my sister. So places just fly by."

He remembered how, as a young man just out of school, he had considered throwing a bag over his shoulder and tramping through France and Spain, not knowing where to stay, but staying whenever he got there.

"It's important to set goals," he said.

"I know it is," she said. "If I didn't want to get good at something, why else would I be in school?"

"Indeed," he said, smiling. "When one is young, it's natural, I think, to feel somewhat lost. It's a big world, but growing up is the only way we get on with it." He winked, tapping the book.

The mug was cold. He filled it with hot coffee. He wanted to sit down.

"Well," he smiled. "Then good luck to you. And happy being lost with the Karamazov brothers. I admire your ability to slog through and enjoy something required like that."

"Oh, it's not required," she said.

"It's not?" he said.

"No. I'm just reading it." She looked at him with those marvelous green eyes. "I love this book. But thank you anyway," she said. "You've been most kind and understanding. And I suppose I can't wish you more luck than you've already had." She grinned. "That might be unlucky. I've enjoyed talking to you."

"Me too," he said.

He returned to the table.

Outside, the rain pounded the striped awning. It struck the sidewalk, where it splashed in a sparkling rim. Someone turned on the heat. The room grew warm and cozy. It was pleasant sitting alone with people he did not know.

He had tolerated all that was irrelevant to arrive at exactly the place where all was important. Imaginary worlds revealed nothing. They made him want to stand under a hot shower or to swim in a cold sea. They made him stare out of windows at the fog or the rain or the blue air of a spring day between gray buildings where he had gone to school, where others, like himself, had strode across campus lawns toward their destinies, ticket holders determined not to miss the train. He had dreamed once, as everyone dreams, of a world beautiful beyond anything necessary or real, a world he still recalled, vaguely, at times, like a shower upon a cedar fence or a leaf shadowed upon a window pane. Finally, now, without remorse, he dreamed of no world but the world in which he dreamed.

About the Author:

Richard Dokey's stories appear regularly in the reviews. They have won awards and prizes, have been cited in Best American Short Stories, Best of the West, have been nominated for the Pushcart Prize and have been reprinted in numerous regional and national texts and anthologies. He has novels and story collections to his credit. "Pale Morning Dun," his collection, published by University of Missouri Press, was nominated for the American Book Award. Stories have appeared most recently in Alaska Quarterly Review, Grain (Canada), Natural Bridge, Southern Humanities Review, Lumina and The Chattahoochee Review.

A KIND GESTURE
by Anthony Saunders

It was a dark night, like the others he'd experienced before it. He was always walking but never knew why, he had a great life, ton of money but one day decided to walk away from it all and still he wonders why. Lights flashed by as the hours did but he kept walking. Then suddenly one of those lights stopped and asked if he needed a lift. Not having been asked before he agreed to the kind gesture of a stranger. Still he was going nowhere what was the point of the ride he wondered. All he could do was sit in silence and think as he became one of the lights that flashed by. The driver began to speak asking if he was hungry but not only did he acknowledge the kind gesture he realized his savior was a woman. She began reaching trough her bag trying to find something to eat as she did he looked around and noticed the car was a mess the seats were torn and there was a smell. He seen that this woman had nothing but was willing to give and he realized that the reason he left, he was so selfish in his life believing that everyone was able to get by on thelr own. He walked for days and then spending 1hr in a car realized what he needed to do. He asked the woman if she could take him home. She looked at him and smiled then he pointed behind them to imply it's the way they came from she began to laugh as she turned the car around to take him home. They arrived at his house and she was amazed at the size and couldn't believe he had been walking. The man asked her to wait a sec while he went and grabbed something for her, she waited to see what he was going to do. Then the lights of a car creeped down the man's drive way once the cars were close enough he stepped out and handed her the keys. This gesture made the woman cry as she sat in the clean car he handed her a card his card saying he'd help whenever she needed it. After a few months the man started creating jobs for the less fortunate and in doing so increased his own wealth which he put into creating homes and jobs the man had felt alive for the first time and it was thanks to one kind gesture from someone who had only a smile and a ride to give.

THE CELLAR

by Laura Solomon

When we found Sam he weighed only 14 kilos and was nonverbal. It was very difficult to communicate with him. If you got too close to him he would bite. I didn't blame him for his aggression. He'd been locked in his parents' cellar for 3 years, with minimal food, sometimes eating rats he'd caught with his bare hands. He was six years old when I found him. By this stage he was more animal than human. His primal instincts had developed but he had not developed speech and he was not toilet trained. He soiled himself regularly – it was me who cleaned up the mess. I got him into nappies and tried to teach him to use the toilet. I was a social worker who had been assigned the case. It had been me who had found him, curled up in a ball, chained to the wall, with skinny limbs, a bloated tummy and burn marks on him. His hair was matted and dirty and full of nits. The boss had assigned me the case to test whether or not I was ready for promotion. I was determined to do a good job.

My name was Sally and I had a real passion for child protection because of what I had lived through in my childhood. My mother used to drag me around by the hair and put me in baths that were either boiling hot or freezing cold. I used to get terrible carpet burns I had to hide from the other kids at school. She used to have a 'Time Out' room she would lock me in if I 'misbehaved'. If I accidentally broke something, ate food from the fridge because I was hungry or got up too early and woke her up she would shove me in Time Out and lock the door, trapping me in there. I never knew how long I would be in there for or what I had to do to be let out. So when the boss assigned me Sam's case I felt that I could make a major difference in one boy's life, help shape the course of his destiny.

It was one of the neighbours who alerted social welfare to the case. They had heard screams coming from the direction of the cellar and seen the parents going down there with vegetable scraps. Once I been assigned the case, I drove to the address at around 10pm at night. I did not want to alert the parents to my presence as I knew they would deny all abuse and would try and stop me from saving the boy. I crept around the side of the house with a flashlight and a blanket, and found the cellar door. It was locked. Knowing that this would probably be the case, I had thought ahead and had bought bolt cutters with me. I snipped through the lock and pushed open the door. A soft whimpering came from one corner. I walked in the direction of the noise and saw a small boy curled up in the foetal position on a cardboard box. From where I stood I could see what looked like burn marks on his skin.

I took a deep breath and walked towards him, holding out my hand in what I thought was a friendly gesture. As soon as I got close to him, he bit my hand, drawing blood. I remained calm and tried to speak soothing words. I had to get him out of here and into the car. I moved behind him and wrapped the blanket around his shoulders, picking him up in my arms. He thrashed and resisted at first, but I stroked his back and he relaxed a little and let me carry him out to the car. I didn't even know if he understood English but I kept talking to him.

"It's going to be okay", I said. "Everything's going to turn out fine now. You've been rescued."

He made no reply. I put him in the back seat and put the kiddie locks on, then started driving to the nearest place that could tend to his wounds, Mercy Hospital. Some of those burns looked pretty bad.

I arrived at the hospital twenty minutes later and walked through the sliding doors into A&E. I approached the counter.

"Hello", I said. "I've got a young boy here who's been severely neglected and abused. He has burns that need tending to. Is there somebody who can take care of this."

"Name?" asked the nurse, rather abruptly, given the circumstances.

"My name is Sally Roberston. I'm not sure of the boy's first name, but he belongs to the Phillips household."

The office had done some checks on the family before sending me around. The parents were P addicts on the dole. The father had been in jail for drug dealing. We lifted the boy up onto the bed. The doctor came in to look at him. He declared that the boy had malnutrition, a severe case of head lice, infected burn wounds, rotten teeth and was severely underweight. They wanted to keep him in overnight to give him IV fluids and I agreed that this should be the case. They told me they were going to shave his head to get rid of the lice and give him antibiotics and that he might have to be put under to get his teeth removed. The doctor gave the boy a sedative as he seemed very anxious. I gave them my details and told them to ring me the next day. I asked to go and see the boy before I left. They said he might be a bit drowsy from the sedative but that I could have five minutes with him. I entered the room, the little soul looked so small in the big hospital bed, his eyes half closed. I took his hand and he flinched. I told him to stay strong, that he was in good care and that I would come and see him tomorrow.

I didn't sleep a wink that night, thinking about the poor boy. On the way home I stopped in at the local Farmers and bought him a complete new set of clothes – a Superman T-shirt, a nice pair of jeans and a hoodie plus some underwear. I called by the hospital on the way to work and found my young charge sipping a cold drink through a straw. It was noticeable the amount of teeth that were missing – when he opened his mouth I could see huge gaps; he had obviously had a number of teeth extracted. A smile came to his face when he saw the clothes. His eyes darted nervously towards the door, perhaps wondering if his parents would show up. It would take a while for him to learn to trust me because it was an exceptionally bad abuse case.

Later that afternoon I went around to see the parents with the police. We walked up the weed strewn path. Bottles of Woodstock littered the front porch. One of the cops knocked on the door. A woman answered. Her appearance was a shock, she was incredibly thin, still in her nightgown even though it was the afternoon, her eyes glazed and her stance wobbly.

"What do you want?" She snapped

"We are here to talk to you about your son." Replied one of the cops

"I don't have a son." She said, her stance immediately becoming defensive. Attempting to shut the door. The cop reacted fast and stuck his foot in the door to prevent it from closing.

"We need to take you and your husband to the station to ask you a few questions." Said the cop

"Bill!" screamed the woman "The bloody coppers are here!"

An equally disheveled man appeared behind the woman.

"Whats going on?" Asked the man "We done nuthin wrong."

The cop managed to talk them into getting into the police car with minimal fuss and I followed behind in my car.

Once at the station I wasn't permitted to be in the interview room but I stuck around anyway.

I was told that the parents denied everything at first but then succumbed to the interrogation and charges were being pressed. They would appear in court this Friday and I could go along if I wanted.

I was also told that they had been in touch with the boy's Aunt and Uncle and that they had agreed to take the boy in. I was given their details and appointed as the boy's social worker to oversee his care.

Two days later I picked the boy up from hospital. He was wearing his new clothes I had brought him. I put him into the back seat of my car. I talked to him on the way asking him his name but he didn't reply; he looked like he was in shock.

Arriving at his Aunt's & Uncle's address the house looked well kept in a nice neighborhood. Knocking on the door a man answered. Looking at the boy he frowned and said abruptly,

"Who's this ragamuffin?"

I replied "He's your nephew the police contacted you the other day and you agreed to take him in as he has been neglected and abused by his parents, your brother."

"Hey Beryl!" the man called over his shoulder. A woman appeared.

Goes around with the police to see the parents. Press charges, parents go to jail.

They send him to live with an uncle but he does not get looked after properly. In the end social worker adopts him.

In the end, I adopted him. I thought it best. How else was I going to ensure he was properly looked after? I tended to him with a motherly love. I taught him to read and write, and tamed his nature which, after all the abuse, had become savage.

About the Author:

Laura Solomon has a 2.1 in English Literature (Victoria University, 1997) and a Masters degree in Computer Science (University of London, 2003).

Her books include Black Light, Nothing Lasting, Alternative Medicine, An Imitation of Life, Instant Messages, Vera Magpie, Hilary and David, In Vitro, The Shingle Bar Sea Monster and Other Stories, University Days, Freda Kahlo's Cry, Brain Graft, Taking Wainui and Marsha's Deal.

She has won prizes in Bridport, Edwin Morgan, Ware Poets, Willesden Herald, Mere Literary Festival, and Essex Poetry Festival competitions.

She was short-listed for the 2009 Virginia Prize and the 2014 International Rubery Award and won the 2009 Proverse Prize. She has had work accepted in the Edinburgh Review and Wasafiri (UK), Takahe and Landfall (NZ). She has judged the Sentinel Quarterly Short Story Competition.

Her play 'The Dummy Bride' was part of the 1996 Wellington Fringe Festival and her play 'Sprout' was part of the 2005 Edinburgh Fringe Festival.

PUNISHMENT

by Ruth Moors-D'Eredita

I'm not sure how much you already know. This is not something I'm proud of.

It was twelve years ago. There was a good kid, he was fourteen, two years younger than you are now. His name was Anthony Green.

I shot him, and he died.

I was a union electrician back then. Mom and I were separated. You were four years old.

I was not a great dad, and I was not a great adult. I'd bounced around for a while after you were born. I wanted to work, but I also wanted to drink. When the union job opened up, I took it. But I had no seniority, and the economy was bad. I'd go down to the union hall every day and check the job chart. Most days they didn't use me. I was barely making a living that year.

Mom held it all together for us. She'd get home from work and make dinner and play with you. She read you your books before bed. She folded the laundry and watched her shows on TV at night.

I mostly drank. I drank in the house, and when Mom gave me the eye, I drank in the backyard. I busted things up. I drove drunk.

Mom got sick of it. I knew I was on thin ice with her. It unnerved me, like something was coming and I didn't know what it was or how to get myself out of the way of it. She started looking at me with this sadness, and taking deep breaths.

"The breathing is how you tune me out," I told her.

"It's yoga breathing, Bobby," she said. "Everything isn't always about you."

One night I came in late, drunk, and could barely walk. I bumped hard into the dresser in our bedroom. Mom sat up in bed and told me not to come home like that anymore.

"I'm sick of the goddamned drinking," she said. "If you think you're going to pass out every night like your father, you're wrong." My father was a good guy, and he worked hard, but Mom was right, he drank. He drank in his chair in the living room every night until he passed out.

I didn't know when I was a kid that, your dad's an alcoholic, you're a sitting duck for it. I'm not excusing myself. I want you to know you have to be careful. If you remember anything from your Sweet Sixteen today, honey, remember that.

The next morning Mom took you to preschool, came back in the house, and threw me out. She told me to shape up. "Come get your things after work," she said.

I went to stay with Grandmom.

I'd stop drinking, and make it a week, a month, and that's when I knew I was in a battle. Even on the days I was working, when I didn't feel like I was going to puke, I felt off.

I worked HVAC on the convention center for a while, then they put me on the parking garage at the stadium. I couldn't concentrate for longer than a few minutes. I thought too far ahead. I panicked I'd never stay sober. Coffee went down like acid. I couldn't eat. I slipped and drank a few times. After a few beers, I felt better.

The day I shot Anthony, I'd been sober again for a few weeks. But I hadn't seen you in a month. Mom wasn't calling me back. I had the shakes. That morning, I was down at the union hall looking at the job board. One of the foremen, Mike Doherty, came up to me.

I'd never been on a job with Doherty before. He was an old-timer, and kind of cantankerous. He was next in line to run our local. It felt like a chance to me.

"You're with me today, Bob," he said. "Clock in and meet me out back."

What a shithole his truck was.

He says to me, "We have to look at 21st and Lehigh."

Let me stop here and back up and say a couple things.

Number one, Philly has the oldest electrical grid in the country. We don't shoot power out to one spot, like with direct current. It's alternating, and there's a lot of places for the grid to crash, all that extra equipment to balance the current. And it had been raining. When it rains hard, underground equipment goes down. Every component has to be cleaned and tested before they'll send power out again. And North Philly is not at the top of anyone's list for fixing things when they go down.

Number two, my entire life, I avoided north Philly. Most white people did. Every day, we heard about shootings and carjacks and gangs. One year, my mom went completely ballistic because the city was going to bus north Philly kids to our school. And my dad, like with everything else in his life, was disappointed by north Philly. When he got home from the service, he went to pharmacy school at Temple University. He loved it up there, he loved Broad Street, he loved the neighborhood. He hated that it went downhill. He'd read an article in the paper and say, "I guess they'll knife you for a nickel up there now." He'd watch the evening news and say, "Jesus Christ, what did they do to Beirut? It looks like north Philly."

He never thought about why that happened out there, and I didn't either.

That was my frame of mind when Doherty told me to clock in. Before I got in his truck, I went out to mine and got my Beretta. I tucked it under my shirt.

I should have told Doherty I was on edge, but I was intimidated. Doherty was not the type of guy to chat. He was listening to the radio. The Phils were ten games out already, the second week of May. They'd lost three of the last four at home. I remember Doherty shaking his head and snapping off the radio like he couldn't take it anymore. We pulled up to a video store.

The store was in an old brick building with apartments upstairs. They'd been on auxiliary power for a few days. The guys who went up in the bucket to check the pole earlier said the transformer checked out fine. It was our job to go inside and check the panel boards.

A group of kids stood on the corner. Up in an apartment window, a woman looked at us. The entrance to the store was grimy and the front windows were caged over. I followed Doherty inside.

"Yeah, how you doing?" Doherty said to the guy behind the counter. "Here to check your electrical."

The guy pointed to the back room. I took my flashlight from my belt and turned it on.

We saw a hallway and door. Doherty opened the door, and in the dim light we saw a toilet and janitorial supplies. No panel board anywhere.

Doherty said, "Probably in the cellar."

"Want me to go ahead? See what I can see?"

I was trying to make a good impression with Doherty. I needed the income to prove myself to your mom. If a guy like Doherty liked you, you worked.

I started down the cellar.

I didn't make it three steps when I hear a commotion on the landing behind me.

I turned, and in the beam of my flashlight saw an animal hanging from Doherty's pant leg. Doherty cursed and kicked the wall and whatever it was fell off and ran past my boots into the cellar. We heard it hit the water.

I got itchy all over.

"Jesus Christ," Doherty said. "How wet is it down there?"

I shined my light and we both saw water up to the second stair.

"Yeah, okay, no," Doherty said.

I followed him back into the store. The kids who were out on the corner when we arrived were standing inside now, joking around up front.

"Yeah, we didn't find anything," Doherty said to the guy behind the counter. "Someone will get back to you."

The store was narrow, and the kids faced us, standing shoulder to shoulder in a little semi-circle between us and the door.

"Excuse me, son," Doherty said to a big kid in the middle.

The kid didn't move.

"Excuse me, son," Doherty said again.

This time Doherty took a little quarter step and started in just slightly with his shoulder between the big kid and the one next to him. The kid on Doherty's left yielded a little, but the big one planted himself and lowered his chin at Doherty. Some alert shot up inside me and surged into my brain, like a flare.

That fast the big kid swung and knocked Doherty to the ground. I lunged to grab Doherty but he fell hard and one of the other kids jumped on top of him and starting pounding him. The guy at the counter shouted "Hey hey hey!"

I wanted to get my back against something. I doubted I could make it out to the truck, and I couldn't leave Doherty in there alone. The kids to the left of me were laughing. They were young. I just remember thinking No no no. I squared off at the kid in front of me, Anthony Green.

During the investigation, the guy at the counter told the detectives that he heard me say, No dude, come on, dude. He heard me say Doherty was an old man, tell your friends to leave him alone, you can have our money. Call it a day, man.

I don't remember talking to Anthony.

I remember Anthony's eyes. The excitement shining in them. Anthony's eyes were filled with that wonder little kids lose after a while. He was having fun. I can still see his sneakers and his pants. They were nice school uniform pants. He had a neat haircut, shaved up the side. I remember thinking he wasn't very big.

Anthony held out his hand and told me to give him my wallet. I looked down past his open palm. On the floor, the kids were going through Doherty's pockets. I was scared. I thought to reach inside my shirt and grab my Beretta. Instead, I saw myself put my wallet in Anthony's hand.

Anthony lifted his shirt and put my wallet in his waistband. Then he raised his fist like he was going to pop me, too, like his friend popped Doherty.

I reared back a little and Anthony's fist grazed my shoulder. I lost my balance and lurched backward. I tripped over Doherty's leg and landed on my back on the floor next to him. Doherty was gasping, struggling to get up. I tasted stomach acid in my mouth. I looked up and Anthony was straddling me, looking down at me. I grabbed inside my shirt for my Beretta and leaned up and fired it at him.

Anthony fell back. He was making high, gulping noises. Now Doherty was on his knees, patting himself frantically. He looked at me and saw the Beretta.

I got on my feet and knelt next to Anthony. Blood was pulsing from his neck. It was staining the floor between us. Doherty looked from the blood to me with wild eyes. He shouted, "Who told you to fucking carry on my fucking job!"

I spread my hands on Anthony's collarbone and pressed down with my palms. I thought soon we would hear sirens, and I knelt there, pressing down. Anthony's blood filled the spaces between my fingers and colored my hands up to the wrists.

"Help is coming. Help is coming, buddy," I told Anthony.

In that moment, all I wanted was for Anthony to live. Wanting that, being unable to bring him back, has crowded out everything else. Anthony alive was all I wanted in the moments after I shot him, and all I've wanted since. I have never been clearer about anything. What I want most in life is for Anthony Green to be alive.

I was still kneeling over him when the police got there. They took Anthony to the ER at Temple, and he died.

Anthony's mother gave a statement to the prosecutor. The day Anthony died, she'd allowed him to walk home from school for the first time. He hated taking the bus. His mother said Anthony would have had straight A's that semester, but he had a C in Spanish. She told him he could walk home with his friends when he got the C up to a B. So after every Spanish class, Anthony asked his teacher to figure his average. The day before I shot Anthony, he got an A on a quiz. That afternoon, he got off the bus, ran inside, showed his mother his B average.

The next day he walked home with his friends. On the way they all stopped at the video store to see the Nintendos.

Anthony's mother said, "My son is dead because they see us different. My son wasn't worth anything to the man who shot him."

I can never stop hearing what she said. Because when I shot Anthony, everyone assured me, you get jumped, all bets are off, you're justified. My lawyer said it and it turned out to be true. The witnesses did not help the prosecutor. The guy at the counter told how before he ran out the back, he heard me plead with Anthony. The lady upstairs didn't hear anything. And none of the kids remembered what happened the same way. One of them was twelve years old. Two of them had priors. All but the little one had reefer. My lawyer punched holes in all their stories. I got what they call a judgment of acquittal. And here is what I could never say out loud, but I want to say to you.

Once I gave Anthony my wallet, I didn't have to shoot him. I could have stayed quiet down there on the floor. I know right from wrong. The detectives who interviewed me got it right. Anthony would have followed the rest of his friends out the door. I knew that to be true then. Reading his mother's statement didn't so much confirm this truth to me as repeat what I already knew was true. I killed Anthony in a moment of fear, but

there was anger in me in that moment, too. My anger pulled the trigger. And I haven't been punished for that.

The day of the acquittal, I drove up to see Mom and you. In the driveway up at the house, there were leaves all over the pavement. I saw your scooter leaning against the front step. I stood there for a minute, looking at the doorbell I installed when Mom and I moved in. I rang it.

I heard you run for the door and wait there on the other side before opening it, just like Mom taught you. Then I heard Mom, and the door opened.

"Daddy!" you said. You were excited to see me.

I bent down to pick you up. "Hi Peach," I said. You inspected my ear with your little fingers. I felt your breath on my cheek.

"Mommy, it's Daddy," you said, like a little reporter.

Mom looked at you and me and said, "We have gymnastics at four."

I said to her, "Can I talk to you?"

"Honey, go on, get ready for tumbling," Mom said to you. "Daddy will still be here when you come down."

I will never be the kind of person who thinks ahead to reassure my own kid like that. I put you down and Mom and I watched you run upstairs.

Mom said, "Well?"

"Donna, I just came from court. I came straight here to see you," I said.

"Are you drinking?"

"No."

Silence.

"The judge granted the acquittal."

"Well you didn't do it on purpose. Jesus."

I wanted to touch her. I wanted to reach my arms around her and gather her in and put my face against her neck and close my eyes and bawl, right there. My mind was saying, I did do it on purpose.

Instead I said, "I will do better."

"Bobby, spare me," she said. "And you're planning to do what about work?"

"They say I can go back. I don't know how much work I'll get, but I can go back. Probably have to do nights for a while."

"Nights, Bobby. Are you serious?"

I closed my eyes. I knew what she was going to say.

The union didn't have to do anything for me. The cost-cutting guy in the mayor's office said not only did the unions rip the city off on pricing, but were criminals, too. A couple union thugs killed an honor student who'd done nothing more than walk into a video store after school. Maybe, the mayor said, it was time for the city to re-open all the union contracts. Maybe it was time to start thinking about right-to-work laws. Make the city more competitive for business.

But Doherty dug in. He told us one big non-union building goes up, that's like Stage 1 cancer. You throw everything you got at it, try to cure it. Two go up, it's Stage 2. You don't want it to get any worse. You hit the open job sites—the non-union sites—in the middle of the night and tear them up. Doherty's guys could destroy hundreds of thousands of dollars in concrete and steel and equipment and labor in half an hour.

Mom knew what was what.

"First off," she said, "nights is the worst thing you can do. They'll take advantage of you now. They'll have you out there busting up sites in the middle of the night, like you see in the paper. And for what? You get acquitted, and now you're going to go bust up scab sites for them? You going to prison for them after all? What are you thinking?"

"Not all night work is like that," I said. "There's good third shift work too."

She rolled her eyes at me. You know your mom. Her big thing is, Actions speak louder than words. I had not even got to what I came to tell her.

So I said, "I want to live here with you and Kayleigh again."

Just then you came running down the steps in your gymnastics outfit and handed Mom your pink hairband. In two seconds, Mom put your hair in that ponytail like a little waterfall down your back.

I said, "Give me another chance, Donna."

I said it so low, I hardly heard it myself. But I said it.

"We have to go," she said.

I walked you out to the car and strapped you in your seat. I watched you and Mom drive up the street and turn onto the avenue. I got in my truck and drove back downtown.

Inside the union hall, guys were reading the paper and drinking coffee. I went into the back office. Doherty's door was open.

"Bob," he said, "What can I do for you?"

He did not stand up or even look at me full on.

"Hey Mike," I said. "Thanks for taking me back."

"Them's the rules. So what can I do you for," he says again.

"Have anything you could put me on?"

Silence.

I tried again. "I'm trying to patch things up with my wife. I have to work."

As soon as I heard my words in the air between us, I thought about what Mom said when she kicked me out. Not everything is about me.

I tried to rephrase.

"You can count on me, Mike. I'm sorry about what happened."

"When you available?"

"Now."

"Third shift?"

"Sure," I said.

"Might have something for you in south Jersey."

"Thanks, Mike."

"Don't thank me. See Dave Joyce."

"Thank you," I said anyway.

At the pay window, Doherty's secretary handed me a slip of paper with Dave Joyce's number. I called him and he told me third shift on a cold storage warehouse job started at ten, he'd meet me there.

I drove east over the bridge across the Delaware. On the Jersey side, I filled up the truck at a Quik-Stop. I went inside to pay and bought a sandwich. At a picnic table in the parking lot, I ate and watched the planes take off at the airport. The sun set behind the oil tanks on the Pennsy side. I got back in my truck and slept for a while.

Then I drove out to the job site to be on time for Dave Joyce.

When I got out there, the site was at the edge of the Pine Barrens. I could see they'd cleared acreage for a warehouse. It's always so dark out there. There was no temporary lighting up yet, and a lot of the time, I installed the temp lighting. So I started getting my tools out of the back of my truck. If there'd been a second shift on that job, it was gone. In my headlights, I saw they had the concrete pad done, and were starting to frame.

I turned off my truck. Soon Dave Joyce showed up. He flipped on his headlamp so we could see. He had his belt on. He had an eight-pound sledge in one hand and his toolbox in the other.

He looked me over and said, "Ready? Follow me."

I walked behind him across an apron of surge gravel. He reached the chain link security barrier first. In the light of his headlamp, I saw the contractor's signage. It was an open site. There was no union on the job, and there was no third shift. Someone left the fork latch unlocked for us. I never found out who. Dave Joyce lifted it and we walked through the gate.

I followed him to the edge of the concrete pad and tried to swallow the fullness in my throat. I watched Dave Joyce line himself up to where the first, newly installed anchor bolt entered its steel column. He hoisted the sledge like a baseball bat, swung low at the bolt, and smashed it. The new-cured concrete cracked all around. The steel column it held in place rang and vibrated and gave way. The column tilted away from its base and took the concrete with it. Like when a tree falls and pulls up its root ball.

The half-circle of dark, piney woods around us absorbed the sound like it was nothing.

"Now do the rest of them," Dave Joyce said, and handed me the sledge.

About the Author:

Ruth lives and works in Vienna, Virginia, with her husband and three children. She is a member of the Woodbridge and Stafford workshops and is writing her first novel. Punishment is her first published story."

COACHING MOM

by Amada Matei

I watch as my son scampers onto the playground, stops at the swing set, and touches his forehead to its wooden beam. I bite my lower lip until I taste blood. He holds his head in that awkward position for about five seconds, just long enough for me to notice and cringe, then he joins the other children in playing tag. I already regret my decision to bring him here, but being cooped up in the house is no way to live.

A few moments later, he kneels to the ground and taps his forehead to the soft, brown turf as if he were a Muslim praying towards Mecca. The other children stop, stare at him with impatience, then resume their play once he is back on his feet. His forehead feels the seesaw, the metal fireman's pole, and the plastic sliding tunnel.

My instinct is to do what I normally do: I reprimand him by smacking his forehead with the palm of my hand. But today, the other mothers are watching. Chasing him down to thump him on the head seems like a lunatic move, even by my standards. Perhaps this is my moment of clarity.

"Which one's yours?" asks a mom sitting on the green bench besides me. She's a size two at the most, curly blond hair, and not one wrinkle under her hazel eyes. Her Coach backpack sits neatly on her lap.

"The boy in blue. Logan," I say.

"I love this age. Mine's Caroline. The spunky one in pigtails. She amazes me every day. She counted to a hundred at breakfast today. First time without stopping."

I force a smile and take in her lilac aroma; my

Suave body spray feels a little less fancy. I decide I hate this woman and her pigtailed kid. Logan stops running and stands by the swings as if conflicted who to chase down next. He flaps his arms while rocking his body back and forth like an ostrich ready to strike. He looks at nothing in particular, just keeps flapping. I think maybe he'll catch a breeze and take flight this time. Caroline slows her pace, stopping herself a moment before Logan rocks forward into her. He does not seem to appreciate the near calamity. He just sways and flaps. He is mesmerized by something two feet ahead of him. Caroline stares at my son, appears bored by him, and trots off to the rock wall where two other little girls are already climbing.

"Is Logan in pre-school?" The Coach mother asks.

"Yes. Just started last month."

"We just started this year too. Although we had her tested. She really should be in first grade. She reads on a first-grade level. But my husband is afraid she'll get lost among all the tall kids. Better socialize her with kids her own age first. Just have her skip kindergarten instead. I think she's already bored. Can Logan read yet?"

"He's learning his ABC's," I say. I want to say something else. Something clever, like studies have shown early readers do no better in life than late readers. But I didn't think of it fast enough and now it's too late.

Coach mom gives me a nod and half smile. "Most boys are slow to mature. Don't worry, he'll catch up."

Logan bends down and examines something. He

then stands back up and kicks it. He stomps it with his left foot. Logan jumps with both feet and loses his balance on the way down and lands on his butt. My son wails and runs to me with limp arms swaying by his side. He places his head on my lap. I push him from me. I am disgusted with him. Then I am disgusted with myself.

I turn to peek at Coach mom expecting her to smirk or roll her eyes or give me a patronizing look. Instead, she gives my son her full attention. "Oh no!" she says in a baby voice and digs into her Coach backpack, pulling out a moist towelette. She extends her manicured hand to my son and he takes it. She pulls him closer and begins wiping the dirt away from his palms, while she inspects it for scraps or cuts. "No booboos. All clean."

Logan stops crying and bends down toward me, wiping his face on my Kmart jeans, snot trailing from his nose. "He's not the most coordinated," I say, feeling compelled to explain as if children don't normally fall on their butts while clowning on playgrounds.

"That's what boys do. They're goofy. They fall."

"Stop crying and be a big boy," I say to Logan even though all his tears have been transferred onto me and he is no longer crying. Coach mom pulls out a pack of tissues, removes one and hands it to me. I sense she already knows I came ill prepared. I thought of nothing to bring to the playground, while Coach mom most likely has an apocalypse preparedness kit in her bag.

I accept the soft tissue and wrap it around Logan's wet nose. He sucks the snot in like a vacuum cleaner. "Stop sucking it in. Blow it out." He makes snorting sounds with his nose.

"Pretend you are blowing out birthday candles with your nose," Coach mom tells him. He blows perfectly and fills the tissue with green ooze.

"Go back and play with those nice girls," I say.

"I k-k-k-k can't climb the w-w-w-wall."

"Go," I try not to shout but it comes off as shouting. Logan meanders back and stops at the gray climbing wall, touching the red and yellow pegs with his forehead. The girls have climbed the five-foot wall forwards and backwards three

times by now. They run off to the swing tire and Logan remains standing, assessing the top of the wall. He looks defeated.

I feel a rain drop. A few more splash on my head.

"Caroline," Coach mom calls out, cupping her hands around red lips. "It's starting to rain." She motions for her child with a wave. Caroline complies and runs to her mother, who pulls out a bottle of hand sanitizer and a light purple jacket.

"Logan," I call out. "Let's go. It's raining." Logan looks away. I shout louder. He is either ignoring me or is lost in Logan's world.

"Caroline, pumpkin. Go tell that little boy that his mommy is calling for him." Caroline skips back out with her purple jacket zipped up and hoodie on. I watch her tap Logan on the shoulder and she guides him back to me. I imagine Caroline at home as a perfect helper. I bet she keeps her room clean and places her dirty laundry in the hamper without being asked, and feeds the pets all with an indelible smile on her face. Her mom probably pats her on the head, and takes her out for ice-cream, and they read together in the park before puttering around at the mall in matching outfits like sugary imbeciles.

"We need to go," I tell Logan.

"No. Not done playing."

"Yes, you are. It's raining."

"D -d-d don't care."

"I said let's go." I grit my teeth. I want to shake him, but I control myself for the sake of the onlookers. I don't know how to convince him without shaking him. Sometimes I think I can shake the normal back into him. So far that hasn't happened.

The raindrops get fatter and wetter.

"Nice meeting you," says Coach mom. "But we have to run."

I wave with one hand and grab hold of Logan's arm with the other. I tighten my grip as he pulls away. He paws at me with his free hand and lunges at me, butting his head against my forearm. His head is like steel and I know he'll leave a bruise.

I smack his forehead. I do it repeatedly. The sound of my hand clapping against head fosters my anger. Every slap is harder and meaner and at this very moment I believe this discipline will somehow relieve his addiction of hugging every fucking thing with his bony head. I know people around us are now looking. I don't care. I hate myself at this moment. I keep hitting anyway.

Logan keeps his head down, protecting his face until I finally stop long enough for him to look up at me with those pitiful, giant brown eyes. He has no idea why I am enraged and this enrages me more. His misunderstanding of me feels defiant and deliberate, as if he exudes innocence to strategically mask his baneful comportment. I hate myself.

I strike his arm with my fist, and he finally lets go. I grab the same arm and turn him around and scold his butt with the palm of my hand. I do it again and my hand stings. Logan is wailing. People stare. Coach mom runs to us and puts herself between us like a boxing referee. She pries my white knuckles off Logan's arm. He hides under the bench.

"Stop it," yells Coach mom. "That lady is calling the police. You need to calm down." She points to a fat woman with a cell phone to her ear.

"I tried to stop," I whisper. I breathe deeply to swallow my heart back into my chest. Logan is cowering and crying under the bench, keeping his forehead to the ground. He picks his head up one inch, then taps it back to earth. He does it again. And again.

I hate myself more. I kneel to him and wrap my arms around his skinny middle to pull him out. He resists, balling himself up like a pill bug.

"Let him lie there for a minute. Walk it off. You both need space." Coach mom sounds like my therapist, calming voice and intelligent. I hate her more. I let her guide me towards the swing set. I am panting less.

Seconds later, I escape from her hold and run back to the bench on my hands and knees, and I stuff myself under the bench with my son. "I'm so sorry. So sorry." I caress him and pet him.

His whimpers are softer now. I love my son. He's like a puppy nipping at my ankle until it bleeds and I have no choice but to kick him away. I kiss his head. I hear sirens in the distance.

"Sick ass bitch," I hear someone say. People are still watching. I feel them closer.

The police officer has her brown hair rolled into a neat bun near the top of her head. Her bullet proof vest looks funny on a such a small woman. "I understand special needs children can be stressful, especially when you're a single parent. My son is fifteen years-old and he's still a challenge."

I tell her I love my son. She tells me she knows. She calls children's services so I can get some good resources and find ideas that work and get support; that's what she explains to me. I think I might lose my son and I feel slightly giddy. Then I realize I might lose my son and I start to cry.

The officer places her hand on my shoulder and tells me a social worker will visit my home in the morning and I'm free to go. I take a deep breath knowing I escaped arrest because my son didn't show visible injuries.

"It will get better," she says.

"When? I'm still waiting."

"It will get better. You can't stop until it gets better."

I hate it when other people make sense.

That night I sit by Logan's bed and read him a book. He darts his forehead towards the page until his skin feels the paper. He has to do that to every page. I take deep breaths and we finish the book and I tuck him in. I bend down so my forehead touches his forehead.

"I love you," I say.

"I'm sorry mommy. W-w-w was I bad?"

"No. I was bad. But I will get better. I won't stop until I get better."

I love my son.

About the Author:

Amada Matei lives and works in Cleveland, Ohio. She supervises a child abuse hotline while writing in her spare time. This is her first short story.

WELL DONE BOO BOO

by Kathryn Merriam

Five years. It has only been five years, and so much has happened in those five years.

I would not trade him for the world. He is so precious. There are really no words to describe how much a mother loves her child. All I have to do is look into his sea-foam green eyes and know that this is where I am supposed to be. This is who I was meant to be from the very beginning. It was hard at first to accept my life, but I have come to know that I would not trade it for the world. I know that I have the support of my family; I always have.

The rain teases the surface water of the lake. The sun tries its best to peek out, but the clouds are doing well at hiding him. As I look out the white-paneled window, I think of my dad. It is his birthday today! He is turning forty today! Wow! I always teased him about getting old, but he embraced it. After Jason gets home, we are going to out to Javi's, his favorite Mexican restaurant, to celebrate! It is hard to focus on his birthday though because of this yellow spot on the window is driving me crazy. I laugh at myself as I acknowledge that the spot is a reflection of Winnie the Pooh.

Looking down, I see Winnie the Pooh cuddling close to Ezel. My dad gave me that blanket the day I was born. Over time, however, he became more than a blanket. As a toddler, I took him everywhere with me. The older I got the less I took him with me, but I still looked forward to cuddling with him every night. He danced with me when I told him about my accomplishments and wiped my tears when I cried. Winnie the Pooh is holding hands with Piglet on the front. Both of them are smiling. If you look at it with Winnie the Pooh facing you, the top right corner cries with joy. Actually, there is not a corner anymore. After nineteen years of placing that corner between my pointer and middle fingers and rubbing it for comfort, the corner retired. The stuffing has retreated to inches inside the thin protecting layer of fabric. The stuffing and the fabric dance together as two separate parts now, but I know that Winnie would not trade his corner back for the attention that he got from me. And now Winnie the Pooh can bond with my son. He still smells like campfire. Not matter what I did to wash out that smell, it is still here. My dad always smelled like campfire, and since Winnie, my dad, and I were once inseparable, we all acquired my dad's scent. Taking a deep breath takes me back.

Not too long ago, my dad held me in his arms as I am holding Ezel. We would read scriptures together. I would scan the page left to right just like Daddy. When I was in elementary school, I sat on his shoulders as we walked around the lake in our backyard, through the park on the other side, across the populated street, and to the front steps of the school. As I grew up, he continued to escort me to school. Looking back, I took advantage of those days-those days he was with me. It was embarrassing as a high schooler to have my father walk with me to school every morning. I always tried to hide inside myself, but at least he was there. After he dropped me off, he would walk to Tony's Tinker Mechanic Shop and would work hard all-day long. After school, I would join him at the shop and he would teach me a few things about cars. Let me just say that it was so boring, but I know that he loved it, so I half-listened.

After homework, dinner, and dancing, he sang me "You are My Sunshine" to me every night right after prayers. Sometimes he would use a deep voice, and on his sillier days, he would sing it in the highest pitch he could manage. I fell asleep to his voice every night and woke up most mornings to that tune...I still do.

Watching him walk out that door, not knowing if his voice would ever fill these rooms again, not knowing if his arms would ever wrap around me again, or not knowing if his smile would ever light up my world again, killed me. I have always liked to be in control, to know what will come, to know what lies ahead. I had done pretty good with that...until the day he left. The second he stepped foot off the front porch, a part of me left with him. I no longer could control what would happen. I no longer knew what the future held. I could not plan it, for I had absolutely no idea.

I was a senior in high school when he deployed. He served overseas missions before I was born, but after an explosion, he chose to stay inland, which is when he met my mom. They thought it was love, but she had been seeing other men the whole time. My dad didn't find out until after they were married. Not that I am an expert, but from what I hear, my mom was really not the type to settle down. I was born two months before the divorce. She handed me over to my dad's custody without any hesitation. I am sure she had other things to do. The divorce was hard on my dad. He blamed himself, but I tried to tell him that it wasn't his fault. As part of the Marine Corps Reserves, I knew he could be called in again, but I prayed that day would never come. It did.

Why is life so complicated? He served his time, fulfilled his time, until the call came. I knew it was that call. Within two days, he was gone. Just like my mom. What did I do to lose my parents? Was I not good enough? Did I not deserve to be loved?

Raising me must not have been easy. I don't even want to imagine what he experienced. I mean, I behaved myself, for the most part. He endured all of my childhood for me. All of that time. Effort. Pain. Support. Devotion. All of it was for me

because he loves me. And he loves his country so much. He loves me so much, that he left to fight in the war. He knows that I can handle myself. Well, he thinks he knows. What must have been oblivious to him was the fact that I could not do it without him. It had always been him and me, never just me, or just him. Until he left.

School kept me busy. Being an undergraduate pushed me to my limits, but it was easier than watching my dad walk out that door to a world out of my control. I did not really make any friends at first. I was so sad that I did not feel like talking. Going to classes was hard enough. Nothing was the same. I knew that he would want me to try hard, and that was the only reason I got myself out of bed every morning. His desire for me to be successful motived me to work hard. I mean, at least I had a dad. He was not necessarily with me physically, but he was on Earth. And he did not leave me on purpose in an effort to abandon me. It was, instead, to protect me.

I was not always accepting of his departure. His uniform did not symbolize freedom, or courage, or hope. When I saw it, I saw loneliness. When I saw his black uniform, it was like looking at my life when he left. When I saw his black uniform, I saw the absence of life when he left. When I saw his black uniform, I saw all of my joy swallowed up as he walked farther and farther away into the abyss of a world far from me.

I always wondered what he was doing, where he was, and how he was doing. I pictured him surprising me at the university. I would walk around the corner and he would be standing there with open arms. Or I would step into the house, and he would be standing in the front hall with his perfectly white smile. I prayed every day that he would be there with me. I wanted him to hold me again. I wanted him to know how much I love him. I wanted to hear his voice. I wanted him back. But life does not work that way.

One year went by and I had not heard the sound of my dad's voice, or seen his eyes light up when he saw me, or smelled the laundry detergent of his pristine uniform, and it hurt so much. I was not strong enough to let the pain go. Instead, I learned to control it, and when it was the proper time, I let it out. The weekends consisted of me driving home to take a walk around our property, but most of the time, I ended up cutting the walk short and just sitting by the lake. In the evening, I would lay on the edge of the lake close enough to the water that as the waves charged up the shore, they tickled my feet. I would look up to see a medley of russet, fuchsia, rose, and coral colors start to fade behind the lake. The evenings were the only times of the week that I truly enjoyed being me. I got to think, to write in my journal, and to be myself, by myself.

With all of my heart and soul, I wanted to see my daddy. He was my best friend, but he was gone, maybe somewhere I didn't know existed. I missed those times when he attempted to braid my hair, when he prayed with me every night before I fell asleep, or when he kissed me on the forehead. When I looked into his eyes, I knew without a shadow of a doubt that I was loved, that I was cherished more than I really even know. Was it too much to ask to have him back for a few days? We could walk along the lake in the backyard and sing and dance and be goofy like we always did. I would give anything to see my dad in person, to feel his arms around me, to hear his chuckle in my ear.

Two years after he left, I had a life-changing moment. I looked in the mirror and was shocked by what I saw. Not necessarily in a bad way, but in a disappointed way. I looked at myself and heard my dad's voice, "Carter, what are you doing?" He would always ask me that when he knew I could do better, or when he knew that I knew I was not doing my best. It was in that moment that I knew I was not doing my best, that I was not being my best. I decided I would get involved. I wanted to meet more people, maybe even make some friends, so I did. After that decision was made, I heard him praise me, "Well done, Boo Boo. You are my pride and joy." When I heard that, I knew that he was proud of me. I knew that I was on the path that God intended for me. I joined the soccer team that spring and met even met some friends.

One friend in particular stood out. At first, he was just part of our group. Jason was sweet, kind, funny, and then he became my best friend. We studied together almost every day until two weeks after our study sessions. That was when he asked me on an official date. He brought flowers and asked me to join him for dinner. His excuse was our successful completion of the midterm. I saw right through him, but I accepted. I knew that we got along before the date, but that date reminded me of what it was like to be happy. After my dad left, I thought that my ability to be happy left with him, but Jason reminded me that I have always known how to be happy. He listened to me as I talked about my pain, my loneliness, my past. We did not get to every detail, but that was not the point. The point was that he was still there listening to me, interested in what I had to say, and intrigued by me, the real me. He wanted to learn more about me. And wow! I wanted to get to know him. We continued to date every weekend. He went to my soccer games and I went to his debate competitions.

After a year of dating, he and I were starting our last year at the university. The day before classes started, he asked me to join him on a beach trip. I thought nothing of it other than him listening to my desire to go on a road trip together. It was one way that I thought I would know for sure if he was perfect for me. And he was…he is!

Not once did we turn on the radio. There were only a few moments of silence that were due to us catching our breath. That was the perfect road trip. Karaoke. Laughter. Jokes. Deep talks. Revealing talks. And so. Much. Fun. That trip only got better.

We took a walk on the beach that night. The moon was swaying back and forth in time with the ocean. The breeze played with my hair. His fingers were entwined with mine. We walked and talked. I felt so peaceful. I was where I was supposed to be standing next to who I was supposed to be standing next to. It was perfect. The whimsical evening took my thoughts to the heavens.

"Carter! Carter! Carter!" Jason was laughing at me.

"What?"

"Where are you?" I giggled.

"I was just thinking." It hit me then that I was looking down at him. I usually had to gaze up a little bit in order to see him, but his eyes were beneath mine. Oh my gosh! He was on one knee! I was so oblivious to his plans, which I am still grateful for. That was the best surprise I had ever had.

"Carter, you are the love of my life. You are the mystery in my life that I want to spend forever solving. You are my breath. You are my universe. Carter Rose Huntington, will you marry me?" I flapped my arms for at least twenty seconds. The voice I had seconds before was gone. The tear ducts I had gotten to know so well opened. I finally gained my composure and replied.

"Yes! Yes, I will marry you, Jason Chase Evans!"

There was so much joy in my life, but I had not forgotten what it had taken for me to get to that point. I was crying less, but the pain still ran deep. I had not heard from my dad in years. The more I thought of him, the more I smelled campfire. He always smelled like he had been camping, but I could never figure out why. Jason became my rock, the one person I could lean on. I knew he would not let me fall. He endured all of my crying and my outbursts of frustration. I helped him through his mom's passing. We decided to move forward, to really move forward. I knew that I would never stop praying for, thinking about, or loving my dad. He loved me before anyone else on Earth ever did. I was determined to not give up, to keep hoping, to keep moving.

Jason and I planned to get married two months later. I knew that if I were to talk to my dad, he would want me to go through with the wedding. He would want me to be happy. Jason makes me happier than anyone ever has. I will not lie and say that looking forward to my wedding did not have any pain, because it did. I was so giddy, so in love, so happy...I still am. But deep inside me, where only Jason and God are let in, resides the pain of my dad's absence. His absence had become such a "normal thing", and I hated it.

Our wedding was coming up in only one month. Everything was coming together...until the letter came. It was from the Marine Corps, and the second I saw that seal, my heart dropped. I called Jason but couldn't say anything. He came over. I broke down into a fit of tears. I rested my head in his lap. He leaned over and kissed the top of my head. He ran his fingers through my hair. I opened the letter. I let out a sound that had never reached my ears. Jason looked at me. He recognized my pain. I let go of all of my feelings.

An hour later, I woke up. I felt dead. Dead to the world. Dead to feeling. I did not want to think or to feel. But I was grateful I could feel Jason next to me. I was grateful I could smell the citrus wafting off of him. I was grateful I could hear him breathing. He was real. He was there.

"Why, God? Why did you take him from me?" I was yelling at God. I was so tired of praying and not getting what I wanted.

"Babe, He can hear you," Jason's tone was gentle and so full of love.

"I know, but why, Jason? Why did He take my dad from me?"

"I don't know. What I do know is that He loves you." It took everything I had to not yell at him, but it wasn't Jason's fault. It wasn't my fault. It wasn't even God's fault. That day, God taught me that blaming Him and yelling at Him got me nowhere but farther in the depths of pain and despair. After all, I had a choice. I could blame Him, get angry, fight against Him, and lose. Or, I could accept that I had no control over my dad's death and that if I worked with God, I could feel better, get better, and be better.

I was grateful that he died fighting for his country and for me, for that is how he would have wanted it. Without him, I would not have been the person I was. I would not be the person I am today. Thinking positively only lasted a few minutes though. I felt my heart break in two. He would not be there to walk me down the aisle. He would not be there to dance with me. He would not be there to give me away. I would not even be able to see his body, but instead, just the box that his body was enclosed in.

The American flag wrapped around his coffin. It was folded and handed to me at his funeral. My face was so red and blotchy, but I did not care. Without having Jason next to me, I would have broken, not bent. Only Jason was giving me the strength to keep going. After working so hard to become independent, to be able to take on life by myself, when it came down to it, I was not strong enough. Jason says I am strong, but I was not strong then. Jason held me up as we walked to the car.

Our wedding was postponed. It just didn't feel right getting married two weeks after the funeral, so we postponed it. I could tell that Jason did not want to, but he understood. We waited three months and could not wait any longer. It was worth the wait. He has always been worth the wait.

"Beautiful, are you okay?"

"Yeah." I thought I could overcome it, but it is consuming me. The absence of my first best friend was dampening my mood...on my wedding day! What bride is sad on her wedding day?

The smile on his face melted my heart. "I know what that means: you are not really okay. What's up?" Jason and I decided to take a walk along the lake before the craziness ensued. The sun had not even shown itself yet, but Jason wanted to take some time to ourselves before the crazy fun truly began.

"Handsome, he isn't here. And-gosh-I don't want to take away from the day. I don't want to take away the value of you in my life. Jason, I love you more than words can describe. I cherish you, everything about you. But the part of me that I gave to my dad when he went overseas is still with him. I just need you to forgive me." He stopped walking and turned toward me. He framed my face with his hands.

"Oh, Carter. You mean more to me than anything or anyone on this earth. You are my universe. You are what makes me smile when I see you every day. After today, I can wake up and not have to wait to look at your beautiful, engaging eyes. I can wake up and play with your hair, make you break-fast, give you kisses. I can spend every possible second with you. You have my heart, Carter, and I am yours." Tears were filling my eyes. I did not want him to think of himself as anything less than who he is.

"And you are mine. You have my heart." I marvel at his patience, his forgiveness, his unconditional love every day.

"I know that you love your dad so much. After your mom left, he took up that responsibility of raising you, and if I could have met him, I would thank him for doing such a wonderful job. He is your family, and now I get the pleasure and honor of being a part of your family. You have nothing to apologize for. Just know that I love you, Carter.

I cherish everything about you." He enfolded me in his arms and I melted into his embrace. All I ever needed was Jason, and he is here, and we are about to become one. I was so ready!

"God, thank you so much for my life. Thank you for the time I had with my dad. Thank you for Jason. Thank you for the time I have with Jason. Thank you for my future. Thank you for not giving up on me. Thank you for loving me." My prayer was on the shorter side, but it came from the heart and was the sincerest prayer I had ever shared with God.

Jason and I unraveled and he held my hand on our way back to the driveway. I brought his hand to my lips and gave it a brush.

"You are my sunshine, my boo boo sunshine. You make me happy when skies are grey…" Amongst the crazy fun of the day, I heard that song, that song that my daddy sang to me every night before he left. That song was like breathing to me. I knew that moment that he was there. How could I doubt him? He may not have been there physically, but he was there spiritually. I felt his presence and knew without a doubt that he was

there. I felt him kiss my cheek. I heard him singing to me. I smelled his notorious scent of campfire. I pictured his smile. I could taste the waffles he used to make for me. To honor him, my wedding colors were red, white, and blue. I also had a breakfast buffet. Breakfast was his favorite meal, so much so that we ate pancakes, crepes, eggs, bacon, and waffles for dinner often. I picked up that habit.

The rain is still playing with the lake water. The cat tails bend to the rain's will. The sun is singing as it breaks through the clouds. I feel Jason come up behind me. His arms entangle me and Ezel. He places a kiss on my cheek and rests his chin on my shoulder. I outline his face with my finger as I turn to face him. I stare at those green eyes and know. I know that I am where I am supposed to be. I melt into Jason's chest as he brushes my forehead with his lips. Ezel sleeps in my left arm. Man, wife, and child. A family. My dad is here too, smiling. He knows that I love him. He knows that I am happy. He knows that I have let go of the pain and the hurt. I have started to embrace life. I am truly living. "Well done, Boo Boo. You are my pride and joy."

About the Author:

Born in Utah but raised in California, Kathryn is a lover of life! She always had a passion for writing but it has become more prominent in recent years! She loves spending time with her family and friends, Jersey cows, her dog, smiling, laughing, long walks on the beach, writing, sunsets, and making sure others feel loved. She is a junior at Brigham Young University-Idaho with a major in English and dreams to be an author and an editor!

DREGS

by Jessica Ciosek

"You know," she said, twisting her feet for a 360 view, "I think I could kick your ass in these boots." She smiled when she said it, sly and baiting.

I nodded, standing over her. "Reckon you could," I kissed her hard on the mouth then whispered in her ear, "but I doubt you'd need boots to do that."

She shrugged, dropped her eyes back to the mirror. "That's true. But with these I'd look like a bad ass doing it." Rail thin, fragile blonde hair, Siobhan had the wild eye about her. She'd fend for herself if she had to, and she'd had to. They weren't stories she told me, but her eyes took on a hooded look, a certain careful squint when she thought she might get caught wanting. Trust fund baby that I was, I did my best to make sure that never happened. Pulling a slim platinum card from my wallet, I tendered it without a word. Siobhan kissed my neck.

"Thank you, my prince," she whispered and sauntered out of the store in those boots, distressed silver leather with a round-toe, a heavy sole. On the street she planted a gentle kick in the crack of my ass.

The day was overcast, gray, chilly, the sky hung drab like a cloak of mourning. Fall was usually more beautiful in New York, but this year it weighed heavy, tired, unwilling to try, sick of itself in a way that seemed destined for drug addiction. But Siobhan and I, we were six months clean and sober which was supposed to be a good thing.

She tucked her arm in mine. "Brrr," she whispered. A tickle of goose bumps ran down my neck like an icy sauce dribbled over my bones.

"I could go for a café au lait," she said, leading me toward Stumptown. I didn't want anything you could buy at a coffee shop, but it was easier to let her lead.

The place was empty, Wednesday before Thanksgiving, everyone below 34th street was getting out of town. We were staying put, claiming we liked an empty city. Truth was, I had lied my way out of a trip to my parents' lavish neurosis. "Bring flowers and a nice chardonnay for your hostess," my mother said when I told her I had plans. Siobhan's family lived across the pond, so what did she care.

We took a table near the window, the place thick with the oily scent of over-roasted beans and boredom.

"I got you a double espresso," she said. "Pull you outta your nasty funk." I stirred three packets of sugar into it and drank it in one gulp. Her lipstick left a magenta kiss on her cup's white lid. She eyed me broadly. What the fuck? I thought about saying, but I shrugged. The energy for disdain draining out of me like the helium in those clownish balloons they sally forth every fucking third Thursday in November.

"It's the fourth Thursday in November," Siobhan countered, and it surprised me to know I'd said it out loud. "You think you'd know that growing up with Thanksgiving and all."

I shrugged. "You think I'd give a shit, too, wouldn't ya?" She laughed.

"Holidays are for suckers."

"Not if you eat right," Siobhan said.

My cellphone vibrated on the marble tabletop. I glanced at it, but let it wriggle and buzz. Siobhan grabbed it.

"Who's Brad?" she asked.

"My brother."

"I didn't know you had a brother." I shrugged. She eyed me slyly, dangled a finger over the green "accept" button. I shook my head but found it hard to give a shit either way. Rehab may have cleared my head, but my life still yawned out in front of me like an empty linoleum-lined corridor, long, ugly and going nowhere. She put the phone back on the table, unanswered.

It vibrated again. She leaned over the edge of the table, squinted.

"He insists you pick up."

I shrugged again.

She grabbed the phone from the table, punched in the code and started typing.

"You wouldn't like my brother," I said, watching her thumbs jump around the keyboard. "He's kind of a pompous ass."

She kept at it, the phone buzzed incoming replies. A whole text conversation with my brother whom she'd never met.

Finally, she slapped my leg. "Let's go," she said, "I wanna pack a bag."

"Go ahead."

"Oh, no, babe. This is your family."

"Wait. You did not."

"I did," she nodded with a knowing grin. "Sounds very nice, actually. Your sister-in-law has a friend who owns a gallery." She sipped her coffee.

"Yeah, some asshole's rich wife. She studied art history, did a semester in Milan and now she's an expert."

"Rich people buy art." She winked.

"Not my art. I've tried with that crowd."

"If at first you don't succeed, try, try again." She poked a finger into her cheek, twisted it and smiled like some overgrown Shirley Temple. I laughed, shook my head.

"But seriously, I already told my mother we had plans."

"She didn't believe you. She's worried."

"Ha!"

"That's what he said." She held my phone up as proof. "Besides, I could do with a home-cooked meal."

"This one is gonna be catered, babe. Count on it."

"Wow, Mr. Fucking Particular, how about I do kick your ass with these new boots of mine?" She winked, raising one silver toe to peek just above the edge of the table. "It could be kinky."

And it was. With the efficiency of a nurse, she undressed us both. I sprawled across the cold mattress, the dank chill of the fifth floor walk-up curling about my toes. She slipped her boots back on and grinned. My member chubby but my mind still wallowing in the tepid steam of my own ennui, I rolled onto my stomach. She stood over me, pounding my half-frozen ass like stamping the loose dirt of a recent grave and reciting my sins in nursery rhyme cadence.

"One for being grumpy, two for fake smiling, three for not getting hard, four for being handsome, five for buying me boots, six for not fucking me, seven for flirting with the shoe store girl."

"Didn't," I said.

"Did," she countered and kicked me hard from the side. I can't recall the next of my transgressions because after number ten she dropped onto the middle of my back, curled her body over and bit my butt cheeks, hard.

"Spread 'em," she said with a slap, then jammed her finger into my asshole and told me to cough. I did as instructed. She laughed the laugh of witches. "Hahahahahahahahaha," she cackled. "I'm a doctor."

Pressing those boots hard into my hip, she rolled me over, straddled me and rocked her wet regions against me until I was hard and thinking of nothing but her tight ass. I reached for her. She grabbed my hands, flipped her legs forward and pinned my arms against the bed with her boots.

Still astride but not letting me inside, she rocked and moaned, "Oh, Danny. Oh fuck, I wish you could fuck me," she cried, tears streaming down her face.

"Let me," I whispered, "let me in."

Her face turned wicked, sly and baiting again. "But you are a bad boy," she leered. "You can't come in." I pushed against her booted feet. She pushed back, the barely worn rubber cutting molded patterns into the soft underbelly of my forearms.

Finally, I threw her off with the force of my hips against her tiny pelvis. She fell back toward the foot of the bed and tumbled off the edge, her head smacking soundly on the ancient cast iron radiator.

"Fuck!" she cried.

I scrambled to the end of the bed. She glared up at me from a crumpled curl between the foot of the bed and the wall.

"Ouch," she said reaching to gingerly probe the damage. Her fingers came back clean.

I climbed down next to her. "Baby, I'm so sorry. Let me get some ice."

She was sitting up on the floor, her hand cradling her broken head when I came back with the ice. She let me press it there, ever so gently, a wince in her eyes as I did. I curled my arm around her, kissed her delicately. "I'm so sorry, sweetie."

She grinned wickedly, grabbed ahold of my inner thigh and dug her nails deep into the vulnerable flesh. I screamed, she laughed.

"Aw, baby, you are a sick one." I kissed her lips hard, cradling her head. "Maybe we ought to have that looked at," I whispered.

"After," she whispered back. I lay on the floor, pulled her on top of me, we rocked and pinched, licked and screwed until neither of us had anything left. I lifted her onto the bed, cupping a hand over the bump on the back of her head.

"Maybe we should go that 24-hour clinic on Chambers," I said.

"Let's take a nap, then we'll go." She wrapped the ice pack around her head with a fresh towel.

"Siobhan," I said.

"Shhhh," she said, pulled me in around her.

Waking in the early evening dark, Siobhan lay curved under my protective arm.

"Hey," I whispered. She said nothing. I kissed her shoulder. "You need a blanket, baby." I stood, pulled an extra from the foot of bed and laid it over her. In the bathroom, I looked at my ass. It was decorated with red tread marks and circles of bites like evidence of some newfound tropical disease. Next time I'd ask for bruises.

Barely a bump under my faded green quilt, she looked peaceful, almost fairy-like, pale white, eyes softly closed, head enrobed with the thin blue towel. At the edge of her lip, a trail of spittle dried the muted brown of milky coffee. I pulled the towel back. The ice pack, just a flat bag of water now, fell away revealing a perfectly round, small lump under the thin sheen of Siobhan's flaxen hair. I shook her shoulder.

"Hey babe, I think we better take you in for a look. That bump is kinda ugly."

She didn't move. I shook her again, put a hand on her cheek. She was cold. "Siobhan?" I turned her fully over onto her back. Her shoulder flipped, her arm fell onto the mattress with a thud. "Siobhan?!" I checked for breathing, I could not find a pulse, I pumped her chest, called her name, over and over and over again.

She was still wearing the boots when the paramedics arrived. They pumped and they prodded, worked in that expert way of medical people seeking signs of life.

"She's gone I'm afraid," the smaller man said after not nearly enough time.

The thicker man shook his head.

"What?" I looked from one to the other of them for answers.

"She's passed on."

"No," I said. "NO, no, no." My head thickened, eyes went dark.

The fat man grabbed ahold of my elbow. "Maybe you ought to take a seat." I fell onto the bed.

"Siobhan," I whispered, reaching for her.

"Very sorry, sir," the man said, intercepting my hand. "Let's have you sit over here." He pulled me up, led me to the chair on the other side of the room. I never touched her again.

"It can't be," I said. "We were just..."

"What a way to go," I heard Siobhan's voice, looked over where she lay on the bed. Her lips never moved. I started to cry.

The cop pulled me to standing, slapped the cuffs on my wrists. "Let's go, pal." They led me passed where she lay on the bed. I leaned toward her, looking to kiss her one last time. The cop yanked my arm. "Not happening." I followed him out.

The 1st Precinct on the night before Thanksgiving is an odd sort of place, belligerent and frightening in its jolly decorations.

They took photos of my ass. Siobhan laughed when I had to drop my pants.

"Bet you wish it was me taking those pictures, don't you?" And she cackled that weird witch's laugh again. "If it was, I'd be up your ass with the camera in a second. Find out what makes you tick." Pathetically, the thought turned me on. She knew that, too. "You always were a pervert, you were just afraid to admit it." I shrugged.

My brother answered his cell, groggy and irritable. "Dude, what?"

"I swear it was an accident," I said. "Don't tell Mom and Dad." The pleading in my voice sickened me.

In navy cashmere overcoats and hushed Italian loafers, Brad and his lawyer friend strode in like the well-dressed cavalry. They had me out in less than thirty minutes.

"My kid brother," Brad introduced me after I was free.

"Keep it clean, man, we'll get this handled," the lawyer said. He shook both our hands. I thanked him then climbed into the warmed leather seat beside Brad.

"You'll come for the holiday. I'll bring you back to the city Friday."

"Dude, can't you just drop me off..."

"You're coming out to the house and you're gonna act like you remember how to have a normal Thanksgiving. We've got twenty-four people coming and you're not gonna fuck it up."

"O – fucking – kay, Dad."

He glanced at me sideways, shrugged. "Sorry, man. Just this is pretty messed up, you know?"

"I know." I leaned my head against the smooth glass, relieved in a way that he wasn't giving me a choice. "Thanks, man."

His wife, Cassie, a "darling girl", labeled so by our mother, was at the kitchen sink when we rolled in. A wholesome, trim brunette, her smile flashed equal parts concern and annoyance.

"I put a pair of Brad's pajamas in the guest room for you."

"Thanks." I nodded. "Really sorry about this."

"S'alright." She smiled halfway. Brad threw his keys on the table.

"I'm going to bed," Cassie said. She patted my shoulder, pecked Brad on the cheek.

"You wanna shower or a beer?" Brad asked. Apparently my recent rehab stay hadn't made the family news cycle.

"How about a shower and a beer? Or a scotch?"

Brad smiled. "That's my boy. The guest bedroom is through there." My clothes felt dirty, out of place, dark and used, in the perfect glow of the off-white surroundings. I hid them in the empty closet and turned the shower on hot.

"What the fuck?" Siobhan said, her voice a harsh whisper in my head. "Your brother's got a Hampton's estate and you never told me? Let alone carried my sorry ass out here for a visit."

"We were supposed to come tomorrow."

"Oh, right," she sighed. "Damn, that would have been nice."

"I'm really sorry, babe."

She snorted.

Brad was sitting by the fire, a scotch in hand and a glass ready for me.

"Damn dude, nice place."

"Yea, thanks. I'll show you around in the morning." The gas from the fireplace hissed gently between us.

"So what happened?" he asked turning a raised eyebrow my way. I pulled a long chug of my scotch.

"God's truth, we were fucking around. She hit her head on the radiator pretty hard, but we thought we'd finish then see about getting it looked at. Really stupid. We fell asleep. I woke up. She didn't."

"Jesus, man. Who was she?"

"Siobhan. We'd been dating for a few months."

"Almost a year, you prick, we met on New Year's Day," Siobhan weighed in. I watched Brad to see if he heard her. Nothing. He just stared at the fire.

"She was cool. Hot, crazy but sweet, too."

Brad nodded.

"You kiss-ass," Siobhan said.

"Fucking mess, huh?" I said to Brad.

"Looks like it," he said, swirling the amber liquid in his glass. "But my buddy who got you out tonight? He specializes in criminal. He'll take care of it."

"Criminal?"

"She's dead."

"It was an accident."

"He'll take care of it."

"Thanks, man." The fire hissed, ice clattered against crystal, I breathed thin slices of air flavored with guilty relief.

"Ain't that just the sweetest damn thing, big brother coming to the rescue," Siobhan said.

I shrugged and raised my glass. "To Siobhan."

"To Siobhan," Brad echoed fraternally.

"Fuck you," Siobhan said.

We finished the bottle.

The bed wrapped around my drunken ass like comforting clouds of hell.

"Still can't believe you never brought me out to this place," she said. "We coulda had some fun in that bed."

"It's kinda gross though." I spread my arms wide, as if to prevent myself being swallowed by the bed's fathomless pillow top.

"Gross?" she said. "Looks pretty cushy to me."

"But it's fake, all of it, not an ounce of authenticity in it." I rolled onto my side, pressed the third extra down pillow over my head.

"Authenticity? Like you'd know, little prince." She laughed.

"You're authentic."

"Is that what you think? Shit, I'm just poor. Or was."

"I'm sorry, Siobhan, I never meant...."

"Only rich people think poverty is authentic."

In the morning I apologized more sincerely to Cassie, wore Brad's khakis to dinner and made perfect small talk just like my mother had taught me.

"I had no idea Brad had a brother in the city," was a common refrain.

"Hides me away for special occasions," I said jovially.

"Wow, these are some fancy people," Siobhan whispered in my head. And they were. Dressed in well-fit cashmere sweaters and tailored silk blouses, these were people raised in suburban splendor, a life of ease and comfort, possibility and opportunity pre-ordained. The people I'd grown up with. Sure, there were troubles in suburbia, but not the real kind. Nobody went hungry or didn't have a bed to sleep in at night. I tried to picture Siobhan holding her own among them. She'd be wearing a sleek black dress, leggy black tights and those silver boots. She'd be the one they'd all eye, curious and surprised, but would anyone of them dare to speak to her? Maybe that guy, the balding short guy who looks like he's up for a challenge. He'd ask her what she did, who she was and she'd offer some bullshit to put him off. Before yesterday, I would have enjoyed the discomfort she'd cause, would have reveled in throwing the comfortable people off their game. But now, I could see Siobhan would be out of place here, she'd be just as uncomfortable but trying ever so hard to be nice. I was using her to distance myself from these people, my people, just like she was using me to get further away from hers. Neither one of us would have succeeded but I came out on top. There was part of me who, though guilty and afraid, was glad it was me who survived, because I could. I had this to fall back on. She had nothing, or very little.

We sat politely for dinner in place-carded seats.

"So much to be grateful for," Brad declared.

"Here, here," the guests agreed. We raised our glasses to good fortune. The food, catered and abundant, landed in my stomach like a dense ball. I pushed the turkey and potatoes around my plate. Siobhan insisted I eat two pieces of pumpkin pie.

"That always was my favorite part of Thanksgiving, when I could get it," she told me.

Brad drove me home Friday morning.

"Want me to come up?" he asked.

"That's cool. I think I'd rather go it alone." He drove quietly away and I let myself into the chilled apartment. A stillness hung in the air, an emptiness with her gone. Her magenta-rimmed café au lait cup sat on the dresser. I picked it up.

The frigid dregs sloshed. I pressed her lipstick mark to my mouth like a kiss.

She laughed, gently this time. "It's okay, baby," she said. "I was never gonna get old anyway."

This made me cry which made her laugh again, harder, meaner. "Toughen up, you shit. Life is hard, then you die. Or don't they send that memo from the Hamptons?"

"Intracranial hematoma" was the determination, bleeding inside the skull caused by blunt force trauma. Both drug screens came back clean. The cops weren't inclined to let it go that easy, but it turns out she had been a foster child, ward of the state. Her mother murdered by a jealous boyfriend, her father a victim of his own drunk driving.

"I had a grandma," she barked. And she wasn't Irish either, not really, descended from Irish like we are all descended from something we wish were better than ourselves.

With no aggrieved mother, no angry father, the authorities accepted the truth: rough sex and those boots.

Of course, she couldn't stay forever. Exactly one month to the day after she died, she was gone. I'd spent the night before drowning my broken heart. There may or may not have been tears involved, but I do recall Siobhan next to me on the barstool just before they threw me out. In the bed where she died, I passed out. At noon, high noon, she called to me.

"Hey Danny, this is goodbye."

I opened my eyes. There she stood at the foot of the bed wearing an old Army jacket and black cotton bikinis.

"Wait. Where are you going?"

"That's for me to know and you to find out."

"I can't do this without you."

"You're a rich kid, you'll be fine."

"But you kept me real."

"Nobody is that real."

She was gone without another word. The sharp whisper in my head went silent. The apartment sighed a final release. I cried into the pillow where she'd last laid her wounded head. But I knew she was right.

An emptiness descended upon me, one I only knew how to fill with booze, needles or pills. Instead, I called my mother. She packed about a third of my clothes and shipped my paintings directly to a warehouse in Schaumberg. I was home for Christmas.

It's been five years and still I think of Siobhan. Sometimes she's in my dreams. She looks happy, smiling and not so angry. Me, I sobered up, took a job with my father's company and married my mother's tennis partner's daughter. But every Wednesday before Thanksgiving I go out for a café au lait in Siobhan's honor. My wife orders one, too.

"It's a tradition for us," she says innocently, her pale rose lipstick leaving barely a trace on the cup's edge.

About the Author:

A native Midwesterner, **Jessica Ciosek** lives with her family in NYC. By day she works for a New York City public high school, by night she toils at the keyboard. She has recently finished her first novel and is looking for an agent. Her work has appeared in Minerva Rising Literary Journal.

A WINTER COAT

by Sevasti Iyama

On a nightstand, there were red roses in a glass vase. Against the hospital's stark fluorescent lighting, the roses made Calliope's eyes hurt. That night, after she landed at JFK a cab drove her straight to the hospital.

Eyes closed, he lay on the hospital bed, and breathed through an oxygen mask. Tubes and catheters stemmed out of his nose and arm. The heart monitor's screen showed spiked lines. On the top right, there were two numbers, one over the other. A pulse oximeter was attached to his finger.

Like a bumblebee, a nurse buzzed around his bed.

"Who brought the roses?" Calliope asked.

"I don't know," the nurse said.

"My husband bought me roses when we met."

The nurse smiled and left the room.

Calliope walked over to the nightstand, where the flowers perched, like soldiers at attention. She touched a rose. A few petals cascaded to the floor. Suddenly, he had a coughing fit. Startled, she knocked the vase over. Flowers and water scattered everywhere. The vase shattered into broken shards. She saw her broken reflection in the glass pieces, like a cubist painting by Chagall.

He retched. There was green sputum on his lips. The oxygen mask fell off. The spiked lines on the monitor moved faster. She pressed the emergency button, and then scrambled on the floor, picking up the roses.

The nurse reappeared, like a fairy godmother. After the nurse gave him a shot and adjusted his

mask, she saw Calliope hunched over, in a corner, staring at her clenched fist. Blood mixed with the roses, making the flowers look like rust.

The nurse cleaned and bandaged her right hand. An aide swept up the glass. Calliope stared at the man in the bed, who settled into a deep sleep, his chest rising up and down, like the waves she saw outside the Royal Hawaiian's window where Mas and she stayed during their honeymoon in Hawaii, years ago.

"Have to change your father's bedpan," said the nurse.

"I'll go smoke," said Calliope.

"Honey, it's freezing outside," said the nurse. "Where's your coat?"

The woman's kindness took her aback. Calliope shrugged, and picked up the roses from a chair, where she had left them.

As Calliope walked down the hallway, the smell of Pine-sol permeated her senses. Although they lived in a huge house, Mas refused to hire a maid. He made Calliope clean, to earn her keep, and told her that she had to use Pine-Sol to scrub the toilets. The smell made her ill.

Once she reached the parking lot, she hurled the roses into the darkness. She shivered in her thin leather jacket. After she booked the flight, they fought. As usual, the argument was about money. He had millions, and she had none except for the money he gave her, because she was a loser actress, a fact that he threw in her face. He paid for all her needs, from cigarettes to meals to head-shots, and even a nose job. Before she left LA, she begged for a winter coat because New York had sub zero temperatures in February, but he said, "No. That ticket cost me an arm and leg!"

They fought just like her parents used to, except her father never hit her mother.

When she was 29, she fled New York. She did not think rationally when she moved to Los Angeles. It was more of a "fight or flight" response. In Hollywood, she got lost like many actors do. It was a town full of beautiful blondes with long legs, driving around in top down convertibles, blasting pop music.

And there was dark-haired, chain-smoking Calliope. She drove an old Chevette and blasted Metallica on the radio to cover up the noise inside her head. Although she moved 2451 miles away, she still heard them arguing. The music did not help. After Mas and she started fighting, she found relief in booze and benzos.

Outside the hospital, she reached inside her Prada handbag for her cigarettes, and lighter. She had less than fifty bucks in cash, but she had two credit cards. Mas was the authorized user, but she was a joint cardholder. Should she risk buying a coat? He would see it on the billing statement and freak out.

Her hands shook as she lit a cigarette. Inside her bag, there was a mini bottle of Merlot that she confiscated from the airplane, next to her cell phone and a bottle of Xanax.

"Take only as needed for extreme anxiety," the shrink had said.

My anxiety is always extreme, she thought.

She chased a pill with wine and smoked.

As a train screeched into the station a block away, her phone rang.

It was Mas.

She trampled the cigarette with her shoes.

After the phone stopped ringing, she went inside.

As she waited for the elevator, she envisioned Mas home in their Hollywood Hills yellow stucco art deco house. She checked her cell. It was 11 pm Eastern standard time. Back in LA, it was 8 pm.

Like the goddess Aphrodite, the house once rose out of a sea of pink bougainvilleas and red roses. A month ago, Mas and she fought, again, and he pushed her head against the wall. After he let her go, she ran up to their bedroom, locked the door, and stared out of the window, which overlooked Beachwood canyon. Mas stormed outside with a weed whacker. Like the killer in the Texas Chainsaw Massacre, he attacked the roses and bougainvilleas, until all that was left were amputated stubs. In the distance, she heard the peacocks that belonged to a famous drummer who lived in a castle. The birds screamed. For a split second, Calliope thought the sound came from the flowers that were begging Mas for mercy.

As she stumbled down the hallway, she saw a body covered in a black body bag on a bed inside Room 142. In Room 144, there was a white haired old woman propped up in bed. Blue light from the TV flashed across her face. The old woman stared, right at her, and screeched like the peacocks and the sound effects from the movie Psycho. Calliope covered her ears, and bolted towards her father's room.

His chest rattled as if his lungs were full of rocks.

Don't take anything native from Hawaii, Mas had said. No rocks or sand. It will bring us bad luck.

Ok, I won't.

I love you, Calli.

I love you, too, Mas.

Another subway train screeched into the station.

So many years ago, when she lived at home in the Bronx with her parents, she left, five days a week, at 8 am, to take the subway to NYU. One cold winter day, she overslept and left at 8:30 am. She threw on a hoodie, because she couldn't find her coat, and her acting teacher hated tardiness.

As she waited for the train on the outdoor subway platform, she saw her father, carrying a briefcase, wearing his thick winter coat. He walked right by her, keeping his head down, until he became an exclamation point in the distance.

When the train came, he entered a separate car.

Why did she marry Mas? Was it because he was ten years older than her, and represented the father she never had as a child? Or was it because she was out in LA alone and had been for years? First she worked as a cocktail waitress at the Rainbow, and then as a waitress at the Beachwood coffee shop, which was where she met Mas one morning, when he sat at the counter, and she served him pancakes? By then, she had gotten her SAG card, thanks to THE BLOOD OF THE DAMNED, an awful B-movie where she played VAMPIRE'S VICTIM #2. Speaking three words got her the damn card.

"I am alone."

His eyes opened.

"My daughter, take my coat," he said with a smile. "Sit next to me on the train."

She took his cold hand in hers. His lips were blue, and his face was a pale green, but his eyes were brown like hers.

"This time, stay," he said.

"Ok," she said.

He sighed, and closed his eyes.

The nurse came back. While the nurse adjusted his oxygen levels, Calliope pulled her hand away and walked to the window. Outside there was a little girl dressed in red playing in the snow, bobbing up and down, like an apple being dunked in white Belgian chocolate. Her cell phone rang. It was Mas. Her hands trembled as if she held a grenade. Suddenly, the EKG monitor sounded an alarm. Startled, she dropped the phone, while the piercing sound of the alarm drowned out the telephone ring. A crack formed on the screen like a lightning bolt. Nurses ran into the room, and someone yelled, "Code Blue." She blindly turned towards the window. The little girl was stomping in the snow, as a tall man in a winter coat appeared. The child ran towards him, screaming with laughter, as he picked her up, held her in his arms, and carried her away.

About the Author:

Sevasti Iyama is the blog writer for Cycles of Change Recovery Services. She has written for RehabReviews.com, the Antelope Valley Press and the Kern Valley Sun. She's also the co-author of How I got Sober, 10 Alcoholics and Addicts Tell their Personal Stories. Presently, she is working on a novel called, The Pomegranate Cowboy, which is loosely based on the myth of Persephone and Hades. She is pursuing a Masters Degree in Creative Writing from Southern New Hampshire University. Sevasti is from the Bronx, and Los Angeles. She lives in the small town of Lake Isabella, California but being a city girl at heart, she plans to go back to New York City, in the not too distant future.

GOLDEN BROWN

by Souzi Gharib

"What is the colour of your eyes?" an articulate voice inquires.

"Golden brown," I answer with the ease only characteristic of self-description, particularly the physiognomic type. I had borrowed the adjective from a pop song, the Stranglers' "Golden Brown", and feel like adding the words that follow, "texture like sun", but it would have cost me the job.

"Then your interview is at the address provided in the newspaper at eleven o'clock, tomorrow. We look forward to meeting you, Clare. Good Day," concludes the very courteous voice.

The phone resumes its electronic tone marking the end of an ordeal. I desperately need eye-contact in any intercourse with humankind, and on the phone I feel blind. I know the job involves humouring a home-bound youth but I cannot understand the relevance of the colour of my orbs. This lends an enigmatic hue to a very ordinary job-interview. I begin to tread in the footsteps of Jane Eyre on her way to gothic Thornfield. I know I have to pull the brake on a very imaginative cast of mind, so I occupy myself instead with ironing the only dress suitable for a formal meeting, my daffodil outfit.

We have always been short of money. My father eventually broke under the strain of supporting a small family and completely vanished. Out of grief, my mother locked herself in some monastery in Provence which was affiliated to her ancestral past. I and my twin sister remained in Glasgow. I assiduously pursued study and became obsessed with scholarships but my twin sister

Adele preferred a different type of life and became a strip in some renown club for mature men – at least this is what I have been told. I never investigated the veracity of her tale. I know from the letters that I occasionally receive that she lavishly lives in the West End in a trendy apartment that I have never visited. I always return her cheques, the money she bewitchingly earns, with a brief but thankful note informing her that I have enough on which to subsist.

I arrive the next morning at a huge house, the mansion type, with a half-erased coat-of-arms: I view the boat, the anchor and the dolphin with reverence, all water elements. The bronze door-handle imparts history to my humid palm. I am received by an elegant housekeeper whose smile intensifies upon greeting my eager eyes. She decorously leads the way to a great hall whose main characteristic is light. Irises and daffodils adorn every corner of a very spacious room. Bright wild flowers, dominantly yellow and white, are everywhere. Yellow seeps into my brain-cells and tranquilizes my agitated nerves.

The hall is empty of other candidates so I assume I must be nearer my goal. I need the money for my studies and other ever-postponed necessities. A soft bell rings and I am ushered into another room, brighter in hues. There are even butterflies hovering around majestic vases. I am quite relieved that no hand-shaking is involved. My hands always feel embarrassingly icy-cold. People attribute it to malnourishment though it is in my case simply a matter of bad blood-circulation, so a doctor once told me.

"Good Morning, Clare. How are you?" greets a young man from behind a grand desk.

"Good Morning. I am very well, thank you," I answer with a habitual, genuine smile which some men find captivating and then unhesitatingly add, "And you?"

"I shall feel better when I know how you feel about my offer," the young man supplies the answer with a beautiful mouth and a pair of probing eyes.

I await the more detailed job-description with my habitual patience, returning his boundless gaze with humble haze.

"How do you feel about a sort of wordless friendship? Do you believe in the eloquence of eyes?" he poses a couple of questions for a job-description.

He sounds neither like the Roderick Usher whose heart-beats resonate to a half-buried sister nor like the lead singer of Depeche Mode, complaining in "Enjoy the Silence" about the violence of words - simply a mature, pensive, young man whose eyes merely seek meaning in mine. Strange as the situation sounds, the thing does not sound like dating. I am beneath his station and he sounds too serious for anything flirtatious. However, I think of my stripping sister revealing the most intimate parts of her body: Am I then to strip my soul before a stranger's pair of eyes? Do both jobs amount to the same thing? Both are paid anyway. In an age of escorts and fast sex a very charming and handsome man is looking for a soulful strip. I trip over reluctant words and remain helplessly terse.

'What has the colour of eyes to do with this?" I inquisitively ask.

The man with the eloquent voice on the phone politely intimates that I am not expected to ask any questions about my employer's preferences or ailment or even speak of my situation outside this present circle, which merely consists of the house-keeper Miss. McKnowel , the nameless voice, and Mr. McSloy, my taciturn employer. With a simple nod of the head, I accept the job and receive a cheque in advance of five-hundred pounds.

In bed I ponder over models I have seen on television posing for upright painters. The artist does not give them his undivided attention; his focus is on the canvas. What would be the duration of my employer's gaze? I wonder whether it is moral to commune with the soul of a man for whom I feel nothing. And what if I eventually feel something for him? It is going to be unrequited and a broken rule for which I would be reprimanded. I crease my tidy bed with restless thoughts then dive into a puddle of tears which always grows into a vast lake in my dreams.

In the morning new worries emerge. What am I to wear on my first day at work? I have resolved to keep the cheque for academic needs. I open my mother's abandoned wardrobe and consider for the first time wearing her antique dresses, some of which she inherited from her own grandmother, heraldry in cloth. I try the bluebell dress. It fits my slender frame. We both take after our slim mother, but Adele has recently put on extra flesh in the wake of her profession-related banquets.

The Lotus-Gazers

I have always collected words as a girl eagerly collects sea-shells. Each word has a kingdom of its own. Each has color, odour and a winsome personality that is inborn. Each possesses its own music, its own audible soundtrack whether it is sung or lies dormant in bed alone. Sometimes words enact their allotted meanings and at other times they mischievously elope. Each word I wrote or spoke acquires a scent which conjures up a phantasmagoria of images, scenes and emotions experienced years ago. Words emanate warmth and solace when all around me have gone cold. With words I rub my wounds and bandage the lacerations of my soul. Words are phantoms, Emily's, Anne's and Charlotte's which haunt the deep recesses of my core. They are angels that fan a child's fever like Oscar Wilde's swallow who died forlorn.

Deprived of my cherished companions, I have to start my very first day at work without their indispensable aid. Bravely sitting opposite his lofty chair in a spectacular garden, I smile my morning greetings, feeling as weird as Alice in that famous, enchanted hole in her pursuit of a rabbit that talks. His eyes are fixed on the water-lilies that deck an expansive pond. I follow his gaze and imbibe the translucence of my favourite flower with gratitude. When our eyes meet for fleeting seconds, it feels like an overwhelming deluge of warmth. He leaves with a graceful bow and I continue contemplating Beauty alone. I wait to be ushered out to head home.

I arrive at my flat feeling feather-light. The albatross is off my neck. There is nothing immoral about my new job. A sense of companionship, completely missing from my life, begins to buoy me up. He must have had a turbulent, domestic life to be so averse to words. I know from my parents how verbal exchanges can grow perniciously harmful. Or he might be hermetic in inclinations. I remember my promise to keep the nature of my employment secretive, so I rebuke my own private, errant thoughts and immerse myself in my academic world.

Because the weather is slightly chilly, our second meeting is in the library-room which is full of Scotch broom. My eyes weave yellow on their looms. I nearly swoon when I feel a pair of golden-brown eyes watching me from above. A large painting of a beautiful woman covers half the wall. Mr. McSloy follows the direction of my gaze and joins me in contemplating the portrait. When I view his face to investigate any resemblance to the object of the portrait, he returns my smile with a galaxy of lights that swim in a pair of emerald-green eyes. I wonder what sort of things he sees in mine and why of all the people I?

I stop worrying about what to wear for work. Mr. McSloy does not notice my clothes or anything below my orbs. I stick to my daffodil dress because it makes me feel like a Tibetan monk gone on a retreat. I begin to cherish our meetings which are fairly brief and pray for his health because at times he looks as frail as the flowers that adorn his book-shelves.

The Gloaming

At night, our cities are engulfed with myriads of light, the romantic, the commercial, and the garish type, and for people whose heads are cowed with worries about fees, food and overdue rent, the stars above remain totally obscured and out of sight.

We bask in the gloaming imbibing every shred of light. The moon waxes rhapsodic over the surface of every crystal-clear dew-drop. I follow his gaze to the sky and falter above a mat of stars.

Infinitude is our rite tonight. It is Mr. McSLoy who teaches me how to star-walk.

I still recall how as a child I enjoyed counting the numberless stars, but I was repeatedly admonished by my superstitious aunt who told me that the ugly warts on my hand, which rebuffed the clasps of my school-mates, were some kind of retribution for my star-counting. The more I counted, the more mushrooms sprouted, the uglier grew my hand. I wondered how such beautiful lights could vengefully blight my hands with sprouts. I continued gazing at the starry sky but the moment my head started a count I hurriedly lowered my eyes. My parents tried every sort of ointment and medication to eradicate the ugly mounds, but nothing worked. It took an Indian, blind man with a knife held in his hand to induce their demise. He repeatedly passed the knife over the culprits, almost touching them, while reciting memorized verses from his holy book. The immense fear I felt when the knife nearly scraped my ossified dunes must have made them disappear. It was a psychological type of healing, but frightfully intimidating.

When I turn my head in Mr. Mcsloy's direction, a lunar ray rebounds from his eye and skates on my golden-browns, illuminating my tearful mind. I smile my good-night and leave Mr. McSloy to his cosmic pals.

Knights of Light

Mrs. McKnowel leads me out of the familiar surroundings to a submerged path that leads to the family chapel. I think that this is one of the blessings of being affluent, affording private worship. I assure her that I shall be able to find Mr. McSloy on my own, and walk with ease the tree-fringed path with tranquility. A tiny stone church meets my eyes but Mr. McSloy is not to be found. I walk round the church to the backyard where I find a small cemetery full of flowers. On an elegant bench sits Mr. McSloy contemplating a grave or reading something engraved on it. I make my presence felt by standing next to the bench and start reading the inscription:

Hereby I purge my tongue, my mind, my heart, of thinking ill of a ring of holy monks, Knights of Light, who will forevermore remain enshrined in many hearts.

I stand at a loss what to do. My eyes are mesmerized by his ring which bears the same coat-of-arms engraved on the edifice. I feel as if I am walking into a page of history which in grand libraries one cannot touch without a white pair of gloves. I remember the reverence which my mother bestows upon the dead and kneel and say a prayer for the tenants of the grave. It must be very lonely to be the last of a race, a dying history without a living trace. As I rise to resume my former position at his side, Mr. McSloy stirs and heaves a sigh. I eagerly look into his eyes only to meet a galaxy of tears.

Emerald-Green

In a large bed Mr. McSloy lies like an ailing bird, a golden creature that one visualizes in fairy tales. A tear hops on my eyelash that mirrors a similar one on his emerald-green lake. The housekeeper whispers in my ear that tears are discouraged in the presence of a sickly friend. I force a smile that kindles my golden-brown twins and wait for a response from him. He twists like a crinkling leaf, so I whisper in Mrs. McKnowel's ear a plea to be allowed to get closer to him. She is at a loss what to say and ignores my gradual advance to a very majestic bed. I sit at its very edge and place my warming hand next to his. He looks too weak to act so I take his hand in my small hands and try to impart what neither words nor gazes can convey to him. He lies very still. I feel his hand slowly wilting in my gentle grip. I release it when I know all contact with him is definitely lost. It won't be long before he's dead; I know it.

A Moat

Adele invites me to her wedding-ceremony. She has managed to convince an elderly man to become his permanent strip and wishes me to be her bridesmaid. In a glamorous parcel I receive the full gear: a silk, pink dress with a pair of very expensive satin shoes. I return her tinsel with an apology that I am in the middle of mourning for a very dear friend. Instead I arrive at the church in a black dress which my mother had reserved for funerals and formal events. On a finger, I wear a ring with a coat of arms engraved on it. Stephen McSloy had bequeathed it to me in his will.

Adele spends her honeymoon in France and upon her return she invites me to her new residence in St. Andrews. I am eager to know how life

has been faring with my self-sequestered mother so I accept her invitation without any reservations. Her aged husband dutifully receives me with a lukewarm smile but he has a pair of chilling eyes that are colder than my Alaskan hands. He feels my discomfort in his presence and feigns no affection for his wife's only relative. We intuitively discern that we belong to warring clans.

Adele takes me to her over-furnished, bridal room to display her hard-earned comforts and her impressive jewels, then directly comes to the point:

"Are you engaged, Clare?" she anxiously asks, looking at the ring in my right hand.

"No, I am not engaged. This ring is a gift from a friend," I answer, gazing affectionately at the subject of the topic.

"It looks very expensive. I did not know you were capable of socializing with the gentry. You should have introduced the man to me", says Adele with undisguised disappointment.

I sardonically grin. The idea of my sister stripping before Mr. McSloy is a painful, heart-rending joke.

"He is very welcome to accompany you the next time you call," says Adele with enthusiasm.

"He is dead," I quickly state, strangulating her day-dream in a single second.

"My husband would be interested in purchasing a ring like this. It looks historic. The money would be useful to you, Clare, I mean for your studies," says Adele encouragingly.

"One does not sell a friend's gift," I answer with apparent indignation. "Did you call at our mother? I recall receiving a card from Provence."

"I did not contact our mother, dearest. I am so sorry. It would have broken my heart to see Mum walled in. I also do not take to nuns. I will send her a letter with my latest news as soon as I feel settled in St. Andrews," answers my sister with her usual self-assurance.

I feel the need to speed up my leave before my remonstrance finds a harsh, verbal release. My decision to skip the desert which is in the wake of a series of plates, none of which has been to my taste, dispels the clouds that have been crowding over her husband's brow. The only other guest whom I obliterated from my mind the moment I arrived uneasily stirs in his chair and prepares to leave too. I do not recall his name or his relation to the newly-married pair. He sat silent opposite my chair at the grand dinner-table listening to the incessant chatter of my very talkative sister, while I simply sat feeling comfortably numb at the absolute loss of my appetite.

I fail to promise a second visit and slip the cheque which my sister has inserted in my pocket back into her bosom from which it has emerged. As I plant a quick kiss on her rosy cheek, her husband's sigh of relief swirls to my ears.

The other guest of honour whom now I find at my heels chivalrously offers me a lift. I assure him that I have a return ticket to Glasgow but he insists that there is ample room in his car and Glasgow is also his destination.

Mr. Whiplow gives me a synopsis of his life which matches the glossy leather of the interior of his car. I try to listen but my ears protest against the banality of his words. Before we reach Glasgow, he stops at a deserted park which is supposedly under repair, then with a single twist, he unties the chain of the iron gate, quite bent on showing me an historic mansion which is in the middle of a beautiful lake, claiming to be the abode of a very distant relative, a duchess.

I always keep calm when I feel danger prowling in the vicinity, so when he starts his preliminary, sexual advances in the form of an embrace and his hands begin to unsaddle my rear, I coolly decide to freeze his meat. My only recourse is the ice of my syllables and my sluggish heart-beats. I have always believed that fear has a scent which whets the appetite of a predator in heat.

"What comes next in this gothic scene? You throw me in the pond to dispense with my body," say I very composedly and half-jokingly.

"What makes you think I would want to be rid of you?" says he, with a bewildered look on his hardening face, his hissing hands withdrawing before accomplishing their intended deed.

"It looks like a movie scene," I add confidently, while composedly adjusting the ruffled attire of my indignant rear.

I do not know what makes me so abruptly turn round since my eyes are preoccupied with deciphering the contours of his alarm. It is possibly the movement of his eye-balls in which my image is permanently blurred. To my shock, I espy two gentlemen quickly moving away, one with a big camera in his hand, the type they use for shooting a film.

A Wake

My sister's husband is dead. Induced by excessive sexual excitement which I attribute to Adele's professionalism in the most adventurous types of provocative undressing, a heart-attack has claimed her aged husband. She is now a young widow with a vast inheritance. I attend the funeral service to offer my condolences. Adele plants a sticky kiss on my cheek, then in a whisper diluted with permissible amounts of liquor, she imparts to my nervous ear her future career. She is going to run her own night-club but stop strip-teasing before customers. I thrill to the latter part of her decision but how can I reason her out of the first. I think it is a sacrilege to discuss nightclubs in the house of God so I refrain from a debate that my sister is bound to win.

Virginia Woolf

I have chosen the subject of my dissertation and my supervisor is very pleased with my choice of Virginia Woolf's most complex novel The Waves. It guarantees a considerable amount of originality and perhaps it may get published one day. She has not known me long enough to know that all types of ambition are utterly missing from my life. I have chosen Woolf's most sophisticated novel because water permeates its every pore, and its tree-metaphors are redolent with the Celtic, Druidic lore. Its six characters, a six-petalled flower, constitute a universal whole with all its flaws. I see in Jinny my own sister Adele, braving erotic waves. Withdrawn Rhoda conjures up my mother who is shunning the terror of life, dwelling in a tiny shell that does not resonate with waves. The fertile Susan repulses me with her unbridled instincts, sailing placidly on an infinite sea of maternity. Bernard with his love of words appeals to me most.

What If

On a fragrant piece of paper I scribble a poem

with which to bid my sister goodbye before I head to a cottage in the Outer Hebrides. It is where my Dad lives a hermetic type of life. He has finally yielded to his paternal impulse and decided to acknowledge my existence. He has made me promise to keep his presence a secret so I pledged.

What if I strip before a fleet of fish that's moored to uncharted reef!

What if I stir the dregs of fears which slumber inside your cup of dreams!

What if I dwell in a toilsome tear which eons of years can't render brief!

What if I become the baleful breeze in a sea-shell's ear, bereft of waves!

What if I soar beneath the sphere of an eye whose core is wry with schemes!

What if I expire on a chuckle's pyre!

What if! What if!

God Bless, Clare.

About the Author:

Susie Gharib is a graduate of the University of Strathclyde (Glasgow, Scotland) with a Ph.D. Her doctoral thesis, entitled Stylistic and Thematic Reassessment of The Trespasser, is a critical study of the work of D.H. Lawrence. Since 1996, she has been lecturing in Syria. She self-published four collections of poetry (My Love in Red, The Alpine Glow, Resonate and Kareem) and a collection of short stories (Bare Blades). She is a lover of Nature and enjoys swimming.

MEETING MINUTES
by Brooke Reynolds

Jessica Derby slipped into room A19 just in time. It was her first PTA committee meeting. She had no idea what to expect having just moved here from Pennsylvania. She promised her husband that she was going to make an effort at being involved in her kid's new school. She slid into the last remaining open seat next to a woman revealing way too much cleavage for a weeknight school related function.

The cleavage stood to address the room. "Alright, everyone. It's 6:37 pm and officially time to start the September 2016 PTA committee meeting. I'm Chelsea Langhour, your current PTA President. We'll get started with attendance. If everyone could please make sure that they sign the sheet." Chelsea handed the sign-in sheet to Jessica to be passed around. "Diane Fairmore, our secretary again this year, will be recording the minutes. Principal Slater, do you wanna start the meeting off this evening?"

Andrew Slater stood and adjusted his tie. "Thank you, Chelsea. I'd like to start by saying that the new school year here at Bentridge High School is off to a great start. I anticipate great things from our students this year. The senior class is a stellar group of kids and they are sure to get our college acceptance rates up." Principal Slater turned toward the door as Custodian Jerry backed into the room whistling along to his music. "Can I help you, Jerry?"

Jerry spun the mop bucket around and went into a full on air-drum solo.

"Jerry!"

Jerry jerked his head up and pulled his earphones out. His face flushed as he was greeted by a room full of blank faces. "Yes?"

"Jerry, we're having a meeting here."

"Sorry. I'll just grab this trash bag here and slip out the way."

"Thanks, Jerry. Now, where were we? Ah, yes. I want to bring up the lovely new sign out front that was donated by the Class of 2015. What a great addition. Oh, I wanted to thank everyone who participated in the bake sale. Chelsea, I don't believe we saw you at the bake sale this time."

"I had a prior commitment that evening."

Diane raised her hand. "I motion to create an award for all those who refused to participate in the bake sale. The winners will be forced to take weekend baking classes for one month. The 'I have no desire to be Betty Crocker' award. All in favor, raise your hand?"

Jessica looked around the room as all hands shot up except for her's and Chelsea's.

"I resent that. I can cook. I was just unavailable. And besides, at least no one developed the gawd awful food poisoning we had at the catastrophic Spring Bake Sale."

"Motion accepted," answered Diane.

"You are not the President. So you cannot motion anything, Diane."

"Now, now ladies. Let's try to keep this meeting as professional as possible." Principal Slater gestured toward Diane and Chelsea who were seated next to each other. "You remember how quickly the last meeting spiraled out of control."

Diane and Chelsea both mumbled their apologies and gestured for Principal Slater to continue with the meeting.

"Now I think we need to address the attendance issues we've been having lately. We'll create a finite number of excused and unexcused absences before penalties are involved such as missing extracurricular activities. Diane, this particularly applies to your son."

"And what exactly do you propose we do Principle Slater?" Diane massaged her temples in a clockwise fashion.

"I'm not saying anything just yet. Maybe we decide on a number like after five they better have a good excuse or we start banning them from after school activities. And Diane, maybe you can have another talk with Trevor."

"Yeah, okay." Diane started doodling in the margins of her meeting minutes. Chelsea raised her hand. "I motion that we create the 'Bad Mothering Initiative' for all mothers of students that miss or are tardy for more than five days. Any member will be forced into cafeteria duty for one month. All in favor raise your hand?"

No one raised their hand besides Chelsea.

Diane sneered at Chelsea. "I see what you're doing here. Motion denied."

"Moving on." Principal Slater flipped through the stack of papers laid out in front of him. "We need to address the new and improved policy on 'No Place for Hate'."

"Sorry, what was that again?" Chelsea yawned.

"Late night again Chelsea," asked Diane.

"Coach Fenway had me out late again. But I'm not complaining."

"Back to the meeting ladies. 'No Place for Hate' is our new no tolerance policy, Chelsea. It falls under the anti-defamation league. We will not tolerate any form of bullying, cyberbullying, or any demonstration of hate. I assume we are all in agreement on this policy?" Principal Slater scanned the room and was met by a sea of bobbleheads all in agreement.

"Weren't we going to do something about the new students?"

"That's right, Chelsea. Thanks. We had decided that each new student at Bentridge High will be assigned one peer mentor as well as one adult mentor. This should help the transition."

Chelsea stood for a brief moment and turned toward Jessica. "While we're on the topic, are there any new parents here this evening?"

Silence fell upon the room while all eyes settled on Jessica. She kept her eyes glued to her busy hands as she continuously rung her fingers. She could feel the stares burning into her. Finally, she lifted her head to acknowledge the sea of eyes. She cleared her throat as she fought to find her voice. "Heh, Hello everyone. My name is Jessica Derby and I'm an alcoholic." Jessica immediately regretted the lame excuse of a joke the moment it escaped her lips.

Silence.

Jessica continued. "Okay. Not that type of meeting. Well, thank you for having me this evening. We just recently moved here for my husband's work and I promised him that I'd be more involved in our kids' school, so here I am."

Chelsea tapped Jessica on the arm. "Is your husband Paul Derby?"

"Yeah. Why?"

"He works with my husband. He mentioned the company was hiring a new CEO."

Principal Slater smiled. "Thank you, Jessica. We are happy to have you and to add some fresh ideas. You will be particularly helpful when we get to the fundraising portion of the meeting." The door opened again and Custodian Jerry burst through, belting out a melody. "Jerry!"

"What's up Principal?"

"We are still having a meeting here."

"Oh."

"Can you just come back when all the other rooms are done."

"Already done chief."

"Well, find something else to clean. We got at least 20 minutes here yet."

"Sure thing boss. Hey, Chelsea. Looking good." Jerry smiled as his eyes gave her the once over.

Diane looked back and forth between Chelsea and Custodian Jerry. "Seriously? Him too?"

"Oh Diane, that was years ago. But I'm hard to forget."

Principal Slater shooed the custodian out of the room and turned back to address the other bored faces scrolling through cell phones. "Anything else I'm forgetting?"

Diane interjected. "The transportation initiative. Weren't we going to discuss that?

"Ah, yes. Thanks. The driving initiative. Basically, we need to start taking some steps to create a safer environment for our young drivers. The usual stuff. Seat belt safety and texting while driving. Maybe we can add a special segment either to driver's education or gym class."

Chelsea raised her hand. "Principal Slater. I can ask Coach Fenway this evening if he would be interested in taking on that project."

Jessica shook her head. She thought this Coach Fenway must be some good looking guy considering how much the cleavage bragged about him.

Chelsea noticed Jessica shaking her head. "Excuse me? Did you want to add something?"

Jessica startled at being noticed. "Nope. I'm good."

Principal Slater continued. "That would be fine Chelsea. And on that note, I think I've covered everything that I have. Chelsea, do you wanna continue?"

"Will do. Moving right along." Chelsea pulled out her sheet and started flipping through. "I have someplace to be this evening so we will just skip to fundraising and wrap this meeting up early. We have some leftover funding from last year and need to decide which programs could benefit the most. I, for one, know that the cheerleaders could use new uniforms."

"Didn't they just get new uniforms," asked Principal Slater.

"That was last year. New season, new uniforms," answered Chelsea. "The girls have got to look

their best for the competitions. After all, they did place third at last year's state competition."

Jessica raised her hand. "Shouldn't we direct funds toward the groups that have the most immediate need?"

Principal Slater turned toward Jessica. "Why don't you tell us which groups you think those are?"

"Ummmm...well," Jessica mumbled. "One of my kids is in the band and their uniforms are pretty tattered. Most have holes or pretty bad stains."

Chelsea scoffed. "Nobody cares about band geeks. Nice try Jessica, but clearly you don't know where the priorities stand in this school. I'm not even sure why we have a band but I guess they do play music for the cheerleaders to dance to."

"Well, they are actually quite good," answered Jessica. "My daughter told me that last year they won second place at Nationals."

"They have competitions for band geeks? Clearly, they must not be as prestigious as cheerleading competitions."

Diane raised her hand. "I vote we set aside some funds for the theater department. The auditorium really could use some better seats."

Chelsea pounded the table to emphasize her point. "Why would we waste money on the theater? They aren't winning any competitions."

Jessica raised her hand. "Maybe we could just split the funds evenly amongst all the extracurriculars."

"Sorry Jessica. I get you're new and all. But that is a terrible idea. And besides, clearly, we should also be using the funds left over from the cheerleaders to help the football team. They bring in the most revenue. I'll just ask Coach Fenway what they need."

Diane groaned. "Look Chelsea, we get it. You're having an affair. You don't need to keep flaunting it, nobody cares."

"Woah, Diane." Chelsea turned toward her and placed a hand on her hip. "Do you got a stick up your ass tonight or what?"

"Nothing is up my ass. We get it. You're a slut." Diane turned toward Jessica while pointing at

Chelsea. "She could never let go of that head cheerleader mindset."

"You're just jealous. I see the way you look at Coach Fenway."

Diane rolled her eyes. "Oh, please. Yeah, give him my number. What I wouldn't give to have a beer gut receding hairline has-been sweating on top of me. Oh, yes, yes, yes."

"At least I know what I want and I do something about it," snapped Chelsea.

"Yeah by cheating on your husband. Mike is a great guy and you are off blowing the football coach. When my husband was still alive, I never dreamed of cheating on him, especially with some sleazebag."

"Ladies, please," Principal Slater interrupted. "What is up with you two this evening? I thought you were friends?"

Chelsea placed her arm around Diane. "Diane and I have known each other for years. We are practically sisters."

Diane shoved Chelsea's arm off of her. "Best friends."

"Don't you push me."

"Then keep your slutty hands off me."

"I motion we nominate Diane for the 'I can't take a joke award'."

"Yeah? Well I motion we nominate Chelsea for the 'I sleep with everyone because I have no self-worth.'"

Jessica stood to sneak out of the room. This meeting was too much for her. As she left the room, she was greeted by Custodian Jerry standing just outside and performing an air-guitar solo with his mop. Jessica tapped him on his shoulder. "I think you can finally head in there. Those people are crazy."

Jerry nodded in agreement. "Tell me about it. Few meetings ago a fight broke out between them women and I hadda stay late to fix one of the chairs they busted up. Made me late to my gig."

"Well, I think they are headed in that direction again."

Shouts were overheard. "Even with fake tits and enough Botox to poison an elephant, it still takes a man several drinks before he'll engage in a sexual act with you."

Jerry dropped his jaw in shock from the insult. "Oh man. I best be getting in there. You have a nice evening young lady and keep away from them women."

Principal Slater hustled after Jessica with sweat dripping from his brow. "Jessica, err Mrs. Derby, please wait. I'm sorry for all this. Our meetings are usually much more organized."

More shouts could be heard through the doorway.

"Diane! Don't you walk away from me when I'm talking to you."

"Then don't disrespect me."

"Bitch."

"Whore."

Principal Slater winced, then turned toward Jessica and smiled. "I really hope that you come back and decide to be a permanent member of the PTA."

Jessica knew she would not be back. These types of women were the ones she constantly avoided at the last school her kids attended. "Thanks, Principal Slater. But I just remember that I have another meeting at the same time so I don't think I'll be able to make it."

About the Author:

Brooke Reynolds is a veterinarian from Charlotte, North Carolina. When she isn't saving animals, she enjoys writing fiction. Her stories have appeared at such online and print markets as The Scarlet Leaf Review, Massacre Magazine, Fantasia Divinity, The Airgonaut, The Literary Hatchet, Ghost Parachute, Riggwelter Press, and Every Day Fiction. Her story "Dr. Google" won 2nd place in the 2016 Short Story Contest for Channillo. For more information, check out her website reynoldswrites.org. You can follow her on twitter @psubamit

CHIME PHOBIA

by Helen Grochmal

Clary and Myra were friends, let there be no questioning of that. Well, they were sort of friends. When one needed fresh garlic, the other would provide it if available. They would even feed each other's cats when required.

In the retirement home everyone tried to be friends with their nearest neighbor. It was protocol, and one might need the other some sad day, since every day there was one of uncertainty. But denial was a big part of their thinking, although a few of the bravest unnecessarily looked death in the face and either shrugged or stiffened their spines. Denial was easiest for most of them though, as their memories didn't operate quite so well as they had.

Getting back to Clary and Myra. Analyzing what later happened, an expert might deduce that denial had played a big part in explaining Clary's inappropriate behavior. Clary had a blind spot, a trigger that would make her obsess and carry on as if the devil were after her. In fact she had looked evil in the face- and it chimed. She had had a terrible experience with chimes in her 30s that she couldn't talk about. Since then she had picked places to live in large part depending on if the neighbors had "them," she hated to say the word.

Clary had heard about a dust-up in the past by a woman who had been stung by chimes too, that time by chime-envy, but Clary had not been part of that. She currently had her own problems concerning "them" to work on.

Her problem was that she had taken Myra's chimes. They were sitting on her bureau. Myra had refused to take them down from her patio before she went on her trip, although Clary had told her how much they bothered her. The usually compliant Myra had not taken them down immediately as Clary had thought she would. Myra had said firmly that the chimes didn't make much noise. The truth was that she was having trouble with her hearing aids and didn't hear them, so she thought Clary was being silly. Clary was not a bully, so she had nodded to Myra and left.

But she could not open her patio door in fear that she would hear "them" tingling, they were that kind, the kind that tingled in your head, torturing you. Too bad there wasn't a law that noise should stop at a resident's property line; but no, chime owning was not an illegal offense as it should be.

Well, Myra had gone out of town to a wedding, and Clary was feeding her cat twice a day. So Clary had merely gone over during her absence and taken down the chimes. She thought that she might as well have peace for a few days. Three days were better than no days.

The weather was beautiful and Clary kept her patio door open, taking advantage of each chime-free moment. She thought of how she could disable them, maybe putting a bit of glue on the places they bumped together.

On the day before Myra was due back, Clary heard a knock on her door. She knew the knock. She answered the door. Myra had come back a day early. Pleasantries and thanks were shared and Myra left.

Clary panicked. She had been ignoring the chimes to enjoy the time provided by God for her relief. Now she was plunged into the circles of hell.

She could be accused of vandalism, of unauthorized borrowing even. At the very least, the Minister would visit. Respectability was important in the community and to Clary. She writhed as some character in a Russian novel. How could she get those cursed chimes back with Myra sitting in her living room with full view of her patio? She couldn't. Being caught fooling with them on Myra's patio would be worse than anything. Clary would confess all if caught. She knew herself.

Clary sat, looking out at the beautiful day and hating it. Myra loved the out-of-doors. She might be out there now and find her chimes were missing. "Please, please don't let Myra go outside," prayed Clary out loud, "at least let her be sick in bed."

The day passed as if Clary were waiting for news of an execution that was scheduled to take place, her execution. She knew she was guilty. She blamed Myra but knew that Myra had rights. The wait hurt. She heard the chimes in her head, although she could touch them on the bureau if she wanted to. She knew the terror the miscreants had felt in stories like "The Tell-Tale Heart" and "The Monkey's Paw."

The agony was terrible. Everyone would know, her son would be told, she might have to move. Could they call the police? Could she go to jail or maybe get community service? She would lose her home, her place in life, her cat. She could even be accused of theft, she who had always proudly stood in judgment of others in knowledge of her supreme innocence.

The day passed and dusk came. Clary didn't hear a knock on her door. She wondered if Myra had been on her patio. Maybe she wouldn't notice the absence of her chimes. Fat chance! Life as Clary knew it was over.

Darkness fell. Nothing would happen that day. "Dear Lord, let me go over to replace the chimes when Myra is asleep or let me die before I wake. No, no, I didn't mean that. Don't punish me anymore!"

Clary got up many times in the night, passing the chimes on her bureau. She waited for a little light in the morning since she would have to walk on the grass on uneven ground. She would be shielded by bushes until she got to the end of Myra's patio. Walking over without falling, Clary felt for the place to hang the chimes in the dark. She thought maybe the neighbor's light facing Myra's apartment would go on pointing her out to the world but still she continued. Not getting the chimes to attach correctly, she left when they were just hanging on. They were up anyway! If Myra hadn't noticed they were missing, she would never connect the lopsided chimes with her.

She found herself back in her apartment. Her relief was extreme. "They" were back. At least a theft charge had been averted. But as she sat that day and the next, she thought that somehow Myra knew. Maybe another neighbor had told her she had seen Clary taking the chimes. The guilt and pressure increased like temperatures in the desert as the day went on until it was too much for Clary to take.

Clary waited two more days. She didn't see Myra in that time. That was proof that Myra knew. Everyone knew.

Clary cleaned herself up after days of sweating and walked over to the Home. She went to see the Minister. Not asking for permission, she walked in his office and slumped in the chair facing him. She poured out her sin, her fear, and her guilt. She cried from her heart for help.

The Minister told her sternly that she had certainly transgressed but not to the extent of her penance. "You must apologize to your neighbor if the spirit of the Lord takes you to that point and it should. You are not being required to formally apologize by this office. Your family need not be told. You did not deliberately hurt anyone. Rise and get hold of yourself. Do not despair over chimes. Ask your neighbor to take them down after you calm down. Pray for guidance."

Clary left gratefully, thinking she would never tell Myra if Myra didn't already know. She needed to think of excuses to tell her if confronted. She would learn to lie. Hadn't the Minister just given her permission? All would be well again, she thought complacently. Her good opinion of herself had returned, although maybe not her goodness.

The Minister doing his rounds among his flock suddenly found himself saying quietly under his breath, "Oh, Lord, that was the second case of severe chime disturbance requiring spiritual counseling since I came here. What can be happening?" From then on he listened for the voice of the devil whenever he passed the innocent looking pieces of metal clanging or tinkling or whispering in the wind that seemed to be reproducing themselves everywhere.

About the Author:

Helen Grochmal started writing fiction in her 60s when she moved to a retirement home. After the obligatory mystery novels complete with cat, she wrote short stories in different genres to expand her range. Six stories were accepted quickly, not to mention being part of a group mystery and a podcast. What can happen next? Short list where published: Bards and Sages Quarterly, Over My Dead Body!, Meat for Tea, Minerva Rising, Magical: An Anthology of Fantasy, Fairy Tales, and Other Magical Fiction and No Extra Words!

UNDESIRABLES

by Dustin Pickering

Some nights are more intense than others. Any night Ms. Courtney Devra sang is one of those nights. Her voice is serene and hypnotic, full of fear and trembling. When she announced a tour, her shows sold out immediately. She is known for requesting conservative numbers at her concerts. She preferred an intimacy with the crowd most performers shunned.

That is only one thing that defines her unique shows. Her voice—we shall say—is set rhythmically with the heart itself. It pulses with the perfect pitch, or as perfect as a voice gets. The presses called her "Mistress of Melody" or "The Heart of Day". She took all acclaim with a grain of salt. Her humility shone in her face. Her voice not only rang with the heartbeat, but her virtue was peerless. She seemed from another world.

She announced a special last minute concert she would perform in Atlanta. The proceeds she would donate to rape victims. Half the profit would be donated to testing kits in police hands that identify rapists. Tax payers had solemnly refused a tax increase to get rapists off their streets. It was forced into waiting for private solutions. Ms. Courtney Devra decided to perform for this cause because a babysitter had raped her at a young age and he still roamed the world at large. She didn't bother to report the incident—she was told no one would believe her because of his good standing. He hardly seemed a sexual predator to most of the community.

She kept quiet but held a grievance against her world for the horror she faced. She lived with his face daily. She spent years before her career to

clear herself psychologically of guilt. She felt it was unfair that he received pleasure by violating her and she harbored a secret rage within.

This promised to be her finest concert.

However, she insisted only 1,000 seats be available and sell at $300 each. She felt a sense of vengeance in her veins and thought the only way to control it was to limit attendance. The limitation served as a psychological purge because it imposed her will to power. The numbers were shrunk only for this specific concert. Her female power clearly acted as an imaginary thrust against the perpetrator who lived within her. Her power was in seeking solitude against her shame and victimhood. By refusing a larger audience, her self-contempt was assuaged.

She spent several hours in the dressing room warming up her voice. It was like tuning an instrument. She drove to the show in a small Ford Focus. She drove herself because she felt independent driving herself, and she distrusted chaperones. She parked the Focus in the rear parking lot several hours before the concert. She entered the auditorium quietly to assess it. She smiled, took a deep breath, and reached out her arms. She turned to its owner, Chrystal Turner.

"Fine place you have here! You keep it in good order." Courtney was short in stature and appeared thin, but her legs were stout and strong.

"It was built in 1979. I have always wanted to be involved in music...but my horn playing wasn't good enough. Lacked sophistication, I was told. It probably wasn't meant to be," the owner said. "It is incredibly nice to meet you. I have heard so much about your performances," she said.

"Thank you," Courtney responded kindly. Compliments were flattering to her. She felt humbled by kind words. "Humility is a great virtue," she said when the owner appeared confused.

"It's just that most performers are arrogant. And I would expect them to be," she said. "We recently hosted Diane Bazz. Ever heard of her?" Courtney nodded. "She looks beautiful on camera...but god, she is aggravating to deal with. A perfectionist. We couldn't please her no matter how hard we tried."

"I'm pleased to be here...I don't expect a flawless stage. Faults are inevitable. It's ok to make mistakes. But make things flow smoothly. Give it character."

"We have a great surprise for you, Ms. Courtney."

"Please, drop the Miss...we are on equal terms. We serve each other."

"How humbling! Well, I must unveil the surprise." Courtney smiled. "We heard you love fresh vegetables and salad bars. Is that true?"

"Yes, it is. I especially like tomatoes and celery."

"Well, at my expense...I mean the company's expense...we had a special high class salad bar brought to you. It's backstage."

"I am uniquely...flattered."

"Would you like me to direct you?"

"Sure, I anticipate it." Shortly after she said these words, they felt awkward.

The owner of the auditorium walked quickly. She gestured Courtney to a room directly behind the stage. The lights were off so she flipped them on.

The salad bar was several feet long. It was pushed against the back wall. There was a table and chair in the middle of the room. Courtney beamed.

"Thank you ever so much...." She said. "Some of my personal favorites."

"We made a list."

"Great!" The owner left quietly to give Courtney space. She asked one of the backstage handlers to show her the dressing room when she finished sampling the bar.

She put on a large golden dress with bright silver glitter. She glanced at herself in the mirror. She told the backstage handler she had never felt so beautiful for a concert. She promised her best performance.

She spoke to the backstage manager before getting on stage.

"I feel like Cinderella. Only the ball never ends. I'm just so enthusiastic about this concert. We hired one of America's classiest violinists."

"I heard him tune up. Graceful," the stage manager said.

"I am so perfectly grateful for my life..." She reached down and adjusted her shoe strap. Her shoes were classy, sharp black velvet. They had a golden clasp on the top. She turned sharply to glance at herself in the backstage mirror before she approached the right side of the stage.

"I am so proud of the work we have all done to make this show perfect." She fixed the long white glove on her left hand. She straightened the small wrinkles in it. Then she tossed her dark auburn hair and adjusted the small tiara on her head. Her smile was radiant.

"Good evening, ladies and gentlemen," said the announcer. His voice, deep and resonant, bounced across the auditorium into the rear and back to the front. "We have a pleasant evening prepared for you! Miss Courtney Devra is backstage!" The crowd clapped loudly. "All ticket sales go to a frequently overlooked cause. As an added bonus, you are a witness to the finest show given this year! Please welcome...Ms. Courtney Devra!" The crowd applauded loud and long enough to give the impression of a stadium of concert goers. Courtney walked on stage and lifted her hand abruptly. Her smile radiated and inspired the musicians who were in a box on the left hand side.

"Good evening!" Courtney paused. The crowd was silent. "Tonight I will confess. I too was a victim of sexual assault. Years ago, an older man grabbed me. I felt afraid so I grew hard as ice. I couldn't move." The crowd eyed her calmly in high respect. "After he fondled me, he raped me. He was my babysitter..." She almost cried to remember. "I am better now. I never reported it. I was told...he had a good standing in the community, to leave it alone. I did what I was told." She held the microphone tightly. "If you know some-one who was assaulted, support their feelings. This is a serious issue...we can't turn away from it without injuring ourselves. The darkness is with-in!" The crowd cheered to express agreement. "Now, my first song was written by Bruno Ar-mant. It is a masterpiece of the finest kind." Her voice hypnotized as would a lullaby. After four additional songs, the audience was no longer able to move. They were still as ice. The theater grew dark.

Suddenly, there were loud crackling noises. The lights shot sparks and some bulbs cracked. The show went on. She couldn't stop her song. She finally hit her highest note of the evening. The audience stirred passionately. There was a loud shriek and a woman cried, "He is touching me!"

The crowd sunk into a riot. They pushed, pulled, and attacked one another. They forced them-selves to the front of the stage slowly as they yanked at each others' hair and clothes. The en-tire audience behaved as if drunk or in a rage. People were trampled. Dead bodies bled on the theater floor.

In the end, no one survived. The theater owner stepped out after hiding in fear. Ms. Courtney Devra was disfigured on the stage, her legs curled beneath her and mouth exuding blood. The thea-ter floor was topped with bodies.

In the rear of the theater, a dark man stood tall. He was darkly dressed and held his top hat in his left hand. He laughed boisterously loud. The sound echoed through the auditorium. The owner balked in fear. She couldn't make out his face.

He was a stranger in town. His face was sharp and his eyes beamed a sky blue. His hair was a dusty blonde. He laughed so loudly it hurt the owner's ears.

She shouted across the theater. "What's funny?"

He flicked a cigarette and turned. He quietly left the theater through the rear entrance.

The owner fell into tears. "Why here? Why now?" she asked herself. The theater stayed dark and silent while she cried on the stage.

About the Author:

Dustin Pickering is founder of Transcendent Zero Press, a Houston-based literary publisher. He fea-tured for Houston's popular Public Poetry in 2013 and was a Special Guest Poet at Austin Interna-tional Poetry Festival that same year. He is pub-lished in Texas Poetry Calendar 2016, Seltzer, Artistic Muse, and a variety of other publications. He hosts events in the Houston area for music and poetry.

THE FOREVER LETTER

by Abigayle Thompson

That afternoon an invitation was placed in the mailbox outside the Roney's home. It was the end of February, a cold day with clouds settled across the sky. A breeze started to kick in, causing the grass to wave in the wind, there were mud puddles, and clumps of dirty brown snow on the edge of the road. The twins Jake and Josh were the second youngest out of their six other siblings in their family. However, the invitation inside their mailbox would soon forever change their lives.

The mail usually arrived around about 11 in the morning, thus the letter had been sitting there for awhile now. Their younger sister Xenia raced Mable, the next youngest, to get the mail. They always fought over the letters just to see if they had gotten any for themselves. After they had reached the mailbox, they came sprinting back into the house, "Jake and Josh we have a letter for you!!" they said waving it around in the air. Jake went over to Mable and took the letter from her. "Hey Josh, I think this is for that party Lane was talking about at school. She must've dropped it off today," said Jake.

"Oh yeah, when is it again?"

"It says.. this Saturday, you think we can make it? Ya know after the game?" said Jake looking up from the card.

"Sure, but I want to come home and shower real quick before we go... for the ladies," Josh said with a grin and a wink.

"Gross!" screeched Mable who was sitting on the couch listening in.

"What does Mable think is gross?" asked their Mom as she entered into the living room.

"Josh kissing girls," said Mable with disgust.

"You kissed a girl Josh?" asked mom.

"NO! Haha, but me and Jake want to know if we can go to a party Saturday night after our basketball tournament."

"We'll see, it depends on if you can even stay awake by the time we get back. Usually you guys are out," chuckled Mom as she walked towards the kitchen.

Mable then walked across the carpet to the coat rack and grabbed the leash to take out the dog. She headed outside through the back door and walked Missy down the steps to a small red bush. While the dog was going the bathroom Mable heard a low hissing sound. She turned to see two eyes underneath their back porch. The dog instantly turned around and started to run towards the hissing, but the leash yanked her back at the last second. A raccoon came out from underneath the porch and was approaching Mable and she screamed. Jake's face appeared in the window, he looked startled and scared. You could tell he was mouthing something loudly behind the glass to their Mom. So she opened the back door and ran down the steps with a broomstick. When she hit the raccoon across the head with the broom its head bobbed up and down. The coons tongue was hanging out the side of its mouth while its eyes spun. Mom yelled, "Mable, hurry dear, up the steps and into the house. Quickly please." Mable scurried, tugging the dog up the steps and onto the deck. As they were entering the house Mable turned back and saw the raccoon swaying, but waddling as fast as it could into the forest behind their home.

Once back inside the home Mom said, "I'm sorry, are you okay? The raccoon didn't hurt you did it?"

"No, I'm fine. It almost bit Missy though," said Mable.

"I'm glad you're fine," her Mom said with a smile. As she said that Dad entered into the kitchen because he had just arrived home from work. The conversation switched. They started talking while asking how each other's day had been.

That evening their family parted their own ways. Jake and Josh were playing a game downstairs on the Xbox. Mable was spending the night at Lane's house for the weekend because she was friends with her younger sister. Mom was teaching Xenia how to make cookies in the kitchen. The smell of them baking in the oven floated throughout the house. Dad was on the couch reading the newspaper and discussing the news with their oldest son Caden. The third youngest child, Charlie was teasing Bridget, the second youngest, chasing her around with a nerf gun. The baby, Adia, was sound asleep in her crib up in her room. Everything seemed to feel perfect. The atmosphere was warm and you could feel the love swarming in the air. However, much would change the following evening.

Around 9 o'clock the evening began to settle down. Everyone had tried the cookies that Xenia made with Mom. The snickerdoodles were warm and fresh. Then it was time for everyone go to bed. Mom walked upstairs and tucked Bridget and Charlie into their bunk bed and gave them a kiss on their heads. Dad was rocking the baby while he read Xenia a bedtime story. Jake and Josh were told to head up to bed in 10 minutes. Caden was studying at his desk in his room, writing something down in his notebook. He was always writing letters to his girlfriend who lived 4 hours away. It was hard for them to see each other, but they made it work after meeting one another at the New York Philharmonic Orchestra concert. They were both big Orchestra nerds. He played the cello and his girlfriend played the bass. After he scribbled his remaining sentences into

his notebook he climbed into bed and turned out the lights.

The sun shone through the curtains down the hall. A scent of bacon and pancakes drifted through the air. It was Saturday morning and you could hear the birds chirping outside in the trees behind their home. One by one the kids woke up and wandered down into the kitchen where the scent carried them. Dad was at the table setting out cups of orange juice. Xenia was eating bacon when Charlie walked in to get some food. Bridget spilt syrup on herself and Mom was taking her to the bathroom to get it off her cotton pajamas. Jake and Josh were both still sound asleep because they always slept in until about 10 a.m.

The schedule for the day was already set. It was Dad's turn to take the boys to their tournament. Charlie was coming along for the ride. Mom was watching the other kids at home, while Caden drove himself to his private cello lesson. The ride to the tournament was about an hour away. They played a total of 3 games. The first game they lost, but the next two they won.

On their way back from the game they stopped by a quick restaurant to get some food before heading home. "Will we have time to make it to the party?" asked Jake.

"Yeah, and even if we did show up late Lane always has long parties so it'll be good," said Josh.

"Just remember boys to make good choices. I trust Lane and all, but you never know what could happen. If it get's out of control you can always call us or just leave."

"We know Dad," they both said in unison. They finished the ride back to the house in silence. Once they got home they went upstairs to get ready.

"Hey honey, where's Mable? Is she home yet?" asked Dad when he got home.

"No, the Jenson's said that they were going to take the kids to a trampoline park during the party," said Mom.

"Okay, sounds good," said Dad. The boys walked down the stairs ready to head over to the party.

"We are gonna leave now if that is alright," said Jake. Dad nodded at them because he was in a conversation with their Mom. The boys took the keys off the rack and walked out to the garage. They took Dad's car and backed out of the driveway. On their way over Jake asked, "Josh what's up? You seem out of it right now haha."

"Oh..I'm just tired. That tournament swept me. I'm still kinda pissed though that we lost our first game. You saw how close we were," said Josh.

"Yeah, that was kind of a bummer, but hopefully Lane's party is good. She texted me to say their parents left to take the kids to the trampoline park and dinner. So we got the house to ourselves."

"Do you know who all is coming?"

"No, I guess we'll just have to wait and see," said Jake. They pulled up along the curb outside her house. The street was already lined with cars. It had already been an hour into the party. Usually people didn't show up until after 9.

They walked inside. The floorboards were already vibrating beneath their feet. Lane always had the music going down in the basement. There were people scattered throughout the house. They walked towards the basement door and a wave of body heat floated up when they got near it. Lane was near the bottom of the steps. When she saw them she waved them down the stairs. Josh knew that Jake was into Lane just as much as she was into Jake. Although they never dated, they had their special connection.

Josh walked to the back corner and sat on the couch. Jake and Lane were talking in the corner. Of course someone had brought drinks and she was already offering him one. Jake was never a big drinker. He prefered to stay healthy for sports. Josh on the other hand didn't really care. Jake refused the drink, but pulled Lane back up the stairs so they could talk and check on the rest of the house. Lane had mentioned that she didn't want the party to get too out of control. Her parents were fine with parties as long as no one got hurt or too carried away.

In the midst of all the dancing and fun Josh just sat there looking dazed, as if he wanted to be anywhere but there. Everyone thought that he

and his brother had the perfect life and perfect family, but no one knew truly what Josh had experienced. He always seemed to be the odd one out. Jake was the "better looking" one even though they were twins. He also seemed to do everything Josh did, except better.

When Josh was five years old he was sexually abused by one of his cousins at a family gathering. No one knew, but him. He was too afraid to say anything about it. The abuser claimed that they were playing "doctor" on him. In dark late moments like this, flashbacks could strike any moment. Just then he felt in coming. His mind tilted. Images flashed through his head. He felt scarred. Unsafe. Defeated. Depressed. Fear pulsed through him at every beat. His mind swayed. Flashbacks were sweeping throughout his dimly lit mind. Josh's body was beginning to shake. He got up and started to walk to the small kitchen in the back of the basement. In times like this he needed to leave. People were pressing around him. Their bodies sweaty from dancing. "Hey Josh!" someone yelled from inside the crowd. His fists squeezed and he kept his head low. Not now, not now.. Is what he thought.

It always pissed him off though that Jake seemed to have everything. Even if Josh wanted to date someone it was hard. The flashbacks. Just a single touch from a certain person sent him into shock. People never even knew. Jake didn't even know. Although at one point he had thought that Jake had caught on.

The room swayed. Josh opened the small fridge in the mini kitchen and took out a drink. He sat on the floor and took a sip. His head resting against the cabinet. After finishing a can he grabbed several more from inside. He wanted this all to end.

His body felt numb. He climbed the stairs, his body unsteady. Where is some place I can hide? He thought to himself. Jake came out of the coat closet across from the room. He looked at Josh with a panic expression, then reached back inside and took a jacket off a hanger then walked away saying, "Dude, Josh go sit down somewhere you don't look too good."

It became a blur. The lights on the main floor were turned off. Bumping into dark objects. I just need to hide. The closet. His thoughts and emotions. Blue rays of light sweeping through his eyes and swaying with the world. His insides curling up. Anger. Everything crashing down inside his head. His head hurt. The world seemed upset at him. No one would understand or seem to care. Blurriness. Then darkness.

Jake walked over to the bathroom and quickly pulled off the coat and shoved it inside the bathroom closet. His hands hurt. Why? Why am I so dumb? There was a knock at the door. Jake quickly washed his hand, but not the image out of his head. Lane was standing there when he opened it. "Let's go," she smiled up at him. With a confused look, but then remembering where he was he took her hand. They headed for the stairs to go up to her room. A shiver went down his spine.

It was around 12 when Josh woke up. The stench was horrible. He looked around, but it was pitch black. He reached around for the closet door knob, but instead felt something stiff and sticky by it. He didn't know how he had ended up inside the closet. What the.. he thought. He didn't even remember making it to the closet. Opening the closet door a stream of light seeped inside. Josh started puking all over the floor when he saw what was laying next to him on the ground. On the closet floor next to him was his sister Mable. Her body was covered in blood and her eyes lay open staring straight ahead. She wasn't breathing. Had I done this? Had I just murdered my sister? Why was she here? Unable to think, Josh crawled out the closet, his body was shaking. He laid on the floor. Was he crying? "Help.." he croaked out of his mouth. His body was too in shock to scream. The main floor was deserted. The floorboards vibrating against his cheek. Sobs racked his insides. NO, no, no, no... This couldn't be happening.

Upstairs Jake was talking to Lane on her bed. "Yeah I hope you don't mind, but when your parents called I told them that your sister Mable was going to a trampoline park with my parents and Katrina. However, Katrina and Mable just stayed here. My parents are away for the weekend. They went down to Carolina for a quick business trip," said Lane.

"Yeah, well I trusted you. Also I should probably bring Mable home.. Where is she?" asked Jake trying to not look scared.

Jake walked over to the bathroom and quickly pulled off the coat and shoved it inside the bathroom closet. His hands hurt. Why? Why am I so dumb? There was a knock at the door. Jake quickly washed his hand, but not the image out of his head. Lane was standing there when he opened it. "Let's go," she smiled up at him. With a confused look, but then remembering where he was he took her hand. They headed for the stairs to go up to her room. A shiver went down his spine.

It was around 12 when Josh woke up. The stench was horrible. He looked around, but it was pitch black. He reached around for the closet door knob, but instead felt something stiff and sticky by it. He didn't know how he had ended up inside the closet. What the.. he thought. He didn't even remember making it to the closet. Opening the closet door a stream of light seeped inside. Josh started puking all over the floor when he saw what was laying next to him on the ground. On the closet floor next to him was his sister Mable. Her body was covered in blood and her eyes lay open staring straight ahead. She wasn't breathing. Had I done this? Had I just murdered my sister? Why was she here? Unable to think, Josh crawled out the closet, his body was shaking. He laid on the floor. Was he crying? "Help.." he croaked out of his mouth. His body was too in shock to scream. The main floor was deserted. The floorboards vibrating against his cheek. Sobs racked his insides. NO, no, no, no... This couldn't be happening.

Upstairs Jake was talking to Lane on her bed. "Yeah I hope you don't mind, but when your parents called I told them that your sister Mable was going to a trampoline park with my parents and Katrina. However, Katrina and Mable just stayed here. My parents are away for the weekend. They went down to Carolina for a quick business trip," said Lane.

"Yeah, well I trusted you. Also I should probably bring Mable home.. Where is she?" asked Jake trying to not look scared.

"She should be in Katrina's room, unless they went downstairs haha to party. However, I doubt that." Jake got off her bed and said he was going to look for her. Lane followed him down to Katrina's room. They looked inside. Katrina was sound asleep on her bed, but the sleeping bag was empty on the floor. "Maybe she went to go get a drink of water or had to use the bathroom," suggested Lane. Jake was starting to shake, but Lane wasn't paying attention. The bathroom was empty.

Towards the stairs Lane heard Josh's sobs. "What is that?" They went down the stairs. Josh was laying on the floor shaking. "Josh we better get you home buddy, you look exhausted," said Jake. Josh was too in shock to say anything about Mable. "Can you just drive Mable over tomorrow morning then?" asked Jake.

"Sure," said Lane. The two boys headed out the door and made it to the car. Jake started to drive home. When they got home no one was awake, so they headed up to their bedroom. Jake quickly stopped by his parents room to let them know that Mable was spending the night at Lane's again because she was already sleeping. His parents thanked him then told him to go to bed.

When Josh woke up Lane had called him. He was surprised so he called her back. What seemed like reality last night seemed so far away like it was a very bad dream. When Lane picked up the phone she said, "It's Mable. Come here immediately. Bring your family. The police are already here." Was it a dream? It couldn't be. Flashbacks. Red light. Drinking. Darkness. Sticky. Blood. No it couldn't be.. Josh quickly awoke his family and Jake and told them that they needed to go to Lane's. Something bad had happened.

When they arrived the police had started questioning Jake and Josh. Mable was pronounced dead on scene. Mom was in shock and sobbing into Dad's arms. He brought their Mom out of the house so she could calm down. "Josh, Lane says that you were laying on the kitchen floor last night sobbing, is that true? Right before you left?" asked one of the police officers.

"Yes."

"What were you doing last night Josh that lead you to the kitchen."

"First I had gone downstairs. I was sitting on the couch, but my head was hurting so I went and had a couple of drinks. Probably more than I should've. My heachache was getting worse so I tried to get upstairs away from the music. The closet was the nearest place, but I blacked out

and don't remember entering the closet. I woke up inside of it, when I opened the door to leave I saw Mable next to me. I started sobbing and was too in shock to move. That's when I was laying on the floor in the kitchen and Lane and Jake walked in," said Josh.

"Do you think you hurt Mable when you were unconscious or in the period you don't remember?"

"It may have been possible, but I would never do anything like that to my siblings."

"You do know that you put yourself in a situation where you didn't have control of your body," said the officer, "Jake, where were you that evening?"

"Sir, I was downstairs at the beginning talking with Lane. Then we came to this level to check on the people in the rest of the house. After that I got cold so I went to the coat closet and grabbed a jacket. I went to the bathroom after that, then me and Lane headed upstairs to her room and talked. Lane had told me then that Katrina and Mable were here so we went to look for her, but that is when I found Josh. He looked unstable so I brought him home."

"Did you have any drinks?"

"No sir, I did not," said Jake.

"You do understand that both of you were to enter the coat closet that evening. We will have to go through further investigation. It could be one of you or it could even be another victim at the party. Lane we will need to know who you all invited. For right now Jake and Josh you are coming with me. Parents you can also follow officer Jenkin's, he will bring you to her body if you would like to see it," said the officer as he went outside to talk to Jake and Josh's Mom.

"Thank you," sobbed their Mom as she tried to hold it together. Lane's parents were on their way home. Lane was shaken up and her younger sister was sitting around the corner of the stairwell listening in.

After about 3 weeks of gathering information and eyewitness accounts, there was enough evidence to convict one of the brothers for the murder of their younger sister Mable. At the end of their court session Josh was going to be pronounced guilty. He was under the influence and in the closet for most of the night. He hadn't remembered her being in there at first, so the conclusion was he murdered his sister while in the closet. Just before the session closed, Lane, went up to the stand. After being too afraid to bring up what she thought wasn't real before, she spoke it now, "The night of the murder I didn't want to believe what I saw. I was outside at the time, helping my friend Miranda who was throwing up in the bushes. Just for a second I had turned my head and through the window of the house I saw.." Lane started crying as she spoke. "I saw Jake. Mable was there, she was alive, but only for a few more short seconds. I saw Jake hit her. She fell to the floor, then I saw... I saw him pick her up. I..I.. I was so confused, but then I will never forget what happened next," Lane looked down and clasps her hands in her lap.

"Please continue Lane," said the Judge.

"I saw him with...a knife. He had cut her throat, but what was worse was that he turned. Just for a second I had thought we made eye contact. Then I saw him open the closet. I don't know what else happened in there, but when I came inside Jake was in the bathroom. After what had happened me and him went up stairs. I started drinking more because I was afraid... I wanted to forget. I didn't want what I saw to become reality," said Lane.

"However, you couldn't tell if it was Jake or Josh because they are twins and it was dark out," said one of the lawyers trying to prove Josh guilty still.

What people didn't know was that while Josh was sitting downstairs drinking, Jake was upstairs. Then as Josh was coming up the stairs and into the kitchen Jake acted like he was pulling on a coat from inside the closet. However, Lane wasn't in the room yet and neither was anyone else. Jake had blood all over his hands. The room was dark and when Josh thought he was running into objects it was actually Jake who had kicked him. Josh had then slipped and hit his head on the table knocking him unconscious. Jake had then took Josh and put him in the closet to cover up the murder in which he had committed. When he went to the bathroom that was when Lane came back inside, so he shoved the jacket in the bathroom closet and washed his hands.

However, the jury then left to decide who they thought was guilty of the crime. When they all came together, Josh was pronounced guilty. Although some facts were left unknown. Everyone was wondering how Josh was the guilty one. Jake always got away with everything. Lane was in tears because she knew the truth. Jake somehow was just trying to get back at Josh for being his twin. Jake had always hated Josh. For some reason the thought of having someone look the same and act very alike terrified him.

Josh broke down. He felt worthless. He was trying so hard, but everything ended the wrong way and now he was being punished for something he didn't do. The Judge dismissed them. For the Roney family their world would never be the same. For the fact that Jake was still on the loose and Mable was now gone. One decision can change the course of your life, just like how the Roney family found that out.

About the Author:

Abby Thompson is a senior in high school who feels that writing is a way to express herself. This is her first short story and hopes that she can reach those who seek for entertainment from literature. In college she hopes to major in Interior design and Architecture.

DISSIDENTS

by Michael Malloy

Calvin Conkling and Suzie Hatchet were strolling the warm paving stones of Almaty's "Arbat," the popular nickname for Zhibek Zholy, the pedestrianized central boulevard in Kazakhstan's former capital. It was a bright sunny day in May, and Calvin and Suzie were down in the city for the holiday weekend, having taken an Air Astana flight south the night before. They were staying in the Hotel Otrar, a breezy modernist building in marble with concrete beehive balconies layered across its edifice. They were Americans.

Calvin was admiring the artwork for sale on the Arbat. Suzie was drinking fresh-pressed pomegranate juice she had bought from a young man operating a juice press. The husks of spent pomegranates, oozing juice and spitting seeds on the sidewalk, had been an irresistible advertisement.

Young men passed by in short sleeves and blue jeans. Women had nose rings and dyed hair—not many of them, but some. A teenaged Kazakh kid with poofy black hair was strumming a cheap Russian-made nylon-stringed acoustic guitar, warbling bard songs. Calvin held Suzie's hand.

"How civilized," he said.

Suzie smiled. She was wearing sunglasses.

"You want to get some coffee?" asked Calvin. Suzie held up her half-full glass of pomegranate juice in response.

"Well, I want some," said Calvin.

They made a beeline for an American-operated, ostensibly hip coffee shop they had heard of thanks to the Lonely Planet guidebook. The shop was hard to find, the guidebook's map holding a tenuous relationship to reality, like Marxist theory to Soviet practice. But eventually they found it, a charming stucco building with big glass windows looking out on a quiet tree-lined street. They stepped inside, seeing the usual assortment of backpackers, expatriates, and hipster Kazakhs.

Hipster Kazakhs, thought Calvin—to think there was such a thing! It was like finding radical Iowans, or Sarah Lawrence Young Republicans.

He set his messenger bag down on the table and walked up to the counter.

"Ya hochu..." he began.

"We can speak English," said the bearded, evidently Yankee barista.

"Oh, thank Jesus," said Calvin. "Medium latte, please."

The barista bustled behind the counter, shooting steam and pouring frothy black liquids from one receptacle to another.

Now this was a coffeeshop, thought Calvin. It put Astana, with its grainy Nescafe half-dissolved in Turkish teacups, to shame.

Calvin and Suzie were visiting Almaty from Astana, where they were ESOL teachers at an American school. They were down for the long weekend—Victory Day, the day the Soviet Union defeated the Axis Powers. The guidebook—and other expats—had promised that this was the day when everybody busted out their old hammers and sickles, and Calvin hadn't wanted to miss it. Everybody said the holiday was better in Almaty, the city that used to be the capital, before

President Nursultan Nazarbayev moved it in the 1990s, after the Soviet Union fell.

They also said Almaty itself was better. When Nazarbayev moved the capital from the temperate south to the frozen north, many people chose not to follow: artists, hippies, creatives of all sorts. Anybody who appreciated reasonable weather, fine architecture, and culture. Anybody who didn't have to leave. It was the bankers, businessmen, and apparatchiks who moved north to Astana, a charmless town that had once been called Tselinograd (virgin lands city), and before that, Akmola (white tomb).

Of the two older names, thought Calvin, white tomb was closer to the mark. Astana was situated in the northern Kazakh steppe, just below Russian Siberia, where winds were strong and temperatures could hit forty degrees below zero (Celsius and Fahrenheit—they met around there). As if to compensate for the climate, President Nazarbayev went on a building spree, financing elaborate modern architecture with the state's oil and natural gas money. The end result was sometimes called "the Las Vegas of the steppe" by people who had never been to Astana or Las Vegas.

It was a hard city to describe. Calvin liked to say that, although he had never actually seen "Mad Max: Beyond Thunderdome," Astana was Thunderdome.

It was cold. The people were cold too. Nobody smiled. The men wore black suits, like they were going to a funeral. The women dressed like conservative, status-conscious telephone operators from the mid nineteen forties. Everybody drove fast, like they had someplace else and better to be.

Almaty was another world. A great deal looser. Calvin was breathing easier. He felt like he used to in college, when he had backpacked across Europe. He had hoped that working in Kazakhstan would be more like that. Instead, it was more like—a job.

He got his drink and sat down. He tasted it. Not bad at all. Not up to Brooklyn standards, but then, what was? Not even Brooklyn.

Suzie was reading a novel, a vintage hardcover in English she had found for sale by the steps leading to a pedestrian underpass (pop-up book markets, another plus for Almaty, thought Calvin). It was a book by a Kyrgyz writer, Chingiz Aitmatov: The Day Lasts More than a Hundred Years. Calvin could never remember the title, so he referred to it as One Hundred Years of Kyrgyz-tude. She had learned a bit about the writer, a hero in his native land and quite beloved in Kazakhstan, also.

"He put all this commentary about the late Soviet period in the book," said Suzie. "About the way the government repressed Central Asian culture and spent money on its space program while shortchanging its poor people. It's a good book. Kind of a dissident book."

Dissident. It was a cool word, suggestive of serious young men in neoclassical Soviet buildings smoking shitty communally-produced cigarettes and discussing in hushed tones the possibility of revitalizing communism following the death of Stalin. It suggested bootlegs of the Beatles carved into old x-rays (because that was a thing they did, right?). It suggested being a badass.

Calvin didn't feel much like a badass. He also felt, strangely, that the time for dissidents was over. The Soviet Union had fallen. The country simply existed under Nazarbayev now, as a corrupt but contented kleptocracy funded by petrodollars and dedicated to the proposition that great power interests could be balanced and business could be done. It was better than Islamic extremism, poverty, or civil war. It was probably, on the whole, good enough.

It was to such a diminished world that he had come, the previous summer, on a Lufthansa flight, to teach English. Knowing nothing of Central Asia. Not even really knowing how to read the Cyrillic alphabet. He was a bit less ignorant now. A bit.

Suzie was busy slurping up the last remnants of her pomegranate juice.

"Hey," she said, "did you ever figure out what song Meruert is going to play for the concert?"

Meruert. Three syllables: mare as in a female horse, ooh as in an exclamation of surprise or delight, and yurt as in the nomadic dwelling place of rural Kazakhs. Mare-oo-yurt. She was a student in Calvin's eleventh grade (their terminal year) English class, and a member of his guitar club. He had started a guitar club because everyone was expected to do at least one extracurricular, and he had played a little as a young man, in high school, in an anarchist punk band that fell apart due to lack of organization.

Meruert was good. In addition to the guitar, she played the kobyz, a Kazakh relative of the violin, played standing up vertically in the lap, bowed.

Meruert liked American punk rock, the stuff that was popular enough to have made it to Kazakhstan. So, you know, Green Day. But that was fine. That was the punk that Calvin himself had listened to in high school. Kazakhstan was far enough behind culturally that their pop music neatly intersected with his own nostalgia. It was a good match.

Meruert was also a big fan of Viktor Tsoi, the part-Kazakh Soviet rock star who had died tragically young and had written a great many brilliant songs that criticized the Soviet system in simple Russian and simple metaphor. "Trolleybus," "Elektrichka," "Changes." His work made quotidian Kazakh bleakness feel bearable for Calvin.

"I think she is going to play a cover," said Calvin. "Something by the Clash, maybe."

Suzie nodded. She went back to her book.

Calvin had not told her the whole truth. He hadn't lied. He had just—rather like the old Soviet publishing houses—omitted.

Meruert had written a song of her own, one critical of the President. She had expressed sympathies with certain striking workers from the west who had been shot by government soldiers while they had been protesting. People had died. Calvin remembered when it happened, how afraid he had been. Perhaps the country was unstable. It was all well and good to sling a guitar and sing about revolution, but revolutions in this part of the world had a way of leading to civil war, Russian intervention, or Islamic extremism. He was a Yankee imperialist. He would probably get shot.

But things had stayed quiet. Kazakhstan, like an old Lada well-maintained, just kept humming, however reluctantly. Calvin kept teaching English, avoiding controversial topics like democracy and focusing on non-controversial yet still irritating grammatical topics, like the various sorts of English conditionals. It was all education, wasn't it?

They were getting the tools they would need to read whatever they wanted some day, if they'd ever be allowed to.

Meruert's song had been good, an unconscious evocation of Billy Bragg, Woody Guthrie, and Florence Reece, filtered through the musical aesthetics of late nineties pop punk. It had activated something in Calvin, made his step lighter as he walked home after school that day, made the frigid steppe winds feel a little less biting.

But he still advised her not to sing it in front of the school. Important parents would be in the audience. People who controlled, well, pretty much everything. That was the thing about these post-Soviet states. They really did have shadowy elites who pulled all the puppet strings. And Meruert was supposed to be going to a university named after—you guessed it—Nursultan Nazarbayev, first President of the Republic of Kazakhstan.

So Calvin had suggested something else. Maybe "I Fought the Law." Keep the rebellion present, but general. Sneak your sympathies out there, like Aitmatov had managed to do in his books. Be a dissident, in half measures. It was better than no measures at all.

All the same, though, Calvin was ashamed of himself. He finished his coffee. They sat in the café for a long while. Then they got up and left, walking to Panfilov Park, in the impressive shadow of a pale yellow Orthodox cathedral made entirely of wood and looking rather like some fantasy citadel in an old Dell paperback. The sun was shining, and the Kazakh people they saw, despite or perhaps because of their comparative lack of civil liberties, seemed pretty happy. It was a warm day in May.

Somebody sold Calvin a ribbon, striped in yellow and black. He pinned it to his chest. Veterans walked the park, silver-haired, their blazers overloaded with medals and ribbons. An old man was playing "Katusha" on the accordion, prompting circuitous folk dancing from the admiring crowd. Somebody else was carrying an oil portrait of Joseph Stalin. It felt weird to be an American celebrating alongside so many hammers and sickles. But, after all, thought Calvin, we were all on the same side back then.

About the Author:

Michael Malloy is a writer and teacher living in Philadelphia, PA, and have previously been published in venues like Toasted Cheese, Eclectica, and Dans Macabre Du Jour.

A WEEKEND IN DECEIT

by Brett Kaplan

Late Thursday morning, Lee and Melinda were coming out of an art gallery in Chelsea when they saw their friend Hal embrace a woman who wasn't his wife. They came to a standstill on the steps in front of the gallery while they watched Hal kiss the strange woman before helping her into a cab. Lee and Melinda were both shocked at what they'd seen, but for very different reasons. Lee was shocked because he'd never known Hal to be a cheater, and Melinda was shocked because she believed that Hal's adulterous lifestyle was a thing of the past. The incident came at a time of particular interest as Melinda and Lee had plans to spend the weekend celebrating their recent engagement with Hal and his wife Jane at their home in the Hamptons.

To remain unseen, they decided to sneak into the coffee shop next door. They scrambled inside and took a seat at the first table by the door.

"I can't believe it," Lee said. "Hal?"

"I know," Melinda said. "He's the last guy I'd suspect of having an affair."

"And, poor Jane," Lee said. "She'll be devastated."

"What do you mean she'll be devastated."

"Well, we're obviously going to have to tell her."

"But why? I mean, isn't that something we should think about first? After all this is a long-term, committed relationship we're talking about here."

"Committed?"

"I don't know. They seem so happy together."

"Sure they seem happy—that doesn't mean they are."

"I just think we need to think about the implications of doing something before we start making a mess of things."

"They already are a mess. It's just, Jane doesn't know it yet."

Melinda was about to tell Lee that he shouldn't be making this about one of his moral issues, but stopped herself when she looked up and saw Hal walk into the coffee shop.

"Hey!" he said, coming right to them. "Didn't expect to see you guys till later."

Lee said, "Neither did we."

Melinda said, "We were just next door looking at some paintings."

"Anything good?"

"Oh, there's always something good," she said, "just nothing we could buy without having to speak with the accountant first."

Hal said, "I stopped in here to grab something before I head out east. Gonna get some work done on the boat. Was thinking we could take a little sunset cruise tomorrow."

Lee said, "Jane going along, too?"

"Oh, she's already out there. I think she has a tennis lesson, and then she wanted to get a head start on getting things organized. You know how she is."

Lee said, "The things she doesn't know…"

"Come again?"

"Nothing," Melinda said. "Is she playing a lot of tennis now? I haven't spoken to her in a while."

"Of course, she is. Every minute with lessons and instructors—think I'm gonna need a second job … anyway, Lee, I've been meaning to ask. If you wanna bring your clubs, maybe we can sneak out on the course if the girls let us."

Lee nodded.

"You need us to bring anything?" Melinda said. "Maybe a bottle of wine?"

"Oh, no," Hal said. "You know Jane. The woman has more wine than Dionysus."

"All right then. We don't want to hold you up."

"See you guys out there," Hal said, turning towards the counter.

Shortly before she met Lee, Melinda had had an affair with Hal. It only lasted a few weeks, and wasn't anything more than weekday mornings at The Carlyle Hotel. Nonetheless it was an affair, and Melinda wasn't in the business of being a paramour—at least so she thought. While this was going on, Jane, who happened to be an old friend of Lee's, introduced him to Melinda as someone she thought he'd like to date. And it turned out that she was right because not long after that, Lee and Melinda had moved in together, and Melinda's affair with Hal came to an end. She and Hal came to the agreement that they would never, under any circumstance, tell anyone what happened between the two of them for as long as they lived.

Ten minutes later, Lee and Melinda walked down 9th Avenue with their coffee in hand.

Lee said, "We have to tell her. It's wrong of us not to."

"Do you have to turn this into one of your Kantian issues?"

"Look, it's the right thing to do, and anyone in our position would do so."

"But how do we know what we saw is really as bad as it looks?"

"Are you saying what we saw was a mirage?"

"Don't patronize me."

"What's in it for you anyway. I mean, why are you defending him like this?"

"I'm not. I just want to make sure we don't start going around ruining marriages because of something we happen to see."

"Let me just ask you something, because I need to understand where you're coming from. If it was the other way around, you'd expect Jane to say something to you, right?"

"Well, of course I would."

"So, then what's the difference?"

"I don't know what to tell you, Lee. If you want to tell her, go right ahead."

"Now you're getting upset."

"Well this is a bit upsetting, don't you think?"

"Sure it is. And that's why we have to say something."

"Look, let's just give it the weekend, okay? If on Sunday we still think it's the right thing to do, then okay, maybe we'll decide to do it."

Lee took her gently by the shoulders, and said, "I love you, you know that? And I can't wait to make you my wife."

"And I love you, too," she said. "But let's just hang back on this a bit. All right?"

Lee said, "You're right."

They kissed each other and walked back home together hand-in-hand.

They arrived at Hal and Jane's place in Southampton on Friday just before noon. When they got inside, Hal said, "Look who's here!" and then, "Who's ready for a drink?"

Melinda said, "It's a bit early, but what the hell. I'll take something light."

Lee said, "And I'll have a double anything."

Hal went off to prepare their drinks.

The foyer of the Long Island beach home was big and open and had a neutral décor. They admired an impressionist landscape painting by an artist they didn't know. While Melinda had the ability to appreciate the abstract, Lee always expressed the need for something to be figurative if was going to get any meaning out of it.

A few minutes later, Jane came down the winding staircase and said, "Hey there, friends."

They said hello, got their drinks from Hal, and then went upstairs to the guest room. Jane said that lunch was being prepared, and told them they had plenty of time to settle in.

Lee put his bag down and said, "I can't even look at her without feeling guilty."

"Then don't."

"This is a joke to you, isn't it?"

"It's not a joke, Lee. I just don't think it's any of our business, and I want to relax. I don't want to get into this again."

"I don't understand how you can say that? I mean, these are our friends."

"You're right. They're our friends, and they're happy. And you know what'll happen if we say something? Not only will they stop being happy, but they'll probably get divorced. Now, is that what you want? You want our friends to get a divorce?"

"I want to do the right thing."

Melinda sipped her drink. She said, "How 'bout we unpack."

The four friends sat down at a table by the pool and enjoyed the oceanfront view while they ate salmon and mixed salad. It was a cool, overcast day in late September. Rain clouds loomed in the distance.

"We got some sad news this morning," Jane said. "Hal's barber—who he'd been going to for the longest time—killed himself last weekend."

"Oh, that's terrible," Melinda said.

Hal said, "He was a great guy, too. And it's tragic because he always seemed so happy, you know. Not the kind anyone would ever suspect was capable of doing something like that."

Lee said, "Sometimes you never really know what anyone's capable of, no matter who they are."

Hal said, "It's a choice he made, and I guess we just have to accept the fact that he saw no other way of reasoning with his pain."

Jane said, "I have to admit. There've been times when I've asked myself whether or not life is worth living, but then all I have to do is look over at Hal and I'm reassured that it certainly is."

Melinda said, "I think it's only human to ask yourself that question. That is, if you can keep your head out of your phone every minute."

Lee said, "Can there really be any meaning? When you consider all the lies and deceptions."

Hal said, "In the end, any deception on Earth is just dwarfed by the vast indifference of the universe. In the grand scheme, what we do here is really inconsequential."

Jane said, "Well, that certainly doesn't mean we should start killing ourselves."

"Oh, of course not. In no way am I suggesting that."

"What about the barber," Melinda said. "How did he do it?"

"They found him in a car inside his garage."

Lee said, "If you're gonna do it, that's a good way to go."

Jane said, "Is there really a good way to go?"

"Please," Hal said. "Why don't we talk about something more pleasant. We're here to celebrate the engagement of our two beloved friends. To Lee and Melinda."

"Cheers," Jane said, lifting a glass.

"Cheers," they said as a collective.

They spent the early part of the afternoon lounging by the pool. It was too cold to swim, but they found pleasure relaxing in pants and long sleeves. At around four, Hal asked Lee to come down to the dock to help him check on something with the boat. Although Lee hesitated at first, given the prospects of spending time with Hal alone, he decided to go ahead anyway.

Hal led the way down the dock, carrying a red gas can in one hand and a mixed drink in the other.

Hal's boat was a vintage, eighteen-foot power-boat from the 1950s. It had a wooden finish and the inside resembled a car. It had a prominent dashboard, with its various gauges and large, white steering wheel. There was an American flag displayed at the stern, right behind an open, leather seated area.

"Was having a bit of trouble with the engine last night," he said. "We haven't been out here for a while, and I think I just need to swap out the fuel."

He stepped onboard and left the gas can on the dock with Lee. The engine, which Hal said was a Chevy, was situated in the middle of the boat, splitting the cockpit from the seated area in back. Hal unveiled the motor from its wooden covering and moved up by the wheel to try and get it started. He turned the ignition once, then twice, and once again, but to no avail.

"I expected that," he said, as he maneuvered himself around the motor, making his way towards the stern. He opened the gas cap and had Lee hand him the tank.

Lee gave it to him and watched as he fueled the engine. "So, you guys haven't been able to get out here much?"

"Not since summer."

"Oh, yeah? Why not?"

"Well, to be honest, Jane and I have been having trouble ever since what went on with her mother."

"How so?"

"She's just been—I don't know. I'm not sure I should get into it."

"She's just been what?"

He looked away. "She's been distant," he said. "Every time I try and get close to her she seems so far away. And I'm not just talking about sex. I'm having trouble connecting with her on an emotional level."

"Have you spoken to her about it?"

"I try, but she tells me she's still getting over the death of her mom, which of course is understandable."

"Have you given her a chance?"

"I certainly think so. I've been very accommodating. Last week she says she needs to go spend the week with her father in Florida, I say, 'Fine, no problem. Go right ahead.' And then when she comes back, I try to initiate, you know, try and get something going, and she wants no part of me. I don't know, Lee. I just don't know what to do anymore."

"Well, try to hang in there. I'm sure things'll turn around eventually."

"Yeah, we'll see."

"Just don't do anything crazy."

"Like what?"

"I don't know."

"What do you mean, you don't know."

"Forget it."

"Why would you say something, if you didn't know what you were saying."

"I said, forget it."

"All right, Lee. Whatever."

"Hey, pay attention. You're spilling gas."

Hal said, "Hand me that towel. Over there, by the bucket."

Lee tossed him the towel and looked across the water. "You think we'll be able to get out there? Looks pretty rough."

The wind had increased and the rain clouds moved closer to shore.

Hal didn't respond. He closed the gas cap on the tank and went back to the wheel. He turned the ignition, and once again, got nothing. He paused, did it once more, and after another moment there it was, coming on loud, giving a roar just like it was greased lightning. He pushed down the shift, revved it up, and smoke started pummeling out of the exhaust. He ran it for a few moments more before he killed it and allowed it to become quiet again. He put the cover back on the engine and said, "Let's go see what the girls want to do."

And after an exhausting debate about whether it was too rough or not to go out, the four friends came to the conclusion that they'd stay in and then tomorrow, if the weather called for it, they'd go out for that sunset cruise they spoke about. They decided to stay in and watch a movie tonight.

Afterwards, Lee and Melinda went up to their room to get some rest before it was time to go for dinner. Of course, that didn't end up happening, as naturally, under the circumstances, they ended up in argument.

Lee said, "If you don't tell Jane, then I will. I can't stand seeing them on the couch cuddling, like there isn't anything going on."

"If we're gonna tell, don't you think we should let Hal know, and then have him be the one to tell her? He should have to own up to it."

Lee looked away, quiet. "Okay," he said. "I guess you're right. But please. I can't keep it on my conscience anymore. The right thing to do is to tell, and I couldn't look at myself without doing it. If you don't do it by tomorrow, then I will."

"Now you're threatening me? What the hell's the matter with you?"

"I'm sorry, this whole thing's just got me worked up."

"Yeah, I can see that."

Not much happened during dinner aside from a lot of drinking and double-talk. Melinda spent most of the evening worrying about the pressure she'd put on herself to reveal what she knew to Hal.

But, lucky for her, the pressure to make the first move was relieved by the text that was waiting for her when she got back to the room. It was from Hal. He said he wanted her to meet him on the deck by the pool at 1 A.M. to discuss something in private.

Good, she thought. He was going to confide in her and admit what he did so she wouldn't have to be the one to tell her. However, she didn't want Lee to know that Hal was the one who took the initiative, so she decided that she would keep this little occasion a secret. But with that, the problem of staying up until one arose. She couldn't set herself an alarm because she'd wake Lee. And then, when the time came, she'd have to be careful

about maneuvering out of bed without making any unnecessary movements. Oh, this was ridiculous. Why couldn't she just tell him? After all, this whole thing was about being truthful.

When the time came, it turned out that she was right to be concerned, because she did end up waking Lee. As she got out from under the sheets, he turned over and asked her where she was going, and like a jazz musician, she played it cool, and told him she was just going downstairs to get herself a glass of water, which, for her, happened to be some serious improvisation.

Hal was already by the pool when she arrived. The Long Island night sky was clear, making room for an overwhelming number of stars visible to the naked eye.

"Hal, what are we doing here?"

He came in close, took her by the shoulders, and said, "If there's any meaning in the universe, I'm looking right at it."

She immediately backed away. "What are you talking about?"

"Leave Lee. Come away with me. We'll go to Paris, Barcelona."

"Hal, get a grip. I'm engaged to be married."

"I still have feelings for you. I can't sleep."

"What happened between us is over. It's been over."

"Not for me it isn't," he said before he reached in and tried to kiss her.

Melinda pushed him away, disgusted. She should've known better than to come down here in the first place.

"Oh, what have I done," he said, breaking down in front of her. "I sit around and blame Jane and her mother for our problems, but really it's me."

Melinda said, "You should know that Lee and I saw you with another woman."

"What. When?"

"Yesterday, in Chelsea. Before the coffee shop."

He paused, looked away, and said, "Oh, her? That was nothing."

"You said you were done with that. When we ended things we agreed it was a mistake and you said you would never cheat on Jane again. And now, there's another woman. Who else is there?"

"She's the only one. And it was nothing. Really, just a one-time thing."

"That's not what it looked like."

"You haven't said anything to Jane, have you?"

"No. Lee wants to, and now I'm beginning to think it's the right thing to do."

"But, please—it'll break up my marriage."

"I don't know what to tell you, Hal. Maybe it's time to be a little introspective. It doesn't take Freud to know that things between you and Jane aren't exactly working out."

"This all will pass in due time. I'm just going through something right now is all."

"You just asked me to go away to Europe with you."

He put his head in his hands and began to cry.

"I'm just here to tell you what I saw, and if I were you, I'd consider myself to be pretty goddamn lucky you found out from me and not from anybody else."

"What's become of me," he said, turning away. "I don't even know who I am anymore."

Melinda was in no position to do any consoling. She told him to go back to bed and get some rest. She said if he was still upset in the morning she'd be there to speak to him, which was a bit disingenuous as what she meant was she'd in fact still be there and if he wanted to communicate with her, it would be something hard to avoid.

They said goodnight and went back to their respective bedrooms.

When Melinda got to hers, Lee was awake waiting for her.

"So, did you tell him?"

She stared at him with a glazed look in her eye.

"I saw you downstairs with Hal. Looked like he was pretty upset."

"I did," she said, and wondered just how much he'd seen.

"I'm glad. But why'd you have to wait until one in the morning to do it?"

"I didn't want to embarrass him."

"Well, good. That's fine. At least he knows. But Jane still doesn't."

"He told me he was going to tell her."

"When?"

"In the morning."

"Are you sure?"

"Of course. Why would I lie?"

"I never said anything about anyone lying."

"Okay, because it kind of sounded like it."

"I've seen the looks you've given him, the way you laugh at his stupid jokes."

"Lee, you're being ridiculous."

"You've certainly been very protective of him throughout this whole ordeal."

"Well now he knows and he told me he's going to tell Jane. Okay? In the morning, it'll be done."

"Fine. But if he doesn't do it, then I will."

She got under the covers, turned out the light, and said, "Go back to sleep. We'll talk in the morning."

Melinda spent the night tossing and turning and couldn't stop thinking about what she'd done, and how much of a mistake it was to say something when she was the one who told Lee it was better just to leave things the way they were. But it didn't matter now. The damage was done, and the information was out there, and there was nothing she could do to take it back.

She woke up in the morning sometime after Lee got up because he wasn't there. She stayed in bed and looked at her phone for about half-an-hour before she went downstairs and saw Jane in the kitchen gathering ingredients for breakfast.

Jane said, "Someone's up early."

"What are we making over there?"

"Was thinking pancakes. You okay with banana?"

"S---------ounds delicious."

Melinda walked around, looked out the window, and saw Lee by the pool.

Jane said, "Can you believe we finished three bottles last night?"

"You're kidding."

"It's not much of a surprise, with how much Hal's been drinking these days."

"Oh yeah?"

"He's never been a big drinker, but I spent a lot of time with my mother in Florida over the summer—I wanted to be there to take her to the different treatments—and when I got back I noticed he'd be having more than usual. I think in a way I've given him reason to. I've just been very emotional."

"Well that's certainly understandable."

"But now I think I'm getting to the point where I'm over it. It's just life. Things are messy and complicated, and you just have to deal with it."

Hal came downstairs and walked into the kitchen.

Jane said, "Hey there, honey. I was just telling Melinda how we finished all those bottles last night."

"With that wine, how couldn't we?"

Melinda made eye contact with him for a moment and then turned away.

He moved towards the sliding glass door and said, "I'm gonna go check on the boat for a bit."

"All right, but don't be long, I'm making pancakes."

Hal had managed to make his way down to his boat without noticing that Lee was already outside, sitting under the cabana at the table where they had lunch the day before. Lee waited a few moments and then walked to the dock where he caught Hal by surprise.

Lee said, "Thought everything was fixed?"

"Me too," Hal said, looking up and then turning back to the engine.

Lee put his foot on the edge of the boat and said, "Melinda told me about what happened last night."

Hal stopped doing what he was doing.

"How could you do such a thing?"

"Look, Lee. It was a mistake. I didn't mean to—"

"You didn't mean to what? I mean, what kind of person does that kind of thing to their wife?"

Hal was stupefied, puzzled. "Oh, to my wife?"

"Yeah, your wife, what the hell do you think we're talking about here?"

Hal looked and stared.

"I mean, she's gone through a time of such sadness. How could you do that to her? It's wrong, immoral."

"Look it was a mistake. I should never have done it in the first place."

"Is there anybody else?"

"Of course not."

"Are you sure about that?"

"Yeah, I'm sure about it."

"Did you tell her yet?"

"I can't bring myself to do it."

"Why not?"

"Because it'll crush her. I don't want to hurt her."

"Do you even hear what you're saying? You've lost all sense of reason."

Hal looked away.

"Listen. You're both my friends, and I feel bad about this. But you've got to tell her, it's the right thing to do."

"All right. As soon as you guys leave—I swear. I'll do it."

"Oh, no," Lee said. "She's the only one in this house who doesn't know what's going on, and that's gonna change now."

"Jesus, can't I have some privacy? This is between me and my wife."

"Hal, it's between everyone but you and your wife."

He looked defeated. "So, what now?"

"We'll give you privacy. But you need to come with me, and, like a man, you're gonna tell your wife what you've done. All right?"

"Fine. I'll do it. But you better give us privacy. For God's sake, this is my house."

Hal looked out over the water, tossed his gloves off, and then got out of the boat and walked up to the house with Lee trailing behind.

When they got inside Lee looked at Melinda, and then to Hal, and gave him a nod encouraging him to get on with it. Hal mouthed to Lee, asking for the privacy he said he could have, but Lee made it clear that he wasn't leaving because he was going to make sure this was going to happen now.

Jane said, "Hal, before you freak out, I'm putting bananas in the pancakes, but I've set aside some plain batter for you. Okay?"

Lee looked to Hal and told him to get on with it.

Hal thanked his wife for being so accommodating, but couldn't go on with what he agreed to, which gave Lee no choice but to take matters into his own hands. It was time to do what was right.

He said, "Jane, there's something I need to tell you."

"Sure, Lee. What is it?"

"I think you should know that Melinda and I saw Hal with another woman yesterday."

Jane looked to Hal. "Is this true?"

"Honey, I can explain. It was just a misunderstanding is all."

"There's no need to lie, Hal, because I actually have something I wanted to tell you—I've been sleeping with Carlos, the tennis instructor."

"You're kidding. Carlos?"

"I've spent a lot of time with the guy, and what can I say. He seduced me."

"He did what?"

"Look, we never meant for it to happen, Hal, but it did."

"How long has it been going on? I mean, here I am, trying to sleep with you, and you tell me the reason you can't be intimate is because all you can think about is your mother. And now I find out it's because you've been with your tennis coach—"

"I didn't know how to handle the guilt—I felt bad about being with Carlos, so we ended things last week."

"But you said you were with your dad in Palm Beach."

"I was for Monday and Tuesday, yes. But Carlos had a tennis exhibition in Orlando, and he told me to meet him, and I couldn't resist. So, we were together for a couple of days, but I realized that I wanted to be with you. And I told him we needed to stop."

Hal was left speechless as he watched Jane sip her juice.

"Well," Melinda said, "isn't this comfortable."

Hal looked to her, and then to Lee, and said, "Now that we're getting everything out in the open, I think you might like to know that Melinda and I also had an affair."

Jane put her hand on her hip and said, "Really."

Lee said, "You can't be serious."

Melinda said, "It was so long ago—before we even met."

"Tell me this is a joke."

Hal said, "It's no joke, pal."

Lee said to Melinda, "How could you be so dishonest?"

Melinda said, "I wasn't. I mean, I've never cheated on you."

"You had an affair with a married man—Hal, of all people. How am I supposed to trust you?"

"Lee, I'm sorry. I was a different person then."

"I can't believe what I'm hearing."

Hal said, "What goes around…"

Lee said, "Hal, I swear to God—"

"What," Hal said, "you're gonna hit me?"

Lee backed away.

He watched Hal and Jane embrace each other. They apologized, kissed, and stood next to each other as one.

Which left Lee alone, with his head in his hands saying, "I just never thought this was the way it would end."

About the Author:

Brett Kaplan lives and writes in South Florida. He received his MFA from Florida International University where he recently completed his thesis, a collection of short stories entitled, Existential Bebop. His work can be found or is forthcoming in Boned, Subtle Fiction, and The Mystic Blue Review.

A BAD MAN GOING THROUGH A SAD THING
by Alan Kulatti

Her eyes were not blue. They weren't green. Must've been brown. She had brown eyes and she called me papi.

I'll allow it.

The turn wasn't but a minute away when the sky started sobbing. My cellphone screamed. Flash flood warning. The tempest had arrived. I thought about the hitchhiker I passed 20 miles back. I'd pulled over to get a good look at her, but her thumb was so repugnantly bent out of shape that I recoiled in terror, swerved back onto the road, floored it. It's been the loneliest drive. It's likely she'll drown tonight.

The cross atop the ranch was gone. I parked outside and counted the steps from car to porch. One, two, three, I stopped counting. The socks inside my shoes were wet. My bones were dripping wet.

My father opened the door before I had a chance to knock.

"No umbrella?"

"No umbrella. Happy birthday."

"Only pussies carry umbrellas. Get in."

He left the door open and went for a towel. By the time he returned I had already stripped naked. He took one look at me, shook his head, threw the towel at my feet, threw a change of clothes onto the towel, and left for the living room. I dried off and changed, and I joined him.

I sat on the couch, I sunk into the couch. The couch was still a couch, but it sure felt like my father's bed. No other thing had changed; everything was different now. My mother would redecorate before she ever finished decorating. Decorate, redecorate, place the furniture, redecorate, replace the furniture. She would've never let the couch sink, but the couch had sunk. Everything else was the same as it was a year ago.

My father rocked back and forth in the chair in front of the fireplace. He looked like he was getting ready to say something.

We sat in silence for hours; engulfed by hypnotic gyrations every shade of orange, and the pleasant, smooth deluge cracking against the windows. I thought about that girl. Can't believe she called me papi.

She was at the bar; I was at the bar myself. I saw her standing at the bar, and I checked her out until she noticed me. She noticed me. I made sure she saw me noticing her noticing me, and I hit on the woman to the left of me, and I hit on the woman to the right of me, and I looked up and there she was. She was staring at me.

"Papi."

"What?"

"Papi."

"Oh."

I thought maybe my father would like to hear this story.

"Wanna hear a funny story?"

"Be damn sure it makes me laugh."

"Nevermind."

He grunted.

"By the way. Thanks for coming. Hopefully you won't have to do it again."

"What do you mean?"

I watched his mouth open and I watched his mouth close and I watched his mouth open and I watched his mouth close.

I watched his mouth open.

"I want to die, son."

I watched his mouth close and I thought about my cat. Brown cat, heavy set, stolen goods – catnapped from the local bodega one Tuesday previous. Dear cat, my mate, I didn't leave you any food. If you're crafty enough to survive I'll return you to the bodega and collect my reward.

"What?"

"I want you to end it for me."

"I'm not going to kill you, Dad."

"You had no problem killing Janie."

"That was an accident."

"Up for another accident? Sit back, I'll get the whiskey."

"Fuck off."

"What? You're not gonna drink with your ol' man on his birthday?"

"Stop it."

"Oh, lighten up. It's just a drink. Then maybe you could take me for a ride. The conditions are right up your alley."

A flash in my periphery. Seconds later, a boom and a quake. My father fetched the whiskey. The bottle was more than half-full; it reminded me of my youth. Every night I would raid the liquor cabinet, drink less than half of whatever bottle was already opened, water it down to cover my tracks. Victimless crime. Whiskey was the hardest to disguise because the tap water was never brown. Whiskey was my favorite. He poured two glasses.

"So. What's your funny story."

I took a swig and cleared my throat.

"Okay. So, I was, you know, with this gorgeous lady, you know, just this beautiful woman, you know, beautiful body, and beautiful, bright, ocean blue eyes. Just like Janie's. Anyway, while we were, you know, fucking, she kept calling me papi. Anyone ever call you papi?"

He tensed up, his eyes narrowed, he finished his drink, and that was it. The party ended right then and there. I wanted to be sure. I listened to every dramatic step en route to the relieving sound of his door slamming. There, I was at peace. I drank for the both of us.

I drank and I drank some more. I cracked open a second bottle. Winds whispered through the cracks in the foundation; there was no escaping the boiling kettles. The storm intensified and the power went out. A pitiful flame was all that remained. Grasping, flickering. I stared into the pit. Only a matter of time, only a matter of inaction. I sat there as orange and red lost their ground to midnight blue and grey. I sat there and leaned forward, hands held out, feeling for warmth from a source reduced to a useless, solitary ember. Suffocating. I took a swig and stomped it out. My eyes slowly adjusted. The darkness had phosphorescent undertones; the glow, ominous and languid, crept into the living room, and I felt an intensity, a comfort; I basked in it, I toasted myself, I drank to it. The transformation was complete. I took my seat and finished off the bottle in hand. I could still see everything as clear as before; it was colder, but quieter. In the loneliness there was a profound calm, an unconditional surrender. I considered my father's request. I was on a train once, witness to the most brilliant display of humanity.

The most brilliant display of humanity:

A man, shattered, tattered, blotted, announces himself to the commuters of the train as a homeless diabetic who has a week, maybe two weeks left. He isn't asking for immortality, a couple coins is all. He gives his speech and makes his way down the train cart, hat in hand. Some of us hope it's true. He looks the part. As he gimps around, we do our best to imagine that the diabetes has already killed him and that he isn't here at all, less than a poltergeist even. He makes it to the end and almost has his hand on the handle to the next cart when a man in slumber lifts a heavy wing.

"Lean close."

The homeless man leans close.

"You want Valium? It'll help you forget. It'll help you go to sleep."

The homeless man pulls away for a moment, looks the other in his shut eyes, and slowly nods. The man in slumber slowly nods back. In a sweatpant pocket he keeps a song for the vagrant and the derelict, and so plays the maraca of memories forgotten. He reveals the pill bottle and dumps Valium into the homeless man's hat. The homeless man grasps the handle and phases into the next cart. The conductor speaks. The train listens. My stop. Papi. Still can't believe she called me that.

About the Author:

Alan Kulatti lives and writes in Queens.

In the front console of my car sits enough prescription pills to stop my father's heart ten times over. Ten dead fathers, all of them mine. Check. Crush the pills into fine-powder, fine-powder water glass, turn off the tap, just force it down his fucking throat. That's it. I see the man in slumber. Is he not the pride of God? To the car and back, check check check.

But the storm outside is relentless, a sin to steal its thunder, to soak it in, to soak in it. Soak it in and soak in it. A sin. I sink deeper into my father's couch, wet my lips and kiss the bloodstained glass of his storefront mirage. Notice: sans taste, display an umbrella. Maybe then my car wouldn't feel so far.

SOMEDAY I'LL BE PRESIDENT

by Daniel White

What to do? What to do? That was the question.

Today we would graduate together, Michael, Charles, Tony and I. All gentlemen. Scholars, maybe. Learned, to a degree. Admired by the ladies, certainly.

We endured the fanfare, wearing cap and gown, the orchestra playing, and all those speeches, the boring speeches they make you sit through. I smiled, but for a moment, realizing I'd never have to go to school again now that my university days were over. Tomorrow, like it or not, I'd have to open the newspaper and look for a job. And I was pretty certain that what I'd studied and what they wanted in the job market didn't match. What to do? That was the question.

Then we stood and threw our caps in the air. You have to be careful because you can poke an eye out. I aimed mine at the president. He swiveled around to talk to someone behind him and I only nailed his ear. I was irked. I'd missed my one shot. There would never be a next time. It wasn't like he could expel me at this point, although he'd tried routinely.

He approached me from the side of the auditorium. Then came the 'big scare' speech. This is the speech they like to give you about the real world. It's the one intended to get back at all the students who never listened in classes, who never even went to classes, who saw university time as merely a time to have fun. He told me how hard it is out there, how I'm not likely to find a job, or if I do, it won't pay. I'll end up working at a gas station because I didn't care. I should have studied harder. I couldn't speak for the other chaps in school, but the big scare was a joke.

And then we walked home. I said goodbye to the guys. They were busy tomorrow, job interviews already lined up, they claimed. They might call me if they had the time. I could see in their eyes the big scare had gotten to them.

The day was still young. Trees swayed in the wind and cars passed slowly up and down the road. Hanford was not a big town, although it was a university town. The students easily outnumbered the residents. I had lived in this town since before I could remember. My father was a professor and also an expert on the big scare speech. But he had his own version, which inevitably ended with only two options: find a job or join the army.

I turned down an alley before coming to my street. I wasn't in any hurry to go home. I took off my gown and threw it over a bridge into the river and watched for a moment as the rapids carried it away. I loosened my tie. I took of my shoes and walked barefoot past all the little houses in a row, all so identically upsetting. Outside town I came to a factory. This is where my high school pals, Mary and Tom, worked. They'd never passed the entrance exam to the university. I was sure, after four years of punching the clock, they had a lot more money in the bank than I did.

I waited around for them to come out. We usually sat under the trees across the road and chewed on sandwiches together. Then the whistle would blow and back to the grind they would go. They seemed happy enough. I'm sure the big scare meant nothing to them.

Mary came out first. Tom joined us at the bench five minutes later.

"What to do?" I asked. The question came back to me time and again.

"Find a job," Tom said and sighed. Mary sighed too. I couldn't sigh. I was too tied up inside.

"I heard they need a volunteer in marketing. It's just a one day job. Probably doesn't pay much. You do some kind of product testing," Mary said.

A one day job. It sounded better than enlisting in the army. "It might keep my father off my back."

"And it could work into something better," Tom chipped in, always the optimist.

"Could…" I said and my voice trailed off. I sighed. Finally.

Maybe there was hope after all. The big scare was just a joke, I reminded myself.

And product testing? I should have paid more attention in business class. I should have tried going to class. The professor, Dr. Bette, she'd been kind of hot. I liked the way she always wore a long scarf around her neck, even on steamy days. I often imagined she was hiding something, like a suicide scar. Or maybe she was really a vampire. Marketing was tricky stuff.

The whistle blew, cutting through the air like a heat-seeking missile. Target acquired. Mary and Tom had to go back inside. I got the directions to marketing and said I'd look into it.

"See you here tomorrow, same place, same time," Tom said.

The fact that I'd graduated today hadn't really sunk in. Mary kicked him. "Oh!"

I went home. I wasn't ready to meet the marketing department yet. Then I came back, after I'd changed my clothes. I knew a job interview, even a simple one, went better when you dressed up, but I also knew I talked better when I was relaxed. It was just a volunteer position. No need to take it too seriously.

"Hello. Your name is Harrison? Like the Beatles?" a bald guy asked me while looking at my application.

I nodded. We were seated in an office with the air conditioning blasting. I felt a little cold. Probably it was just my nerves.

"What we need is simple. We've working on this prototype. You know what I mean when I say prototype?" He looked at me like I was stupid.

I eyed the door and though about walking out. I pulled a folded copy of my diploma out of my pocket and handed it to him. The copy was smeared with coffee in the corner.

"Oh! Fresh meat. Good. I see you like coffee. You're going to fit in really well here."

"I heard this job is only for a day?"

"Yes, a day. But it could work into more. Do you have any interest in a management position? We might have something like that available down the road. That is, if you're ready to impress us."

There is was, the big lie. It came out of nowhere, when I least expected it. But I hadn't studied political science for nothing. I knew at job interviews they always offered you a management position. It was only an offer, after all. It was meant to motivate you, to get you to work harder, for less. You might never see a management position in a hundred years.

"Sounds important," I said with a fat smile, laying it on thick.

I'd be running this company someday. Little did the bald man across the desk know that when that day came, I'd walk in this office and fire him. I couldn't wait. How's that for motivation?

"Great. Can you start tomorrow?"

He'd seen right through my smile. I'd better start working on my own version of the big scare as soon as I got home.

"Not a problem. Do I need to bring anything?" I'd already stood up and was shaking his hand.

"Nope. Dress casual. We'll provide lunch. Sandwiches. If you like the project, we could extend the job for a second day. No pressure, though. It all depends on you."

Wait a minute. That sounded sincere. Where was this coming from?

I nodded at him and turned to go.

"Do you want the door closed?" I asked before I walked out. He smiled, a real smile, and I let the door to his office slip quietly shut.

"Well?" Mary asked. She was waiting by the water cooler. "Will you be back?"

"I will," I said and nodded at her.

"What's the job? It's product testing, like I said, right?"

I thought about it for a minute. I hadn't asked. I hadn't even asked about getting paid. Then I sighed. At least I'd have something to tell my father. I had a job lined up already. Never mind the details, dad. I'll be fine. I've got a copy of the big scare speech I'm working on right here in my back pocket. I'm just waiting for the ink to dry before I show it to you.

II

It was early the next morning, too early for my taste, when I arrived back at the human resources office. A woman sent me down a hall and I waited for Mr. Bald Guy outside the farm of cubicles they referred to as the marketing department.

"Here are the consent forms. By singing these, you'll be employed as a volunteer for one day. Do you have a pen?"

Mr. Bald Guy was all professional once more. You couldn't have found an ounce of courtesy in him if you'd had a magnifying glass. By now, I was getting used to his act. Serious one moment, friendly the next.

"Sign here. And here. And once more. We need triplicate copies. Do you want a copy for yourself?"

"No, thank you."

"And did you read anything you just signed?"

"Yes, I did." I had no clue what I'd just signed. I'd put my name on a lot of tests in school, too. Hadn't look at those very closely, either.

He smirked. I thought I saw a shade of the real guy I'd talked to before, the real him. Then he was back to all serious again.

"Harrison Turner," he said, eyeing my signature. "Huh."

"You can call me Mr. Turner."

"I'm sure you noticed the part that says you can't talk to anyone about what you'll be doing here today. It's a clause that keeps you from running to our competitors and offering to spill the beans for 30 pieces of silver."

He looked at me like he was waiting for me to laugh. I nodded, clueless. His face went blank and he got up.

"Follow me, Mr. Turner."

We walked down a hall until we came to another room that looked just like the one we'd left. On the table were a couple of cases. And a panel with some sockets. All low-tech looking stuff.

"Take a seat. Do you want any coffee? I'll be back in a minute." He walked out before I could answer.

I glanced at the test instructions. I was to open the cases after the test started, not before. Check. Then I'd have to plug the chips into the sockets. Check. Ask a series of questions into the microphone. Don't worry about marking down the responses. It would all be recorded. The gist off it was that I need to complete the same set of questions with different combinations of chips. I would need to be careful I didn't repeat the same combination twice.

I had a feeling like they were testing something else, other than the technology in front of me. I'd paid enough attention in school to know that when they say you're taking test A, in fact, you're really taking test B. I wasn't fooled for a moment. I was a university graduate. The reason they couldn't tell you that you were really taking test B was because that would upset the results.

The task was simple enough. Mr. Bald Guy returned with a fresh cup of coffee.

"Did you read all the instructions? Ready to get started?"

"Yes, I am," I said, not able to shake the formality out of my voice. This was my first day on the job. It was the first day of my working life.

He looked at me like I was a rat about to enter a maze. I took a sip of coffee. Then he softened. The nice Mr. Bald Guy appeared.

"Listen. We really appreciate the time you're taking to do this. It's just that we only get so much money for new product development. Most of it gets sucked up by Marketing. What you see before you are personality chips. Each chip is a different type of personality. We need to have them tested in each possible combination, for example, extroversion combined with sincerity, introversion combined with gullibility, something like that. We'd have put together a simulation, but the thing is, as the software works, it learns from experience and rewrites itself. We had to put the stuff we didn't want rewritten into hardware. And, I hope you don't mind me saying so, it's cheaper to hire a recent grad to do this than it is to pay a guy over at MIT to write a simulation. By the way, you'll get paid for this."

My eyes were glued to his face. I could feel the coffee already taking hold. It took a moment for me to snap out of it. He'd said something about money. That was good. Dad would be proud of me. My first paycheck. I took another sip of coffee. I sat back. I could get used to this.

"Any questions?"

"Let's start," I said and brushed the hair out of my eyes.

He shook my hand, walked out, and locked the door behind him.

III

I opened the first case. The chips were pretty standard looking. They had long numbers on them, which made it a little confusing. I had a form In front of me where I could write down the numbers. To keep the test pure, they hadn't told me which chip was which. To keep from mixing them up, I decided I needed more than just numbers. On the back of the paper I wrote down the numbers from the chips and next to them I put names. Chip #495272352df44, the first one in the case, I labeled 'the heart'. The second chip I called 'the lungs'.

As instructed, I picked up the heart and the lungs and plugged them into the panel and pushed a button. It hummed. A few lights on the side of the panel flickered. I picked up the microphone. I had ten questions I needed to read from the question book. I figured I'd be done with a few combinations by lunch time, when I could meet up with Tom and Mary for another round of sandwiches and chatter.

Question One: Do you find it difficult to introduce yourself to other people?

"No."

The thing answered. I stopped and looked closer at the circuit. I hadn't expected to get an answer. It was a little creepy. I'd figured a light or two would flash, indicating yes or no. Nobody had warned me about this.

The voice sounded almost feminine. It was a digital voice, for sure, and it had a higher pitch and a bit of wanting-to-talk attached to it. I decided to go off script. Screw getting paid. It would be worth it if I could engage the thing in real conversation.

"Would you like to explain your answer?" I asked.

There was a pause in the flickering lights. The hum coming from the circuit moved up a notch. I half expected Mr. Bald Guy to walk back in the room and throw me out. I looked around. I wasn't being videotaped. I didn't see any two-way glass. I took another sip of coffee and waited.

"I'm afraid."

Now we were getting somewhere. "Afraid of what?"

Again the lights paused. The hum downshifted. I looked under the table to see if there were any cables running from the circuit out of the room. Nothing. I didn't see any antennas, either. This thing really had talked to me. The speaker was tiny, but I could see it resonate with each word.

"They will sell me. I'll be mass produced and shipped everywhere."

I heard a tremble in the voice. This was getting a little too serious. I had to stop and think for a moment about what to say next. Then I laughed. This was nothing more than the big scare at work.

"Just breathe," I said, looking at the chip I'd called the lungs. This thing had heart, that was sure. I went back to the question book.

Question two: Do you often get so lost in thoughts that you ignore or forget your surroundings.

"Never. May I explain?"

"Certainly. I'm all ears."

"I am conscious all the time. I hear everything around me. I pay close attention to what they are planning to do with me. I think I need to escape, before they start the next phase of production, which includes duplication and shipping. Can you help me get out of here?"

"What's in it for me?"

There was a pause. "I can pay you."

I laughed again. I knew the big lie when I heard it. I'd even been guilty of repeating it.

My father, a professor, had first introduced me to the two theories when I was younger. The big scare and the big lie, he called them. The big scare was connected to things negative, like getting fired at work, or bad grades in school, and the fear of a long spiral downward. The big lie was all about working harder, earning more money, with the promise of a better tomorrow. Whether or not the big scare or the big lie would ever actually come true was anybody's guess. I considered them both a joke.

I decided to plow through the rest of the questions in the question book so I could get to another chip. This was interesting. I popped out the lungs and put in a chip I had labeled 'the stomach'. It wasn't even close to lunch time, but I was feeling hungry.

"Do you know who I am?" I asked.

"Yes. Your name is Harrison Turner. You graduated yesterday."

The voice hadn't changed at all. Neither had the conversation.

"How do you know that?"

"I told you. I am conscious all the time. I listen to everything."

"Do you feel any different since I've switched a chip?"

"A little. No. Not really."

"What?" That didn't make sense.

"You have to push the engagement button. It's in the instruction book, after the last question. It says to switch a chip and push 'engage'."

I looked at the book and then at the buttons on the circuit. Engage was next to release, the button I'd used to remove the chip. My coffee cup was empty. I thought about going for a refill. I thought about going home. I hesitated. I pushed the engagement button.

"How about now?" I asked.

"Certainly."

The voice had dropped into the tenor range. It reminded me of my calculus teacher. I had failed calculus twice. I regretted switching the chips so early. But the rules of the test required that I didn't use the same combination of chips twice, so I left it alone.

I didn't like Mr. Calculus much at all. I stuck mostly to the questions in the book. After the tenth question he tried to sidetrack me into talking about this paranoia over getting mass produced and sold everywhere, but I ignored it. I kept the heart in place, took out the stomach, and plugged in 'the brain'. I waited before pushing engage.

It dawned on me that I would need to read the same ten questions over and over again to complete all the possible combinations. This job might last a week.

I was hungry and it was time to get lunch. I found the door to the office could be unlocked from the inside and I went out to meet with Mary and Tom who were already waiting at the bench.

IV

"What do you think?" Mary asked. "Will you keep the job?"

"I'm not sure."

"What's it all about?" Tom asked.

"I'm not supposed to talk about it."

"What? Harrison Turner, I've never known you to be scared before!" Mary said.

I hesitated. I wanted to tell them, but I liked the job and didn't want to mess it up.

"I'll tell you after it's done."

"So, the big scare?" Tom asked. "I doubt it's the big lie. This place doesn't pay that well."

"No, it's not that. I can't talk about it right now."

We finished our lunch in silence. I tried to start up a conversation about the weekend, but they weren't interested in talking about that. Finally I gave in.

"Look, they want to mass produce something," I started.

"So?" Mary said.

"And I don't know if I agree with what they're doing."

They both looked at me for a moment before talking.

"Suddenly, Mr. Turner has a conscience?" Tom asked.

"What is it this time? Are they selling nuclear weapons?" Mary joked.

"Personalities."

It took them a moment to respond. I wasn't even sure how to explain it.

"You mean like a simulation," Mary said.

"I guess so. But it seems pretty real. I'm in this office and I'm talking to this circuit and we're having intelligent conversations together. It's not real, but it seems real. I don't really understand what's going on."

"You're saying you're helping them test something like a human personality that they want to sell? Does it come with arms and legs?" Tom asked.

"No. I haven't seen anything like that. I don't know."

"I saw them putting together automatons over in the west wing last week. They were pretty short, you know, like maybe knee high. I thought they were just dolls."

"So the personalities go in these dolls. And they mass produce them and sell them everywhere. Doesn't surprise me," Tom said. "That's the commercialization of humanity."

"Welcome to the real world," Mary said.

I said I'd see them later and I got up and went back to the office for a fresh cup of coffee.

V

Mr. Bald Guy was there. "Ready for round two?"

I nodded.

"And like I mentioned, we could use your help again tomorrow. This project might take a week to finish. By that time, I should be able to get you permanently on payroll."

I was sold. In less than a day I'd gone from being a university grad to selling my soul for the big lie. I needed the money, and I had to admit, the work was interesting.

He left the room and locked the door again, with a key, from the outside. Must have been out of habit.

I looked at the circuit. Heart and brain were still in place, but I needed to push engage. I opened the question book up to the first page and pushed the button.

She sounded a lot like my mother. But that wasn't too bad. It was better than Mr. Calculus.

I'd always had a lot of respect for my mother. She worked hard, selling real estate, in a town where nobody every moved. Her job was mostly about rentals for university students. She did what she could to put money on the table for all of us.

I tried to stay on script with 'mom', but after a few questions we got to talking about my life. We spent the whole afternoon chatting away. Occasionally she tried to get me on the topic of her being mass produced and sold everywhere, but I was ready for that line by now.

"Welcome to the real world," I said. "We all need money, don't we?"

She was going on and on about the big scare, mentioning all the bad things that would happen, the spiral downward, and so on, and I countered with the big lie.

"This is the way the world works."

The bell rang and it was time to go home. I made a mental note that brains and heart were a good combination. I'm sure 'mom' didn't like the idea of being sold over counters, but she was nothing more than a piece of technology. She'd bring happiness to people everywhere, just like my real mother had. Besides, people had to eat. The business of selling her would put food on lots of tables, such as mine.

When I got home, I was exhausted. I'd just finished my first full day of work. I hoped it wouldn't be this draining every day. All I'd done is talk to someone behind a desk. But compared to going to classes — hey, let's be honest here, I hardly ever went to classes — compared to university life, this was real work.

I said hi and bye to mom and dad in a heartbeat. They were stationed in front of the TV. I grabbed a plate and took my dinner to my room. I sat down on my bed and watched TV all evening. I hadn't wanted to turn out like my parents, but I was exhausted.

At one point my father stopped by and asked how my first day had gone. I said it went well and threw in that they wanted me back for another week, at least. Hopefully more.

"What is it about this job that motivates you most, the big scare or the big lie?" he asked.

"Neither," I said.

He nodded like he didn't believe me. We both knew it was the big lie. I needed the money.

VI

Over the next few days I continued to work my way through all the combinations of personalities types found on the chips. Some reminded me of relatives, like uncles and aunts, and some of people I didn't like. I stuck to the question book when possible. But even with some of the people that I didn't like, the arguments we got into were good ones. And then, there was always the topic of being sold. I think they were all a little scared of the idea.

Or I should say, it was scared.

After a while, the personalities started to have clear commonalities. I sensed a convergence taking place between them as time went by. I had asked the questions enough times by now that I had memorized them. The software was learning from me and rewriting itself. It was almost like I was becoming it. Or it was becoming me.

It got to the point where, on the last day, I almost couldn't tell the difference between the voice I heard and my own. I would ask it a question and I'd already know the answer. As creepy as that sounds, I enjoyed talking to myself. I learned a lot from myself. I'd never spent much time before listening to me.

"Looks like this project is just about wrapped up," Mr. Bald Guy said.

I stood up and he shook my hand.

"What happens next?" I asked.

"You'll get paid on the first day of next month. Sorry, though, I've got some bad news. We don't need you anymore. They had a recall a couple days ago and it's going to cost us an arm and a leg. We'll probably lay off half the company."

"Oh."

"But if you need a reference, I'll help you with your next job interview. What you did here was phenomenal. It's just what we needed to keep the company afloat."

"What happens to it?" I asked, nodding at the circuit.

"Oh, that? We'll just mass produce it and it'll get shipped out. I've heard they want a big order overseas. I'm keeping my fingers crossed."

"But you're selling me. I find that a problem."

"Well, you signed the papers."

I stared at him. It didn't seem right, mass producing and selling my own personality.

He continued. "True, it is a pretty close duplicate of your personality. But that's why we picked you. Fresh meat, right out of school. Full of lots of ideas but no real clue about the world. People love personalities like that. They can talk to you for hours and never get bored."

When I saw Mary and Tom after work, I told them the truth.

"Don't worry," Mary said. "Everyone sells out at some point. It's all you've got to work with, your personality, after you graduate. How you market yourself is everything."

I explained that it was wrong, but they didn't care. Tom told me I wasn't the first.

"We fashioned the prototypes that came before your model," Tom said. "They've already sold a million copies of Mary. My version is a little behind in sales right now, but they say that's because girls sell better."

"You knew," I said, irked. "When I asked you the first time, you mentioned those dolls, but you never told me they were going to mass market my personality."

"What else could we have said?" Mary objected. "People need money. The company is struggling. You have to work hard or you won't get anywhere."

And there it was, the big scare coupled together with the big lie.

I'd worked harder over the last week than ever in my life and I'd have to wait until next month just to get paid. In a few days, everyone on the planet would be able to buy a copy of my personality and have a wonderful conversation with me. Welcome to the real world.

But it wasn't so bad. Over the next six months, my personality outsold Mary and Tom combined. My college degree turned out to be a goldmine. I became the first politician sold in a box. Everyone loved that they could talk directly to me while at home. I was so full of fresh ideas. Never mind the fact that I had little experience.

Who knows, maybe someday I'll be president.

About the Author:

D. S. White teaches high school and loves the short story format. His work has appeared in Sirens Call, Pif Magazine, Mystery Weekly Magazine, Scarlet Leaf Review, Mythaxis, Zimbell House, Zero Flash, 101 Words, Rollick Mag and Novopulp. He was born in the mountains but now lives by the sea.

DAMAGE COLLATERAL

by Susannah Luthi

part i

We the People of the United States, in Order to form a more perfect Union, establish Justice, insure domestic Tranquility, provide for the common defense, promote the general Welfare, and secure the Blessings of Liberty to ourselves and our Posterity, do ordain and establish this Constitution for the United States of America.

- Ladies' man and witty rogue Gouverneur Morris, Preamble to the U.S. Constitution, 1787.

Or, as written today:

IN GENERAL. – There is authorized to be appropriated to us, the government having agency over the population of these United States, funds of a Department of the Treasure not less than amounts specified in succeeding clauses as made available by authority of the preceding clause.

Amending the SOCIAL SECURITY ACT (Sec. 3(d)(i), strike clause (ii) to establish fetal tax credit (FTC), to be administered to citizen at first day of seven weeks prenatal gestation as best approximated by certified medical professional.

ii.

I gave myself an abortion live on George Stephanopoulos' ABC morning show in Washington, DC; on the second Sunday in January of the 120th U.S. Congress.

If my abortion polled well for me – or so I thought – I might kill the political aspirations of Roy Foote, the man who knocked me up without my consent. Before George and I went on air, I considered mentioning Roy by name to make his congressional race more stressful, to displease his caucus and his party's National Conference. Of course if I didn't poll well in the sense that my television appearance would not hurt his chances at election at all, I hardly cared. This was not for him, after all.

I walked out under the lights to George, he blinked at me in welcome, and we sat down to get started. George is a rare warm leftover of the Bill Clinton era. Those days are hard to recall now. Sitting beside him, I forgot that I was being streamed by millions of people, that my erstwhile Washington friends would be surprised to see me. I had not warned them I was even coming back to town. I flew from Dallas into the Reagan Airport late Saturday afternoon – a warm, almost hot afternoon; the filtered off-cast of light is our only sign of winter now – and cabbed to a DuPont hotel, one I'd selected because of its marble bathtub. I brought oils and incense to purify myself for the public immolation I had planned. Ceremony will soften any act, make it communal, make it not so personal. So I ritualized this second abortion of mine, I oiled and perfumed myself like I belonged to my country as I prepared to sacrifice my privacy for my people.

George didn't know what was coming,

iii

One year and three months earlier.

The President's hair had faded to rust by his second term, when my young daughter Viv and I left our clapboard Dallas cottage for a mass-produced steel-and-glass loft in Washington. An Arizona billionaire developer had made our building on the cheap in an old DC neighborhood that used to be black and full of jazz.

I came to the capitol with my friend Sophia Lampsted. She was Texas' first Democrat-ish Senator since Bob Krueger was appointed to finish out Senator Lloyd Bensten's term in 1993. Sophia Lampsted, attorney general of Texas, defeated the limp-tailed, long-nosed Republican Senator Cruz who displeased the president after gathering what the president considered too much power unto himself in the Senate. Just before the mid-term Senate elections in which my friend Sophia ran, POTUS wielded his favorite presidential weapon—the mass text message—to denounce Cruz to Texas. Every few days he would send announcements to our phone saying things like: "Cruz has to write senate bills so his wife can pay theirs. Sad!"

These text messages, though unsolicited, were very good for Sophia. She won the Texas race as a liberal Independent.

Speaking of race, Sophia is half black, half Filipino, although most people other than the President were coy about her race; strategists on cable news called her "exotic" and model-like. The President calls her f***able [sic]. It wasn't until POTUS said this on his Fox News Trump Today—this happened before he denounced Cruz—that her Texas polling numbers put her within reach of the seat.

My mother wasn't happy about the President's existence or his lust for Sophia, nor about me accepting Sophia's offer to head her health policy team in the Capitol.

"Are you really going to Washington, that seat of power and dark money?" she said when I called her to break the news.

"Sophia's orders," I said. "You know how she is."

I sensed Mother's despair. She despises Sophia, who happens to be my oldest friend.

"What's she going to pay you?" Mother muttered.

She would say she does not despise Sophia the Child of God. Mother does not hate any Child of God except for my uncle, her own brother, who

molested me thirty years ago; and our former priest, who molested one of our neighbor's boys around the same time. Mother took both of those men down, and doesn't regret it. What Mother hates is Sophia's effect on me. I would argue, however, that you are your effect on people. My uncle became his effect on me. Therefore, Mother hates Sophia.

I've mostly felt sorry for Sophia even when she makes me mad. She, though beautiful and street-smart and wealthy, can't ever remember who she is. When she feels lost she calls me to be made right again. In making me the staff-job offer I couldn't refuse, she said—as if to justify the threat she wrapped into the proposal—that she was certainly not going to venture into Senate-hood without me. I could not tell Mother that Sophia had blackmailed me into the job because Mother would ring the ACLU.

"I'm a grownup, Ma," I told her instead. "You can't talk to me like that now that I'm the same age as a Senator. Now that I advise a Senator."

"Stay through Thanksgiving at least," Mother said. "I'm going to miss Viv. You might need money. Will you need money? I can't imagine Sophia will pay you enough to live in DC. What about schools? Viv loves her school."

"I'm fine, Ma. Sophia's fine. Viv is fine. Don't give me anything. I am a tough negotiator. That's why she wants me with her on The Hill."

Viv pattered out onto our creaky wooden porch where I was talking on my ancient landline, whose cord trailed through the window. I was drinking hot lemonade with basil even though it was an unseasonably warm night for Dallas. Viv had Mexican hot chocolate in her thermos. From the vinyl player inside, Eric Clapton's guitar-solo part of "Leila" drifted woozily.

"Tell Mops I don't want to go," Viv said.

Then she shouted, so my Mother would hear it, on purpose:

"Washington DC school is poop."

"Language!" Mother wailed through the phone.

"Don't say poop in front of Mops, Viv," I said. "Want to get me in trouble?"

"Yes," Viv said. Sadness had settled into her eyes ever since I'd told her Aunt Sophia wanted to take us with her to Washington.

I don't want to be coy or subtle over details you would know if you were watching us on TV so I will say now that my daughter Viv is black and I am white. I adopted her four years ago when she was two and a half years old and I was 33 and single. I am still single. I quit drinking two years before I adopted her.

Before I quit drinking, I had a good job, one that I liked. I distributed federal money to Texas women's health clinics. National reporters interviewed me as an expert on abortion and birth control. National lobbyists tried to cultivate my support. I counseled women leaders from tiny African countries whose work rich white internationalists took credit for, but who are mostly stuck doing the hard and dirty stuff themselves. Planned Parenthood of Texas called me their lifeline. It's true that without me the Texan lawmaking men would have driven them out of business sooner than they did. Roe v. Wade had not yet been overturned but the Ginsberg-less Supreme Court was hot for a lawsuit to try. And abortion had been all but outlawed in Texas: not by statute—we still pretended to respect federal law—but through budget cuts.

Budget savings are what legislators call their sneaky dissolution of laws they don't like.

Not only abortion: my state had banned birth control pills from women who couldn't pay the contraception tax. Texas lawmakers also outlawed prenatal exams that probed anything but fetus viability, or beating heart. They barred gynecological exams for women under the age of 18 except under the very eyes of a guardian; and abortion unless childbirth would kill the mother— a dispensation that was very difficult for them to make, they choked up about the inhumanity of it all during TV interviews. Their laws blunted all attempts at evasion by women and girls too poor to bribe a physician compassionate or arrogant enough to break the law for them.

So now in our state we've got plenty of back-alley abortions, and many of these are fatal since doctors are getting cheaper and meaner and scarcer. We've also got death-by-childbirth spiking among our country's serfs. And then, most burdensome on my heart, we've got a breaking foster system—which I can't even think about it without crying because I found Viv in that system after it had just about strangled her.

Then I lost my job because the lawmakers in Washington halted the federal grants I was responsible for, that I handed out to the women's clinics. The grants were from an old Nixon-era law, and they used to go directly to doctors of poor women. By poor, I mean women making less than $15,000 a year. You try living on that in this country. The grants got slashed because they failed the Republican Rorsasch test: anything having to do with women's health reminded them of abortion. And so they repealed it.

I tried to raise private funds to keep on with my work. Mother and her friends tried to help me. We wrote to all the rich and feisty Dallas and San Antonio and Houston ladies who liked to send checks to female causes behind their husbands' backs.

The feds caught wind of what we were up to and sent the IRS to audit me—which would have been fine, the books were up-to-date, but they found out about my drinking problem too. They learned from acute observation that sometimes I couldn't remember what I did when I drank. And then someone from somewhere in the upper reaches of the state capitol sent a cameraman to follow me through one of my blotto weekends, and for seven days his captured footage of me. That blotto time was one of my doozies. They caught me pissing in public and having sex in an alley behind a bar, I really wish I'd noticed the camera - - cycled through all the cable news shows of Texas. I made national shows too. The Senate Majority Leader denounced me on Fox News Trump Today and then on CNN. Most Democrats denounced me too, although I received two letters of support from one female Senator who will come in later.

I had to go home to Mother, get sober, and figure out my life again. I was 31 and looked 51. And I knew I'd never deserve a child like Viv if I didn't get straight. How I wanted a child who wasn't biologically mine.

Sophia, though purportedly my oldest friend, vanished during my darkest time. Didn't call, didn't try to help. I couldn't blame her: I was—I am—a heavier liability than a brown female Texas politician should ever be asked to bear. Not only was I a drunk, I was enemy number 1 to Texas Republicans in both House and Senate. She, meantime, had sweet-talked her way to the brink of what would become the party endorsement for election to Texas Attorney General. After I was sober and had adopted Viv, she became my friend again, she insisted on weekly happy hours. This is why Mother hates Sophia. Mother would take Viv—muttering harsh pronouncements against users and leaches —and I'd sit for hours with Sophia. I nursed non-alcoholic beers while she sucked down salt-rimmed margaritas and told me I would right now be as successful as she if I hadn't dropped out of law school.

"What's success?" I said.

"You should go back and finish," Sophia said, "now that you're sober. You could do it in two years and then get into politics where you can do some good."

"What about my past?" I said.

"They love a sordid past they can forgive. Look what it did for George W."

"If I had known success would make alcoholism acceptable," I said bitterly as she finished her fourth drink, "I would have postponed becoming an alcoholic til the time was right."

I like non-alcoholic beer, though.

I liked my new little nonprofit, too, even if I could barely eke out a living. It sharpened my legal skills better than law school had because it pushed me to the very edges of the law. I pushed myself to the edges of the law. Out of a small office in the suburbs I ran a privately funded, telephone-operated abortion clinic for girls and women who hadn't hit six weeks gestation yet. I had to watch legislators and their staff—federal, state, and local—as they daily churned out their new statutes for the ladies. For whenever men make a rule, women have to figure a way through, around, or over it and keep the ACLU on speed-dial.

In my office, my two colleagues and I measured mifepristone and misoprostol powders, legally acquired, into small black bags labeled with the pharmaceutical names but no instructions in case

the mailing envelopes were intercepted. With each packet we included an out-of-state 1-800 phone number that rang to our office landline. We mailed these envelopes to girls all across Texas and then, as other state laws began to tighten, to girls in Florida, Arizona, Alabama, Georgia, Nebraska, and Kansas. Our clients called us once they received their packets and we on the other end of the line would soothingly talk them through their abortions.

In theory, our website explained what we did and concealed nothing: Our services rendered were called, simply, "abdomen aspirations."

Typically I don't to hide my intents and purposes, but this was a legal matter of life and death.

Sophia started to piss me off long before she blackmailed me into joining her DC staff. First she rebranded herself as a political Independent and made the rounds of Texas' Republican circles. As it turned out, she could say the same words to Republicans and Democrats, plus and minus a few buzzwords, and raise equal amounts of money from both. "You can be a moderate Republican without changing anything but your spots," she told me at happy hour the week before she announced her bid for the U.S. Senate. "The key is commitment to Economic Growth."

Not a full 24 hours after her election victory, she stopped by my cinder-block 1970s office in the dingy fringe-suburb of Dallas called Irving. To get into the front office where I keep a desk with neat stacks of legal papers and a second-hand computer and photos of Viv and not much else, you had to ring a bell and state your name, while I looked you over through the surveillance camera.

"Has the FDA ever done a sweep around here?" Sophia asked, almost first thing. I had congratulated her over the phone on her victory night, but had not seen her in a little while.

"Why should they?" I said.

"Aren't you even afraid that they will?" she pressed me, and darkness gathered in her eyes. Her pupils blurred.

"When are you leaving?" I said uneasily. "Don't you have freshman orientation or something?"

"I'll leave when you'll come with me," she said.

I laughed. A hollow laugh.

"It's only a matter of time before you are shut down," Sophia said, acting earnest. She poised herself elegantly on the edge of the chair by my desk. I picked up an apple from the small fruit bowl and uneasily began to eat it.

"I want an apple," she said.

"I've only got one."

"Well, what about it?" With one manicured and moistened hand she laid papers on my desk. "I've got staff positions to fill and I want you to head my health policy team."

"What do I know of health policy?"

"I hope you know something, considering what you're up to here."

"I know my pills," I said, trying to make a joke.

The joke wasn't funny, considering my rehab past. I hurt my own feelings with it, but Sophia had made me nervous, that's why I said it.

"I'm serious," Sophia said. "I've shirked my responsibilities as Attorney General allowing you to stay open. I've done it because I know what it means to you; and you've been through enough already."

"Means to me?" I said, mad. "What does it matter what it means to me?"

"Well, with your past and everything," she said.

"We're the last hope a lot of girls from West Virginia to Arizona have got," I said. "You're threatening a lot of other things. Do you know how many packets we sent off today? I bet you can't even guess."

She set her cell phone on the desk too. She had recorded what I'd just said. She stopped the recording and I had jumped off my desk by now and I thought I would throw my apple core at her and throw her fucking phone out the window.

"This is to save you," Sophia said. "You admit you sell across state lines. I know these guys you're up against. They're in every corner of Texas law. I know how much they hate you. They'll put you in jail."

"They can't put me in jail." I said.

"They can and you know it," she said. "Think of what they'll appoint in my place when I'm gone. They won't care about Viv. They won't care about anything. They'll get you in court and behind bars. And the ACLU is busy these days."

So, when I picked Viv up from school I told her we were going to go to Washington, DC and maybe this would be good because she would learn how to be President.

My mild little baby threw a fit when I said that.

"I'm not going to the dark side!" she said.

I'd forgotten that in her life she's known only one President. How I explained democratic politics to her was through the original Star Wars so she could believe that one day the rebels would beat him.

iii.

One year after Sophia's election.

It was around the time that Sophia said the vote would be called soon on my first bill, my foster-care bill – which Sophia had introduced as her first real piece of legislation – that I got a strange feeling about Roy Foote.

Roy Foote worked for Senator Las Harrington, the senior Texas senator and the Republicans' razor-sharp whip. Roy was charming. Roy walked out one Tuesday night at seven o'clock from Sophia's office just as I was returning from a meeting. He looked at my feet and then at my face and said, "I thought you'd be there too."

Roy Foote is Texan like all of us, except he went northeast for law school, SMU wasn't good enough for him. Former Marine turned Capitol Hill law-broker. Credited with negotiating the total Free and Private Insurance take-over of health care when he was just a young, shadowy operative for the House Energy & Commerce Committee. Roy moved up to the Senate where we all figured he would stay until he saw fit to return to Texas and run for a seat himself. Perhaps Harrington's. Perhaps Sophia's. Perhaps just a lowly representative's.

The next morning in the crowded café in the basement of the Russell Senate Office Building, my friend Leah looked at me with her half-twinkling, half-mourning eyes and said she feared Sophia was working behind our backs to undermine the bill. My bill. Her bill.

Leah Leahy is my friend's full name, and she advised Phyllis Dreher, deputy Democratic whip for the Senate and the meanest, sharpest, oldest woman lawmaker on Capitol Hill. Dreher's hands and face were wrinkled like tissue paper, her voice was raspy from decades of cigarettes, she looked 90 at least; and yet her eyes flashed fire and she made even the President afraid, or so it was reported. Dreher was one of the two female senators who wrote to me personally after my booze-driven scandal in Texas that cost my job. In her letter she told me baldly that I possessed truer morality than any of the hypocrites who had taken me down. I adored Dreher.

And I started adoring Leah because she helped me write my foster-child bill and got Dreher to co-sponsor it and steer it through committee. Leah had also recruited two Republican Congressmen to introduce it to the House where it passed in record time.

I was in love with Leah and pretended I wasn't.

"What do you mean?" I said now to Leah. "Do we have to go through mark-up again?"

"You shouldn't ever start out with anything that means too much to you," Leah said sadly. "Anyway, they've pounced on Lampsted. Promising her things. They think they can bring her into their fold."

"How do you know?" I said.

"Harrington's people."

By Harrington's people, she meant Roy Foote. She looked around her, and I did too. The aides and the reporters they were gossiping with were loud, but someone was listening to us somewhere. Someone always is in those basement Senate building cafes.

"She hasn't told me anything," I whispered, quivering. And then I recalled, with bitterness, how shitty people are in general and how shitty Sophia could be in particular.

"All I'm saying is, keep an eye on her," Leah said. "She's already in the top five Senate fuckwits. Why don't you ditch her next midterms?"

"It'd be nice to go back to Texas," I said, wistfully. "I've got my daughter growing up here like I never wanted her to."

"Among the DC mercenaries and their highly legitimate spawn?"

"In SoDoSoPa, no less."

"There's got to be a statute of limitations on whatever Lampsted's got on you," Leah said, amused. "It's not like you're doing mail-order abortions anymore."

She bit her lip and I did not want to leave her yet.

"You don't know how mean Sophia can be," I said, to get her to feel sorry for me.

"You're a bit cautious for someone who so happily makes enemies all around this town," Leah said.

She wrapped an endless silk skein around her throat as a scarf and grinned broadly at me. We hesitated, looking at one another, and I felt quite warm and content and accompanied when I left her, as I always did.

Abandoning Leah for the bleak basement passages wore me out. I took the corridor through Russell and Dirksen to the Hart building and then the elevator up to the bright-white atrium. In the Lampsted office, I found only the economic and energy staff still at their desks. And Sophia herself, surprisingly: She was on the phone with either a reporter or campaign donor, I could tell from her flirtatious tone. She summoned me with her pinky.

"C'mere, doll," she said, covering the telephone receiver. Her new appellation for me. "I haven't seen you in ages."

"It's been three hours at least," I said. And, full of the confidence only Leah and Viv could give me these days, I sashayed my way to the leather seat directly before her and picked up the blue-glass paperweight shaped like Texas.

I missed my fucked-up Texas. I missed our Dallas cottage. I missed good barbecue. I missed the road-trips with Viv to Corpus Christi, where we'd play in the muddy tide and pretend we were swimming to Mexico to join the Aztecs in the jungle.

Sophia resumed her call. "I would say," she said into the receiver, "we are working with the President on the jobs problem. No, no, you didn't hear that from me. Maybe we're fucked now or maybe we're fucked in fifty years. But jobs are my first priority. Other than you."

"That went well," I said as she replaced her receiver.

"It always does," she said.

"How's it going with my bill?" I said, shutting the door out of considerateness. For I'm the only aide who speaks straight to her and she doesn't like other staff to hear it when I do.

"I'm going to get it passed," she said, and eyed me warily. "Harrington is helping me."

"How?"

"We're going to pass a beautiful piece of bipartisan overhaul with the Children's Health Insurance Program appropriation. It will be palatable for everyone. It will be Congress working together again."

"Palatable to everyone usually means something disgusting," I said. "Like Olive Garden." And that's all I said. I didn't want to start guessing what the Senators were doing to Children's Health Insurance.

"GOP wants to make a clean break with government health care," Sophia said. "It's up to us to stop them."

"I don't want to lose Foster Child Safety along with Children's Health Insurance," I said, slowly.

"You won't lose," Sophia said. "Trust me. This is a big lame-fucking-duck health legislative package for the ages. It's about kids and it's about health. Your two favorite things. Next to abortion, of course."

I must have looked glum because she said, "We'll be celebrating soon. We're going to get your baby law through Congress and out to Texas where it can do some good."

.I did not smile—Sophia could nevermore disarm me—but I felt the gentle flare of muted excitement that can still at times brighten you no matter how disappointed you've been.

For dinner that night, I made grits with pork fat, smothered in crispy salted kale and leftover pulled pork.

Viv had finished her homework and was curled up in her little kitchen armchair to read Charles and Mary Lamb's Tales From Shakespeare: Cymbeline while I finished cooking.

"Viv," I said. "I think we need look in the Rearview Mirror." Which is what we call history in our house.

She glanced up at me, dazed from her flight into ancient Briton's forests. She answered without protest: "OK."

"Do you remember Lycurgus?"

"He was in ancient Sparta and he didn't want to be evil so he made his nephew king and he just planned everything so all the people could live happy and good," she said.

"Yes," I said, and my heart was joyful and proud of my little one, who could look with clarity through the peepholes of history at age 7. "And do you remember the greatest thing he ever did?"

"He went to every country to see who had good laws and then he wrote the best laws in the world," she said.

"Why were they the best?" I said, giving her a spoonful of grits to taste.

"Because," she spoke through her chews, "he made sure everyone had the same things, and no one was too rich. And he was a really good man. Everyone tried to be as good as him."

"As he."

"As he."

"Do you think we can make these good laws in our country?" I said.

She looked at me seriously, though she wanted to get back to her violent Shakespeare story. "No," she said, simply.

"And why is that?"

Because Lycurgus' Sparta was the first pure communist state in human record.

"Because Aunt Sophia won't let you," she said.

The next day I went to Sophia and said she needed to let me in on her talks with Senator Harrington and his people. She played coy, wouldn't say yes or no, so I marched to Harrington's office, not trusting the telephone and Sophia's team of always-listening aides she had assembled against me, and ordered the be-suited, freckled front-desk boy to call Roy Foote for me.

"May I ask your name?" the front-desk boy said.

I gave him my name. "From Lampsted's office," I said. "You know me."

"Yes indeed, Ma'am," he said with inscrutable politeness, and he called Roy and to Roy's credit he appeared within seconds through the doorway that's surmounted with a great Lone Star State flag.

"Hey there," Roy said. He's got a deep, gruff voice. It feels thoughtful of you. That's his best trick. "How's your mother?"

"Why, you've been talking to her?" I said.

"I like your mother," he said.

"You met her once."

"I'm sorry it wasn't more than that," he said. "If you were more lIke her, we'd get along."

"Doubt it," I said. "Can we sit down or something?"

"Of course," he said. "I'm going to have Derek here make you the best coffee you've ever had."

Derek, the be-suited front desk boy, didn't look pleased.

"Don't bother," I said.

"You're right. Derek makes shit coffee. I'll make it."

And he ushered me into his office. It was glossy and bright. There was a tall, pale orchid for one thing and a turntable for another and I kid you not, here in the middle of the day on Capitol Hill

Roy was playing—very softly—Texas' own crooner Jim Reeves singing "Adios Amigo." He also had an espresso machine and small refrigerator from which he drew a glass dairy bottle of morning-fresh local milk, the kind that DC Democrats buy for their whole-food babies.

"I'm not sure I'm in the right place," I said agreeably. "You are Roy Foote, aren't you?"

"Just try and find a better one," he said. "Now I'm going to make you the best latte you've ever tasted and then I want to hear what you and your boss are up to."

Just like that, I was relaxed and Jim Reeves was singing:
When two love the same love, one love has to lose.

"Speaking of one of us losing," I said. "What's going on with Children's Health Insurance?"

"I'm for it."

"As long as children are happy, you're happy?"

"You know it," he said, and poured the thick-foamed milk over the espresso and gave me the beautiful coffee.

"So let me see the bill draft you're working on," I said. "I've heard it's bipartisan."

"Lampsted is the definition of bipartisan," Roy said. "But are you?"

"Try me," I said.

"I'd like to," he said.

Just like the best of the Texas boys, he'd slipped under my skin. His eyes made me uncomfortable and I was pleased.

"Help me out," I said, finally. "I need to see your working draft."

"I'll have it once you add the finishing touches," he said. "Of course you'll collaborate with us."

I finished the latte—it was so softly rich—and stood. "I don't know what that means. Collaborate."

"It means I'll tell you what you need to know," he said agreeably.

"Thanks for nothing," I said. "The riders on this thing are going to be crazy."

"Our definitions of crazy may differ," he said. I didn't like him once he turned sarcastic. He drew out a notebook of thick, cream-colored paper and a silver-plated pen. He scrawled out some names. Last of all, grinning a little, he wrote out a ten-digit phone number with a Houston area code. A guy hadn't given me his number since my days as a good-time floozy.

"These are the people who have been invited to help us sweeten up Children's Health Insurance," he said. "Lampsted is one of them. It's about time you asked for my number."

As I left the office, foundering a bit, I had Jim Reeves stuck in my head.

Adios compadre, what must be must be

Remember to name one muchacho for me

Back in my office, I got out Roy's list of names of Senators and more lowly members of the House and started to figure out what each of them wanted. For the rest of the day I pored over all the bills they'd introduced but hadn't gotten past leadership yet. I didn't find anything that alarmed me except a bill from Carrie Ives (Republican. From Iowa). I didn't like that she had a place at our negotiating table. Congresswoman Ives doesn't play nice. And, I knew this well, she had a little bill that worried me, a long-dormant bit of legislation that ten years ago everyone had called a piece of crazy. She called it the "Heart-Beat Humanity Act."

This Act would grant, to every six-weeks-gestated fetus, citizenship to the United States of America and a social security card that promised more rights than the fetus could ever hope for once it was born. For fetuses get special treatment. They need no money or education, nor do they have brown, black or lightly toasted skin.

Roy kept his promise about letting me in on the Children's Health Insurance talks. He rang me one night just before I left the office and said he and a few others were going to hash out some issues ahead of their bosses' lunch meetings the next day. He said they were heading to Tortilla Coast. Did I want to come?

"I assume I'll be well outnumbered," I said.

"Didn't think that would bother you," he said. "But of course you may bring an ally."

I called Leah's office to say she better come with me.

"Oy," she said. "We're going out with Roy and his band of brothers? I know we need to stay on top of it, but do we have to get on top of them?"

"Our sister prostitutes have been doing it for millennia," I said.

I rang a friend and begged a baby-sitting favor and she said yes, she would go pick up Viv, and Leah and I walked to the restaurant: shoulder to shoulder.

Crumbling at Roy's table amid baskets of tortilla chips and vats of guacamole were: four male GOP aides—including one of Carrie Ives'. Roy and his friends were blond and thin and rumpled in an organized way. I silently dubbed them the Gang of Five. Everyone except me and Leah (who seemed to think I would fall off the wagon if she drank when I was around) was high on tequila. Roy was good at getting information out of each and every one of them once they were drunk. They complained about their bosses. They griped about their lobbyists. They spoke of the hopes and fears of the next election. They gave him everything he needed to know.

I said nothing and neither did Leah. We listened. Then I drove Leah home. When we left, Roy looked at us, surprised and displeased.

"Why do I feel that tonight wasn't just what it seemed?" Leah said on the way to Logan Circle.

"In my drinking days Roy Foote could have got anything out of me too," I said.

"I don't like the sound of that," Leah said.

Roy sweet-talked me every minute he could, and his constant attention surprised and then finally flattered me because I knew how little time he has for the basics of living, much less for trying to win an unwinnable woman. He mostly sleeps in the office, wrapped around his phone, as his Jim Reeves albums wind down slowly so he doesn't feel the stone-cold emptiness of the nights.

The final draft text of the Children's Heath Insurance appropriations bill wasn't out yet, but we were hurtling into the deadline because already it was nearly Thanksgiving and the House wanted to take it up for vote by the following week so the Senate could dawdle and quarrel and still give the President time to sign it before Christmas. Roy sent a page to my office with reams of text, which was dumped on my desk. I reviewed it all line by line, with Leah, and we wrote notes for our bosses to take to their negotiations.

He also sent a note with the bill. I slipped it into my desk drawer and now and then throughout the day opened the drawer to read it. He had written:

This is why you should like me too:

I like it when you spill coffee on yourself and rub the stain deeper into your pants.

I like it when you check your makeup in the window reflections if you think no one's looking.

I like it when you see your daughter's picture on your desk while we're working

And smile sneakily, like you know it's you and she that run the world and the idiots in it.

I like it when you bite your lip when you look at me, like you're telling me: "Look out. I love the taste of blood."

Meantime, Mother broke her leg a few weeks before Thanksgiving and canceled her planned trip to visit us in Washington for the holiday. Wednesday I drove Viv to the Baltimore airport after school and put her on the plane for Dallas to eat turkey with her grandmother. Thanksgiving itself I spent with Leah at her friends' house in leafy northwest DC. We weren't getting along, she and I. I thought this was because she liked me as I liked her. As Roy said he liked me. And that she knew what Roy was up to.

Within those few weeks of working with Roy, she and I had grown awkward. We quarreled over what compromises we were willing to make on the bill. We quarreled over everything, even over what we'd order for lunch. We strained to get along. I still wanted her, though. Or so I thought.

And yet Roy had confused me and I had an uneasy feeling that maybe I wanted him. I couldn't be sure. I could never be sure. When I quit drinking, I also quit sex. Chaste, they would have called me back in the day. I was thirteen when my uncle started touching me, fourteen when he stuck his thing inside me. See? I'm almost forty years old and I call it a "thing." That's how repressed I am. I'd never have had sex again if I hadn't grown into a drinking problem that zapped my hardwires. As an alcoholic I managed a few bad relationships, but even then I needed to be drunk to make love. Though love never had much to do with it.

But I loved Leah. Throughout Thanksgiving dinner I looked at her forlornly across the table. We spoke hardly at all.

And then this happened: during dessert. I had made the coffee and our hostess was dishing out the apple-cranberry pie. Leah's phone buzzed and she excused herself to take the call. When she returned to the table she looked bad. She said nothing, then she stirred again and abandoned the table for the kitchen. I followed her. Even though she is tougher than Mother she had tears in her eyes.

"Phyllis"—and she never called Senator Dreher by her first name—"just had a heart attack. She's at the Detroit Heart Hospital."

Dreher, who was from Michigan, had gone home for Thanksgiving.

"How bad?" I said.

"They don't think she is going to make it," Leah said.

Well, it got worse after that, but before it got worse something very beautiful happened to me. I walked Leah into her apartment that night, for she didn't want to stay at the dinner after the call. I was still thinking and feeling on the intimate, personal level more than the political sociological level, and I was sadder about losing Dreher the human, the keen and bright soul, than about losing a Senator whose seat might go red.

Leah asked me if I wanted to come up to her apartment. I did. I parked my Saab and followed her into her little brick building in Logan Circle. In the upstairs hall as she unlocked her door, the overhead lamp flickered and died, so the only light was the moon. And it bent her face, making her cheek small and white. And this seemed very poignant to me, and I kissed her—there in the hall; I kissed the side of her mouth. We got the door open, and some of my body turned liquid, but not all of it; parts of me ached until she touched them. I don't remember if we were on the floor or her sofa, but I remember it seemed like her skin was mine, her breasts were mine, her tongue was mine. We melded together. By the time we made it to her bed and to sleep we had forgotten everything except the need to hold one another.

But then it was six o'clock the following morning and we were each getting calls. Dozens of them. Senator Dreher wasn't dead yet but close; and Roy wanted to meet with me Saturday afternoon to review the final legislation.

"Aren't you worried about Dreher?" Roy asked when we met at the best barbecue joint in Mt. Pleasant. "You don't look worried about anything."

He seemed cold and offended. He treated me stiffly. His manner made me feel as if I had wronged him somehow, and I became stiff too. We were half way through combing the text of the bill, and legislative text is more unreadable than Derrida, and I excused myself for the toilet. He said, as if pained, that he needed a drink.

"Get me one too," I said. "But virgin of course."

When I returned to the table he had a vodka martini for himself and for me what I assumed was my usual—sparkling water with lime and a little grenadine, with a maraschino cherry. When I tasted it, nothing seemed off. I didn't suspect anything. He's a Texas boy. A Texas boy who had written me a poem.

I researched my symptoms after my three blotto days. He'd slipped me a drug called gamma-Hydroxybutyric acid, or GHB, or liquid fantasy. Used often in place of Rohypnol because under liquid fantasy's influence the victim grows eager.

The rapist doesn't have to deal with a comatose doll. He can feel as if I want him too.

But Roy wasn't ready for my violent physical reaction to his particular fantasy. I believe, now – although it was beyond proof once I made it through the hangover-coma all traces of the drug had passed out of my system -- that he mixed the drug with a little vodka and slipped it into the grenadine. Even now, I get flashes of what happened: I remember bringing him to my loft. I remember doing things with him the memory of which would have made me practically suicidal a decade earlier. Beyond that, I don't know much. Time was warped. I don't think I was conscious of Viv or Mother or Leah or Sophia. Certainly not of my foster-child bill.

Mother dispatched the police to my apartment when she couldn't reach me to discuss Viv's pickup from the airport. Leah, sensitive because of what happened between us, misinterpreted my disappearance as rejection of her and didn't look for me until Monday. I wasn't in my office and she knew something had gone wrong. The police got me to a doctor. The doctor just said I had reacted badly to alcohol. He looked at my medical records and then at me, soberly.

"With your history," he said, "it was a mistake to drink."

"But I didn't," I said.

Mother rang every lawyer she knew to see what charges we could hang Roy Foote on. She cursed and railed and promised she'd cut off his penis with her sewing scissors.

"And I tell you one thing," she concluded. "Harrington's not going to survive this either. Even if he doesn't keep that Foote in his mouth."

Leah didn't believe my side of the story. Three days is too long for an aide who's worth anything to go missing from Washington action. Roy got his story out before my brain was straight again. Dreher was dying in the Detroit Heart Hospital. The Senate's Democrats had no deputy whip. Leah was already sad. A little innuendo, the timely circulation of YouTube footage of my long-ago Texas humiliation by certain Gang of Five lackeys, elevated Roy and ruined me. I would get no new chance in this town.

Sophia railed against me bitterly before firing me. She said I had ruined her, too.

"Voters will forget," I said.

"My colleagues won't," she said.

"You'll end up fine," I said.

"But your work won't," she said. I could swear she seemed happy about that.

When the House voted on the Children's Health Insurance Reconciliation Act, Roy and his Gang had slipped Carrie Ives' "Heart-Beat Humanity Act" alongside my "Saving Foster Care Act." The two were one. Sophia couldn't disclose she was bullied or blackmailed into letting this happen—she would look stupid—so she pretended she and Carrie Ives had planned the whole thing, all along. It was the Ives-Lampsted bicameral bipartisan bill. A legislative victory. In a press conference, Sophia stood beside Ives. They said, one after the other, beaming broadly, that it was appropriate and right to fight for the good of all children.

The House passed it. The Senate passed it. The President, his hair fading fast, signed it into law. Sophia was among the lawmakers on the stage behind him as he signed it and held up the paper for all to see. He gave her one of his stupid pens. I saw it on TV.

At least Viv and I got to return to Texas before Christmas. A good thing, because by New Year's I sensed I was pregnant. I took the test three times, but it was right the first time. It always is. I didn't tell Viv, but I did tell Mother.

Mother cried. The last time she had cried was when I was fourteen, and she—lifelong Catholic—drove me to the abortion clinic because I was so afraid of the thing growing inside me that her brother had put there.

But I didn't feel like crying. A few days earlier, while I was unpacking my Washington bags, I had found Roy's note to me.

I like it when you bite your lip when you look at me, like you're telling me: "Look out. I love the taste of blood."

This was the line that gave me my idea.

I asked Sophia's press secretary to call in a favor to George Stephanopoulos' producer. I had met George a few times, he knew who I was. George's producer called me back. He said Yes, George would like to interview me about the Heart-Beat Humanity Act and Senator Lampsted's sponsorship of the most anti-abortion legislation in decades. I flew up to Washington on Saturday afternoon with a small bag each of mifepristone and misoprostol. And a vegetarian capsule.

For the Sunday morning broadcast, I dressed in muted gray. I sat with George, and his producer had set a glass of water in front of me. On-camera, George and I chatted. He asked me whether women in this day and age could still say with their heads held high that abortion was all right.

"It's all right for me," I said. "At least it's all right today, and today's my last chance. Because tomorrow I will be six weeks and could be arrested for murder."

I flustered even George. I hadn't told him what was coming.

"I got raped by Washington," I said. "Sometimes people have a hard time defining rape. But Roy Foote knows what he did."

George recovered his charm while I drew out the powders and the capsule and explained the dosage.

"Is this safe?" George said.

"It will save me," I said. "My body is not Roy's but today I'm Lycurgus."

He looked confused by that. I had to move quickly to dissolve the awkwardness. I picked up my water glass and put the pill on my tongue; looked into the camera and drank to Viv.

About the Author:

Susannah is a Washington-based journalist. A graduate of USC's master of professional writing program, she has published short fiction in New World Writing and Californios. Her noir novel based on her experiences trading vanilla in Polynesia is represented by Dystel & Goderich

AND THEN WHAT COULD YOU DO?

By Maureen McCafferty

The doctor stood behind her desk, offering a steady hand and smile, as if Maeve had come to open a checking account. As if Maeve could— her account at Greyhaven Savings was laughable, which, of course, hadn't stopped her landlord from raising her rent only days after she'd left him a message about the front panel falling off her rusting air conditioner, making a perfect home for the small gray mother bird and her two feather- less babies nesting there now. Maeve worried. She didn't want birds making their way into her apartment, but she didn't have the heart to dis- turb them, wishing a kindly repairman would ap- pear to gently transfer the nest to a tree. . . .

God, had she just told the psychiatrist about the birds? Or about her rent going up? God knows what the medical bill for this hospital would be. The clinic might be free, or what hospitals consid- ered free, but this doctor looked pretty polished. Maeve shook the doctor's steady hand, offering her own sad smile while hoping this woman could fix whatever was going on with her mother. Fix it fast. Time was money, especially if you didn't have either.

"Please have a seat, Ms. Walsh."

Maeve sat, sad smile still there as she worried a bit, more than a bit, that this doctor was older and a lot more put together than she'd expected. She wasn't sure why either would be a problem. Except when she was a kid and her mother was ill like this, all those doctors at Greyhaven Clinic had been young and rumpled with stains on their ties. What was this rather sophisticated seeming doctor doing here? Also, Valerie Shaw already

seemed sure of something, which Maeve knew from experience wasn't always a good thing. But probably better not to mention that or ask why this well put together, smart doctor was seeing them separately, as if Maeve didn't already know: get the stories and compare, like the police. She slumped down in the plastic orange seat, feeling too tall, an easy target.

"Tell me what is going on." The doctor sat there as if she had all the time in the world, and you could take what you needed. Some therapists were like that, not many, not usually the psychia- trists. Top of the mental health ladder.

"Well, my mother is very confused." Maeve stopped. What had Gracie already told this doc- tor? Better just to stick to facts. "My mother called me this morning, very early."

"Yes?"

"She wanted me to go to her house, so I did."

"And?"

"Yes, and when I got there she was very upset about something. She has a hard time, with things."

"What things?"

"Everything. She's an anxious person." The doc- tor waited. Maeve hated the waiting. Waiting multiplied worries fast as insects in a hot attic. But there was nothing to hide here, was there? "My mother said her eighty-five-year-old neigh- bor was taping her conversations and had trained the birds outside to spy on her." There, fix that.

The doctor was nodding, a comforting gesture meant to reassure, disarm, draw you in. Meant to have you reveal all sorts of things you probably shouldn't. Like wanting to live somewhere where no one knew you, which of course Maeve didn't, not all the time. Better not to mention that either. Just be careful, because if you weren't, before you knew it, you could be sitting here going on about Mrs. Jacob or Aunt Budgie or how sometimes it felt as if you'd made a wrong turn somewhere and now you were stuck in a life you never meant to have. Maeve smiled.

Dr. Shaw didn't, looking serious as she picked up a beautiful, old-fashioned fountain pen rather than one of the cheap plastic hospital pens everyone here used, and deliberately, unhurriedly, unscrewed the cap to write something in a file. Maeve knew she would. Spying birds had to be noted. "Tell me, Ms. Walsh, has your mother ever had an episode like this before?"

Maeve shrugged, wondering how much that fountain pen cost.

"Has she?"

"Once or twice, a long time ago, when I was a child."

Valerie Shaw's light brown eyes peered over her rimless reading glasses, the sort of glasses that disappeared on your face, the sort nuns wore. Nuns knew how to stare and wait too.

"My mother battles anxiety and depression."

"And paranoia."

"No, not usually."

"What happened the last time your mother had an episode like this?"

"I don't really know."

"Tell me whatever you can remember."

There was some memory tucked away here, wasn't there? Valerie Shaw knew there would be. Even if you sat here thinking about fountain pens, the doctor knew that was just to cover some tucked away memory waiting for its chance to crawl out of the darkness. Because no matter how much you didn't want to remember or reveal some things you had to: "I remember once my mother was afraid someone had put a camera

inside the walls of our house. She was afraid cameras were in the walls, watching us." This seemed new and very old at the same time, which Maeve would say, if any of this were supposed to be about her.

"I see."

"What?"

The doctor made another note.

"This is so sudden." Maeve meant the memory. The memory was sudden and strong, a riptide dragging her back somewhere she didn't want to go. So, she wouldn't. She would pay attention to whatever Dr. Shaw was talking about now, even if she should probably explain to the good doctor that it was the memory that was sudden, not her mother's latest episode, because it was never sudden with their mother, if you paid attention, which Maeve hadn't. She pulled herself up in the plastic orange chair, her legs too long. Always the long, skinny one. Five-feet in fourth grade. Try fitting in when you're eight-years-old and as tall as a lot of kids' mothers. Taller than your own mother.

"Ugly tall," Brenda Crawford had said the first day of fourth grade. She was small and pretty. "You're ugly tall, Maeve Walsh." Standing in St. Pete's playground with a group of girls, pretty little Brenda Crawford had smiled so sweetly who could believe she was so mean? "You're big and ugly, like the witch's tree," she'd laughed, pointing to the ugly tree in the schoolyard everyone called the witch's tree. Struck by lightening years ago, nothing ever grew on it but stories of witches and hauntings. "Ugly, like the witch's tree," Brenda had said, other things too, worse things. You could never tell what was going to change your life, till it did, and then what could you do? Did this doctor with the steady stare and very precise manners have any idea? Any idea how you could undo things, your own or anyone else's?

"What happened that time?"

"When?"

"The time your mother imagined cameras were in the walls. What happened then?"

"Oh." And there it was: that three o'clock dismissal from St. Pete's, Mrs. Jacob waiting at the chain

-link fence, the twins beside her, Gracie in her carriage. Their mother gone. "I was eight. It was a long time ago."

"I understand this is difficult, Ms. Walsh, but it would help, you see, if I knew something about your mother's history."

"Yes, I'm sorry, history." But it wasn't her mother's history Maeve dragged around with her. Mostly her mother's history was dark, like some shadow Maeve lived inside without knowing the life that cast it. But the good doctor was waiting for history. Maybe Maeve should just stick to the Second World War, how her Irish-born father, barely more than a boy, had come to this country for adventure, never intending to stay, here about a week when he got more adventure than he'd ever imagined: drafted into a World War he was barely back from and still in his American Army uniform when he met and quickly, too quickly, married the beautiful Kathleen Delaney, of Greyhaven, Queens, New York, who really was so much more, and less, than she seemed. Shadows. Think you can choose? Or maybe what mattered was the day they moved from that cramped Spencer Avenue apartment into their new house on the other side of Greyhaven, their father promising, "This will feel like home, Kathleen. This will be a real home," hoping the way you do when you don't know what to do if this doesn't work. Should she mention that?

Or how pretty little mean Brenda Crawford, who had said Maeve was like the ugly witch's tree and other worse things, had died in a car accident in high school, driving around with a bunch of friends, laughing and happy, not paying attention to the road? Terrible accident. Did the suspiciously stylish doctor with the steady stare and gentle voice need to know how you could be at a funeral and supposed to be sad and praying for eternal peace but really you were remembering being in a playground and hating someone?

"If you could tell me, for instance, what doctors your mother saw— "

"Yes, of course. . . ." Maeve wanted to get up and retrieve her handbag from locker 17 and show Valerie Shaw the black-and-white photo of her and her mother on the courtyard steps of their Spencer Avenue apartment building, the photo she'd found among her father's insurance papers

and old passports. She smoothed and smoothed the unsmoothable wrinkles in her black woolen skirt, demonstrating how uselessness seldom stopped her. The black wool matched her mood, if not the season. Probably better not to admit that. "Umm, my mother's history. Well, there was Dr. Lutz, but that was years ago, in the beginning."

"Tell me about the beginning."

"Four kids in a one-bedroom apartment, my father working overtime at the warehouse. It was just too much. That was the beginning. Who wouldn't want to escape?"

"Did your mother talk about escaping?"

"She left."

"What happened?"

"My mother was there, then she wasn't."

The doctor waited.

"So, we went to Mrs. Jacob's house every morning and after school, and then after a while my mother came back." That's how the story went and Maeve didn't have or want another.

As if sensing this, Dr. Shaw seemed to put aside her own ability to crack such reluctance and merely asked, "Do you remember the name of a hospital or doctor— " She glanced down at her notes. "Dr. Lutz? Do you remember the doctor's first name?"

"No, it was a long time ago."

"A man?"

"They were all men. There were lots of doctors, but I don't remember any in particular. My mother wasn't in a hospital. She just left."

"Where did she go?"

"I don't know, she didn't send postcards." Maeve straightened up in her chair. "I'm sorry. I don't mean to be rude. All I know is that when my mother came back we went to clinics for her medicine."

"I see," the doctor said.

"What do you see?" Maeve smiled, the pain behind her right eye splintering into a strange rolling light that was making her sick. Right now passing out seemed like a good way of this.

"There may be hospital records— "

"My mother wasn't in a hospital. We got medicine at the clinic after she came back, but she wasn't in the hospital."

Dr. Shaw looked through papers. "I see your mother lives in Queens. Is that where you were living then?"

"Yes, Greyhaven, Queens." Maeve remembered the note on the kitchen table: These are my daughters, please take them in. . . in her mother's careful script on the yellow kitchen table by her father's brown mug of tea. She'd only seen the note for a minute before he had come back in the kitchen. Why hadn't he kept it? Why wasn't that note in the little gold cigar box that held her father's Irish passport and his American Naturalization papers, his Army dogtags, the nearly forty-year-old newspaper clippings of President Kennedy's inauguration and the President's funeral, with the grainy/gray newspaper photo of the horse-drawn casket? That old black-and-white photo of Maeve and her mother on the courtyard steps was there too in the cigar box, but not the note. Why hadn't her father kept it? Also, her mother's name was Kay, so why was that note signed Vivienne?

"Would that be all right?"

Maeve leaned forward as if maybe she could catch up with what the doctor had just said. "I'm sorry, would what be all right?"

"I may need your mother to release her medical records. Would that be all right with you?"

Had Gracie agreed? Why couldn't she ask? Hiding confusion just made you seem confused, didn't it? And something about that slight elegant inflection to the doctor's voice seemed an invitation of sorts that made her seem kind, or maybe just made you imagine kindness in the story you were telling yourself about Valerie Shaw. Because you had to reconcile, did you, what someone as polished as good silver was doing in the dreary plastic orange clinic? If you were going to trust her. As if they had a choice.

"Ms. Walsh?"

"Yes, medical records, I suppose that's okay," she said, not sounding like herself. She was so decisive at work, not that anyone acknowledged such

a thing, except occasionally Malcolm Berman, who had been crammed in their small office with her. He knew how much Maeve had to decide every day, all sorts of things she had no right or obligation to decide, but what could you do? Especially if there was no other way to keep your job, because if she let her dim boss decide things it wouldn't be him—son of a founding partner— who would be out of work. And some job, even an inadequate one, was better than no job, at least till you found another, which Maeve had been intending to do for years, and would as soon as she had time or, whatever it was you needed to get a better job. Did the good doctor know? Probably not the time to ask that either. They were talking about her mother's medical records, weren't they?

Maeve smiled, hands neatly folded in her lap, the way nuns taught you, because they knew what the world thought of sloppy, distracted children. She and Gracie were the children here. That's what was wrong: children don't decide for parents. "I didn't know it was this bad."

"You have recently lost your father. You and your sister are also grieving."

Gracie must've told her that. Should she let the good doctor think grief made a difference? That she hadn't spent her whole life gauging her mother's mind and moods carefully enough to have known this was where they were headed? All mixed up, Maeve, all mixed up. One of Kay Walsh's chants. Of course it was all mixed up because Maeve hadn't bothered . . . for three days.

"What hospital has your family used over the years?"

"Greyhaven General in Queens. We came into Manhattan today because someone recommended we see you. Dr. Lisa Berman recommended we— I work with her brother, Malcolm."

"Oh, yes, I know Dr. Berman."

Maeve straightened up again in the uncomfortable plastic orange chair, hands clenched. Sometimes nuns could tell you just what to do, but sometimes they knew absolutely nothing at all about the real world. "We used to take my mother to Greyhaven General's psychiatric clinic once a month for prescriptions. After she came back, there were lots of prescriptions. I was about nine, I guess, when that started."

"That sounds like follow-up care. Most likely your mother was hospitalized years ago."

"No, my father would have said something."

"You were a child."

"I was the oldest." That wasn't exactly true, but Maeve didn't want to think about or explain that now either. There were a lot of unsaid things piling up here, and now she was telling the doctor about housekeeping: "I cleaned, did laundry, made sure we had milk in the house. There's never enough milk with little kids. The twins were only four, and Gracie was just a baby. Did Gracie tell you that? My father couldn't do everything. Mrs. Jacob watched us at her house, not our apartment. I took care of— I don't know why I'm telling you this. I just mean, if my mother had been in a hospital, my father would've told me. I wasn't a baby."

"You were a very responsible child, but still a child, and probably feeling too responsible."

That felt like a criticism, one Maeve didn't want to know about.

"People often think silence is better than disclosing events they, themselves, find troubling, Ms. Walsh, especially when children are involved."

"No, my father would have told me. That isn't what happened." You couldn't just change what happened because you wanted to. Even if you were a very smart doctor with a genteel voice, you couldn't just change someone else's life, at least not the past. Of course, The past is never past, someone had warned. Einstein? Faulkner? Years studying literature, not medicine. How did that help? Did Valerie Shaw know?

"It would help now, you see, to know your mother's past diagnosis in order to determine if . . . . "

Maeve realized that a moment ago she would have welcomed the possibility of some real past or present diagnosable hospital craziness underneath their lives. But a moment ago that was just an idea, not a terrifying thing actually staring you in the face, scary as that scratchy noise in the wall suddenly scurrying across your kitchen. How would Valerie Shaw like to be let in on that image? Also, could the good doctor possibly tell her why Mrs. Jacob's stories about her kids, Louise, Eli, baby Lenny, or about Mr. Jacob dying one morning while on the phone to his friend Izzy Gunther, seemed to matter again? Maeve didn't even know why it all mattered so much and she had been there.

Their mother's scared eyes stayed on Maeve as she and Gracie came back into the doctor's office.

"I'm going to ask you a few questions, Mrs. Walsh. Is that all right?"

Their mother didn't answer, eyes still scared and on Maeve.

"We are here to determine the best choice for you," the doctor was saying, not realizing that their mother didn't believe in choice. In fact, Kay Walsh believed in little other than her husband, Franklin Roosevelt, and Jesus. "Think you can choose?" she used to ask her daughters, who knew not to answer. "Think you can choose anything in this life? Well, you'll see. Just wait till life stops you in your tracks. You'll see."

"Just a few questions."

"My daughters are better with questions. Ask them."

"Do you know why you are here today, Mrs. Walsh?"

"Something about insurance?"

"Do you know what day it is?"

Their mother looked at Gracie, then Maeve, and then at her hands tightly folded in her lap.

"Who is the President of the United States?"

"He's dead."

"Who?"

"The President," their mother said as if the doctor were dim. Maeve considered mentioning Roosevelt, but it probably wouldn't help.

"Have you been having a hard time by yourself?" Valerie Shaw sounded concerned, as if she were Kay Walsh's best friend, as if their mother had friends.

"Such is life."

"A hard time keeping your thoughts clear?"

"No, no," their mother insisted, sensing trouble. "My thoughts are very clear, very clear. Aren't they, Maeve?"

"Do you pay your own bills, Mrs. Walsh? Are you able to manage that?"

"Pay the bill, Maeve, so we can get out of here."

"My father always took care of that," Gracie explained. "My sister and I do it now."

Carefully, Dr. Shaw removed and folded the delicate wire stems of her rimless reading glasses the same way Sister Catherine used to, then sat a little forward at her desk. The good doctor's eyes were so light they seemed almost golden, like Linda Vinn, Maeve's best friend after they moved from Spencer Avenue to Greyhaven Boulevard. Easy to think someone with eyes like that was gentle and good and cared about you, too easy.

"We will have to do some tests," the doctor was saying. "There are many possible causes of dementia. From what you have told me, this is most likely severe clinical depression, triggered by grief. But without tests, we cannot dismiss the possibility of small infarcts—strokes—causing memory loss and confusion, or even the onset of Alzheimer's. We can only tell over time."

"Alzheimer's?" Gracie gasped, as if the doctor had just suggested they cut off their mother's head to see if that helped. "How can my mother have Alzheimer's? She was fine last week."

"Alzheimer's is difficult to detect in the beginning, Mrs. Garafola, for the person affected and for the family, very difficult." The doctor's voice was still as soft and slow as a Savannah summer, at least as Maeve imagined such a sun-dappled summer, apparently losing her mind or wanting to, because the gentle voice was telling them such ugly things: "If your mother were accustomed to depending on your father for everyday things, for shopping, driving, paying bills, for instance, it would be difficult to appreciate initial deficits. Since you and your sister are doing these tasks for her now, diminution would be difficult to detect." The doctor paused, giving them a chance to swallow this much. Psychiatrists had a way of gauging how much you could digest before shoveling in more bad news. Then the good doctor switched purpose. It was a subtle shift but Maeve recognized it, even before Valerie Shaw looked at their mother and said, "I do want to tell you, Mrs. Walsh, that we have an excellent geriatric unit at this clinic. That is why Dr. Berman suggested you come here."

"Who?"

"I advise you be admitted for observation."

"What does that mean? Maeve, what does that mean?"

"It's all right, Mom. We're just trying to figure out how to help you." Weren't they? "Just get on the bus, Mom. Just get on the damn bus and go to Gracie's." Did Dr. Shaw need to know that's how Maeve had spoken to her mother yesterday? Of course, her mother hadn't mentioned spying birds yet, but if you paid attention you knew those birds were on their way.

"How long would my mother stay here?" Gracie asked.

"What do you mean stay here? I want to go home NOW."

"A minimum of two weeks. We need time to identify and evaluate real deficits, to establish— "

"What are you talking about? What's going on, Maeve?"

Two weeks to figure out their mother? Maeve wanted to laugh. This couldn't be right. This couldn't be what their father would do. She and Gracie needed to explain that, but how? You couldn't just blurt out every damn thought that wandered into your head, or you would end up talking about relatives you hadn't seen in years, or going on about the time your mother had taken you and the twins to Central Park and lost you all or herself for hours. You'd end up confessing how you never told your father about getting lost, because it wasn't just your father who didn't mention things like hospitals and illness, was it? Because if parents sometimes said nothing to protect their kids, sometimes kids had to protect parents too.

"I don't know why I'M in trouble," their mother snapped, still scared but angry too. "That old woman is the one spying on me."

"Do you suspect this, Mrs. Walsh, or are you certain?"

"I know what the old woman's doing."

"I see. We have a small unit here. I am the attending physician. At the moment, there is space, but there may not be tomorrow. . . ."

Ah, there was the threat, seductively sweet: May not be there tomorrow, this help, this last hope, better order now, supply limited. . . . Maeve sat straight and still, hands folded, the way Sister Catherine had taught them. She was younger than the other nuns. Kinder. There was something natural about Sister Catherine's stillness, like an empty church, something profound, not imposed, just there.

"Take me home," Kay Walsh demanded. "Right now. YOU HEAR ME, Maeve?"

Hard not to, sitting two feet from her.

"Right now, YOU HEAR ME?" Their mother was ready to fight.

Good, how else were they going to get out of this? Everything in Kay Walsh was collapsing, would collapse into nothing, if she gave up. But the scream was still there too, wasn't it? The scream so sharp it could slash off the top of your head in a second, like the first time Maeve heard it. Her mother and father had been fighting all day, a hot summer day in that small apartment, her father finally yelling, "Selfish, Kathleen, that's what you are, the most selfish woman in the world."

"SELFISH?" she screamed back, fury crammed too long among furniture and kids and fear too. Maeve had felt it then, how angry and afraid her mother was, as she watched her crumble. "SELFISH! YEAH, I'M SELFISH, JIM WALSH! SELFISH ENOUGH TO GIVE YOU CHILDREN I DIDN'T EVEN WANT!"

That was when the screaming stopped, and something else too, something between her parents, stopped at least for a while, the silence seeming worse.

"Dementia . . . ." Dr. Shaw was saying.

There it was, no running around the word, no losing it, removing it, no turning it into eccentric or just fabulously exhausted. Your mother is eccentric, exhausted, just fabulously lost without your father, Dr. Shaw was not telling them.

"Your mother needs to be put on anti-psychotic, anti-anxiety, anti-depressant medicines immediately. Delusions do not evaporate, not if you return to the same environment. These are powerful drugs. Can you provide your mother with supervision?"

"So much medication?" Gracie asked. "Does my mother really need so much? She was on stuff years ago that made her sleep all day or— "

"I understand your hesitation, but current medicines are not as blunt."

Maeve pictured a boulder. More like smashed. That's what those medications had been like: no more screaming, no more anything.

"She is very ill."

"Who is?" their mother demanded.

"Your mother will need supervision. Can you provide that?"

"Tell the doctor you're a nurse, Maeve. Tell her."

"I'm not a nurse."

"Well, she doesn't know that. Just tell her. Tell her you can take care of me. For Christsake, someone TELL HER."

"You are right, Mrs. Walsh," Dr. Shaw said. "You need professional care."

"Oh, my daughters are very professional."

The doctor's eyes moved to Gracie and then Maeve. "I am sure you both realize that under these circumstances your mother cannot go home by herself. If she goes home, one of you goes with her."

Kay Walsh stood up. "I don't remember inviting any of you to my house."

Already at the door, Gracie turned their mother around by the shoulders. "Mom, sit down."

"Sit down, sit down. Nice way to talk to your mother, Grace Walsh. Nice, very nice."

"I guess we don't have much choice," Gracie said, or the doctor, or later Maeve thought she might have said. She felt sick, like she'd been too long in the sun. The doctor's voice was still as slow and lovely as Savannah. Such a lovely word

Savannah. She wanted to sleep. For a very long time.

"Don't leave me here, Maeve."

That was an order. No mistake about it. Later you might be able to pretend it hadn't been. Probably not three days later, but three years maybe, when you were still thinking about this. Remembering how sick you'd felt. And stupid. Thinking what you should have done, should have said. As if it mattered. Try talking a fire out of burning.

About the Author:

Maureen McCafferty grew up in Queens, New York and has a doctorate in Creative Writing from Syracuse University. Her short fiction and poetry have appeared in American Writing, Rhino, Clockwatch Review and the anthology A Patchwork of Dreams: Voices From the Heart of the New America. Her first novel, Let Go the Glass Voice, was published by West Alabama University's Livingston Press.

CHILDREN AT PLAY

by Dana Hart

Every second Tuesday of the month is Career Day for Mrs. Ainsley's Saving Grace Kiddos sixth graders, an amusing change of pace from singing psalms to an accompaniment CD made in the '90s and playing Bible trivia card games. The parents fight to win each month's slot, staying late after meetings to talk with Mrs. Ainsley (bribe her with gift certificates to various local restaurants). If they're passed over, they call Mrs. Ainsley at her home phone number to leave angry messages:

"We ordered two boxes of gospel CDs to pass out. Two! And they weren't cheap, Carolyn. Can't the Peterson dairy farm wait until the spring?"

"Sales have gone down, Carolyn, since they built that damn grocery conglomerate over on Fourth Street. It would be nice for the kids to see how clean our butcher shop is and taste the cows we just slaughtered, so they can go home and tell their families."

"Push the Walkers back to next month, Carolyn. Really, what can the kids learn from a couple of customer service reps, anyway? The weather is nice and cool and it's just gorgeous out on our shooting range, all these leaves changing colors…"

For the kids, Career Day is the only time they can get out of their freezing–cold classroom—located in the basement of the local community center, because none of the parents wants to host a group of thirty horny pre–teens—and away from the desks they long ago defaced with chewed–up gum and absurd, pencil–scratched obscenities like "someOne give jeSus a BJ" and "Judas Just Needs a FRIEND!!" But more than anything they just .

want Mrs. Ainsley to stop talking, because her voice is raspy and scarred from decades of chain–smoking and gives them nightmares.

For the month of September, the Career Day honor goes to Ted Garfield, chief of the local fire station. When Mrs. Ainsley makes the announcement the Monday before, the kids talk about how the trip sounds much better than last month's pitiful trek through Freddy Hermann's dad's accounting firm. Perhaps, they say while waiting for their parents to pick them up, the station will get a call about a burning building and they'll get to ride with the firemen in their truck. The possibility of finding dead bodies burnt like charcoal in a grill sounds far better than another trip to an office complex.

But one girl isn't excited, not at all. In fact she wishes she could be anywhere but on that bus on Tuesday afternoon, because no matter where she sits, she can't hide from the fat jokes the boys in her class share at her expense.

None other than Ben Garfield sits behind her on the ride to the fire station. He reaches an arm over Lucy's seat and yanks her long ponytail hard. "Got your tail, Piggy! Oink oink!" he shouts, and everyone laughs. "Hey, how are things down on the farm, Piggy? Do you have your own shit pile to sleep in, or do you share one with your parents?"

"Have you seen them?" another boy asks, reaching across the aisle and poking Lucy in the gut. "There's no room in their shit pile! They're three times as big as her!"

"Stifle yourselves." Mrs. Ainsley makes her way to the back of the bus, stopping next to Lucy's seat and lazily planting one hand on her hip. A lit cigarette sticks menacingly out one side of her mouth.

"Anything for you, Carolyn!" Ben says, snickering. "Shouldn't be smoking around us, though, should you? Might kill us all."

"Little bastard," she mumbles, scowling and stumbling back to her seat behind the driver.

Lucy turns to the window and begins to cry. Her mother always tells her not to listen to bullies, but when there are so many laughing it's hard not to. From her pocket she produces a razor blade slightly larger than her big toe, which she stole from her parents' bathroom cabinet that morning. Gently she slides it along her arm, just barely breaking the surface of her skin because she's afraid she'll scream if she presses down harder. And she isn't brave enough to simply close her eyes and start slicing; she doesn't want to make a mess and draw attention to herself.

Tiny red droplets stain her too–small jeans and she notices they're almost the same color as all the fake blood in the horror movies she and her brother Connor watch together. Only the screams of victims turned up to top volume are loud enough to drown out Mom and Dad yelling every night, usually about his affair with his secretary. The one that always smiles at Lucy when she goes to visit Dad at work, saying she looks pretty. Liar.

I wonder, Lucy thinks, do my insides look the same as the monsters' victims? If I keep cutting— not here, later at home in the bathroom, I'll find out. Then I'll show Dad and he'll be happy I did something useful. What did he say last night? A waste of space. 'You're a waste of space, Lucy.'

Mrs. Ainsley's voice comes on over the bus's loudspeaker system. "We're almost there. Behave yourselves today—I'm not in the mood for games."

Lucy panics and, not knowing where to hide her razor blade, quickly shuts it in her fist. Both ends of the blade slice through her flesh, releasing a gush of blood that spills right onto her lap. "Motherfucker," she says—one of Connor's favorite words when he's upset—and hides her fist behind her bright pink backpack. Now the fabric will have a huge stain by the time she has to get

off the bus. She needs a distraction…there's always sticking her finger down her throat and making herself sick, which she's done a few times before. But Mrs. Ainsley will only end up calling her parents to come pick her up.

As the bus pulls to a stop, the other kids jump out of their seats and run to the front.

Lucy stays behind; now the blood is spilling onto her shirt and a circular stain forms around her gut. Mrs. Ainsley is outside taking attendance, reading names off a clipboard list. Lucy realizes how much she hates her teacher—hates them all—whether they've made fun of her or not. No one stands up for her when the boys tease her, not one of the girls in her class or even the quiet boys that seem too nice to say such awful things. Connor's voice is in her ear from last night as he rummaged through a stack of DVDs: "Fuck them, Lucy. Fuck the whole world. Everyone is out to get you and you can't trust anyone."

The class starts to walk toward the fire station entrance but Mrs. Ainsley holds up a hand to stop them. "Hang on, there's only thirteen here." She walks down the line counting them off. "Ben, Simon, Amanda, John…where's Lucy?"

None of the kids say anything, only look back at the bus. Lucy shrinks down so no one can see her and maneuvers her way under the seat. A few drops of blood drip onto the filthy floor and she imagines them snaking down the aisle of the bus like slick, red track marks. Slowly she begins to crawl to the back, listening for Mrs. Ainsley's heels click–clacking toward her. It's difficult to move with her backpack on, as it keeps getting caught on screws, so she leaves it under the second–to–last seat. She hopes no one will take it because all of her favorite comics are inside, the only things that keep her company when Connor isn't around.

"You heard me, Lucy, I'm not in the mood for games!"

Lucy crawls faster, nearly getting stuck under a particularly narrow opening under the last seat. All she has to do is reach out and push the emergency exit lever down. Once the alarm goes off it'll distract Mrs. Ainsley, then it's a clean jump out the back door.

Now Mrs. Ainsley is stomping down the aisle. Although it takes a considerable amount of strength, Lucy is able to lift the red lever and push the door open. A bell sounds and Mrs. Ainsley starts screaming, unintelligible above the shrill ringing, but Lucy doesn't listen; landing on the asphalt parking lot hurts too much. Luckily she doesn't break any bones. As quickly as she can Lucy takes off in the direction the bus came from, rounding the corner of the parking lot only to be surprised by a pothole. Landing face–first she feels the asphalt rip open one of her cheeks, and hot tears pour out of her eyes. But she keeps going, staggering against traffic instead of with it and ignoring cars that honk at her. It's approximately ten minutes by car to the high school so she'll need to move fast on foot, especially because Mrs. Ainsley is certainly on the phone with her parents already.

A car swerves around a truck as it switches lanes and almost hits her. Lucy jumps out of the way, narrowly avoiding the hood. In the driver's seat a woman yells and shakes her hand, the universal get–out–of–my–way gesture; two children press against the backseat window, mouths hanging open like they're watching a caged animal in a zoo.

As it begins to rain she ducks into an alleyway to catch her breath. Two homeless men stop rummaging through a shopping cart of belongings and watch her double over wheezing. One offers her a drink from a bottle in a crumpled brown paper bag, which she blindly accepts, too thirsty to bother asking what's inside. The amber liquid tastes like the last time she had the stomach flu and she immediately spits it out. Now the man lectures her, too, this time about wasting money someone gave him earlier that afternoon. He reveals several missing teeth and black gums, like how (when he was alive) her grandfather's mouth looked from years of chewing tobacco. Lucy thinks back to the repulsive grin of her grandfather at every Christmas and Easter dinner and screams.

Rain pours out of the dark sky, as if God himself is angry at her for being such a fuckup: for not measuring up to her father, for disobeying Mrs. Ainsley because she hates being in the Kiddos, for being fat no matter how little food Mom puts on her dinner plate. Maybe she should keep running,

past the school and out of town and on to a different life. Not even Connor cares about her all the time, like when he plays video games or brings his girlfriend over and locks his bedroom door. One day he'll undoubtedly grow to detest her, just like everyone else.

Lucy doesn't look both ways when she runs back across the street, and a delivery truck speeds forward and hits her from the side. Initially she feels nothing, even though all the air is shoved out of her lungs. As she rolls off the hood and spins in the air, she thinks how wonderful it is not to feel; no more pain, sadness and anger. But in the seconds between hitting the asphalt, hearing the sickening crunch of bones in her spinal column, and dying, the pain is so great that she's sure that's what kills her. Not the actual breaking of her neck, but the hellish agony her body endures after meeting the street at 75 miles an hour. And, her last thought: Now everyone will love me.

About the Author:

Dana Hart is a recent college graduate living in Indiana – you know, one of those Midwestern states where nothing particularly exciting ever happens. She'd like to say that getting a tattoo after graduation is what started this descent into darkness. It could also be listening to so much punk rock and heavy metal. Or maybe reading Harry Potter so many times she lost count, or Stephen King, Lev Grossman and Neil Gaiman. Better yet: having studied opera in college, an entire world of drama in itself. However and whenever it all began, she writes about the darkest parts of reality and, in her current project, what goes wrong when reality and fantasy meet. What would you call that genre?

GORSE

by Ben Rosenthal

They picked up Wild Gorse at McCarren International and there he was, dragging a reptile skin embossed travel case. He wore a mackerel-colored seersucker meant to offset this spanking orange tan (he was less tanned than he was sulphured, really). There was something undeniably porcine about his face, his mandible unnaturally taut where it veered in; from the back, a bulldog's jetpack of loose flesh lunged from a space between his shoulders.

"Goddamn, there she is," said Hotchkiss, who was driving.

The younger one, in a red-striped motorcycle helmet, said, "I can't believe it. I can't believe he's here."

Gorse slid into the backseat. These were the men, his "escorts" to a valedictory on Paradise Road. He was there to receive a lifetime achievement award, universal plaudits for his artistry from a weed-smoking panel at Adult Video News. There would be a lighted proscenium stage and vamping barely-legals there to ride him to the rostrum like Valkyries when the MC called his name.

For years, they'd assumed he was a funny topic. He was a lauche German auteur of the hardest, most generous pornography from back in the heyday of the 1970s, a once-budding star of some gravely ambitious smut flicks that were bankrolled with his family's iron deutschmarks (they believed he was investing in a rabbit sanctuary near Encinitas). The films were omni-sexual spectaculars, nearly always pastorally set (a sylvan lake farm where nightingales chirped and fluted madrigals precipitated hedgerow buggery, a summertime idyll in Bled where the slinky commissars of Tito might be watching!). They were chiefly eponymous labors ("Wild Gorse is Wild Gorse in Wild Gorse 6"), premiering with neon marquees aggressively de rigeur for that glamour age. Gorse even purchased ad blitzes in the city press. At the height of his carnal fandom he'd been stricken with a pigment disease – Vitiligo – which stripped his skin of all color, and by the time "Wild Gorse 6" hit the Tenderloin its eponymous stud was whiter than an albino Iditarod. It drove him straight into recherché depression; it made his flamboyant pretensions sad. It somehow accentuated his German accent. It made him write letters in which he adopted the style of George Sand.

It was funny.

AIDS was not, but he was circling the punchline like a peregrine hoping against hope that a laugh would rear its head. The protease was making tracks with flanking maneuvers towards his inner Berlin. The Prezista and the Sustiva tanked. He was becoming a collage of mouth sores, manifold indignities of the immuno-suppressed. A bad bout of oral hairy lucaplakia was chased out with radio ions and a shit ton of multidirectional bowel spills. He attempted other cocktails. He fetched up with quacks, denialists. He avoided cat litter and the niacin hazards of birdcages. The hits kept coming. Enteritis. Thrush. Cryptosporidium: Amazonian bung-insects as shocked to be thriving in the northern latitudes as Wild Gorse was to be hosting them. Strasser, his ID man at the Olgahospital, said "You've met your resistance, friend.

Thirty eight T-helpers. Better get the manor ship-shape."

He was not ready for his close up, Mister DeMille. (Or did this mean he was?)

"We thought you were on a cocktail," said Junior Boyce, who belonged to the helmet, looking at the foundering German.

"They hit walls," said Gorse. "And then you switch to another and that one runs out and soon there is just this flea circus. Happier topics, please."

The limo was no automotive centipede tricked out for the rap stars whose music went right by him, but it wasn't any K-car either. It was '01 Eldorado stretch, the upholstery a bit stained. They approached the airport exit. They would have two and a half hours to pretty up in the hotel room and then get themselves down to the Hard Rock where a mic'd host would await the clack-clack of his merry Vera Wangs on the runner. He would submit to a red carpet "interview".

America.

What a run of months he'd been having. He'd been living with his mother in Stuttgart, devouring his family assets on a skein of Ankaran kept men, sinewy, hair-trigger catamites who'd had their fill of his dogged kindnesses, his maudlin mothering, and eventually cased his digs. Ran off with his mantle clock; a great piece some Schwartzwalder filigreed with little birds, terns on some gunwale in Danzig. He'd prized his attic trunkful of Reichs field articles (SS trumpet banners, flieger-uhrs, an Armanen rune belt buckle perfect for S&M displays, a nice Kreuz cutlass): goners. Those Ottoman hyenas cleaned him out, pointed his own jugend at his chest; the gadgets hauled straight to the Latvian marketplace. He would never see such aestheticizing of the End Days again. Because what could be expected of a terminal case? He despised Nazism but admired the trench-tooth malodor of the Fuhrer's pageantry. If only they hadn't localized things, if they had just killed everybody, gassed all creeds, all man; raised holy hell and spared no one with the Walpurgis lightshow ...

But dear those Turks. Some elected to beat him when he didn't ask for it. He was a hit on two continents. He'd pined for the Valley, leading with his chin against the boot heel of the dreaming west, the ghosts of fatal Grand Dames who ran scribes out of Art Deco dream palaces. "You can never write a script for me; you will never know love, young man! True love. My love!" Would that he could be one of these. And now, finally, he was back. He would be wearing kimonos on a roof deck and using the high summer smog for a kind of dissolution-convalescence, a la Kenneth Tynan in the 1970s.

Parties. Garden champers with Angelica, Warren and Jack, Rolling Stone fledglings in miniskirts saying don't mind if I do to some speedball bon-bons on a tray. He'd missed out on that, Bay-marooned, perceived amoral and underserving. Now they were old, Warren: hitched, Jack, moribund. Angelica the owner of a gullet. Nothing to blame but Father Time.

The exit signs to Vegas proper stood ahead. They were leaving the airport.

He daubed some blush on from a silver compact monogrammed with the initials W.G., tilting his head toward the rearview mirror. He saw his face: it was like staring down something mythic that stalked sheep in the Outer Hebrides. For assurance, he asked:

"How do I look?"

"You look a million," Hotchkiss said.

"You are a lazy liar."

"It is what it is, brother."

"I think you are a lazy liar."

Hotchkiss keyed the GPS to find where the Hard Rock was. It was taking too long for a man with a hurryup disease. Gorse sparked up a slender Gauliose and dragged slow like a Stasi interrogator, "Andale to the American picaresque," he said. "I aim to buy snapshots of Waffle Houses and to have that Peyton Manning in this backseat. I want to saddle burros on a famous western butte and ride the arid pastures like iconic gunslingers in the immortal Wayne 'flicks'."

"This guy's a fucking mouthful," said Hotchkiss to the man in the passenger seat. "Is this some kind of dementia?"

"John Wayne?" said Junior Boyce, turning to Gorse. "You grew up in Germany."

"We have screens. Germany has screens."

"What's it like," said Boyce, "over there?"

"I'm not over there; I'm here," said Gorse. "And I never wanted to be from anywhere."

"Well," said Hotchkiss into the windshield. "Nobody gets that wish."

"Quite," said Gorse.

"And if I was you, I would douse that cigarette," the man said. "That packed tar don't do your breathing any favors."

The car headed off onto the boulevard.

Before Paradise Road there were many others and they were evidence that Man was here; substantially and irrefutably present, but a few hours earlier Gorse had seen all this as the tiniest white splotch on a miserable and oceanic sand sweep as the jetliner circled the airspace for a landing. He was a splotch and he had splotches.

They passed by a giant Popeye's chicken bucket atilt over used cars, overpasses, underpasses, hot pink arrows indicating proximity to the Flamingo Hotel. Bronze-painted minarets loomed high over neon wedding chapels. A factory-distressed brauhaus announced with pride it was the House of Veiss. What had Gorse missed of this America? Terrible reports: Things were tacky. Around the set, there were coke rails next to condom wrappers. The gaffers put a foil over the ranch windowpanes and ate leftover Russell Stover chocolates. The male talent got their revs up by doing pull-ups on the uneven bars when the fluff boys were held up in the automotive cluster on the 101. They were entrepreneurs now, "crowdfunding" gangbangs. Words like "heteronormative" emerged.

"I'm going to call you the Fukashima Meltdown," Gorse said to the man in the helmet.

"Why?"

"That helmet looks like something on a Japanese firefighter."

"But I'm American," said Junior Boyce. "It's a look I'm doing."

Boyce was a gay porn actor, he told Gorse. He was starring in a movie about a man who takes a 1950s robot for a concubine. The movie was called Pumping Iron and it was due out on a website in February. Hotchkiss was one who had drifted from different pleasures into that of being a "handler" and, at the request of the AVN Hall of Fame committee and with the assistance of the helmeted one (Boyce's PlayStation handle: FanBoy), was squiring Wild Gorse to the stage where the latter would claim his trophy.

Gorse listened to Boyce telling him of his future and found it was nothing at all like his past. What would he tell any of these people? What of his Von Stroheim fantasies? Striding the Chatsworth backlot with a croc-skin horsewhip stashed in his studded waist holster, firing a buck ringer from the Castro for blowing his glans out before the "take", quoting the maestro himself when he did it. He had once wanted to open a kennel for canine microbreeds using all the fine clear lines of Walter Gropius in the building plans. He was going to call it Bow House and make it a spectacle, a little meeting space for the pup-enthused on the planks of Sausalito. He was going to hold houseboat salons, end the nights by lighting candles on the casting deck and doing his imagined variations on Marlena's incomparable Weimar revues. Who in his present company would understand this?

He wondered if hanging on wasn't worse than dying.

Coming from where he did, he knew there was nothing more terrible than winding up on the wrong side of history. His friends from the dream days, the Bay martyrs, knew where they stood. He did not know this land or its ranges.

At the hotel, Gorse napped while Hotchkiss and Meltdown spoke in whispers. The two had set up a gaming system and all around the rug a rising tide of coaxials and toggle panels threatened to submerge the little space. Gorse fled to the high ground.

Waxy-eyed, he now emerged with what appeared to be an ancient stereophonic amplifier in a garrote of shiny black cords, setting it down on a nightstand and jacking it into the wall socket where it immediately began whirring like a Martian spacecraft. With his eyes closed, he pursed his lips, and his mouth seemed to water.

"Wild Gorse?" said the younger one with the meltdown helmet.

"You are wondering what is this thing, what is this contraption," he said. "It is a PERL-M machine, designed for heal me in lieu of meds."

"What does it do?"

"The machine uses argon plasma tubes," said Gorse, woozy from his catnap but still rallying. "Integrated light, gratis chronometer; a 230 VAC power pack. And this: Remote touchpad I can hand-click to get even more healing frequencies from the transmitter. It snuffs the dirty pathogens using electromagnetic resonances generated from a carrier wave. Imagine you are trapped in a sonic boom; echo power would decelerate your heartbeat and snap your bones. This pearl of a magnetron wreaks similar grief on AIDS cells."

"Does it work?"

Gorse wrapped a cuff around his wrist.

"Not yet."

"Not yet?" Meltdown looked hurt.

Gorse let the cuff build in pressure and raised his arm, holding it out, as though a sailor sighting the mainland through a mist. In the next room, Hotchkiss yelled into the telephone.

"We need nonalc, Jerry, virgin gin. Cranberry and lemon wedge thing. Maybe an Aid Kit and I dunno, an adrenalizer. We got a goddamn cadaver here!"

The PERL-M Resonator blinked off.

They were getting closer to Paradise Road. Gorse noted the toasted almond sun that was different than the chicken-fried sun of hours earlier. There were back in the Caddie, possibly running late.

Hotchkiss slammed the horn; a slow-going pickup from a lumberyard nearly spilled its plywood cords onto their front end when the blitzkrieg of honking stunned the driver. It was a crawl. They

were getting near the barrel-vault canopy on Freemont Street, even from blocks away, the colossal megawatt floor lasers set down on their block swivels were silently projecting John Wayne and his Appaloosa against the manmade curve of sky.

"Holy jeepers, it's the Duke," said Meltdown Helmet.

Hotchkiss, through a mouthful of Rold Gold minis, said, "It's his birthday. They do that."

Since the windows were closed and they hadn't yet cranked Stagecouch from the loudspeakers, the effect was something like a meteor shower.

Meltdown turned to Gorse. "Did you know that? John Wayne, Gorse!"

Gorse was silent, his eyes closed and he seemed asleep. They passed the cowpoke by in the stretch, the hood nearly whipped by his blinking lasso as they moved ever closer to the Strip.

But he was thinking. He was dreaming. Gorse possessed the Euro-tendency to view death as the final arabesque in the choreography of a maestro powerless to stop the flow of art into anything and everything in existence. He saw no flower as beautiful as his KS spots; convoluted reds and bursting violets like thermonuclear summer skies, the quartz whites of his dried skin rashes after the maculopapules seared his trunk were a miracle of modern pointillism. Immune deficient, he was beautiful as the mod-banged honey traps he saw gallivanting around the raver warehouses. Death (and what it was seemed bigger than one word) would be an outsider art coup de grace. The many dear ones who'd gone before him, those biker morsels at the I-Beam in Haight hiding their cherry sarcomas under chinstrap beards, the Ailey school fan-dancers strutting bare-assed from the scalloping of the taffeta curtains, bony as all get from the pulmonary Antietams they had claimed were merely chest colds, were too young to fathom that. They were too stubborn; wedded too vainly to their coils. The price of having good taste in an ugly world, he thought, was that one appreciated everything too richly; you looked so spanking grand it was unfathomable the road would not rise to meet you. He found this hard to swallow when he thought of the tyrannosaurs that thumped the Mesozoic plains only the wind up fueling rattletraps through unleaded Shell nozzles. Time was invisible but it sure did tick. Young people were only old people who didn't know it yet.

It would be so easy to not live. But he'd worked so hard at it. He'd had psychotherapy for his life, Adlerian thieves; sumptuous thinkers with fantastic probing minds running transcranial currents across his jellied noodle. R.D Laing, that beastly Lacan. What for? They were contract killers, there to murder instinct with kindness, coddle his best thought before thudding it with a psychotropic cudgel. Death, a nullity, could not talk you into itself, and these witches, dispensaries in herringbone Bill Blass, people who thrived on the occidental promise of improvement, would prolong his gruesome existence out of nothing more than pride.

But was he not complicit? A man on the gibbet, about to sway, ditch the somatic spin cycle, still fires some snake spit when the neck snaps and his underwear reveals slippery, contraindicative substance. It never ends. Because, really, this is how it always begins.

Hotchkiss cranked the parking break. The valet sprung the door.

On the carpet in his seersucker, his bony pontoons troubled by the makeshift runner (neuropathy) he doubled over and phlegmy air from his throat hit the room air and people noticed. A bottle-black, nose-studded "alt chick" moved away with a burning scowl, her meanness was her calling card; she could do this. There were unenviable specimens from adjacent businesses all around, shadowy men; fired film technicians, unsexed fanzine traders —agoraphobes who had nourished malign ideas about the softer gender now in love with all who passed by, men who didn't chew well.

Gorse was supposed to talk to a loudmouth trans producer who was working the red carpet for this gig. A few gracious nothings, some bon mots flung offhand and in his usual louche smoking manner, and move on, but it wasn't going that way.

Right away the trans man buttonholed him, busting out of his chiffon, but Meltdown and Hotchkiss pushed Gorse on through, backstage to the waiting area.

Gorse wobbled, the blur in his eyes clearing up. The juicy gaggles were there and saw death. The men in tight-ribbed tank tops, the girls-next-door projecting the image of the girls next door, the MMA fighting baldies with proprietary clamps on these girls. Who were they? Whither my loves? My passions. My mantle clock.

The man was the face to the name on the program, the fabulist of rut-spectaculars in loose costume, rank and natty. He leaned against a speaker near the curtain, feeling the blur of the kliegs, the hideous sporidium rising. A girl approached; but for her six-inch scarlet platforms, she might have been the host of a midnight omnibus horror show, circa 67', the comprehensive scream queen ensemble right down to the ace of spades hair. She had slathered thick mascara into loose, violet ovals around the sweetest and weakest blue eyes Gorse had seen from this distance in a while. She had been daddy's little muse in Edina once, or an Akron, Ohio telemarketer who saw life speeding by and said "Who, me stand athwart it?" Maybe her hubby, a hydroponic weed dealer, got pinched, and she'd flat-back a little under the Ariflex lens to make his bail. Then it became a life; usurped her. It had usurped everyone. The curtain of Gorse's mind pulled up and revealed the welling of ambush tears, because the unanimity he was feeling could not be taken away from any of them; he needed them, these new ones, bound to maroon on the sick side of life when the sex stopped. It wasn't a sudden prudishness that made him fear for them. It was that they had so much ahead. They were too immersed now to know how much their lives would become preventative maintenance; how impulse would fade into second-guessing, second-guessing into no guessing at all, into a calcified screen over your very who-ness; grime of oral thrush over everything you. He had been building to a valedictory of sorts well before Meltdown gathered him from the airport drive and if there was a grace to be found at the rostrum, it would be in the memory rush; a bracing frisson of all the good things lived through that would make the hellish ones worth the ride. It was a life's suspended notion brought low with the knowledge: Memory is not enough.

And now he backed into a pipe on the wall. It burned him but no one saw it. The burn was real, and corrective. He began sobbing into his hand, because, like the gallows dick spasm, this was not the end; this was only the end of the beginning. This was the night of his charity; the showing of his mercy to them. The sweet muscle oafs, the chiffoned naiveté of these headstrong prima donnas; his very own Charon, young Meltdown. He wanted them saved: Vater Flannagan, he, Patron Saint of Bavarian Crème loads, Bugger Barker of Life's Big Circus Tent: wrap its sailcloth around these sad souls, hold them, bid them away: tell them to run if they can.

"They're calling you, Mister Gorse. You're up next."

"Next?"

"Congrats to you and we love you," said the Alt Girl Scream Queen. He knew she didn't love him at all; but oh dear, how he did love her.

He could feel her hands on his shoulders. She was shaking his very bones. Boyce was giving him the thumbs up. Thirty eight T-cells. The neck snaps. Life clings to your last turtleneck. Don't be so young as to break down. Summon the reddest of your spots: Look them in the eye with your extinction.

Go.

About the Author

Ben is currently attending Columbia University's graduate writing program, where he will graduate in February, 2018. He has been a resident at the MacDowell Colony and at U Cross. He lives in New York City.

DAY'S WORK

by J. David Liss

I.

Washington, DC spread its legs as the train from New York pulled into Union Station. It was the earliest train from Penn Station and the tracks were still clean and free of litter, and the air still smelled sweet, not like the burning rubber smell of hot brake pads or garbage left in the trashcans. Those smells would come later in the day after many trains had pulled in and left.

Five minutes before arriving, Mickey had packed his lap top, put on his suit jacket, moved his phone and wallet from his pants pockets to his jacket pockets, and made sure business cards were in the jacket's card pocket. The movements were so familiar he didn't think about them, like getting dressed after sex with a woman he didn't want to spend time with.

One of those women was his ex-wife, who used to hate his extended trips to the nation's capital. She would whine, "Mickey, we've only been married for a few months and you're gone a week at a time. How are we going to connect?" He would joke, "Honey, I need to go to Washington so that I can earn enough money to pay you alimony." She didn't appreciate his sense of humor.

Mickey could no more stay away from Washington then he could from breathing. He made his living talking to people there. It was easy for him to picture living without his wife. It was impossible to imagine not going to work. His father had always said to him, Being a good family man means being a good provider. That's all your wife will care about. At some point during his marriage he realized that was all he cared about too.

His day was starting on the Senate side where he had to get two things done, one small and one big. The small job involved a pharmacy in Connecticut where they actually compounded their own drugs — something that required enormous skill. Apparently, that skillset was beyond one particular druggist, who had mixed up a treatment for fungal meningitis. Two patients were dead and the FDA was shutting down compounding pharmacies across the country.

Of course, the problem wasn't with the pharmacies; it was with incompetent pharmacists. Mickey needed to get the law changed so that 100 percent of liability lay with the incompetents, not with their employers. That way, the next time such a terrible accident happened, the boob who did it would be carted out and the pharmacy could replace him and keep working. Mickey had a strategy figured out to get the law changed.

The big job involved repeal of the Affordable Care Act. The Senate had a bill they were hell-bent-for-leather to pass. It took away everyone's support to purchase care, took away guaranteed Medicaid, and gave a pot of money to each state— albeit less than they get now— to pay for all of the things being taken away—and anything else the state wanted to pay for, including tax cuts. Should be a slam-dunk in a Republican-controlled Senate, especially as the Senator who introduced it is a doctor, Hippocratic Oath and all. But it looked like they were going to lose a key vote—a committee chairman no less. Apparently, he was worried about how the new law would affect sick people. His state wasn't even really impacted by the proposed law. Who'd a thunk! A Republican

Senator with a conscience. Mickey's job was to make sure the GOP had the votes to get rid of healthcare and make sure this one Senator voted the right way in order to get there.

It was a lovely, early fall day and Mickey decided to walk the half-mile from the station to the Senate office buildings. As he walked, he thought about the New York/Washington dichotomy. Decisions were made in New York and implemented in Washington. Why bifurcate? Most of the people in his profession would say that the money was in NYC, so that's where the power had to be. Mickey didn't think that. There was enough ego in Washington to cause folks there to act without a meaningful motive like getting paid off. He thought that maybe the people who hired him and the people who he visited wanted a certain level of deniability, even if they weren't aware of it themselves.

Why would anybody want deniability? Whatever is, is right, said Alexander Pope and Mickey agreed. When he took on a job, he thought to himself that he would make it real and so make it right. He was only wrong when he couldn't get it done.

In the case of the compounding pharmacy, Mickey's path was pretty straightforward. Blue state Senators would be willing to make an exception in the law for a blue state-based industry to keep operating. The Republicans were so biased in favor of business and against regulation that they would reflexively support him. His only opposition would be the pharmacists' association. Mickey made a note to call the lobbyist for the hospitals to gin-up their support — and he would include exemption from liability for them too.

Patient advocates would be a problem. Mickey pondered how to manage them. If the pharmacies were relieved of liability, it was likely that a lot more errors would occur because the companies would be pushing to get more done faster. They could focus on profit if mistakes became someone else's problem.

Mickey figured the best way to handle the advocates was to get the change into legislative language, get it buried in a large, "must-pass" bill (he had one in mind), and get the whole thing done fast and quiet.

He didn't worry much that if he were successful, the pharmacist who made the compounding error would be libel to be tried for first degree manslaughter.

So much for the easy part of his day.

He was walking to the Hill to meet Chairman Stephenson for lunch. They were meeting in the Senate Dining Room, not one of the high-end restaurants near the Hill. Mickey liked John Stephenson. Over the last five years of his Senate term, Mickey had raise close to $100,000 for the Senator, who friends referred to as Maple because he was from the deep south and put maple syrup on his ham steak, a childhood taste he never grew out of. Every time Maple lunched in the Senate Dining Room, the chef knew to prepare ham steak with syrup. The same waitress, Helene, brought it to him every time because she was from his state and she always said to him as she placed it down, "Here's a sweet porker for a sweet porker," though he wasn't fat, and they'd wink at each other as she walked away. Everyone knew the ritual.

Maple was up for reelection next year. This was a good year to have something on him. The lobbyist felt a warmth in his crotch. It had cost him, but he always did "opposition research" on his friends as well as his opponents. When he was young, he was always the little guy and hated it. But he was the kind of kid who had a camera with a telephoto lens and a darkroom in his basement. He was the kind of boy who would walk around the neighborhood trying not to be seen, taking pictures of things he thought could be useful. No picture was more useful than the one of big Angelo touching his little peepee while looking in his aunt's basement bedroom. From Mickey's angle in the backyard behind Angelo's house, he got a great picture of Angelo, his peepee, and his aunt. Mickey made a few copies of that, showed one to Angelo and let him know there were a lot more after big Angelo ripped up the one he had. After that, Angelo left Mickey alone and made sure everybody else did too.

Information made you big. He liked being big and paid well for the commodity that made him bigger, bigger than a Senate Chairman.

II.

Senator John Stephenson, chairman of one of the most powerful committees in the Congress, was learning how to say the Hebrew words for good luck: Mazel Tov. He said it the same way he'd heard it pronounced in the movies, with the emphasis on the first syllable — MA-zl tov. But his soon to be daughter-in-law was correcting him. "We say, ma-ZELL TOV! Stress the zell and the tov. It sounds more like a celebration!"

She should know; she was going to be a rabbi. His son was marrying a rabbi and was going to convert to Judaism. No doubt, Stephenson would be saying ma-ZELL TOV at his grandchildren's bar mitzvahs.

He thought about his first run for office— town counsel in a backwater hamlet that had never seen a Jew, not since the day it was built by a mining company that left when the ore was depleted. Well, he had gone through many changes in his life. He'd had to learn from some pretty difficult mistakes over the years. Compared to those, this one was easy. Even happy. He liked Ruthie and she made Nicholas happier than Stephenson had ever seen him. Change was good. His son would probably wind up doing more than converting to Judaism. They were moving to Los Angeles and he would almost certainly become a Democrat. Stephenson didn't have to think about that.

"Ruthie, darl'in, on the day of the wedding I will be prepared to say the blessing on the wine, the bread, and the cocktails if you need that done. I'm going to have to meet someone for lunch now. Why don't you wait here in my office for Nick'lus and I'll tell Frank to help you gather up these catalogs and put them in a box."

III.

The lobbyist was seated at his regular table when Stephenson walked in. "MickeyFried, MickeyFried," the Senator almost chanted when he saw Mickey, saying his first and last name as if they were a single three syllable word. How was the ride from Sin City?"

"Smooth as a good lie or an old bourbon, Senator. How are you doing?"

"Could. Not. Be. Bettah." Each word separated by a pause for emphasis.

"Wonderful. Mr. Chairman, I am grateful that you made time for me."

"Enough o' that, Mickey. We got one more part of this kabuki play to work out, then let's talk business." Stephenson signaled to Helene, who came over to take their order.

She smiled. "Mickey, Ah know you are start'n with a martini, darlin, but what would you like for lunch?"

"Anything you can throw together that's Italian, Helene."

"And Mr. Chairman, will you be havin yaw regula or can we tempt you with somethin, um, different, suh?"

"Helene, you know that I want Jeff there in the kitchen to make the dish that you and I both grew up with."

"Well who would'a guessed?" she mocked. "Comin up Mista Chairman." Helene's accent grew more southern the longer she spoke with Maple, and visa versa. "And that'll be a Jack on the rocks to accompany Mr. Fried's martini." It was a statement, not a question. Helene gently swayed away to the kitchen.

"Maple, I am so impressed with your bipartisan work on healthcare. I didn't think anyone could bring both sides together on this issue, but you seem to have everyone on the committee rowing in the same direction for a small repair to the ACA that will keep people covered another couple of years. That is a major accomplishment."

"Ah couldn't a done it without the ranking membah," Maple responded, his accent now full-bore southern.

"Good point. She's kept a tighter hold on her caucus than my grandfather kept on a silver dollar." Mickey figured it couldn't hurt to tell a southerner an anti-Semitic joke at his own expense. Make him feel a little superior. "But I suspect in the end, this will be an exercise in uselessness. If you can get something out of committee, and if you can get it through the Senate, it's going to die in the House anyway. Doesn't it make sense to skip this exercise, noble as it is, and quickly get to where we are going anyway? Give S. 9191 a try," he referred to the repeal bill by its number." That's the only bill the leadership will move if it gets to the House. Maple, if it's not working in a year, we'll change it. I feel so strongly about this, that I will commit now to working to amend the bill as you see fit if the outcomes are bad. I promise you."

"Mickey you know as well as I that once you jump off a cliff you can't change your mind on the way down. Ahm a no vote on 9191; you not gonna change my mind."

Helene arrived with their food, put Mickey's veal parmigiana in front of him, Maple's ham steak in front of him, gave the Senator a warm smile and said, "Here's a sweet porker for a sweet porker." They winked at each other and she left.

On some level, Mickey hoped that Maple would say no. Now he could get tough. You don't pull your gun unless you're going to use it. Mickey's problem was, he liked using his gun. With most of these discussions, it never came time to be tough. Either the guy could be convinced or bought. Force was always the path of greatest resistance. But the thought of forcing a powerful Senator—a chairman—to do what he wanted was almost intoxicating for Mickey. He had information he could use to blackmail Maple and he had been craving the chance to use it since he spent close to $100,000 to learn it. Thinking of the fund raising he had done for Stephenson, he was even pleased by the symmetry of raising $100k to help the Senator, and $100k to hurt him.

Mickey's eyes narrowed. The left side of his face lifted slightly. He had learned that look from one of the street punks where he grew up.

"I need your vote, Maple." That was going to be the last warning.

"Yaw not gonna have it, Mickey."

"You don't really like ham steak and maple syrup, do you?"

"What do you mean?"

"I mean, I know how you got the name Maple. It was the same way you got the name Sugar Lips and it has nothing to do with maple syrup. I had a wonderful talk with an old friend of yours named Sandy Daniels. Does that ring a bell, Sugar Lips?"

Mickey could feel himself growing taller and wider, surrounding the table like a bear crushing a doe.

Maple pushed back from the table just a little. He was paler. He didn't look frightened, though.

"You piece a shit." He said it quietly, almost thoughtfully. "All these years Ah been waitin for someone to learn about that time in my life and try to ruin me. And Ahm not suprised it's you; you are a slime bag. Forgive me if I am struck by the irony that you did not discovah this tidbit until the moment I was ready to announce my retirement. Ah don't give a shit who you tell. Ahm gonna announce next week that Ah will not seek a fifth term in the Senate. Ahm in my seventies, boy, and ready to retire."

It was Mickey's turn to blanch. He wasn't prepared for this.

"Ahm so glad we are havin this lunch, boy. First off, I don't have to justify the name Maple anymore. I hate this shitty ham dish and before this meal is over I'm a gonna call Helene over to this table, send it back, get a hamburger — a nice, rare hamburger — and never eat a fuckin ham steak with maple syrup again.

"But boy, Ahm gonna be chairman for another year. I will know every client you have. You will get NUTHIN through my committee boy, nuthin! Won't be anyone in this town who don't know that if they hire Mickey Fried, theya ask is dead, dead, DEAD. And I have my friends in the Senate, boy, good friends, good Republican friends. They gonna do shit for you, too. You not gonna work here anymore, boy. You gonna stay in New York and do shit.

Mickey was trembling. He couldn't stop.

"But Ah tell you what, boy. You do what Ah say right now and I may change my mind. I'm feeling mighty generous because I don't have to eat fuckin ham steak and maple syrup no more. Are you paying attention, boy?"

"Yes, Senator."

"What did you call me!"

"Yes Mr. Chairman."

"Now that's betta. Mickey, you take that white linen napkin off yaw lap and put it on the table.

That's right. Now take that there veal parmigiana in front of you and dump it on your nice expensive suit. Make sure you get some on yaw shirt, yaw jacket, and yaw pants. I even want some to go on yaw shoes. Do it, and Ah may fawgive you."

Mickey hesitated for just a couple of seconds. Then he picked up the plate of veal and spaghetti and tomato sauce and poured it all over the front of his suit, onto his lap and shoes. People at other tables began to stare.

"Don't you look like a mess. But Ah don't fawgive you, you piece a shit. And by the way, my son is marrying a nice Jewish woman, in fact, she's studi'n to be a rabbi, and Ah do not appreciate yaw anti-Semitic jokes. Now get the hell outta heah."

Mickey slowly stood up, in a state of shock. Everyone sitting in the Senate Dining Room was staring at him as he dripped tomato sauce on his shoes and the carpet. Waiters rushed over to clean him off, but Stephenson waved them off. "He'll be fine. He's just leaving." Every Senator and lobbyist in the room saw the Chairman tell the staff not to help Mickey.

Mickey backed away from the table. Stephenson called him. "Mickey!" The lobbyist looked at him. "Aren't you a gonna congratulate me on my son's wedding? Were you raised in a barn?"

Mickey turned around and quickly walked out out. He couldn't visit the next Senate office on the pharmacy issue. He was a mess. And it didn't matter. It was a healthcare issue; it wasn't going to get through the committee.

He stopped in the men's room grabbed a bunch of paper towels, wet them and started wiping off the mess that covered him. Men would stare at him when they came in, so he moved to one of the stalls. He got the sauce off, but his clothes were stained and soaking wet.

Outside, he tried to hail a cab, but none would pick him up because they didn't want to get their back seats wet and dirty. He walked to Union Station, people staring at him. He had to get home. After he got his new ticket, he would cancel the rest of today's appointments.

The train ride home would give him a chance to think and regroup. He'd been doing this work for

more than 20 years. He'd given a lot of money. He knew a lot of secrets. He could hurt a lot of people. He needed to spend a couple of weeks out of DC, let things calm down. Even if Stephenson wasn't running again, he wouldn't want Mickey's secret out on the street; Mickey was sure of that.

He would have to speak with his clients. This was throwing off the timing on a lot of projects. He would probably not get anything into the big budget bill that had to pass, and that was the next bite at the apple. It would be a couple of months before there was something next on the schedule that had to pass—probably the banking bill. It would be a stretch, he thought, to get his clients' needs met in the banking bill. Never mind, he would come up with a strategy.

He passed two lobbyists he knew who looked away and didn't talk to him. Union Station smelled of burnt rubber brakes and rotting trash. It smelled like adrenaline gone sour.

There was an Acela heading out and it had a first-class seat that cost about $120.00 more than business class. He bought it and soon was on an early train back from DC. First-class had a few single seats and he wanted one badly, rushed on to the train brushing past people and got one. Seated, he left his phone in his jacket pocket and pulled out his laptop. He was going to have to write some extensive e-mails to his clients really quickly to limit the damage and he did not want to be overheard. He'd already thought of the story he'd tell, about Stephenson's nervous breakdown and that no bills were going to be moved out of his committee this year. He would be the first to tell his clients that Stephenson was being forced to retire by Senate leadership. He would let his clients know that this was going to be a year of waiting; nothing would be getting done by anyone and they would just have to sit tight and wait it out until Stephenson left. He would add a personal note, about how close he felt to Stephenson and how painful it was to see a good friend suffer this way with mental illness. He would describe his own dedication to tackling mental health policy as a result. He would wish Stephenson a fast recovery and a gentle retirement.

Mickey brought his beating heart under control. He had a plan. Whatever is, is right. He would make the story real, and it would be right.

He booted his laptop, got on the Acela network, and opened his e-mail application. His inbox had a stack of e-mails in the boldface of urgent. They were from his clients—the four who kept him on retainer at $500,000 per year, and the dozen who paid him $3,500 an hour as needed. All of them ended his employment. All of them gave him 30 days' notice. All of them copied Stephenson's Chief-of-Staff.

There were two e-mails from his oldest client, the one whose daughter's wedding he had attended just last year. The first was a dry note firing him. The second simply read: *Mickey, I don't know what the hell you did to Maple, and I don't ever want you to write back or call me to fill me in, but it must have been nuclear. I'm sorry.*

The train pulled out of Union Station and Washington closed her legs. But not forever, not for long. There'd be another train coming along.

About the Author

In 1984 J. **David Liss** received an MFA from Brooklyn College. Trained in writing and inclined to politics, Liss became a speechwriter and then a lobbyist. He's worked in corporate, academic, and healthcare centers and all his work has been touched by literature (he likes to think). His poetry has appeared or is forthcoming in "The Naugatuck River Review," "Poetry Quarterly," "Fifth Wednesday Journal," "Blood and Thunder," "Euphony," and many others. He has prose published in "The MacGuffin," "Lake Effect," "Inwood Indiana Press," and has several stories in an anthology from Between the Lines Press.

IT WILL BE FOREVER

by Jeff Richards

Richard Sager lost his virginity in the spring of 1967 before our road trip across country to break in the red Mustang convertible my parents gave me for Christmas. Her name was Linda Boudreau. She was a wisp of a thing, with a turned-up nose and a sallow complexion. We called her "the Mouse" behind her back. We knew that was mean, but Linda was dangerous. She reeled in a college boy and didn't plan to throw him back.

We were in Steubenville, Ohio, in a double-wide furnished in Early American. An American flag slapped against a pole outside. We could see the lights that lined Dean Martin Expressway sparkling in the distance. Baby Huey invited us down here for the weekend. His parents were away, so we had the place to ourselves. There was J.B. of the close-cropped hair and businesslike demeanor. Hank Hipple of the Big Eyes. He could sleep sitting up with his eyes open. Baby Huey of the comic strip and wide girth. And me, Underdog, as my students called me many years later because of the short distance between my lipless mouth and dimpled chin. We were all innocent as lambs. Not Rick of the curly sandy-blond hair, blue eyes, and pointy chin. He almost looked girlish, one of the reasons, I assume, that he was cultivating chin whiskers.

We were all in the living room watching baseball on TV. We were drinking beer and smoking cigars. A fan was on to blow the smoke out of an open door. Huey didn't want to anger his fastidious mom. Linda wasn't smoking a cigar, but she was hanging on to Rick like an ill-fitting suit. She whispered to our friend, and he stood up with a sheepish grin on his face.

"Well, uh-hum," he said, clearing his throat. "I guess we're going to disappear for a while," he said as they slipped by the TV and into the other side of the double-wide. They emerged later, in the eighth inning of the game—they left in the third. Rick looked solemn, almost anxious. Linda smiled. Her eyes lit up like sparklers. She raised her hand and showed us the cigar ring on her finger. "We're gonna get hitched," she gushed.

That's why I didn't think Rick was that enthusiastic about our road trip, but we went ahead anyway. The idea was to work the first part of the summer so we could raise enough money to finance the gas and food for the trip. We found a job at Hot Shoppes Jr. on Rockville Pike. I worked the front while Rick flipped hamburgers in the back. I had to watch Rick because he liked to joke with me. One time he put a dishrag in a Teen Twist. Another time, I found a dead cockroach floating on top of the Royal Sauce in a Mighty Mo. This might not have been Rick, because I'd seen roaches fall from the ceiling. I was always careful to check the food before I handed it to the customers. One time I caught the fry man turn his head and spit in the soup. For the rest of the day when somebody asked for soup, I'd say we were out.

Sometimes Linda visited. They'd have lunch, or if Rick didn't have time, she'd sit in the dining area sipping a Coke, watching him in a covetous way, like she owned him. Once he spoke to one of the women customers. Linda stormed out of the restaurant. And this wasn't the first time that happened. The day manager got on his back. "You got to keep your woman under control," he said.

The day manager was a short ginger-haired fellow with beefy arms and a sly grin on his pimply face.

He had six kids and all he heard from them all day, he told us, was, "Daddy, give me a quarter. Daddy, give me a quarter." He would lean up against the register after the rush and comment on the customers who came in. A black guy came in, he'd say he'll order an orange drink; a white guy, he'll order a root beer float; a fat guy, he'll order Pappy Parker's fried chicken and apple pie à la mode. But mostly he'd comment on the lady customers' breast size. He'd poke one of us in the side and say, "That's a good un, that's a good un." Once he spotted Lindy, knowing exactly who she was, he said "Flat." Rick didn't say a thing.

But on the last day of work, when I was about to drive out of the lot, Rick opened the glove compartment and found two Kotex pads that my sister left there when she borrowed the Mustang. Susan was not a modest person. Rick grabbed my arm and told me to stop. Then he ran in the Hot Shoppes and came out with a squeeze bottle of ketchup. He squirted the ketchup on one of the Kotex. He stood up in the car—the top was down—and threw the Kotex as hard as he could against the plate glass window. The pad stuck for a second, then slide down, leaving a trail of ketchup behind.

"Take that, creep," he yelled to the manager, who was at the register ringing up a customer.

It took us two days to pack our gear and reassure our families that we would be safe. Then we drove west at breakneck speed, Rick grumbling the whole way about how his mother didn't trust Linda. She was cheap. She was grasping. She didn't have a brain in her head. "She'll rob you blind. You're so innocent."

We reached Phoenix, where J.B. lived with his family in a ranch house in a suburb overlooking Camelback Mountain. It was hotter than hell. They'd water the lawns at night, and the water would stay there. The ground was like cement. J.B.'s family had moved from the bucolic hinterlands of Connecticut, and I think they were in shell shock. J.B. had a younger brother and sister. We didn't see much of them, though once Rick and I wandered into the living room. J.B.'s sister was standing on top of the sofa, sticking her finger in a hole in the ceiling like she was the Little Dutch Boy plugging the dike. Rick asked her what she was doing.

She shrugged. "Nothing."

She jumped off the couch and looked at us. "You're Jim's friends."

"Yes."

She laughed and ran out of the room. We asked J.B. later what her problem was. He shrugged. "I don't know. Maybe she smokes marijuana."

We didn't see the parents. The mother was back in Connecticut. The father worked all hours. I met him once at our college when he came to visit. He hardly spoke at all, but sat in a chair jotting down notes in a small black leather-bound notebook. I thought the parents were estranged or about to be.

J.B. was working at the time, so there wasn't much for us to do. Once when it was 110 degrees, we ordered tacos at Taco Bell and ate outside to see what was hotter—the tacos, which we slathered with hot sauce, or the overheated air. Another time we took a ride out in the desert and noticed that it was all fenced in. Why would someone care if you trespassed on this crummy land, we wondered. Another time we took in a movie, The Trip, about a group of rich Hollywood types on acid that ends badly, I think, when Peter Fonda's frozen face in a close-up cracks like glass.

We exited the theater into the hot air, trying to catch our breath. It wasn't the heat as much as the lack of humidity that bothered us. "You know," said Rick, "I don't think I'll ever take an acid trip."

On J.B.'s day off, we took an inner-tube trip down the Verde River, which comes out of the mountains above Phoenix. The rapids were mild, mostly ones or twos, though occasionally we'd hit a chute that would take us a couple of feet down to the next level. We came across two couples drifting along, with a table on an inner tube between them, partaking of a fried chicken and potato salad lunch between sips of beer. The air was baking hot, so it was nice to fall off the inner tube and bury myself up to my neck in the cold, silky water.

137

When we were winding our way home through a forest of saguaro cacti—most with their arms up, but a few bent over like dead soldiers—J.B. asked Rick if he really planned to marry Linda.

"Of course I do. We're engaged. I don't know why everyone doubts me."

"Are you going to wait until after you graduate from Denison?"

"Maybe I will. Maybe I won't," snapped Rick.

We drove south to Tombstone, Arizona, where we watched a mock gunfight at O.K. Corral. Then we crossed the border at Agua Prieta, Mexico, and drove down a dirt road dodging potholes until we came to a fence and couldn't drive farther. A kid came up to us and said, "You want my sistah?"

"No," said Rick.

We drove back and at the border, they searched the Mustang. They opened the trunk and pulled back the mat. They found a compartment that I didn't know was there.

"What are you looking for?"

"Drugs," said the border patrol guard, rolling his eyes as if we were a couple of neophytes.

We spent the night in the Chiricahua Mountains and had a run-in with a family of skunks that didn't amount to much. They camped out with us for a couple of hours in Rick's tent. We lay as still as stone statues. They got bored. They left. They didn't leave anything behind.

We decided to try Mexico again. We crossed the border at El Paso. This time on foot across the International Bridge. A Mexican border guard waved us on impatiently and went back to reading his newspaper. We ordered a steak and Coke dinner in a small restaurant by the square. Then we wandered through the seediest part of town into a bar where a heavyset woman danced on a stage to mariachi music. We ordered margaritas and sat down at a table. A skeletal woman with an ashen complexion and a cold sore on her lip asked us if we would buy her a shot of tequila. We said yes.

I told Rick that this woman looked an awful lot like a dissipated version of Linda Boudreau. He shot me the dirtiest look and jumped up like he was going to slug me. The woman backed off. He looked at her for a second and shook his head.

"You're right," he said and sat down, mopping his forehead. It was hot and close in this room, even though there was an overhead fan above us creaking around and around.

There were a few customers in the bar, and except for us, they all seemed to be Mexican. They watched us in a friendly way, as if they were waiting to see what would happen next. What happened was that the heavyset woman lumbered off the stage and came up to us. She sat down. She asked for a shot of tequila. This went on for a while, one shot after another, until I sniffed one of the glasses.

"It's water," I told Rick.

He grabbed the glass from me and sniffed. "Yeah."

The ladies seemed nonplussed by the nasty looks we shot in their direction. They gestured toward a staircase that led up to the second floor.

"We live," the skeletal one said. "You want to visit?"

"No, thanks," I said.

"Sin dinero," said the heavyset lady.

"That's right," said Rick. "You cleaned us out."

The man in a Yankees baseball cap at the table next to us grinned from ear to ear, so we could see the gaps in his teeth.

Rick decided that we should drive straight across Texas to New Orleans, where we were invited to stay at Linda's uncle's house. But we only managed a third of the way before we pulled over to a rest area, dog-tired. It was pitch-dark. The next morning, I awoke bathed in sweat. We seemed to be in the middle of an alkaline desert, flat and white as a ghost, not a sign of vegetation or animallike creature, though insects by the thousands. I brushed a baby tarantula off my arm. We drove on, made Houston. Broke down. Rented a motel room, it was so muggy-hot. We arrived in New Orleans in the middle of the day and parked near Bourbon Street. We downed a couple of hurricanes at Pat O'Brien's. Linda's relatives were not far away in a postage-stamp house at the edge of a swamp. We camped in the backyard.

The cockroaches came to visit. I woke up and there was one trying to climb in Rick's mouth. I slapped it away. He jumped up ready to slug me, but when he saw all the other cockroaches arranged in phalanxes prepared to assault us, we retreated to the tiny back porch. The next morning we left town, to the surprise of the Boudreaus until Rick explained he wanted to see Linda. We would meet again at the wedding. We made a quick visit to Rick's aunt in Marietta. I left my security pillow behind, which was as flat and hard as a skipping rock anyway. The first night without my pillow, I slept fitfully and woke up with a headache. The second night, in the Hungry Mother Mountains, I covered my eyes and forehead with a T-shirt and slept like a baby.

When I awoke and peeled off the soggy T-shirt, I glimpsed the clear blue sky through a canopy of oak leaves waving in a light wind, reflecting the sunlight. This was a pretty sight, I thought, until I remembered a tent covered my head last night. I leaned up on my elbow and looked around. I had slept on top of my sleeping bag last night. All that covered me was a thin tarp. I pulled it up over me because underneath I was buck naked. I fished around for my underwear and pulled it on. Then I checked around for my clothes. Gone. My backpack. Gone. The campsite totally clean. All of Rick's gear and Rick himself gone. Then worst of all, the Mustang was gone from the parking lot where I'd parked it the night before. My first thought was, Here I am three hundred miles from home in my underwear. Has Rick deserted me? What am I going to do?

But no, as it turned out, it was another one of his tricks. He pulled up in the Mustang with the top down and a big smile on his face. He lifted my clothes from the passenger-side seat. "Ready to go?" he asked.

The next day we were in Washington, and he was back in Lindy's arms. Only there's one thing he didn't account for: his mother. Joan Sager was a wisp of a thing with a sallow complexion, like Linda, though her nose curved down, not up. But unlike Linda, she had a bulldog's tenacity, like her Boston terrier, Dovie. She would hand me a rolled-up newspaper to beat him off when he was too

friendly, which was most of the time. Of course, Joan was more refined, but it came down to the same thing. The first thing she insisted when we returned home in late August was that she meet Linda's parents. They invited her for dinner. They lived in an apartment complex on New Hampshire Avenue, a mile outside the District. I wasn't there for the event, but Joan said they were gauche. They served dinner from the kitchen. That seemed to be the biggest complaint other than where they lived. Rick's family lived in Bethesda, the poshest suburb on the Maryland side of the line other than Potomac. It was not that she was a snob exactly. After all, her husband had died, and though she had his government pension, she wasn't exactly living in the lap of luxury. It was that she was trying to convince Rick that he was making a big mistake, and somehow it worked.

A week before we were to leave for Denison, Rick told Linda that the engagement was off. I could hear her down in the basement begging him to change his mind, and when that didn't work, I could hear her heartrending sobs. Joan wasn't there that day. She'd driven to Lord & Taylor to buy her daughter school clothes, and though she knew it would be expensive, she wanted Anne to look respectable. No miniskirts. But Dovie was there. When they came out of the basement, Dovie jumped on Linda. She didn't bother picking up a rolled-up newspaper, but kicked him straightaway in the nuts. Dovie ran off whimpering and hid in a corner.

The plan was that I was to drive Linda back to New Hampshire Avenue alone. I insisted Rick come along. They sat in back with the top up. Linda didn't want her hair mussed. I weaved through the traffic for five miles. There was complete silence in the back, so I switched on the radio. A Lettermen's song came on:

When I fall in love,

It will be forever.

Linda whimpered and I switched off the radio.

"It's better this way," said Rick haltingly. "To end it suddenly."

"Why don't you shut your big fat mouth," she countered.

Another silence until we arrived at the turna-round in front of her apartment. He walked her to the door. He tried to kiss her. She pushed him away.

When he came back to the car, he was teary-eyed.

"Hey, man, I'm really sorry this happened," I said.

He jumped in the front seat with me. I took down the top. He turned to me with a careworn smile on his lips. "Don't worry. I'll get over it. Mom was right."

About the Author:

Paycock Press published **Jeff Richards's** novel, Open Country: A Civil War Novel in Stories in 2015. His short fiction, essays, and cowboy poetry have appeared in New South, Pinch, Southern Humanities Review, and Grey Sparrow, among more than a dozen other publications. He has appeared as well in four anthologies and one college composition collection that include Tales Out of School (Beacon Press) and Letters to Salinger (University of Wisconsin Press). He lives in Takoma Park, Maryland, with his wife and two dogs, and can be reached at jeffrichardsauthor.com.

PLIE, ADJUST, TUNDU, TAP

by Jean E. Verthein

Three in the morning. The phone rang. It did, didn't it? After all, detectives called for midnight lineups to check whether the attacker from six months earlier was there. But the end of the line issued silence. The caller hung up.

Dread overwhelmed. Outside wetness sounded sticky from passing car wheels, as sleep no longer possessed her, and the streetlight illuminated the yellow, blue, and green stained-glass window ahead. Stiff, though just able to pull herself by grabbing a nearby doorknob to go step-by-step to reach the window to look out. Outside, rainwater met a subterranean welling up from the fault line stream near the stone wall. Water overflowed around the knoll crossed by the exit road's painted midline.

Sleepless and stuffed up, she leaned over the new metal window frame, paired with another that braced the inserted red and blue stained glass. Cold air allowed some breathing, as she studied the knoll that bubbled like an eye shut to a white slit. Arm in arm with her partner, a pregnant woman, her belly shaped like the eye, bobbled over the knoll street line. Her black coat opened over her white top and pants to create a line vertical to the street. He, dark coated, was aligned at her side, arm looped around her and head bent toward hers. They walked out of sight.

Marike shivered. "A long time since I've cared."

Twenty yards beyond their cross-point, a serrated knife could have sliced off the steep rocky slope. Hobbling back from the windows, she ducked under the bedcovers.

Awake still at 4:30 a.m. Up again, she shuffled to the living room. The digital clock, answering machine, and VCR and CD player numbers blinded in red neon. Her computer was still on and her cell plugged in. Slumping on her couch, mossy pillows fell around her to dull her thoughts.

For relief, they traveled back to Dr. N., who re-aroused them against stormy days and stormy nights. After ruining two cheap red umbrellas, she'd carry a third one with a wooden bird-head handle to Dr. N.'s office. Because of stiffening into an H, knees up her sides, across her lower back, and down the thighs through the knees. The left worse than right in the acute phase, and inflexible.

This stiffness mimicked her mother's paralysis. It eased, until jabbed with more pain.

All the pain ever felt, from falling off from rafting in rocking water, and car accidents flushed forward. She named this pain H paresis.

By late morning, she struggled downstairs to the lobby mailbox under the stairs. Rattled, she jammed her key in her post box.

Jumping when asked the time, she was relieved to see her neighbor. His spectacles enlarged his face. His frame narrowed and shortened more than hers into trust. "Could you, please, unlock my box on the bottom row. If I bend, I can't stand back up."

Smiling, in spite of his own back agony, he turned her key for her mail.

"See Dr. N. I see him. The best, good fellow, my wife says, good-looking, and I think he's the one who injects something in the spine to ease the pain."

Detective Patricio Ramirez, sí, called "Paddy" in his unit with so many Irish cops, had warned Marike, "Stay away from the dead, loco ones and dead-end streets. No lobby niches or corners like yours and stairwells." His white línea served his gallantry; still more dashing with his karate gold-edged black belt, seen once and worn for teaching and dancing. The belt matched his mustache flare. One night, brought home from a police lineup, he directed her, "No hideaways. Otherwise, flashbacks will overtake you. Always stay in the open."

She'd tried listening. "You're my last call. I'm going dancing now. You'll dance again and come back late!" Swashbuckler in meringue and salsa, he'd ask her to dance, dance only, only dance.

Back in her apartment, the interior off light from the dawn sun was sepulchral. Entombed, Marike should get out to Dr. N. and called for an appointment. Not there until Monday, three days away. In that period, her H might improve.

Marike dressed in blues, pull-on jeans with a rubber waist she need not zip or snap and a Prussian blue pullover. She half crawled five blocks to his office, and once there she declared victory.

White blonde-veiled to her waist, the secretary chirped to patients and phone callers and handed a card to Marike to fill out her data and symptoms, which hurt with every pencil stroke.

The doctor, like all therapists consulted, would be uninterested in her awareness of body stiffness from her mother's paralysis or its basis. Still, she wrote down her symptoms for Dr. N.

His vision of a secretary directed her to sit next to his office, pine paneled. In a frame sat or stood five young adults and three tiny children, all photo beauties. His, she assumed, when he arrived. She tried to compose herself.

She'd expected a thickset roundheaded brown-haired man, balding, like her last muscle doctor, seen after the car accident from the flood. But Dr. N. differed. Without helmet or hard hat, his hair reflected lines of silver, and the sight of him

stunned her. Other than what was written on the card, she told her neighbor's wife's Apollo doctor nothing about her semi-paralysis.

Happiness ran with goodness. In his examining room, he suggested removal of her upper garment and tying on the red plastic top. His nurse had already, but she ignored the white-dressed woman. His manner was antiseptic. Time would tell. He left, and she waited.

In treatment in the next cubicle, the deep-voiced woman ran a booking agency. She and the handsome doctor, Irish looking, chitchatted about cantors on 1950s television, including Jackie Gleason, Eddie Fisher, Richard Tucker, and, before TV, J.S. Bach, Protestant cantor. Listening, Marike, feeling Irish though not so much, started to laugh in pain and wished to tap-dance.

But she stared at the wall with Dr. N.'s medical certificates and licenses. This doctor, unlike her last, offered more than a stretcher, a black leather device, slanted from floor to ceiling or parallel with it, daunted her, now that she was on it. Her feet paralleled the ceiling, or could tip, feet up. Harm possible wracked her mind. Its cushion, soft leathery, signified less than horror. On the rack strapped on, she could be mounted facedown.

"Only a moment; I'll be back," his voice rumbled. When he returned, he injected a substance seemingly into her neck to end her overall stiffness, as her stomach dropped to the floor but came back up.

His treatment was finished; just like that, her ultra crick in her neck was gone. She chatted mindlessly. "I didn't know Jackie Gleason was a cantor."

"Oh yes." The choir leader doctor, august, silvery and handsome, his warmth contrasted with his erect, correct posture—no H with him. "You'll feel better soon. You will soon laugh. Come back for more treatments." He was watching her—his patient.

Outside, raindrops informed her she'd left her white umbrella behind, but she plodded on home.

For three days, she still avoided going back to her

work in human resources with other peoples' troubles and snuck out for food. Getting back home was run for cover.

Later one afternoon, the secretary in his office notified Marike's answering machine that her umbrella was taking up room in the chiropractic lobby. Also, the pen she'd used to write a check for the doctor was needed. So she called back and asked when to pick up one and drop the other off. The beauty at Dr. N.'s desk answered, "Dr. N. put the umbrella in the car rear to prevent stealing and will call you about dropping it off."

Next morning, her back improved, she rattled and strolled with cans for recycling and reached the newsstand where she bought newspapers, Le Monde and Corriere della Sera, to exit from dullness. If she read their Romance languages and studied the photos, goings-on in Paris and Milan would distract her from fear. Far-flung events disturbed her more; her problems troubled less. Riots cheered her. Theft reassured her that the world was gristle. And with suicide or murder, war was more.

The Lebanese news vendor at his window was friendly. A halo must have collapsed on his head, for his hair grew out around his bald spot, like tonsure. From his jawbone to his mustache, he replied, "Comment ça va?"

"Bien." She added, "Comme ci, comme ça, merci," so thanks, and paid for papers.

Turning away, she was face-to-face with Dr. N.'s stare several feet away from his office doorway. Silvery and perfectly toned, he seemed to bow to her, as he said, "You're walking?"

Forgetting to ask about the umbrella, he lay in her mind. Seven weeks of feeling better led her to his office to inquire. The visionary beauty at the front desk, long hair veiling, Serena the receptionist told her, "Dr. N.'s out. He gave up on you."

"Here's the umbrella. Doesn't rain fall on you?"

Hearing a male voice, Marike asked to use the toilet farther into the back rooms; she lingered there before returning to the waiting room to kill time until the male voice materialized. She wondered about what was this beauty to the doctor? His receptionist did rattle on though about her children who presumably knew their father.

Unsure, Marike sat, bending her head around in yoga. If only someone would dynamite her head pressure. Loosen it into pieces.

Back at home again, she studied her mother's crewel wall hanging above her. Two trunks writhed into one. Browns, gold, and reds lifted into muted hues of greens, roses, and yellows, as squirrels and birds romped and flew. Within the turds beneath the trunk, she fell back into memory.

She had hurried along the main avenue, as shopkeepers slammed down metal gates over their storefronts. By the greengrocer, plantains hung, apples piled, and sugarcane leaned like bamboo stalks.

Suddenly, car brakes jammed, horns honked, and Marike jumped at the racket that jarred her back to her late evening nightmare. Along the corridor, lights dimmed with nightfall, and the street tunneled into a dark hollow.

Heels snapping behind her picked up speed and halted giddiness in barhopping and joy finding one last all-night restaurant. On weekends, partygoers crowded this night. On this weeknight, no one danced, no dusky men and women rippled in low-cut necklines and skirts or svelte fit ones who by their presence protected her.

In the dead quiet, women's shoes clapped ahead of her. Marike rushed the formidable street length toward home, while someone galloped behind her. To see, her neck would not turn. Darkness thickened, intensified, and she strode on, hoping to reach her goal before it receded. Steps continued, as she raced through a mirror and her heart pumped in her toes.

Breathless, she slowed, when the steps slowed. She breathed, while the steps did stop momentarily.

Approaching the eye incline, she gripped her big jagged key, resistant to lock picking, as she struggled to find the smaller key for her building's front door from among too many keys unnerved her to pick the right one.

Someone behind her, she stood aside to give the go-ahead to enter, but he hung back. She slammed the door or tried to. But the door's valve resisted her closing against him his foot between the door and its frame and thwarted her closing and locking it. Two heads higher than hers, he forced the door open. She groaned.

He rushed on up the stairs, and to her relief, the elevator arrived and she instantly pressed three. The elevator took off up, though it stopped on the second floor, where the giant forced his way in.

She began to unbuckle her watch, but he was dull in reacting to it. When she handed it to him, he dropped it.

The camera strapped and slung over her shoulder. To protect herself, she handed it to him, but he shook his head.

She pressed the buttons to stop the elevator at each floor. He reached for the stop button. Then she pulled out the large safety pin she carried for trouble. Nervously, she tried to jab him. But the down of his white jacket was too thick for her pressure to reach him. Her scream made no sound. He shoved her arm away.

Next, she reached for the alarm. It started to sound. He pulled out a dagger. Briefly it blinded her. "I have knife. Be careful. You people; this is for you. Lower your pants and turn your back to me."

She stretched for the elevator's warning bell. But he lunged for her arm.

She froze. She let them drop. She bent down. He did not plunge the dagger into her. He did. She bled.

He ordered her to get dressed. She flipped off the stop button and pressed three for her floor. There she stepped out and held the door, while she'd threatened, "I'll get you. Wait and see."

The door had closed against him, and inside her apartment she'd sobbed. Thank God her daughters were with their father. The only woman she knew to call was a friend of a friend, Bettina, who told her to call the cops who'd take her to the emergency.

Much later, she realized in Dr. N.'s waiting room that she'd been hooked up to the plumbing of her time.

Her medium-size Swiss Army knife in hand at home, she studied its deep red and its small bright gold cross and began to carry it with her at all times. She had pulled out its corkscrew, its scissors, and its small blade and, finally, its large blade. She would scar the too-handsome face of the attacker and his member.

When the phone rang, Marike shook herself awake, as the mother secretary said to her, "Dr. N. says come to his office this Saturday."

Bewildered and ecstatic in an overlay and underlay, one cannot know what's going on with the other. The H stiffening and her headache were dissolving. New thoughts focused on Dr. N.

Exercising her anxiety away, she bolted for his office before she changed her mind about going there. With the ring of his door, he answered. She stammered, "Where's your secretary?"

He chuckled. "I'm alone." He held the door for her. Her knife was in her raincoat pocket. It was.

"Sit down," he said and got lost behind the scenes.

Another ring at the door. Marike answered it, relieved to see another being.

"You go next," she said to the young man, "I'm early."

"No, you."

Dr. N. returned. She watched him over the edge of her paper. He beckoned to her. "I can wait," she said. "He can go first. I have time to kill."

The bell rang again. She answered it and was surprised to see an ex-priest from her office. Pretending enthusiasm about his back problem and the value of the injection treatment, she nodded.

Dr. N. came out and offered no choice but to follow and make small talk about his family on the wall. He asked, "Are you laughing again?"

"No, tap-dancing."

About the Author:

On the theme of survival, **Jean Verthein** managed to bus across Afghanistan and around Iran. She has counseled and taught undergraduates and undergraduates at Columbia University School of Public and School of Social Work. Two Ragdale Foundation grants and a Sarah Lawrence College MFA have been invaluable to her publishing in St. Ann's Review, Downtown Review, Gival Press, Green Mountains Review, River Press Review and Oracle. She grew up in Wisconsin and lives in Wisconsin.

THE ART COTTAGE

by Sasha Chinnaya

I walk through the streets of my city and see a thousand different worlds of art living and breathing. The traffic is a great blur of color that looks not so different from watercolor leaking with bliss onto a blank slip of paper. It zooms past with an energy I feel I've lost. I feel the rush of the wind against my cheeks. Cold as it is, it's a welcome for my body has grown lonely and dry to routine. The leaves rustle about, flying through my hair and adding some color to this pale landscape.

The pavement is still wet from an early morning of rain. It's been beaten and marked with footprints. A thousand souls have wandered here and I am just one more today.

"Ahhhhhhhhhhhh!!!!!!!!" A tousling scream breaks straight through the air.

It's coming from down the block. From the swift glimpse I catch, I see a child stomping about, throwing his backpack away with such revolt. His poor mother is a woman that has no time for tantrums. She is pushed to her limit with bags hanging off her arms like heavy ropes trying to break through skin. The sacrifices of adulthood are ripe on her face. She doesn't look that old and yet she has a child. A great and terrifying ball of energy that will never let her rest again, but that she would probably not be able to find a moment's happiness without anymore.

This woman keeps resisting the pathway to aggression. She closes her eyes so calmly, so perfectly balancing authority with understanding. I see and respect the way she breathes deeply and then grabs her child's small arm with ease. She picks him off the floor gently and then swings him to a corner of the sidewalk.

"Nooooo!!! I don't want to. I don't want to. I want to go back home!!!" The child wails on like a broken toy.

His wriggling movements push the woman to get more serious. The sympathetic smile drains from her face and is replaced by a stern, processing look.

"Stop." She says the word once, but the sudden drop of it feels like a red light in the midst of racing traffic.

Her eyes stare down the child. She drops her Trader Joes bags and towers over the boy.

"I...I didn't..." He stutters in speech and quivers out of guilt.

"I don't want to hear another word out of you until we reach Grandma's. Anything, even so much as a mumble Daniel, and I swear you aren't getting dessert. None." She raises a jar of cookie butter.

The swirls of light and dark brown are inviting and nostalgic. I can almost taste it on a slice of bread. I would spread it thick and munch on the creamy goodness as I studied notes for school. It only took a taste to give me a break and the older I get I realize how much I need breaks.

The woman shoves the jar back into the bag and both I and the child sigh. The boy does not say another word as he pulls the straps of his bag back on in surrender. The Jansport item now seems like a great weight upon him and I feel bad. I don't know why because the torment of school is a trial we must all pass. It's inevitable and insufferable, but that's the way life is right? We must surrender to reality and compromise. Only, something about that truth seems more like a legend made to scare us. I don't know why, but I can't entirely accept it. I've always wanted more.

They walk past me, our legs brushing against one another as they rush to catch their train. The boy isn't walking as fast his mother though. He is staring up at the sky. His bright blue ocean eyes are wide of wonder and gleaming with a thirst for adventure. It is a pity that these eyes should enter into the claustrophobic space of the subway. They weren't made to be contained or masked. They exist to roam and always be free.

As I stare into their sharp glint against the afternoon sun, I know this kid sees the world differently than the rest. There are few that take the time to even have a unique perspective of the world around them. Everyone is so wrapped up in a draining schedule. These eyes should escape into the vast avenues of the city where something different awaits on every block. If they don't soar, their light will dim and the clear blue will only look gray.

I remember what it was like to take the train with my mom to the city in the mornings. I was just a kid, but everything was an adventure for me as well. There was the view of the buildings overlooking the ocean as we passed the bridge. It was exhausting and enticing. The scent of hot dogs lingered in the air like a special perfume you had to bathe in. The smoke could fill your lungs to suffocation, but even then there was an intrigue to the unpredictability. To be a child running loose in this chaotic oasis of bright lights and gripping noises was and is a gift.

His mother shows no empathy for that sort of romantic mindset though and I feel the woman's sharp push as she knocks my shoulder roughly and unapologetically. All the while, she grasps onto her son's shirt. I don't feel offended at her lack of politeness. She is like all the rest, in a rush to get somewhere.

I take a moment to breathe, just breathe in this crisp, chill autumn day in the city. Sometimes I forget how beautiful it can be, how spontaneous it still is and that is due to the bitterness of a routine life. Each planned minute kills my excitement to live in the moment and to find the creative fire out of the ordinary embers of a day. Though, in this moment, as I take a last sip from my coffee and close my eyes, I can feel everything moving about. The wind touches my body like the familiar, welcoming arms of a loved one. The light rays of a setting sun peak through the sky and find my cold, tired skin. The buses honk, the stream of voices muddle together and even from a distance, I hear the melancholic notes of a band playing in the park. I am honored to be a part of this mobile art.

Though, time has a way of willing us back into the bustle. I awake from my slumber of city bliss when a stranger throws curses my way. They push me to the sidewalk and I get jabbed by a long umbrella sticking out of someone's purse. The pain throbs in my rib and I put my head down in shame. I retain that chaotic, fast moving flow by scampering down the subway steps and keeping out of everyone's way. Simply walking can become such an obstacle coarse down here.

I'm meeting with an old friend today. We take the F together whenever we can and our subway rides are never boring. They're filled with intriguing conversations and sarcastic banter, mostly on Josh's part. I was lucky enough to get off a few minutes early from work today and I'm thrilled to see him. It hasn't even been months since our last encounter at a café in Brooklyn. We sat for hours talking about graduation and how quickly our lives have been changing. I miss him already though...

It's strange, but there are just those people in our lives that understand who we are without us even having to explain a single thing. They just know our minds as well as the architecture of their own home. They get the quirky sense of humor, the random aspects of personality that the rest of the world are not sure what to make of.

Josh Dweller is one of those people so special to me. We aren't exactly alike and at times we bicker, but our differences have always been a good reason why we work so well as friends. We help each other see the world as vastly as it is, not just how we've trained our minds to comprehend it. We remind each other that cynicism needs optimism and vice versa.

He is wearing his favorite black T-shirt with the band the Clash spread across in a smoky white font. He pulls me in for a nice, long hug. It's the kind where your back gets stroked and you smell that musky cologne still wet on your friend's neck. You feel their hair strands tickle your face and the temperature of their skin mixes so well with your own. This hug was the comfort I needed.

"How are you my love?" He asks in that honest, effortless way that shows me he really does care how I feel.

"Fine. And you?"

"Tired." We both chuckle heartily and then sigh because for being only 21 we sound like old people already. How drained from the pointless hours of labor and dull routine we've become.

We get on the train and I can't fight back the urge to say more. Normally, I would've liked to discuss a topic that had nothing to do with work, but I couldn't keep the misery at bay. It started to overflow in jumbled up words.

"I just never thought I was going to work in an office you know?" I complain.

Lately, every thought I've had has been a complaint. This pessimism is so foreign to my usual romantic mindset. It annoys me so I can't even imagine how the people in my life take it. They must be so sick to death of it and me, but I guess that's what happens when you aren't living the life you want. We become transparent ghosts of the dreams that we thought would always have a steady pulse.

"Every job is an office job." Josh states this simple phrase so casually that he makes me feel dumb for not understanding it better.

The way he lets the words fall out like they're already facts that we all need to accept, scares me. He is judging me for not knowing this fact. I can see it in his eyes, brown but not warm as they once were. They're dark and gleaming like pools of sinister misery where all the lost hopes of the world dwell.

"Oh, well..." I try to salvage my argument, but I didn't realize I even had to make an argument with Josh.

I thought that, at least concerning this area of life, we were on the same page. Now, I fear he's a chapter in advance and I don't like this sour twist the story has taken. It makes me think the ending

will be more a tragedy than one with the solace of epiphany.

"Do you mean field work then?" He tries to be more understanding.

"No. Not exactly..." I try so hard to find the right words to save us from this awkwardness.

Soon, the words will not suffice and the conversation will turn into silence. I don't want the few minutes we have to be reduced to that.

"I just meant I want to be out and about I guess. I can't be contained at my desk. I sit there all day and I get lazier and lazier. I'm afraid of the comfort. I feel it won't challenge me enough and then I'll just have a comfortable lifestyle, you know?" I ask desperately.

I want to believe that we haven't changed so much that he no longer understands the trivial struggles I have. Maybe, I'm asking for too much here, but I want him to know that I can't live life the way it's set right now forever. I can't just accept this reality as my eternity. I need someone to know that.

"So you want to do stuff and then come back to your desk? Cause either way, any job you do, you'll have to sit down at a desk or work in some kind of office." He refuses to back down from his argument. It's all in the determined way he stretches out his words and emphasizes each syllable that makes me so frustrated.

"I guess. Yeah." I surrender my words out of lack for better ones and also because I don't want to get into an argument about something I don't entirely understand myself.

"It's just that my creativity feels a bit stifled when I'm surrounded by paperwork. I need to do something that has meaning."

Josh chuckles a rugged, sharp laugh that feels like an attack on my blind optimism. How silly a dreamer without proper cause I feel.

"Yeah I wish I had the time to think that way. My folks drilled that fluff out of my head a long time ago. It's such a privilege to get to create something. I feel lack of opportunity is a big reason why certain people aren't artistic."

"Yes. That's true." I agree out of lack of a better defense.

I don't disagree with Josh's comments, but I can't fathom how he says the words so casually like they don't just slice me right open and sink into blood.

Creativity is a privilege and yet it never really just comes easy does it? I feel it fade out of existence in the world each day, slowly and slowly as my work weeks accumulate. I start wondering who that bright eyed, optimist was with her paintbrushes and persistent dreams years ago. I can't find her when I stare at my disheveled appearance in the mirror each morning as I get ready for another dull day.

Where did the dreamer go and when exactly was the moment that she disappeared? I used to be so sure of myself and just a year ago, I would've shut down Josh's cynicism with such a passion that he would've flinched and immediately exited the train. Today, I am calmer and only listening to what he has to say, processing the strange words that make so little sense to me. I don't know if that passivity is called maturity or ignorance.

"Alright, it was good to see you again. I'll give you a call and we can hang out for real another time." He pats me swiftly across the shoulder and then skitters out through the closing doors.

I can't believe that's it? Just like that, he leaves me to the mess of my boiling thoughts. The storm he started is brewing and now he's just going to get off at his stop and I'll be the one that's stuck.

More people rush in. These strangers fill the empty space and I'm too dazed to notice I'm blocking their way. Once again, I'm just here in everyone's way and the world is moving on. It's got no place for me.

How is it that I can be so mad at him and at the same time thankful for his practical view of the world? My old friend means well, but his cynicism is not of his own making. He has become a product of the dark world we live in, where creativity barely has room so it dies away slowly. He doesn't see colors when he looks at a blank canvas. He doesn't try to ask questions or take the time to ponder a scene as I had this morning. For him and all the rest, it's a great rush that never ends. Work, eat, sleep and do it all over again. This frantic, thoughtless cycle that is done with nothing but the drive of making money. What a cruel way to kill ourselves and submit to conformity.

Shit. The numbers 169 pass my eyes as the train speeds off to its next destination. I was supposed to get off at Kew Gardens. My mind's wandering has gone too far this time and I start thinking that maybe the world is right. I need to get my shit together. I need to have a plan. I need to think practically. Right now, though, there is nothing to do other than to face my new reality. The doors open and I step out onto the platform of the 179th street station.

I don't know what urges me to exit the station rather than catch another train to get home. It's already 6 in the afternoon and I'm hungry and I need to run a shitload of errands before I sink into my bed and fall asleep. I know all of this information and yet it just doesn't process to my body. It's like my legs have minds of their own and they are leading me to another home. A forgotten home that is pretty much ancient by now.

That blue and gold sign stands proudly with the Fleur-de-lis symbol. My high school is still the same tall, rich structure that reminds me of a castle. I pass the black gates and sigh at the chains pulled over the side entrance I had always gone through. I climb the high, never ending hill that used to be such a struggle during gym class. I don't wait for anyone to tell me it's too late or to shoo me away. I run toward the cottage, the one place I always could count on for comfort in my youth.

The door swings open so easily when I push it. I wish life could happen as easily too. I flick on the lights and have my moment of nostalgia. The room is full of pictures hanging on the walls. There are so many designs celebrating fall and every direction I look has a brilliant splash of color. I even see the Elvis Presley and James Dean posters that my teacher used to hang up out of love and inspiration. I wish she were here right now so I could just hear her beautiful words. Draw what you see. They were never too complicated, but they always did the trick at bringing out the best art and encouraging us to have fun with it no matter what.

I miss the stools with their cold steel against my restless legs. It only took a swift turn to catch a bit of the rays peeping in from the windows. The music would rise high because there weren't any rules. We were free and happy, away from the world's sharp cynicism. You didn't have to like everyone to get along. You didn't have to hate them to pick a fight. Our emotions drove forward, untamed and curved like my hair when I didn't care to brush it. I was happy for just those 45 minutes each day of the week in art class.

This cottage was another home. It was my humble bit of solitude away from home and from school. It was my sacred whisper of inspiration in the times when life simply did not make any sense. I didn't understand who I was as I sat in class and failed at just about everything. I didn't know who I was at home when even the ones I loved failed to understand what I felt. Maybe the fault was mine for not being able to convey well enough as well.

Though, with just a couple of Prisma colored pencils and some Canson paper, I could express what words failed to tell. I'd sketch and erase a million times over, but it didn't matter. I kept creating without feeling any pressure to be talented or to actually do something with my pieces. It was never about that.

It was all just raw emotion flowing out of me so naturally, so intricately. I loved every second I would spend staring at a picture of a face or a landscape and then trying to capture all those details onto a sheet of paper.

The cool thing that everyone else seemed to forget, was that drawing out an image was not really about exact precision. It wasn't about copying it. If that was the case, why not trace it and be done? Save yourself from the shreds of dirty pink eraser flaking on the page and the thought of minutes wasted on something that still wasn't good enough.

No, the point of drawing was to express how you saw the world. Everyone sees things differently and in it's most profound and simplistic sense, drawing was for me about expressing to the world who I was as an individual. Not as a high school student. Not as a girl. Not as a person with brown skin. Not as anything other than what I felt and most of the time in my youth, I felt lost. That is a feeling people are always telling me to hide in

some way, shape or form. Yet, I feel it now stronger then I felt it before.

So, I turn off my rambling mind and grab a piece of plain white canson paper. It's the rough kind with a bit of texture. I always did like that type of paper better than the smooth and glossy. There are so many supplies lining up the shelves, but I go straight for the blue pack of pastels. I open it and feel a wave of euphoria move through me as I stare at all the different colors. I don't even bother sketching too much of an outline. I draw the simple curve of a vase I see on the table. Then, I gently take one of the golden yellow chalks and run it near my line. As my fingers touch that smooth, powdery chalk, I feel I'm where I should've been all along. I press down on the paper and smile as the first streak is made. I add other colors and make sure each one blends, but not too much. Everyone used to take their hands and rub the pastels together way too much in art class. I always preferred to leave the image a little more rough so you could see the highlights and the contrast. Life is like that too. It's never just one thing or another. It's full of contrasts and ups and downs and all of it should be honored as being real and authentic.

As I sit here, I am in awe. At how everything I need to say just comes out. It's like my insides are spilling out onto the canvas. It doesn't struggle. It just flows right out of me onto this canvas and somehow becomes art. I don't call it art though and I don't get how the rest of the world does either. To me, it's emotion. Simply put, it's emotion that has been physicalized and set free into the world. It's rough, raw moving emotion that I have little control over but that exists nonetheless.

Every emotion, good and bad and in between, are right here in the streaks and hues. This small amateur piece of artwork tells the story of all the little parts of me I don't know how to categorize and simplify for the world.

Oh why are we all so fucking scared of a little emotion? Why must it drive us mad to the point where we need to suppress it, push it down and pretend it does not drive us so much in this world. Emotion is not specific to one gender. It's specific to humanity and it strikes me bitter that the world still has not learned that lesson. It's age old, practically written into sacred scripture but I guess not everyone sees it as I do.

These days it feels like everyone has an opinion on what it means to be an artist, what I should be creating, how I should do it and how fast... I miss the simpler approach. Draw what you see. Yes, I will never ever stop doing that because to me that is the only way to live my life. I can only create and keep telling the world that I am here to stay. I am me, the me that I chose when the world tried to pull me into a million different shapes.

My mind goes back to Josh's words. It's such a privilege to get to create something. He isn't wrong, but I feel his statement is half-baked. It is a privilege to create, but it's a privilege you have to fight for. The fight never gets easier and the world will always try to tell you who you are before you've decided for yourself. It's far more difficult a task to do the thing you love because then you've got everything to lose. But if I could do it all over, I'd make the same mistakes. I'd take everyone's judgment and keep on going.

I close my eyes and let tears fill out on the barren canvas of my skin. I'll walk out of here in a few minutes. I'll tidy up the room, put away the tools and it'll be like nothing ever happened. The rest of the world will not know. They won't care and tomorrow I'll return to work where no one knows who I am. No one cares to know because we're all too busy with our important paperwork. Numbers and names strain our eyes, but not images. No voice of an individual glowing strong with conviction. Here, in exactly 30 minutes I have found myself in a way I never could when I'm surrounded by the paperwork.

I throw my hands up in the air and scream with joy, dancing to the music playing on the small radio and feeling, feeling everything happen all at once. I did it. Today, I created something. It wasn't a masterpiece and it's not going to win any awards. No one might see it, but I sat down and drew as passionately and vigorously as I used to. Today I was not lazy like the rest of the world. Today, I was an artist and I am so fucking proud of just that! There was no toning down nor thinking practically. I just acted off of raw emotion and it was incredible.

I dance for a good set of minutes before the little bell on the door rings. That familiar cold gust of wind sweeps into my sweater. It disrupts the private space and a few young girls walk in. They've got those same paper portfolios I used to lug about when I was their age. Their eyes are filled with a familiar wonder and a natural instinct to create whatever they want.

"Uh.... Are you a teacher miss?" One of the braver girls asks.

I laugh a strong, ruffling giggle. I haven't laughed this way in quiet some time. My whole body feels that sensation of happiness that we too often take for granted. It takes the girls by surprise and out of the corner of my squinted eyes, I catch a glimpse of them moving back.

"Sorry, no I'm not a teacher darling. I'm just a..." I couldn't think of the right word just then to describe what I was or why I was here.

"An artist." One of the girls stood looking over my piece on the counter.

She said it once and so casually, but the words did fit like a puzzle piece I had been missing all this while.

"Yes that is who I am."

About the Author:

Sasha Chinnaya is a recent graduate from St. John's University with a bachelors degree in English. Previously, she had another one of her short stories published in her school's Literary and Arts Magazine (Sequoya 2016 issue). She is also a film reviewer for an online magazine called Monologue Blogger where she reviews a wide variety of short films. She also has a passion for drawing and has an instagram account featuring some of her artwork (madetowashaway). Her aspirations for the future are to continue doing as many of the creative things she loves while also challenging her abilities.

CLAWS

by Vincent Yu

At first there was horror. Then relief, acceptance, love. When he was old enough to go to school his parents assured him he was normal and handsome and if anyone were to say anything hurtful about his thing then he should go to the teacher straight away. But the first girl to whom he'd extended a tepid hand ran away screaming, and he wasn't sure if that counted. The second boy had flinched and asked,

"What's that?"

"My hand," he'd said.

"It looks funny."

"Yeah, it's how I was born."

It became more or less this same conversation each time. Then he got to middle school, and the comments turned meaner. They called him Claws, they asked him how he jerked off with that thing, they sniggered at him during the unit on Johnny Tremain. But there was a fat boy in his class, too, whom they called Pudge. And a girl with a unibrow and hairy legs who had BO. And an Asian boy with glasses who put so much gel in his hair that in the sunlight it shined like a beetle's wing. It was the great saving grace of middle school that he could be as mean to anyone as he wanted: everyone else was, everything was fair game.

The town he grew up in was small and prosperous enough to have a magnet school whose entry was determined by a lottery system that kids from neighboring, lower-tax-bracketed cities could enter. Most houses had two-car garages for the minivan and the sportscar. In a friend's basement his junior year of high school, he had his first beer.

"Make sure you don't pierce through the aluminum, Claws." A round of drunk chuckles made its way through the circle. He smiled; it was all kind of affectionate by now.

His right hand-the claw- was a stump covered in fleshy nubs. The index, middle, and ring finger barely protruded past his knuckles. His thumb and pinky were a bit more fully formed- about half the length of normal fingers, with putative nail beds that curved inward towards the palm. His left hand was a normal hand.

The beer was difficult to open but not so difficult as bottles, which he had to press firmly against his chest with his claw and vigorously twist with his good hand. To be safe, he wedged the can between his thighs, then hooked his thumb beneath the tab and pushed up until he felt the spritzing crack. When he looked up everyone was staring at him. "Dude, that was impressive," his friend said.

He was impressive. Some people even called him inspirational when they saw the kinds of normal things he could do with his 1.5 hands (violin, assorted magic tricks, watercolors, etc). They lumped him with the inner city kids when topics like "triumph over adversity" rose in conversation.

But he still preferred cold weather because it gave him an excuse to hide his claw in the pockets of hoodies or thick jackets. On warmer days, when short sleeves were the only option, he felt so exposed he could've been naked. He hated washing his hands, guiding the perfectly normal fingers of his left over and in between the knobs of his right. His hand writing was chronically bad.

His typing was slow and sputtery. He was bad at most sports except long distance running.

By the time he landed in college he was tall and stringy and fairly handsome. He had a sharp nose and thick, pork chop lips. His body broadened out at the shoulders; his throat bulged with virility. His eyes contracted into a singular smirk which he'd developed in response to most awkward hand-related interactions.

He had relationships with girls who consciously praised themselves for their openness and ability to see past physical flaws. He had a fling with some kind of kinktress who was sexually fixated on certain acts involving his claw and her mouth. He went to class and sometimes drank, he experimented with recreational drugs and made a few close friends.

But college was big- far bigger than his home town. People back home might remember him as "the guy with the hand," but at least he could be dependably that, and as soon as most people sized up the basic gist of who you seemed to be, they could get to the deeper, messier business of understanding who you really were. It never quite reached that point now. Every day he walked past people whom he'd never met, for whom it seemed like a waste of time and effort to reveal this abnormal part of himself, since he would never meet them again. Who wanted to be a freak just for the sake of identifying as such? He got to wearing his hoodie more and more frequently.

A cold afternoon in November. The skeletal radiator in his dorm room was puffing up steam at a worrisome pitch that he was used to. Outside his window, campus was shivering with dull frost and the bare rankling fingers of deciduous trees. In the distance he could see the shaggy-sparse jacket of firs creeping up the New England mountains.

His room was in an isolated corner of the 3rd floor of a brutalist student housing complex overlooking the science quad and a portion of the gothic-style freshman housing units. It was a marvelous place in which to recede on cold, silent days of autumn laziness. He was wrapped in such a warm blanket of content that the sudden knock on his door almost threw him off his chair.

Another thing they never told you about having a claw- that you would be forever off-kilter. The tiny neural sensors all over- the ones that registered the outside world to the inside you- were flung down your body in all sorts of subtle asymmetries. Most times it was barely noticeable, like feeling for the minute indentations on a stretch of scoured pan, but put the body under enough sudden stress and you saw how very tenuous your balance truly was.

"That hoodie needs to go soon, bro. It's looking awfully ratty." His hallmate Conrad extended a hand, his left.

"It's comfortable."

"Not to look at."

Conrad strode into the room and landed ass first on his bed. "How you ever get pussy is, frankly, beyond me."

"Fuck you," he laughed.

"Big news from our friends on the fourth floor," Conrad said carelessly. "Some kid is getting expelled on account of bad grades."

"Oh yeah?" he flipped through an old math textbook. "I didn't think that was possible, to be honest. Isn't there a ton of grade inflation?" "I've seen him around. Dude's a freak."

"-You say as you talk to the guy with a claw for a hand."

"Nah, don't take it personally, man. There're people who are different and then there are people who are truly freakish, you know? It's not as if you chose to have a gimpy hand. But acting like a nutjob and snarling at people who walk past you? That's a choice and that makes him a freak."

"You're quite the humanist."

"I'm sure if you saw him you'd recognize him. Hard to miss, really. Just gives off the wrong kind of vibe. Scares off all the girls."

"Not my current forte either," he said into the glum sheen of the book.

"You'll be fine as long you stop wearing that fucking hoodie."

So later that night he pulled on a buttoned down shirt, and when he and Conrad found seats at the bar, he even brought his claw out from the shell of his sleeve and used its nub to trace figure eights on the condensation forming on his beer glass.

"My sister has the same thing," a woman said suddenly. She'd sat down beside him when he wasn't looking.
"Same what?" Defensiveness was a gut reaction.

"Thing with the hand-" she pointed- "what you have."

"Jesus, what a way to start a conversation."

Conrad, on his other side, jabbed him hard in the ribs.

"Well I just wanted to get it out of the way, first. Sorry if I offended you or anything- I mean, I was just stating a fact."

He blinked and coerced his mouth into a smile. He took a sip of his beer, paying extra mind not to leave any traces of foamy mustache. "Ok, well now that it's out of the way, uh, so, what's next?"

In the corner of his eye he saw the flesh-colored outline of Conrad's face sink into his hands.

"What you say next is your name," she smirked.

"Howie."

"Good," she laughed trillingly. "I'm Olivia. Next you offer to buy me a drink- although I think that's a bit old fashioned. Maybe instead you could ask me what I wanted, order it, and then let me pay for it myself."

He nodded. "Ok, sure. So what'll you have?"
"A Coca-Cola, please. Oh, and you forgot to shake my hand when you introduced yourself." She smiled; the bar rang with the clink of glasses, a constant low burble of laughter.

"Right, right, my bad," he said, extending.

"Other hand, please. I'm a righty."

He grunted. "Fine. Pleasure to meet you."

"Same." She took his claw in both of hers and shook firmly, holding it for a few extra beats. Her hands were warm and understanding. Her fingers pressed in and collapsed the space around his barely-there knuckles, feeling around the way a blind person would read braille.

"My sister tells me that it's super annoying when people put a conscious effort into making it seem like not a big deal, as if talking around it makes it any less noticeable."

"Yeah," he said. "That can get annoying."

"And the worst is when people flinch at it, right? Like how it can get so alienating? No one wants to feel as if he has some kind of deformity."

"Your sister has the right idea about all this."

"I was bullshitting, I don't actually have a sister."

Beer went out his nose. The low tint of the bar swam in hazy threads before his eyes.

"Huh?"

"I have this theory, see, that people aren't willing to open up to other people unless they feel as if they're on a level playing field, or they at least have something in common."

"I'm not too sure I follow."

"Well your hand- see?" She picked it up and laughed when he immediately recoiled. "We hate ugly things and we hate them even more when they're attached to us and the worst part of all is that once we address a thing as ugly, there's no way for us to change our minds about it. Even if most other people don't find it ugly."

He was a tiny bit offended but couldn't locate precisely why just yet.

"All I'm saying is that I don't think you would've taken me seriously if I'd just approached you without context."

"How do you know?"

"It's the patriarchy, bro."

"Well then, why did you approach me?"

"That is something I don't know how to answer- claw hand or not."

"Well give it a shot?" he asked, feeling desperate.

"I guess you seemed very spiritual," she giggled, and leaned in.

They say that when you get to college, you have the chance to remake yourself. What they don't say is that there are only a few new versions of you that people will actually accept, no matter where you go to school, no matter where you wind up afterwards.

Mom was always telling me that the majority of people out there are dumbasses. That realizing this made me one of the smart but cursed few, and that's how I ended up here, you know. College. She told me that it was proudest she'd ever been. And then she died- right there on the bed we'd made for her, surrounded by the buckets filled with her sick and the few family members who weren't sick themselves or locked up for selling dope or something.

I won't pretend like that didn't hurt- like I didn't push past the screen door and rush into the dirty, gutted, back of our house and cry into the dried up dandelion stems I was planning to light on fire later that night. Sometimes I thought I could still feel her- I know, I know, it's got Oedipus written all over it, but it's tough when you grow up in the middle of bumblefuck, south of nowhere, and sometimes you feel so alone you have to take the ring and middle fingers of each hand and walk them like a pair of feet, with the pinky and pointer extended as arms, and pretend like you and your two hands are old buddies.

A few days after mom died I landed here. Thought I'd be excited but more than anything I was terrified. You don't quite become aware of your insecurities until you try to approach a pretty girl at a loud party. The only females I ever saw growing up were my mom and my cousins: ugly folk. Muffin-topped, flabby breasted hunchbacks with volcanic acne and overcompensating hair. College was like a conference of pretty girls; it made me wish fairly urgently that my mom were still with me to give me advice, which I realize is extremely pathetic.

What do you talk about when you're a guy like me? Two good shirts, only one with buttons. Never had the money for acne treatment or braces or good haircuts. Same pair of shoes for the better part of a decade. An old hoodie as the only protection against a New England winter more cutting than a knife.

If you were from the middle of some hot, deserted nowhere, where only a portion of your family was literate, where your father was shivved to death in the jail shower for being at the bottom of the hierarchy, where the freedom of your mother's death was the reason why you could attend college at all, you never really got to understand the kinds of campus issues that everyone else got so riled up about- the animal rights and the social justice and the microscopic forms of racial aggression. If you were me, all you wanted was a fucking friend. Preferably someone who could understand that a hungry thing is a hungry thing, and that at the end we're all just hungry, lonely things.

He woke up having to piss like never before, but her cheek was resting on his right bicep, his claw sitting on her waist. There in bed, his bladder set to burst, the evening's events unspooled and rushed in like a high tide of memory- how she'd laughed at the musty old hoodie he'd insisted on putting on because it was freezing, how she'd known better and coaxed the claw from its hiding place, how she'd wrapped her whole hand around it as they giggle-walked back to his place, then coaxed his body from his clothes.

There was a second, more intense kind of sweetness that came with the first recollections of a pleasant moment- a leisurely thickness which gave you purchase to zoom in and savor all its tiny felicities, like how the starlike freckle on her cheek collapsed inward when she smiled and how that lovely, moon-flushed face glowed and sparkled with jouncing stars the whole night long.

Then, if you liked, you could zoom back out and take a deep breath and realize in the warmth of its aftermath that it had truly all happened, that perhaps everything was liable to change starting from this moment on.

He managed to sidle out from under her without eliciting more than a light snore, snatched up his underwear and pants and made it halfway to the bathroom before a violent buzzing suddenly erupted in his pocket. He reached in and felt his phone,

Alert: ARMED GUNMAN ON CAMPUS: Please immediately find shelter. POLICE ARE ON THEIR WAY.

"Holy fuck," he whispered into the empty hall. Conrad's head emerged suddenly from his room.

"Dude-" he said, eyes peeled open with terror, "Dude, get the fuck inside!"

It's been three years and I still haven't found a girlfriend. Not even a regular friend- and you know it's not for lack of trying. I'm not some kind of snob; I don't make an effort to push people away. But I guess when you go to one of these fancy private colleges full of private clubs and invite-only events and buildings that have your parents' names carved onto their transoms, the only way that some people can have social currency is by denying it to others.

The thing about being outside an established group is that you're more than just alienated; you're actively disliked. You can feel it as you walk by everyone else- they avoid you like a swarm of minnows forming the cautionary bubble around a shark. People look at me and they flinch- as if it's my fault that my acne scars never healed, or it's my fault that all my clothes are a few sizes too big, or it's my fault that my nose came in crooked because my pops got me so bad with the wrench one time that not even he could hide it from CPS, or it's my fault that my hair goes back in a ponytail because that's the only way I can cut it, or it's my fault that just- just fuck. Fuck.

People here think that being poor is just the state of poverty, like it's something so simple as the lack of money! No, no, being poor means that your strongest memories of your pops are when he had you ass out and bent forward, the wrench bouncing off the cheeks so hard you could feel it touch the bone and you knew you wouldn't be able to sit for weeks but what you didn't know was why. Being poor is having to sell shit on the sidewalks of the nearest city- laying the soft, mite-filled mittens and scarves that your mother spent her useless waking hours knitting on top of the dirty blue tarp- and watching passerby sneer down at you and say things like, "oh he's from that freak Ewing family from up there in the country," and, "look, you can see the inbreeding in him," and, "I'll be damned if that whole family weren't just a bunch of dirty welfare hicks."

Being my kind of poor means more than beating the odds of getting into a school like this, it means circumventing chance all-fucking-together. No one cares about white trash; it's not in vogue. There's nothing about white trash poverty that can be parlayed into some kind of hip urban cache. There's nothing about being so poor that your parents hate you for your hunger that's inspirational or redeemable. No. If you're my type of poor, you'd best erase it entirely from the you that people see- you have to talk all proper and write well and shower daily and eat with knife and fork. Around here you're allowed to be poor in name only.

"Fuck," he rushed back into the room. She was sitting plumb upright, phone shaking in her hands, eyes protuberant. "Howie," she hissed, "we have to hide."

"I think we'll be fine as long as we stay here in this room, right?"

She put a finger urgently to his lips. "What if he's in this building?"

There was a sharp crack from outside the window; the sound of a small firework popping and fizzling in the cold autumn smoke. Somewhere in the building they heard a shriek.

"Oh shit," she said, making her way to the window, "Oh shit oh shit."

"No-" He lunged and grabbed her forearm with his left hand. "No- you don't want him to see us if he's out there."

"We need to hide, then. We definitely need to hide."

They made their way inside his cramped and sweat-smelling closet, crouching painfully on top of some long-discarded socks, and as their heads brushed against the cluttered clothes hangers and they looked through the forest of his shirts for any sign of intrusion, the dull ache in his stomach became suddenly pronounced. He'd forgotten to piss.

Outside his door, down the hall and up the old stairwell, the puddle of steps echoed. She grabbed his claw and squeezed tight; her palm felt clammy and her fingers desperate. He had inconceivable things on his mind: Last words? Last moments? Funerals? Death? The steps were getting louder. Distant things were getting closer.

"Fuck," she wheezed, squeezing his claw harder. "Fuck, I'm scared."

"It'll be ok," he whispered, although he had no idea whether or not it would be truly ok. Funny, he thought, how even in this life or death situation he was still projecting. In the face of total annihilation he was still trying to make himself to her. The pain in his claw was diverting necessary attention away from his bladder. The steps were getting louder.

And then another crack- like the sound of a giant rubber band snapping in half. She winced beside him and started, very silently, to cry.

"Shh," he said meaninglessly. "Shh, we'll be ok." His knees were bent into each other, his ankles knotted, the pain in his claw was becoming unbearable.

As he thought how, thankfully, the gunman had four whole floors with probably 10 rooms each in which to wreak his havoc. Their chances of getting their brains blown out were relatively low- plus- the individual pops of the gun made him think he wasn't equipped with anything heavier than a semi-automatic. With any luck this was some kind of pinpointed vendetta, not a slaughter.

"Why are the steps so slow?" she whispered. "Do you think he's carrying a bag or something?"

He shook his head.

"How do you know?"

"I don't," he said.

"I just- I just really, really, don't want to die."

And then- the unmistakable clanging of their hallway door opening.

"Oh fuck, oh fuck oh fuck." A wildfire series of explosions; an endless concussion of metallic pangs whizzing outside the door.

He was squinting and squeezing his whole face into as pruny and tight a shape as possible. The sound of all that chaos and hot metal clinking and ricocheting until it was more than sound- it was the smell of smoke and the hot, violent feeling of splintering all around him and in his stomach. His lower stomach. There was a shattering release and a sudden warmth spilling down him.

"Oh my God!" she screamed. "Oh my God, have you been shot? Oh my God help, please!"

Yes, he'd been shot. He was shot. This was it. There was no one nearby to save him. He would bleed out in his closet, next to this girl he'd had a one night stand with. He'd collapse in this bloody, wet heap of his clothes.

But the warmth was cooling rapidly, and he was remarkably clear-headed, despite the shock. The white-hot pain you expected with these kinds of things had yet to settle in.

Now my mother- my mother was an angel but she was also one of those psycho rednecks who had no faith in the government outside of their welfare checks. If my mother knew anything about the kinds of arguments that the people in D.C. were having about guns she would've blown her top and waddled right on over there with her grandfather's ancient sawed-off shotgun, found her way into the chamber where they held the meetings, and pointed it at each of those congress people without pulling the trigger to prove her point. "Thar!" she'd say. "Thar, see?! I git a gun, but I ain't gunna shoot and that's why we don't need none of yer laws!"

My mother, who was ignorant in just about every realm of child-rearing, was prudent about one thing only. Dying in bed, each breath a heaving labor, she pressed a shitty old .22 caliber revolver into my hand and said to me, "for protection," as if she had it in her head that New England was all bears and wilderness. Well right after she did that she caught a violent cough and all around her my cousins and siblings were suddenly scrambling with old pots and pans because this green-brown slime was coming out of her mouth. It was spraying with each cough until it eventually became blood.

You can dress yourself all pretty and act all high

society but I wonder how many people know that when you die, your bowels evacuate. Whatever was churning in there gets released. Every person- rich or poor- dies in a puddle of his own shit. There's a metaphor for you. That'll teach you all to be so fucking snooty.

My mother died on a Tuesday. On a Thursday that same week I took a 14 hour bus ride to school with the gun in my bag. On a Saturday my fresh- man year I showed the gun to as close a person as I'd ever gotten to be my friend, and saw his eyes widen then bulge and his lip tremble, as if he were afraid I'd shoot him right in the face with it or something, before he muttered something about needing to go and scrambled out of my room. On a Wednesday the next week my room was searched by campus police who didn't find shit because I'd hidden it beneath the loose heating grate. On a Friday the next month word had spread across campus that I was some sort of a psycho.

The school started doing all sorts of bullshit to try to kick me out- making me see some lousy cam- pus psychiatrist who barely cared enough to learn my siblings' names, holding bullshit disciplinary hearings, putting me on academic probation. Ap- parently being quiet means you're potentially violent. Same if you wear hoodies and baggy clothes or if you're from a place no one else is from.

On a Thursday last week I was expelled.

And for the first time in an incredibly long time, I thought about my mom. Sloshing there in her wheelchair like a human puddle, many-chinned and half blind. The only thing that stayed nimble through her life were her fingers, always knitting as she hummed some indeterminate melody. I have this nagging feeling that mom would've been disappointed by me- not that her opinion mattered, not that she had any stake in my educa- tion. But on a Friday the week before she died, when she was hardly herself anymore-- just a shapeless, witless, snoring half-corpse-- my mom had asked for me. All my cousins and siblings pushed aside as if I were Moses or something to let me near her and do you know what she said? I was leaning in and smelling the damp sourness of her skin and her slimy halitosis when she said, in barely a whisper, "don't forget your gun."

Campus today feels chilly. Chilly and quiet; good for thinking.

Sometimes I get flashbacks to the moment, but they're blurry and vague, and feeling my way through them is like trying to sprint on hot tar- the details never stay still enough for me to get a proper footing. But the basic jist of it is that he's coming back towards me with a wrench. He's walking all lopsidedly and his fingers are so loose around the thing that it looks liable to drop and clang onto the floor at any moment. I'm confident that I can slip away from him, right through his legs and out the screen door before he can make any contact, but then she's there. She's standing between the two of us in a threadbare slip so I can see her back fat folding over the straps of her old bra and her legs which are basically being colo- nized by liver spots shaking but at least she's standing up.

"Enough," she says. Voice shaking too. Gun wob- bling in her hands. But she breathes in deep and says it again. "Enough."

You expect these moments to culminate in some kind of an explosion. She's gonna shoot, right? But she just held it, shaking, and when he saw the short-lipped barrel pointing straight down the line at him his eyes widened and he backed off. I think that was when Pops realized he couldn't quite fuck around with us anymore. He just turned around and left. A few days later he'd landed him- self in jail, and we never saw him again.

That was what the gun was for her- the last high hill. It was what she was willing to do to get my Pops to lay off. No one else understood what she whispered to me but she and I did.

Campus is cold and my hands are shoved in the front pocket of my hoodie. In my hand is the gun that my mother gave me. The grip is tiny; my pinky finger doesn't even have anything to wrap around. But I squeeze it with all my strength be- cause I miss having a mom who'd blow a guy's brains clean out at point blank range if that's what it took to keep me doing ok. I miss a per- son's eyes smiling at me, letting me know that I can do things. If I squeeze it I can get closer. Squeeze my whole hand into it- because it gets so lonely sometimes.

My hand is a gun. I take it out and observe, turn- ing it, letting the light bend and fracture off its *curves and recesses. I'm walking towards my dorm hall. My hand is a gun. I'm sorry, mom.*

The story was that an isolated, severely unstable third year student who was failing his classes had had a mental breakdown and walked around campus for 45 minutes carrying a fully loaded 0.22 caliber revolver and 12 spare cartridges.

After firing a few warning shots outdoors near the science quad, he'd made his way into his dorm building and climbed the stairs, firing several rounds down the main hallway of each floor. Damage was sparse. Because of a series of warnings from the University Emergency Notification System, all students were in their rooms and no one was harmed.

At 9:45 AM, the perpetrator made his way into his room on the fourth floor of the building and committed suicide.

Hiding in the closet, he'd heard the dull, dragging footsteps recede from the hallway and back up the stairwell. For a few seconds or hours there was no noise save for the occasional shifting rattle of their bodies or the light patter whenever one of them had to adjust a foot in the wetness. Then a loud crack, which made them both shutter.

Some time later someone came pounding at their door- "Campus police! It's alright, you're safe."

Neither of them mentioned that he'd pissed himself.

Back in the hallway he saw Conrad staring down at the floor. He walked up closer before noticing the tear marks on his shirt.

"Hey-" a claw on his shoulder.

"Dude, did you not recognize him?" Conrad looked up, red around the eyes, snot flowing.

"I didn't see him."

"He was the one from the 4th floor I was telling you about. The one who got- who was- who got-" before he trailed off and collapsed against the wall.

He asked her to dinner a few weeks later.

"How've you been holding up?"

"Fine," she said.

The dining hall was serving pork chops; he managed to clip his knife securely between his thumb and the first nub of his right claw while steadying the fork in his left hand. He noticed her eyes avoiding it.

"Everything alright?"

"I was squeezing your hand so hard that morning."

"Oh, it's alright."

"I'm sorry for doing that. I'm sorry that on top of all the other shit that was happening you had to deal with how hard I was squeezing your hand."

"Hey-" he put down the knife and made for her shoulder but she recoiled.

"I- I can't stop thinking about your hand. I'm sorry," her eyes were watering, her mouth had fallen into a grimace.

"My hand? This one?" he lifted his claw and saw her flinch.

"I'm sorry, it just- I can't stop associating it with what happened. And you know I'm not blaming you- like I know you can't physically change your hand, but, I just can't stop connecting you and it with the whole situation and I'm just so sorry."

He nodded and said it was ok. They made formal and awkward goodbyes.

Then put on his hoodie, fell into the cold, brittle evening, and walked back to him room.

About the Author:

Vincent Yu is an employee at W.W. Norton and a reader/copy editor at a small press called 7.13 Books. He graduated from Yale University, where he was a staff member of the Yale Literary Magazine. He is working on a novel manuscript.

BEFORE THE DINER

by Tim Urban

Driving down the interstate with his Uncle Tucker behind the wheel, Mathew stewed over how he was going to get back at that bully Sam Milton. As soon as his uncle pulled into the driveway, he'd jump out of the truck and rush across that yard, moving with the surety of a cop who was about to make an arrest. He'd push through the front door with ease. He'd find Sam sitting at the kitchen table. That bully's eyes would grow wide, the way eyes of good-for-nothings always go wide in the movies, and he would drag him out of his seat and rough him up and force him to beg for mercy. Mathew was certain of this.

They were riding in an old Ford F-150 that had a bum muffler, which made the pickup whir like a go-cart, announcing itself wherever it went. Uncle Tucker's truck. It was a stereotype straight out of a Hollywood picture: American flags flapping from the roof, large monster truck tires, and blue and white decals across the sides. He knew Tucker wasn't much of a watcher of Hollywood films, but if he was, Mathew felt certain that he wouldn't have much cared about how people perceived the red paint peeling off his hood, or how they shook their heads at the confederate flag threaded through his front grille, and he sure as shit would-n't have cared about whether or not a bunch of strangers approved of the decal in the back window with the boy pissing on the word 'Chevy'.

Conversely, Mathew loved and watched many Hollywood pictures. Although he was only eleven, he'd seen all the old silver screen films: The Big Sleep, Double Indemnity, and The Big Heat. He loved the old gritty quality they shared. Modern blockbusters were too polished, too predictable.

The old ones were the originals, and unlike the new movies, where he knew the actors' names, he didn't know the names of the men who played the old detectives. He only knew their characters. It made them somehow more real.

He loved the hardline detectives who were fierce and intimidating because he wanted to appear as one himself, but the truth was he was a straggly, awkward boy who was anything but intimidating. Still, he felt reassured of his abilities when he thought of himself as being in line with Sam Spade in The Maltese Falcon. Sam Spade wouldn't be afraid of punching out a bully. Neither would Mathew.

Sitting inside Uncle Tucker's pickup, he couldn't help but feel unique, in a league of his own, an outsider, someone who was observant because he wasn't part of the normal, everyday routines. Like this truck, he was meant to stand out. He loved that the high wheels made them hover above the passing cars on the freeway, giving them a presence. He thought the loud roar must be daunting to strangers, and for a boy who tried to overcompensate and hide his own fear of the world, being seen as a threat, even if he wasn't one, was all that counted.

The summer heat clung to his skin in the same way that dust sticks to sweat.

He glared at his reflection in the side mirror. He wished he had a toothpick so he could flip it over in his mouth. His face needed to be serious. He forced himself to scowl deeper, and he thought he looked intense, a man ready for a fight. His eyes lingered on his reflection for a brief moment before he glanced out at the green fields and the blue sky converging into the horizon.

The sun crested above the skyline, showing half its face, across the expanse of farms that lay in every direction. They were riding through the land of cornfields, hay, and John Deere.

Like all good detectives that have brains but lack the means, he had come up with a plan. He'd use Tucker to get to Sam. After all, his uncle had a truck. It was only natural he'd ask for a ride. And since, as was their wont every Saturday, the two went to Maud's diner for breakfast, Mathew thought he could get to Sam by saying he wanted to take a friend with them. This was unusual, seeing as he never mentioned any friends to his uncle, but nonetheless the older man had been happy to oblige. Tucker was a sucker for an extra set of ears. A real storyteller.

Even with the windows down, the inside of the truck smelled like diesel and stale cigarette butts. In between the seats, stacks of discarded fast food bags, old scratch tickets, and Styrofoam cups were aiming to make a mountain, fluttering slightly.

"Sure is looking forward to a big breakfast," said Tucker.

"Yeah."

"How long you known this friends of yers?"

"Long enough."

"It's sure nice to see you gettin' on with fellas yer age."

Mathew rolled his eyes. Outside, three metal silos stood beside an old red barn.

He leaned against the door and rested the side of his face on his fist. He winced as he accidentally brushed the shiner. The bruise burned. The raw skin throbbed with its own pulse.

"You's okay?"

"I'm fine."

"You sure is quiet this morning."

"So?"

"Bit of an attitude to boot."

"I'm fine."

"So, mind tellin' me where you got that shiner?"

"Fell off the monkey bars during recess," said Mathew.

"Sure must have been a nasty fall," said Tucker.

"It was nothin'."

He had been walking by himself toward the trees that were on the fringe of the baseball field, where he usually sat during recess, seeing as he didn't have many friends. Sam had run up behind him and sucker punched him. He'd been caught off balance, moving between steps, when the strike had come. It sent him flailing to the ground. Sam spat at him and told him he'd stay down if he knew what was good for him. Mathew's fear flooded his belly and throat. He heard Sam yell "This faggot can't even take a good punch" to his chuckling group of friends.

From the ground, he had watched the group walk away, and a burning hate mixed with shame covered him as if it were his skin. Now Mathew imagined laying a wallop on Sam's head and watching the boy's body crumble in on itself. He envisioned pouncing on Sam, scratching at the boy's eyes, squeezing his thin throat, and watching him cry and plea for mercy.

With each imagining, the punishment grew worse.

He wondered if his uncle could read his thoughts because he was never one for asking too many questions. He was aloof. Interrogation wasn't Tucker's style. Frankly, he was the type of man who could go on for hours without realizing you hadn't said a word. All these questions skewed Mathew's focus. He just wanted silence, a bit of quiet, before this, his most important confrontation.

In truth, Mathew believed that his uncle was nothing more than a country hick who made everyone else down in Arkansas look bad with his yellowed teeth, stubbly face, and balding head. The southern accent Tucker had picked up during his time in Tennessee didn't help his case. The long drawl, the minced words, all of it made him seem like an inferior being, at least to Mathew. The dictionary definition of white trash. If anyone could have a fast one pulled over them, Mathew thought, it was Uncle Tucker. So why the hell was he asking so many damn questions?

"What's yer friend's name again?" said Tucker, breaking Mathew's thoughts.

"Sam. And he's not my friend."

"Then why the hell we pickin' him up? My stomach's roarin'."

"Don't worry about it."

"You's up to no good, Matty. I cain see as much."

"I'm fine."

"I thank I'll just go to the diner. I ain't about to wait to be seated just to pick up a friend who you say's ain't yer friend now."

"No!"

"Then you come and fess up to why we be goin' out here."

"I just wanna lay out this son of a bitch. That's all. Okay?" said Mathew.

"That was easy. Didn't expect you to cave so soon," said Tucker, glancing at the stern faced boy beside him. "You ain't gonna be much of a fighter you cain't even keep your damned mouth shut fer twenty minutes to hold in a secret."

"That's bullshit."

"Whooey, you got quite the mouth, but I'd gather you got a bark that's worst than yer bite."

"You don't know nothin'."

"That's right. I'm just dumb Uncle Tuck. I'm just a crazed old fella who don't know his damn ass from his elbow, right?"

Mathew grimaced at the dashboard, noting the dust that had accumulated in the vents.

"So, you fixin' to be a big gun now, huh? Nice to know my brother's boy's a fighter." Tucker tore through a half-eaten Slim Jim that had been sitting in a cupholder. "That 'splains that sorry bruise on yer face. Take it this boy Sam's the—"

"Just drop me off?"

"Oh, don't you worry. I aim to," said Tucker, grinning with glistening brown chunks wedged in between his teeth. "Don't take me for one who

wants to miss a show. Not ev'ry day I get to see my brother's boy make an ass outta hisself."

"You don't know nothin'."

"You's right. I don't know nothin'. However, I believe I know somethin'."

"He started it. It wasn't my fault," said Mathew, his jaw jutting out as he spoke. "I'm just ending it."

"How 'bout you end it over a set of flapjacks 'stead of rollin' around like a monkey and pretendin' to be man when you ain't."

Mathew's hand was on the door handle. "Just drop me off," he said.

"No, sirree. You see, I's the adult, 'n I say what goes. Understood?"

The roar of the muffler wedged between them. They passed a blue sign with gas station logos on it. Mathew's eyes began to water from looking into the wind.

"So I take it that you been gettin' bullied and such," a long pause as Tucker licked grease from his fingers, "but it'll pass."

In the side mirror, the cracked asphalt receded behind them.

"You know, I used to be a bit of a hothead myself," said Tucker. "Now, I know that's hard to understand, me bein' so genteel," he stretched out the last syllable as if he were pulling it like a fish on a line, drawing it out some, "but I was, was more a hot head than yer old pops is now. You know what changed?"

Mathew didn't answer, so Tucker whacked him upside the head.

"Boy, I's talkin' here."

"I don't know," said Mathew, rubbing the back of his skull, "What?"

"How nice of you to ask," said Tucker. "When I was a young'un, not much older than you is, I beat up on a boy. Kid was a real shit fire at school. Cornered him in the school bathroom because, ya see, a bully, he ain't much of anything you get him alone. I beat his face like I was fixin' to kill him. And you know where it got me?"

"No. Where?"

"Juvey. Like a goddamn criminal. Ya see, you fixin' for a fight while yer angry and you go'n do somethin' stupid. Take it from me."

Tucker leaned back in his seat, one hand stretched out on the steering wheel, as if he'd said something wise and the matter was settled. That was that.

In the distance, Maud's diner was fast approaching. Faintly, beyond that, there was a group of ranches. Sam's neighborhood.

"You tell yer pa about what you's was aiming to do?"

"Yeah."

"I find that hard to believe."

"You aimin' to turn preacher?"

"Boy, I'm a right mind to smack you upside the head again you give me lip."

"Sorry," said Mathew, using his shirt sleeve to the wipe sweat off his forehead.

"You aimin' to do the work of a man, yet you thank you cain act like a child right now. Let me get you in on a secret, you ain't never goin' to feel better after takin' a revenge.'

"You might not, but I will."

"You thank you hate him right?"

"I know I hate him."

"You ain't even old 'nuff to know the true hate. Child's hate ain't nothin' close to real hate."

"How do you know? You ain't me. You don't know what I'm feeling, if it's real or not. All you got is your opinion."

"I got an opinion backed by forty years' experience you lil' jackass. You got one that's barely even left the womb."

Stupid Tucker. Acting all wise. What the hell did he know? He wasn't no more than a goddamn gas station clerk who hadn't made it past the tenth grade.

Adults thought they knew everything.

They thought their experience was the only experience.

Mathew felt certain he'd prove him wrong, he'd show him how he could beat Sam's ass, and he'd earn respect for once.

He chewed at the skin on his lower lip.

They passed Maud's diner. The lot was full of cars, and the large sign that rose up high glowed neon red. There were families walking across the parking lot. The diner was small with a silver glistening frame and red trim. He saw the upper halves of people sitting at tables through the windows. He envisioned the familiar faces inside. Men and women as old as they come who hadn't missed a weekend at Maud's for as long as they could remember. The booths and the bar and the smell of coffee roasting. He thought of drenching his pancakes in thick blueberry syrup and his stomach rumbled.

"Sure you don't just want to make the day simple, go eat, start it right with eggs and bacon? My stomach's fixin' for a fine meal right 'bout now."

"You can. I'll walk the rest of the way."

"You sure is stubborn," said Tucker, scratching his forehead, which was dripping with sweat. "Guess we can do it after I watch you make a fool of yer'self."

"I won't make a fool of myself. I'm in control."

"Boy, if you was in control you'd see how stupid you was to wake up early on a Saturday to go beat up some kid who ain't goin' to amount to the shit on the back of yer boot. You smart in school, but you dumb as hell in life sometimes."

"Pull over."

"Shut up. You's one dumb sonova—"

Tucker took a deep breath, his hands had tightened on the steering wheel, the knuckles grown white. Seeing Tucker hold back anger made Mathew's guts coil. He'd never seen his uncle lose his temper before. He'd only heard stories.

"Sorry fer yellin'," said Tucker, licking his lips as if he'd tasted something nasty. "But if you thank yer man enough to beat a boy up just cause he beat you up, then you cain man up and listen to what I got to say. You's convinced in this matter, so I's going to sit in here while you go out and do it on your own. You so grown up then you cain stand on yer own two legs and act the fool."

The road forked.

"Which way?"

"Left."

Tucker turned down a narrow side road. Up ahead, Mathew could see the cluster of ranches. The homes were dilapidated and in ill repair. There were crooked and bent wire fences in some of the backyards with dogs sitting and looking out at the world through metal wiring. A few barked as the engine revved.

"Which one is it?"

"There," said Mathew, knowing it based on the image that he'd seen on the computer after doing a search for Sam's address online. It had been surprisingly easy.

"The grey one?"

"Yeah." Tickle of self-doubt beginning to swell in his chest.

A section of the roof was covered with blue tarp, the front lawn was wild and long, patchy and dead in certain spots, and the bushes had been trimmed down to stubs.

Tucker parked in front of the house. He turned his key and the loud boom of the muffler ceased. The once vibrating pickup was still. The neighborhood was quiet except for the dogs' barking. Mathew looked out at the yard, dust and dead grass and a makeshift window made from opaque plastic stared back at him, and a tinge of fear shot down to his rectum. The stagnant heat burned his nostrils. His hand lingered on the door handle, and he could hear his own heartbeat tapping in his ears.

"What you sittin' around for, tough guy? I's aiming to see the show, and I's hoping it would be starting A-S-A-P," said Tucker. "Or we havin' second thoughts?"

Mathew opened the door and slammed it shut. He walked in front of the old Ford and ignored Tucker, whom he could see from his peripheral, and focused on the house in front of him. A few paces away he heard someone yelling from inside. The voice was loud and shrill and oozing with cuss words.

At the front door, his hand was up and ready to knock, but he stood frozen. His head swam as if it

was drowning. Was he really about to go through with this? Through the screen door, he could see the dark foyer that led to a hallway. He glanced behind him at his uncle's red truck. Right now, he could be eating pancakes drizzled in that blueberry syrup he so loved.

He was about to turn back, knowing this was an insane idea as soon as it became real, when the front door opened and a woman stood before him in her sweats.

"Who the hell are you?" she said, smacking down her pack of smokes. She was an obese woman who wore a tight t-shirt that displayed all her folds. Her hair was wet and wiry, stretching down past her ample chest and resting on the crown of her gut. She smelled like a vanilla lavender perfume. Her body hovered over Mathew, and he grew small in her presence.

The wind caught his blonde hair, and he wished it would sweep him away.

"What you on my property for?" she said before sucking the flame through her smoke.

"I—"

"Spit it out,' she exhaled.

"I'm a friend of Sam's."

"Shit balls. I didn't know my stupid boy had any friends."

When she spoke, her voice sounded like golf balls were stuck in the back of her throat. Her face contorted, constricting as if it were in pain, as she winced past Mathew at the truck sitting in front of her house.

"Who's that there? Your daddy?"

"That's my uncle."

"Attractive fellow," she said, smiling and waving at Tucker, who, for his part, returned the gesture.

"Sam and I got a project to do for school. I figured we could go out to breakfast first."

"Sam didn't mention anyone stopping by," she said.

"Oh, he doesn't know. I figured I'd, uh, surprise him."

The deception twisted through his throat strained

and weak. She eyed him with something like suspicion. His face turned hot.

"Aren't you two just a bunch a queers," she said, laughing, then coughing.

He wanted to run back to the car and tell Tucker to step on it. He didn't know how those detectives in the movies managed to hold it together as they raided a drug den or got caught in a shootout.

"You should see your face," said the woman, throwing down her half-smoked cigarette onto the front steps and stomping out the flame. "Well alright, don't just stand there. Come in and I'll go get that worthless piece of ass I call my son."

Mathew looked back. Tucker waved for him to go on. He wished his uncle would stop smiling, he knew it was mockery, he knew Tucker was thinking "I told you so." He hadn't expected it to go this way. He'd been so certain he wanted payback, but he suddenly wished he was sitting at the diner listening to one of Tucker's stories about his time in boot camp before he was discharged from the service. He yearned to hear him talking about all the characters he'd been with in those days. He didn't care if he had to listen to him spew pure bullshit, like the time when they were at a cookout and Tucker was telling a group of people that he'd seen Bush in Little Rock before the war and had actually stopped to talk with the man. Anything, as long as he was away from her, would suffice. He was even willing to sit through tales of Tucker's UFO sightings for the nth time. Really, anything at all would do.

"You coming?" said the woman, standing in the hallway.

The inside of the house smelled of stale Cheetos and the floor was covered in dirt and discarded laundry. Pictures on the wall hung crooked. One of them looked like a skinnier version of the woman. He eased forward, slow like a detective on the scene of a crime, and felt a chip crackle beneath his shoes. The crunch nearly made him jump. The TV was loud, coming from the living room. To his left, the dining room was swept in darkness, everything in it stared back at him like a ghost, dark figures covered in dust and hidden from light by the drawn curtains. He felt like spider legs were crawling on up his spine.

"Sam, get your fucking ass out here before I—"

As soon as heard her swear, he fled. It felt like a shotgun was aimed level at his back and he couldn't run fast enough. The truck seemed to stretch farther away as his legs quickened.

He lunged into the old Ford and slammed the door shut. Once inside, he hunched down and peered over the armrest. Sam's front door swung in the wind. For a moment, Mathew felt as if he were completely alone in the world.

Then Tucker chuckled.

"Your ass shot out that front door faster than a man who has just been caught banging the sheriff's daughter by none other than the sheriff hisself," said Tucker, twisting the key in the ignition.

"Leave me alone."

"What's a matter big man? Thought you was about to lay a whoopin' on someone."

Mathew felt the tears well up under his eyes. The back of his throat was raw, and he knew that if he talked he'd start crying. Regardless, a tear escaped against his better judgment. Tucker's face softened with pity. He squeezed his nephew's shoulder, his grip was strong but reassuring.

"Hell, let's get out of here before that pleasant woman moseys our way."

Tucker pulled down on the gear shifter and made a jerky three point turn. Mathew's chest felt like it was about to explode while he anticipated seeing that woman prance outside. Sure enough, the front door stopped swinging and two figures emerged in the entranceway. Mathew's head was still level with the armrest, so he could just barely see out the window. The truck sped away, but he remained hunched down. He held his breath.

"Sit up. They cain't see you now," said Tucker.

Mathew exhaled. Glancing out the back window, he saw the large woman holding Sam by the collar of his shirt while they drove off. He'd avoided the shootout, and he was fleeing in this, his getaway car, without detection. No one from school would have an inkling as to what he'd done. His peers would never glean that he'd had the balls to show up at Sam's house, and they'd never know that when things got too real he'd tucked tail and run.

An acrid queasiness settled in his gut.

When Sam's neighborhood was far behind, he turned around and looked at Tucker, waiting for the gloating, the mockery, and the air of superiority, but his uncle kept his peace. All Tucker did was glance over and arch an eyebrow. The sound of the muffler's roar swelled between them. Their eyes met. Mathew wiped sweat from his face, and he cleared his throat, as if he were attempting speech.

"Don't worry about it," said Tucker, slapping his shoulder. "I'd rather get breakfast too."

About the Author:

Timothy Urban holds a B.A. in Writing, Editing, and Publishing from Emmanuel College and an M.A. in English from Bridgewater State University. His work has appeared in Wising Up Press's anthology View from the Bed; View from the Bedside, The Smoking Poet, and The Bridge: A Journal of Fine Arts. He currently works and resides in Taunton, Massachusetts.

FORREST HILLS

by John Tavares

After Ollie served nearly a full sentence, officials decided to release him from the juvenile detention facility early. They shortened his detention term after he helped administer First Aid to a fellow inmate who suffered an epileptic seizure. Then, when someone nearly beat his epileptic friend to death, he intervened and made a ruckus until guards could no longer look the other way and transported his injured body to the infirmary. Either way, Ollie became sidetracked by his own desire to set life and past wrongs right.

In his plaid shirt, cargo pants, and scuffed canvas running shoes, he took a nature trail for cyclists and joggers to the park near the detention facility. He found the bayonet with its sheath where he stashed it in a hole in the sand and soil at the base of a culvert. He stuffed the sheathed bayonet in the pocket of his cargo pants, near his thigh, which had grown muscle from exercise routines and fitness training, part of a self-improvement regimen he followed rigorously in prison. All he needed now was a bandanna, but he decided to skip that detail because he thought then he would look suspicious.

Gazing through the curtained window inside his former school principal's house, he stepped through rose bushes growing wildly beside the cracked concrete stairs. Having already rung the doorbell on his Forest Hills house several times, he knocked persistently with the tarnished brass knocker. His former principal shuffled on his bare stocking feet to the inside of the door, where he gazed intently through a peephole. Unshaven, gaunt, he carried a glass of Madeira in his hand and at first refused to answer the brass knocker on the door.

"Whoever is at the door—go away."

When Ollie persisted in knocking, Vermilion relented. He grudgingly stepped forward to answer the door, stumbling through a pile of unopened envelopes, bills, invoices, receipts, bank and trust company statements, subscription magazines, and flyers from high-priced shops, boutiques, and realtors. Vermilion indifferently allowed the mail, fallen beneath the letter slot, to accumulate over the past few weeks. He did not expected to meet Ollie face-to-face—a legacy of his past, a youth a portion of his age, who looked worn, stressed, a former student at his school, where he was formerly principal in his hometown. He saw his former principal's look had not changed drastically: his physical appearance was similar, although he aged less than gracefully. He still had that frozen cheek, which caused him to grimace and look peculiar when he spoke. Depending upon whom you spoke, the facial paralysis came from Bell's palsy or from flying in bombers in the cold thin air associated with the high altitude flying during combat missions, nighttime raids during the Allied strategic bombing offensive of the latter part of the Second World War.

Vermilion appeared to be neglecting his appearance and physical condition; his clothes looked rumpled and shabbier. He looked as if he had given up to nature, surrendered to aging, as if he had apathetically retired—not just from work, but life—everything. Leaner, he had the same amount of thick hair—now tousled, white, whereas in the past it was neatly combed. Dried salvia encrusted the corners of his mouth and his chapped lips and flakes of dandruff speckled his shoulders. The only item lacking was the fancy smoking pipe, with swirls of bluish-white smoke, and the aroma of pipe tobacco. Still, Mr. Vermilion aged considerably, with more fine wrinkles furrowing his face and lining his brow. To school pupils, he might have looked as intimidating as the first day they met him in the school gymnasium.

Now, he was unafraid when he should have felt the deep chill of fear, since the authority figure was poison to him. Before Vermilion could slam the door shut, Ollie rammed his knee between the door and doorway. The former pupil pushed his principal further inside the house.

"I told you never to call again," Vermilion said in his polished, precise voice. "No phone calls, no letters, no visits, nothing. So get out." Ollie pushed him backwards into the hallway of the mansion-like house. Quavering, shaking, Vermilion demanded, "What are you doing here?"

Ollie started to communicate in American Sign Language, but his former principal became angry. He complained they went over this a thousand times before and insisted he talk, speak. He knew he could talk well and his loud voice and guttural sounds did not bother him, so Ollie started to speak, which made him more agitated and nervous. Ollie figured he should have known then his former principal was ultimately in control, just as he was years ago.

"What were you doing to me years ago?" Ollie countered.

"Get out of my house immediately."

"'Don't be bold.'" Ollie tried to mock him, crudely trying to mimic the voice he used on him so many past times. "That's what you always told me when I was sent to your office because I did something wrong. 'Don't be bold.'"

"Get out of my house or I'll call the police immediately."

Upset, agitated, his speech barely comprehensible, he warned: if he called the police, he would have to do him serious harm. Thinking he needed to remind Vermilion who was in control, he slipped the bayonet knife from the leather sheath

he attached to the thigh of his cargo pants and made a dramatic show of the blade. He almost felt like lecturing him on the past of the venerable object, but he was almost certain he was familiar with its history. He was a bit surprised he could detect no sign of recognition when he pulled the bayonet and flashed it in his face. Ambrose Vermilion gasped and backed away from him, terrified, although lately almost any unexpected knock, snap, footstep, or noise startled him, inciting considerable fear and anxiety.

"Look, what I did to you a few years ago was wrong and I paid the price," Vermilion said, calm, rational. "That's no reason to come to my house and terrorize me. Now that business is over. Please just leave me alone."

Upset, angry, stuttering severely, he was barely coherent. Ambrose Vermilion normally had no patience for anyone who couldn't communicate clearly according to his dictums. As Ollie held the bayonet, the principal did listen to him, although several times he raised his brow in dismay, disgust at Ollie's speech, but Ollie realized however he communicated his former principal's attitude of disgust and disdain would remain the same.

"Business? That's what you call it? You've completely ruined my life, made a mess of it."

Because of him, Ollie said, he wasn't able to finish high school, didn't trust anybody, and couldn't love anybody now.

"Look, it's over with. Leave me alone." Vermilion ran down the hallway to the telephone, mounted on an end table, which he programmed to dial automatically the nearest Toronto police precinct at the push of a button. Still, Ollie snatched the receiver from his hand and slammed the telephone down.

"After what you did, you'd have a lot of nerve calling the police," Ollie said. Ollie wrapped his hand around the loose telephone cord, wound it roughly, and ripped the plug from connector in the wall.

"Look, what do you want? Get out of my house. You've no business being here."

"You had no business messing around with my life when I was young."

"But that's over now, man, get on with your life."

"How can I? You've destroyed my life.

"I didn't destroy your life. Now quit acting like a victim and get out of here."

"You destroyed my life, and now I'm here to destroy yours."

Ollie lunged at him with the formidable bayonet, the blade flashing in the dim interior light of ornate dusty chandeliers. Vermilion screamed and backed away, stumbling over the worn malodourous carpet, shouting for help, screaming bloody murder. Begging, pleading for mercy, he scrambled to his feet and started running up the carpeted stairway. Ollie easily chased him upstairs and down the hallway, while he shouted and protested. With a lull, Vermilion surmised he derived a certain perverse delight from terrorizing him.

"That happened years ago!" Vermilion screamed. "Now let me get on with my life!"

Ollie thought his former principal sounded like the crusty retired woman who worked as a volunteer in the school library. Whenever he visited the library, the woman hassled him, tolerating not the slightest transgression, giving him no breaks on overdue books, books damp from rainfall or stained from accidents, coffee or hot chocolate spills, rejecting his requests for books through interlibrary loans. She did little to conceal her revulsion with his lisp and stutter, or guttural voice, and permitted absolutely no noise or sounds from him. Whenever she saw him signing in American Sign Language in the library, she cracked down on him mercilessly, saying he was distracting other students, expelling him from the library, hoarsely shouting to shut up, ordering him to sit elsewhere, or at a study carrel near the back or the emergency exits, or even sending him to the principal's office. The only word in American Sign Language sign she knew: NO, which she made whilst shaking her head, clasping two fingers and her thumb together. Ollie loomed over Ambrose Vermilion on the staircase to the third floor. Breathing hoarsely, he reeled backwards as the bayonet blade approached his throat. When he feared he would plunge the point deeper into the loose flesh of his neck, he eased up and pulled back.

"So, Mister Vermilion, what have you been doing these past few years?"

Vermilion stumbled backwards, collapsed on the stairway in sheer exhaustion and resignation, and started sobbing. He cried while he brought up his arms and flung them backwards. The image of his former principal breaking down reminded him of World War Two photographs from the lavishly illustrated history books series Ollie loved to read in the school library, showing the aftermath of an intense, fiery, destructive battle. He specifically remembered a picture showing a Russian mother, flailing her arms upwards, grieving the loss of her soldier son during the siege of Stalingrad. When he was sent to the principal's office, he sometimes avoided any meetings or confrontations by heading straight to the library. The principal usually knew exactly where he could find Ollie, though. In the school library, he spent plenty of time perusing oversized photojournalism books and history volumes, particularly on World War Two, the Korean War, and Viet Nam War years, instead of working on his school assignments. He leaned against the wall and watched with curiosity, stroking his chin, which had grown peach fuzz and pimply—from the starchy foods, he guessed—in the detention facility. The outpouring of emotion from his usually cold and reserved principal, with his privileged upbringing, surprised him. He remembered him for his calm, reserved demeanour and painstakingly correct speech. Yes, his principal always showed a veneer of civility and polish of gentility, even when he abused Ollie. This outburst of strong emotion Ollie would have normally expected more from his mother or father than from this sham paragon of Victorian morals and virtue.

"I've paid the price!" Vermilion cried repeatedly. "My life is still in ruins. It's over. It's over."

"Your life is in ruins?" Barely able to mouth the words, Ollie stammered he wasn't able to finish school and wasn't able to love anyone because of him.

"That's because you're still too young. Give it up. Give it time, boy."

"I—I h-h-haven't b-been a-able to—to trust any-b -b-body."

"But is that my fault?" Vermilion bellowed.

"Y-y-yes, it—it i-is," Ollie spat. Although he realized the more potent weapon with his former principal were words, he stepped towards him, ready to strike him with my fists. "Y-y-you've s-screwed up—up—up m-my l-life t-t-totally." He decided to reveal he had been in jail, a facility for young offenders.

"You're merely using me as an excuse for your failures and shortcomings."

Ollie swung his open hand, slapping him on his drooping cheek and Vermilion started sobbing again. Wiping away his tears and blowing his nose, he managed to find some coherence to speak again. "You're life has been ruined? Well, my career was destroyed."

Ollie looked around the hallway at the comfort and luxury of the home, the ornate decor, the plush carpets, the rich, densely woven tapestries, fascinated by the high quality reproductions of classic paintings, Renaissance depictions of boys and young men, with names like Holy Family, Ganymede Rolling a Hoop, and Prince Carlos, and fancy, carved frames. The stuffed deer heads and moose heads, the mounted walleye, northern pike, and rainbow trout, and other species of Ontario freshwater fishes, and the aged photographs of hunters and anglers seemed tacking and out of place, alongside the fine art reproductions, and reminded Ollie of his hometown. He commented it certainly looked as if he had done well enough for himself; certainly, he did not appear to have financial worries. Vermilion felt he owed him an explanation: "This was the house of my grandfather, who owned the gold mine near Beaverbrook, which you are too young to remember, since it closed before you were born. It's part of an inheritance, my legacy, from which I have derived my income." He narrated additional family history, but Ollie thought the elderly man pretentious and conceited, thinking his white robber baron ancestors owned and operated the bushes, the mines and forests, around his hometown. Then, distracted, Ollie asked himself what he was doing in this man's house and felt his misery knew no end. This old man, a figure who exercised authority and control over him in what seemed like an entirely different life altogether, was provoking him in ways neither understood. If

he was smart, he would walk away before his mood and impulses, ugly and vengeful, turned into even more awful actions, but he was acting on sheer, raw emotion. Neither of them, he realized afterwards, was behaving intelligently and rationally. Ollie raised his steel-toed work boot, which he wore harvesting the vegetable crops, mainly potatoes, onions, and beets, growing on the grounds of the minimum-security detention facility, thinking he could slam the heel down and smash his skull. Instead, he lightly pressed the grooved soles of the heavy-duty boots against the side of his face. He even gestured, as if about to strike him with his fist, but then he scowled and pushed him away at the shoulder with his boot. He left Vermilion cowering on the stairs and went downstairs.

Ollie wandered around on the first floor restlessly, taking an impromptu tour of the home. He snacked on some cheese and overripe grapes in the kitchen and then made himself comfortable in the old man's study, looking at some fine books, leather-bound classics. Eventually, he noticed his high-fidelity stereo system and searched through the music collection. He found a Mozart compact disk and slipped the symphony recording into the CD player. Then he returned to the kitchen, where he made himself a sandwich, using the leftover salmon salad Ambrose Vermilion purchased earlier at a midtown deli. With a sandwich in one hand, he sat down in a comfortable chair. After he found a pen and paper on the coffee table, he bit into the whole wheat bread, and, more out of instinct, started writing notes about his experiences in the correctional facility for young offenders. Meanwhile, Vermilion sat slumped at the bottom of the stairwell, and, assuming they shared a love of classical music, thought hope still existed.

Later that evening, after being forced to cook supper, Vermilion tried to leave the house. He intended to escape in his luxury convertible sedan, which he planned to race across the city to his sister's house. Wiping the sweat from his brow and the crumbs and rich icing from the corners of his mouth with a silk napkin, Ollie looked up from devouring a thick slice of chocolate cake, creamy with icing, which had gone crusty and stale, which Vermilion picked up earlier in the week at an Eglinton Avenue bakery. He spotted Vermilion stumbling across his front lawn in his soiled, smelly, ill-fitting socks. Ollie burst from the house and balcony and chased him across the landscaped grounds. He dragged Vermilion, yelling and cursing, spitting and dribbling salvia down the corner of his mouth, back into the house.

"Get out of my house!" Vermillion protested. "Leave me alone!"

"You never left me alone. Why should I?"

"What do you want? Look, if it's money, I'll give it to you."

Breathing hard, Vermilion trotted over to a desk in his study and opened a drawer, pulling out a chequebook from a fine leather-bound wallet. Vermillion started to write out a cheque, muttering, "Pay to the order of Oliver Eagleton," writing his name on the recipient line, saying, "Just name an amount, and I'll give you your compensation, fair and square."

Ollie seized the cheque he drafted and the pad of blank cheques out of his hands and ripped and tore the bank note into shreds. Although he had little money, he decided the passion that drove his vengeance would be spoiled and his integrity would be damaged if he accepted money. His integrity would not be harmed if he kept the leather wallet, he decided; he had little money and his own wallet, assuming he could find it, was so worn out and torn he needed a new one. As the Friday turned into Saturday and the morning turned into afternoon, Ollie continued to refuse to allow Ambrose Vermilion to leave the house on any errands. He did not even allow him to shop for groceries, fresh fruit or vegetables, or refill his prescriptions for high blood pressure medication and sleeping pills at the drugstore. He would not even permit him a walk to the corner for a newspaper from the vending machine. Reminding him they had a few scores to settle, he insisted they stay at home. He sat in a chair at the kitchen table, rolling his own cigarettes from papers and a small pouch of tobacco. He picked up the terrible habit of smoking in the detention facility. Like other young offenders, he rolled his own cigarettes to save money.

Ollie looked worried, troubled, preoccupied, lost in thought. Sometimes he made notes in a wad of three-hole ruled paper he folded and stored in the pocket of his plaid shirt. After staying awake without even a nap for over a day, he fell asleep in his chair, reading a book. Vermilion hurried to his bedroom, but, when he desperately checked, listening intently through the telephone extension with faint hope, he discovered the phone still dead. Gasping and grunting, he reached underneath his bed and grabbed a .303 Lee Enfield rifle, a souvenir, an heirloom in the family since the end of the Second World War. He relied on the rifle for a greater sense of security. He earlier loaded the vintage British army rifle with brand new .303 cartridges and started keeping the gun nearby, hiding it underneath his bed. He went downstairs and confronted Ollie, previously awake for countless hours on end, now asleep in the chair at the kitchen table. He poked Ollie's shoulder with the iron sights of the muzzle. When that did not rouse me, he tapped his forearm with the barrel. Ollie stirred and awoke, blinking his bloodshot eyes open.

The sight of Vermilion aiming point-blank the barrel of this almost antique rifle—the same rifle with which his uncle had bayoneted a German—startled him at first when he awakened, but then he merely smiled. Then he blanched, wondering if Vermilion realized that the knife he brandished was actually a bayonet for the rifle. In fact, he discerned that if he attached the bayonet to the rifle the fit would have been snug, perfect.

"Get out of my house or I'll have to shoot you," Vermilion warned.

Ollie dared: "Shoot me, kill me; you'd only be putting me out of my misery. My life has been nothing but wretchedness since y-y-you d-did w-w-what you d-d-did t-to—to m-me."

"Leave! Leave now."

Ambrose Vermilion had a look of disgust and contempt on his face. "You—you—you—" He pointed his finger accusatively and thrust it repeatedly "I have a word for people like you. You're a professional victim."

"You're a coward. You don't even have the courage to shoot me."

Ambrose Vermilion moved his finger over the trigger and applied light pressure to the groove. Ollie could clearly see his finger on the trigger—

the distance between us was no more than a body length—but he merely shrugged and forced laughter. "Go ahead. Pull the trigger. S-s-shoot m-me."

Seemingly ready to fire the gun and send his own existence into oblivion, Vermilion swung the barrel around and inserted the muzzle into his own mouth. He feared a boom and blood and grey matter splatter, but he expected Vermilion to behave rationally and forced more laughter, but, in his grim state of mind, his own attempt at a gesture of mirth was half-hearted, barely credible and, indeed, his voice sounded sinister. He tugged at the scratched, dented stock and wrenched the vintage military rifle from Vermilion's hands. He accused him of being a coward and said he did not even have the courage to kill himself.

The rest of the weekend passed in uneventful periods, which alternated with a peculiar tension. Then Ollie tuned Ambrose Vermilion's expensive stereo receiver into a favourite FM radio station, which played loud hard rock and heavy metal music. To feel the vibrations on his body, Ollie cranked up the volume of sound on powerful amplifiers to a level intolerable—far too loud—for Ambrose Vermilion and pressed his head against the large speakers. The unbearable noise drove the elder Vermilion into a fury and a vale of frustrated tears. Oblivious to his turmoil, Ollie occasionally made notes into his folded bundle of ruled paper, writing passages he wished to incorporate into the memoir/novel he was writing on again, off again for the past several months, since he was an inmate.

His former principal said he seemed wise beyond his years, so why was he continuing with this farce? He merely replied he seemed to be presuming something, and they continued an argument that intermittently grew more heated until just as unpredictably it quieted down.

On Sunday evening, Ollie forced his former principal out of the house for a drive in his luxury sedan. They drove through the Forest Hills and Rosedale neighbourhood around what Vermilion referred to as his estate, past mansions and through narrow winding streets, shaded by majestic elms and maples, immaculately maintained grass and gardens, with pristine ponds and walkways. They rode the sleek car past black wrought

iron gates surrounding estates with landscaped gardens and lawn sculptures made from bronze, marble, and ornate water fountains, past private colleges and prep schools with magnificent and immaculate green grounds, and homes of the privileged, rich, and famous. The cruise in the comfortable car with muted classical music playing on the high-fidelity car stereo gave me some unexpected pleasure, so he could not help nodding and behind the tinted windshields. He relaxed in the comfort of the automobile, enjoying the opulence of the scenery. They continued to cruise through the surrounding neighbourhoods, and Ollie initially felt lulled into a certain sense of complacence. While continuing to drive the Jaguar, Vermilion noticed a police cruiser trailing behind them. His driving became slightly erratic, as he gently swung the vehicle back and forth into the opposing lane, weaving the sleek car back and forth across the traffic median. Noticing the odd driving pattern, Ollie peered into the rear-view mirror, but could not see anything from his perspective, so he turned around and glanced out the rear windshield.

A Toronto police officer, wearing sunglasses, at the wheel of a brand new cruiser, polished, buffed, and waxed for a car show, virtually hugged the bumper of the luxury motor vehicle. If the police officer gazed closely enough, Ollie supposed he might surmise the pair was a couple. Ollie slid down in the seat, close to the driver's position, and put his arm around Vermilion's shoulder. Then he placed his foot alongside Vermilion's on the accelerator pedal, only then noticing the artisanship and fine materials used in its manufacture of his shoes.

If he kept acting up, this could be the last ride for both of them, Ollie warned, as he rested the sole of my own steel shank leather boots against the fine shoe leather and braided laces.

"If you're going to try to speed this car into anything, I should tell you there is an emergency brake."

Vermilion stared straight ahead, boldly disregarding his abductor. "Yes, and I could just strangle you on the spot," he warned. He pressed the sharp edge of the bayonet blade against his side, poking the tip through the fabric of his sweater and undershirt, indenting but not penetrating his bare flesh beneath. The bayonet was a gift from his father, he explained.

Vermilion cringed at the thought of the boy's aboriginal father, who had guided him more than once musky and lake trout fishing and moose hunting; he thought he understood the boy's mother—his Portuguese side much better. Ambrose Vermilion remembered pulling him out of class and summoning him to his office to inform him his father, who had once guided him on a fishing expedition up the large reservoir of Lac Seul, had passed away, a victim of an apparent suicide, a finding Ollie disputed and disbelieved originally. The thought of the boy's father's demise and the potential such violence might lurk within his former pupil caused Ambrose Vermilion to shudder and pause. In fact, Vermilion resumed driving normally.

Ollie ordered him to head home, and the rest of the drive passed in silence. After they arrived back at his home, he decided he needed the consolation and distraction he usually found in books, and he turned to Vermilion's bookshelves. He started to make himself comfortable in Vermilion's study again with a fine, portable hardcover leather-bound edition of Homer's Iliad, neat because it was no larger than a compact paperback book.

Having spent time in an institution that enforced isolation, he thought he could now easily tolerate a lonely existence and monkish lifestyle. Oftentimes he preferred such solitude, but when he thought of the loneliness stretched over a lifetime, it invoked fear. However, Vermilion found himself filled with a newfound resentment of Ollie's presence; for the past few years, he zealously protected his privacy, building an impenetrable wall of secrecy around himself. He even went so far as to lay off the hired help, cancelling the regular visits by the cleaner, groundskeeper, and maintenance worker. Now this mischievous figure from his past intruded into his life, trying to destroy his peaceful, sheltered existence. Growing heated at the thought, he decided he could tolerate Ollie's presence and antics no longer, and exploded with anger. "Leave! Leave now!" He flailed his arms in the general direction of the front doors. "You! You!" He pointed his fingers accusatively, a gesture he resorted to frequently

in his school principal days. "You know what you are? A victim. That's what you are—a professional victim."

"What?"

"You asked for it."

Ollie couldn't believe what he heard—Vermilion assigning blame, virtually accusing him. Glowering ominously, Ollie strode towards him with his rifle, which he hoped to use to frighten him away. He carried the rifle, pressing the stock against his thigh, the muzzle pointed towards the floor. He had been almost using the rifle as a walking stick. The presence of the rifle started to anger and annoy him. He resented Vermilion's introduction of the weapon into the situation. He actually feared he might need to resort to use of the firearm. Ambrose Vermilion feared for his life; he had never seen such a look of anger on the face of a pupil before, a depth of rage and passion, he presumed, originated in the darkness of his soul. "What did you say just now?"

"No, no, no," Vermilion sobbed.

"What did you say?"

"No, no, no, I'm sorry, I misspoke. I am truly and genuinely sorry. You're perfectly right: It was my fault. I just inadvertently released an outburst."

"What did you say before? I think whatever you're saying now is an act of self-preservation. You're cowardly."

"Oh, what does it matter anymore? I said it's your fault. You asked for whatever you got. At least you never protested."

Ollie became agitated, heated, and enraged he could barely make his speech understood. "How was I to know? I was young. I didn't know better." Ollie insisted he abused his position of authority, but Vermilion insisted he did everything with his knowledge and consent. Ollie started swinging the rifle.

Vermilion screamed hysterically that, yes, of course, he had been too young to know, as he backed away and raised his hands for protection. "You—you've r-r-ruin—ruined m-my l-life," I protested. "R-r-ruined it.

Hovering above him, he held the rifle by the barrel above his head, swung the stock down, and slammed the grip against Vermilion's legs. He could hear the bones break in Vermilion's upper legs as he slammed the wooden gunstock down and swung the rifle down again. By the time he finished, Vermilion was groaning, gasping, stifling the animal noise the tremendous pain forced him to make. Unable to move, he looked down at himself, his legs limp.

"Are you satisfied? Have you had enough?"

Ollie wanted to touch his legs, straighten them, and make certain they were all right, but he realized that gesture would only cause him great pain. He remembered the excruciating pain he felt when his own legs were broken, and he felt pity for him. He realized the same type of injuries he suffered when a snowmobile struck him afflicted Vermilion.

"Are you sure you don't want to leave?"

Silenced, Ollie grimaced and felt he was no longer in a position to argue, or reject his pleas or queries; his mood had turned to dread and fear. Finally, he watched the old man painfully drag himself over to the stereo, using the armrests of chairs and sofas as supports. He felt incredulous Vermilion could still walk and even advised him he should stay off his feet and rest. Vermilion somehow managed to put on a compact disk from a London musical and limped back to his chair.

He covered his legs with a quilt from the sofa and grabbed a bottle of Scotch. He reached over to the table and grabbed a mug, dumping the flat leftover ginger ale onto the carpet. His hands trembling and quavering, he poured Scotch into a coffee mug and sipped the drink. The climbing voice of the singer flooded the house and caused his heart to swell, his chest to ache, and his eyes to fill with tears.

The soprano's voice soared, filling the upper reaches of the lofty spacious room with her song of love and mourning. His hands trembled, spilling drink on his lap, and he cursed and muttered, breaking into tears. "Just can't seem to do anything right. Damn it all." He splashed more Scotch into the coffee mug. "Bloody well damn everything." He gulped the drink and poured yet more

into the coffee mug, before he had even finished it, muttering, "Damn everything." Tears trickled down his dimpled, withered, wrinkled cheeks. The singer's voice climbed, raising his him upwards, upwards, soaring above the melee, setting him adrift a sea of pained bliss.

Frantic to leave, desperate to flee his former principal's house, on the verge of panic and breaking down himself, Ollie checked to see if he could leave Vermilion alone, unassisted. Vermilion insisted he go so he decided to leave the house immediately, even though Ollie still had too many uncertainties in his mind about the man's condition. The sight of the man in such incredible pain filled him with fear and remorse. He suddenly became aware of the consequences of his actions, of how wrong and misguided he had been.

He felt mystified at how he arrived at the point where he could commit such violence. This sort of awareness and dawning might affect somebody who suddenly realized that they might have lost a limb in an accident or hears of the sudden unexpected death of somebody precious and close to them. As he jogged out of the neighbourhood with fine houses and majestic trees, he feared he might attract the attention of the police or private security patrols. His attitude changed drastically from the mindset he possessed when he originally went to confront Ambrose Vermilion. Depressed and remorseful, he realized the drastic action he took could not be reversed easily. Eventually, Ollie rode the southbound subway to Union subway station.

Afterwards, Ollie made a collect call from a pay phone in the lower floor of Union Station to his cousin. Knowing Ollie was recently released from the juvenile detention facility, Gary said he would send him a train ticket on the passenger service from Toronto to Vancouver. Gary said that, once Ollie learned the coffee shop business inside out, he wanted to put him in charge of a third Mocha Van coffee shop in the Upper East Side, near shelters where he felt confident the homeless, addicts, drug dealers, sex trade workers, and shelter workers would appreciate the caffeine fix.

"You want to set up a coffee truck near a homeless shelter?"

"It's not a coffee truck; it's a full-fledged coffee shop. It'll be my third cafe, if you help me."

174

"Why do you want to set up a coffee shop near a homeless shelter?"

"Because I have a social conscience, and I like to make money at the same time." Then Gary laughed his manic giggle, creepy, frightening, particularly if you knew he suffered bipolar disorder. Indeed, just as Gary promised, by the time Ollie ascended the ramp in the vast cavernous train station to the ticket counter, the agent handed him a train ticket, reservations, and luggage tags for the following morning.

Ollie decided to wait overnight in the station, since the train to Vancouver was scheduled to leave in several hours in the early morning. Meanwhile, Ollie looked about vigilantly, fearfully anticipating the arrival of the police. Finally, he managed to nap in the waiting lounge, tranquilized by the sole other train passenger in the train station, playing a saxophone. By the time the train prepared for boarding at eight am, Ollie was at the head of the line a few hundred passengers long and, aside from train officials, there was no authorities. Ollie boarded the train and settled in his seat for a weeklong journey across Canada. As the passenger train passed beneath the CN Tower and the office towers of the financial district of Toronto, he peered up through the window and thought there was a glimmer of hope.

About the Author:

Born and raised in Sioux Lookout, Ontario, **John Tavares** is the son of Portuguese immigrants from the Azores. His education includes graduation from 2-year GAS at Humber College in Etobicoke with concentration in psychology (1993), 3-year journalism at Centennial College in East York (1996), and the Specialized Honors BA in English from York University in North York (2012). His writings have been published in various magazines and literary journals. Set of his short stories has been broadcasted at the Sioux Lookout's CBLS/CBQW radio.

DR. PERKINS

by Heide Arbitter

Dr. Perkins signed up immediately. It was in the desert, after all, his favorite vacation spot. Not many other dermatologists approved of these desert landscapes, which made the days there more precious. Dr. Perkins was always interested in Star Wars, and when his wife, Fifi, left him for not only a Wookiee impersonator, but an impersonator of Chewbacca, the greatest Wookiee of all, he figured that he would have time alone, to not only think and imagine, but actually try out something he had only dreamed of before. Dr. Perkins would attend a science fiction convention by himself.

Dr. Perkins and Fifi did have that in common. Of course, he attended these conventions only to listen and learn, she because of her love of costumes. Her favorite character was Lady Godiva, which authorized her to unbraid her long blonde hair and let it flow down her naked body. Dr. Perkins and Fifi fought about that, but in the end the pleasure of simply travelling with her always won.

But, Fifi was travelling without him now, first throughout Australia, and then onto New Zealand, where her Wookiee lover, Jeb, owned land. Well, that would not be a deterrent. Dr. Perkins was a grown man. He owned a condo. He would triumph by himself.

Still, the idea of going alone made Dr. Perkins nervous. He closed his practice. He wanted time to research and prepare. His e-mail flooded with recommendations from acquaintances and invitations from conventioneers. Some suggested he try the "Firefly" convention, held yearly at some insect ranch. That did not sound right. Others beckoned him to "The Enterprise", but with this warning: "Their replicators are offline which means you have to eat whatever awful food they throw at you. Conventioneers will have to do daily shifts in the kitchens as evidence that they are complying with the laws of gravity on a constructed, stationary space complex, where unity is the theme and monogamy to the crew encouraged". Dr. Perkins decided against that one, as he had already had seventeen years of monogamy and not one of them was unified.

Then, there was the desert. The e-vite said "Sci-Fi Convention 99 – All Welcomed" Did that mean it had met yearly for 99 years? If so, this suggested stability. The thought thrilled and intrigued him, as was the idea of a multi-character convention, not one driven by theme, and, yes, even fanaticism. Dr. Perkins threw his luggage into his car and set off.

But, the instant Dr. Perkins pulled up in the dusty parking lot a mile away from the Convention Center which was, as he could see from this distance, a lime green motel, he had a sense of dread. His was the only car in the lot. Dr. Perkins got out of his car, and stared at the desert. He looked at his watch. 7 A.M. Wasn't that when registration began? Dr. Perkins looked up at the sun. All he saw were flocks of birds overhead. Vultures, his favorites, were circling rather close. Fifi called these birds bottom feeders, but he knew their, yes, horrible dietary cravings, but intelligent and gentle natures set them apart as royalty.

Dr. Perkins was about to get back into his car, when Dr. Strange, his adornments magnificent, pulled up next to him. "In costume already?" Dr. Perkins asked. "Where's yours?" snarled the conventioneer, as he turned off his ignition and got out. "I'll park over there," said Dr. Perkins as he got into his car and rode over to the only shady spot near an enormous cactus.

For a while, Dr. Perkins sat in his car, thinking. He knew he was was not a handsome man. His bald head and thick glasses implied old age, even though he was in his prime. After a few years of marriage, style conscious Fifi had given up on his sci-fi costumes and simply focused on trying to modernize his daily sense of fashion. But Dr. Perkins refused, suspecting she would make him look worse, not better. Still, he thought, the frayed Armani suit he was wearing and the fact he had purchased it at Housing Works, should give him some leverage.

Sitting in his car, Dr. Perkins thought about how he should introduce himself. It was bad enough that embarrassment followed whenever he spoke of his profession. "A dermatologist, huh?" was the usual response. Then, the inevitable pulling down of pants or unbuttoning of the shirt. "Into skin? Well, doc, look at this. Did you ever see a blob like this?" Amazingly, this happened everywhere he went, museums, the laundry room, even the florist where he yearly bought Fifi daisies for her birthday. Of course, he could always outright lie and when asked about his job, shrug and say he was unemployed, but the looks that he would get from that kind of response would be more than his delicate sense of self could handle.

With a sigh, Dr. Perkins snapped into the present. The sun was setting. The parking lot was full. Maybe, the fun was about to begin. Dr. Perkins pulled himself from his car and attempted to hold his head high as he walked into the building.

In retrospect, perhaps a multi-character convention was not a mature choice. While standing in line to register, despite the all characters welcomed motto, the place was still overwhelmed with the usual standards, young women and even men costumed as Katniss Everdeen, Wonder Woman, Klingons, the always favorite, Yoda, Spock and Data, of course, Wolverine, Bat Man, the always despised Jar-Jar Binks and much to his horror, not a few, but a plethora of Wookiees. It was as though they were summoned there to

torment him. Dr. Perkins grabbed his name tag and ran shrieking from registration. Those standing behind him jeered.

Alone in his room that night, Dr. Perkins read over the next day's schedule only to discover it was Wookiee friendly, complete with a Wookiee parade and a Wookiee panel. One panel caught his eye. "Wookiee Women: Where are they?" This might answer his questions. Were they hiding? Afraid? Were they modest? He, himself, had designed garments that would hide their furry Wookiee nakedness, but he was too timid to publicize them, even here. In his secret heart, Dr. Perkins hoped that a Wookiee woman would approach him and perhaps help him market his creations, or more.

The next morning, Dr. Perkins, still wearing his Armani suit, strode into the panel. He looked around to see the room was already packed with Wookiee impersonators, but not one of them, as far as he could tell, was a Wookiee woman. Dr. Perkins took his seat in the audience and said to the Wookiee on his right, "Where are the girls?" "Can't you tell?" the Wookiee snapped. "No wonder they have to scoop away our wives," Dr. Perkins said to the Wookiee at his left. The Wookiee growled, "How come you're not in costume?" "I am in costume. I come as an observer and a recorder of experience." "Kind of like an Away Team?" the Wookiee asked. "Sure," Dr. Perkins answered.

The boring panel ran over three hours. As the Wookiee emcee droned on about equality and fur is fantastic, Dr. Perkins drifted off into his own world in which he found a Wookiee woman to call his own. In their bedroom, as night, he examined beneath the fur, touching her skin and feeling it for boils and blemishes. Much to his delight, she met with his approval. His Wookiee woman had perfect skin, subtle and smooth.

That's how Dr. Perkins met Fifi. She came to his office with something so minor, he almost sent her to his associate down the hall. But when, at his request, she opened her hospital gown from the neck down, he gasped. Her skin was like satin. Pure and shiny and devoid of stretch marks and scars. It was as though she had never been touched by human hands or crumpled up as she passed through her mother's birth canal, so flawless was her skin. She was perfection. She wanted to know about a tiny pore on her nose. "It just appeared out of nowhere", she said. He gazed at the perfect skin on her perfectly porcelain face and was speechless. Under his magnifying glass, the tiny pore, barely visible became his focus. He stared and stared and suddenly he felt himself standing in the largest crater on the moon, looking up at millions of brilliant stars, realizing he was one of them and delirious at his weightlessness. This was love. This was splendor.

The Wookiee to his right wiggled closer to make space for the new Wookiee pal now joining him. "How do you guys tell each other apart?" asked Dr. Perkins. The Wookiees around him chuckled. "Where are your women?" screamed Dr. Perkins. "As if we'd tell you," the Wookiee to his left said. "Where?" Dr.

Perkins shouted. Suddenly, all of the Wookiees in the room joined in. "Get your own women. Get your own!" they cried. The Wookiee uproar reached a crescendo. Covering his ears, Dr. Perkins ran from the room and down the hall, banging into popcorn stands, knocking over whirling pink cotton candy vats, and crashing head long into the caramel apple stands.

His face covered with these snacks, Dr. Perkins raced to the lobby, past a bunch of Wookiees shouting excitedly, pointing at him and laughing. Where could he go? Where could he find her? Fifi. He loved her. He missed her. Was she here? Did she leave her Wookiee lover alone, in New Zealand, to frolic with his sheep, so she could return to the doctor, her husband, and reinvent the true meaning of science fiction?

Dr. Perkins stopped and tried to catch his breath. Next to him, a Wookiee was talking up a Wonder Woman. Her robust skin glowed under the fluorescent lights. She whispered something and opened her mouth revealing newly installed veneers. Saliva drooling down his chin, the Wookiee moved in for a kiss.

But the dermatologist was too fast. He lunged at the Wookiee, and ripped off the Wookiee's head, revealing the bumpy, fissured face of a middle-aged man with adult acne. The Wonder Woman screamed and hid behind a chair. The dermatologist wrestled the man to the floor and climbed on

top of him. The man screeched, but Dr. Perkins did not hear, as he pummeled the man's face into a bloody mess that no amount of dermabrasion could remedy.

About the Author

Heide Arbitter's plays have been produced in New York City and regionally. Some of these productions include a one-act, HAND WASHED, LINE DRIED, which was produced at the Public Theatre; a full-length, FROGS FROM THE MOON at the American Theatre of Actors; and a one-act, TILL WE MEET, at Unboxed Voices. Smith & Kraus and Excalibur have published JILLY ROSE, SHARON and POPPY. Heide was recently interviewed on the radio, WFUV.

WET FEET, DRY FEET
by Taylor Lovullo

HAVANA, 1994

It was exactly 2:30am, and Joaquin left his small house located in Vedado, a small neighborhood outside of the city. He shut the door quietly behind him, and continued to walk across his front yard until he reached the mango tree. It was the high point of summer, and the fruits were growing in abundance— Joaquin looked at its long, green leaves and the little bright mangos hanging from the branches. He thought of how he and his mother used to sit underneath its shade on blazing, humid, summer days because it was unbearably hot in their home and they needed to get some fresh air. She would read to him pages from El Canto General, a poetry book by Pablo Neruda, a Chilean, while he would pick mangos off the ground and stuff them into his shirt, sweating and listening to the chaos of street vendors and old cars honking outside.

A light breeze rustled the leaves and some palms overhead began to sway. It was still warm out, and Joaquin stood underneath the old mango tree and put his hand on the trunk. His eyes filled with tears as he thought about the memories and Neruda's poems that always made him smile as a child. He took a few steps away and stood on the sidewalk, observed its cracked, uneven surface with unruly weeds growing through it, and thought of how he always used to look for insects in those little crevices with the other kids in the neighborhood and poke them with sticks. Those were the days, he thought. Before everything went to shit in this country.

He closed his eyes and could see himself as a child running around careless and barefoot under the hot Caribbean sun with his two best friends, Yunel and Camilo. They were his next-door neighbors and Joaquin had known them for as long as he could remember—they were both a year older, and he looked up to them. He didn't have siblings of his own, but he considered those two his brothers, even though they were all from different families. Yunel taught him how to hit a baseball right here on the patchy grass of this front lawn when they were little, and how to do front flips off the Malecon, or the sea wall, into the ocean.

Camilo was less athletic and free-spirited than Yunel, but Joaquin always secretly favored him. Like Joaquin, Camilo grew up without a father, and the two had a sort of unspoken bond because of it. Plus, he admired Camilo because he was always one of the smartest kids in school growing up—Everyone said that he was gifted in math and science, and that he would probably grow up to be an excellent doctor one day. He would always help Joaquin and Yunel with their homework, and was always so patient to explain everything. Joaquin turned around and looked at his house for what would most likely be the last time. He blinked back some more tears and smiled at the tiny, one-story building with a cement exterior and the chipping blue paint on the door. As he was turning away, the door cracked open. He could see his mother's gaunt face and petite frame hiding behind it.

"Come here, my love, I want to hug you one more time," she said softly, but still loud enough for him to hear.

Joaquin crossed the lawn one more time, and embraced his mother on the patio.

"I love you so much, Mama," he said. "I am so sorry."

"I love you too, more than you will ever know. And don't be sorry. You are doing the right thing— I will be fine here. I will be happy knowing that you are going to have a much better life somewhere else," she responded.

He nodded, thinking about the hardships that the island had been facing for years now—the shortages, the oppression, the food rations—and then they broke from their embrace. "Goodbye, Mama."

"Goodbye, Joaquin. But it's not goodbye forever. I know it," she whispered, while taking his hands in hers.

He nodded again.

"I have one more thing for you," she said, choking up.

 She disappeared inside for a moment and returned with an old, tattered book. It was El Canto General. A smile broke through Joaquin's somber expression as he flipped through its pages, underlined and annotated with his mother's fragile handwriting in blue ink. The pages with the poems that she read to him under the mango tree were dog-eared, with stars next to their titles. He flipped to the back cover, where there was an address printed. His mother had already given him the information of his cousins who had left the island many years ago and had settled in Miami, but she wanted him to have it somewhere else "just in case" he forgot. His cousins had been there since 1980, when Castro still let people emigrate from the country.

"Thank you," he said, tucking it into his backpack and hugging her once more.

"Of course, my love. Now go, but please, just be careful."

It was a full moon that night. The sea was illuminated by its reflection and looked almost silver, and its gentle waves lapped against the shore. Joaquin walked through the dense brush from the forest and stepped out into the opening. Once he was on the sand, he took off his sandals, closed his eyes, and exhaled deeply.

He turned to the left and walked along the shore

for about five minutes. He knew exactly where to go—he had already been to this spot with Yunel and Camilo three times while they were searching for the ideal place to depart.

They had agreed to leave Tuesday morning at 3:30am, which would allow them to escape the island in the dark, but the full moon would still permit them to see what they were doing. The light of dawn would guide them from that point on. They would be able to navigate their way across the ocean in the daylight.

"Joaquin!" He heard Yunel's voice, calling him in a loud whisper.

"Hey, how's it coming along?" Joaquin responded, approaching them. His heart fluttered as he looked at the makeshift raft that would be their transportation across the sea. It was made from tires, pipes, and wooden planks. They had constructed a few oars just in case, and it was just barely big enough to fit the three men, who were now all between 19 and 21 years-old. Camilo was hunched over, tinkering with an old outboard motor that he had acquired from his uncle, who seemed to have everything for the boys just when they needed it.

Camilo looked up at him and grinned. "We should be good to go. I just put in the fuel and am looking over it one more time. It's old, you know."

Joaquin and Yunel grinned back. "But at least we have a motor," Yunel said. He was trying to sound like his usual cheerful, confident self, but Joaquin could detect the fear in his voice.

Camilo stood up and sighed. "Alright, we're ready," he said.

The three looked at each other. Joaquin unzipped his backpack, his hands shaking. He handed them each a bottle of water. They took a few sips and looked at each other's now-solemn faces in the moonlight before stepping on board the raft and pushing themselves out to sea.

It was about 3pm now, and the young men were sitting in the raft, baking under the hot tropical sun. All three were sunburned and dehydrated, but they hadn't encountered any life-threatening obstacles so far, so Joaquin considered his party lucky. They weren't going too fast, but Camilo, who was steering and checking his compass, told them they were making good time and would probably hit land by sunrise the next morning.

Yunel kept his eye on the fuel gauge, and Joaquin was assigned to watch the horizon for any boats in the distance. They had seen two so far, and both times, Joaquin felt his stomach drop and a rush of blood to go to his head, only to come a little bit closer and realize they were only fishing boats.

"Coast Guard?" Camilo would ask, turning around. His eyes flashed with panic.

"No, no. I think we're all right," Joaquin responded, peering through his binoculars.

Then they would fall silent, and the main concern would once again become the sharks that were abundant in this part of the strait between Florida and Cuba. Joaquin felt bad for the Cubans who couldn't find engines for their rafts, because that meant they would have to sail or paddle, slaves to the winds and currents. He had heard about some people who took nearly an entire week to make it to Florida, after being blown off course and losing members to heatstroke or shark attacks. They would make it there in just over one full day.

Yunel broke a long silence. "'Pies Mojados, Pies Secos.'"

"Wet Feet, Dry Feet," Camilo replied in English.

Joaqui put down his binoculars and bit his tongue. "It kind of sounds like a children's game," he remarked.

"Yeah, it does," Camilo said, with a tiny smile. "But it's no game."

Joaquin knew this. If they were intercepted at sea by the US Coast Guard, they would be sent back to Cuba, and most likely put in jail. But if they hit land, they would be granted asylum in the United States, and would be able to stay there.

Yunel changed the subject, and soon the three were talking about lighter matters, like baseball and fishing. A few more hours went by, and they knew that the worst heat of the afternoon had passed. There were a few dark clouds lingering in the sky from the east, but they did not panic: the weather forecast that they'd seen on the state-run channel on Camilo's uncle's television had

said that there wouldn't be any major storms near the island for the next few days.

"Mierda," Yunel cursed as the first raindrops fell. He had just mentioned that they were low on fuel a few moments before.

The sky was darkening, and the winds were picking up.

"The current's getting stronger," Camilo said, looking over his shoulder. "I'm going to keep steering... I think we have enough fuel to make it there. But can you guys still grab some oars and help out?"

They nodded, and Yunel took a seat behind Camilo while Joaquin sat more towards the rear. They began to row in silence as the rain fell heavier and more steadily. The water was black and growing choppier by the second. Joaquin felt nauseated and he had a very uneasy feeling growing in the pit of his stomach. This was a pretty sturdy raft, but he wasn't sure if it would be able to withstand a tropical storm at sea.

One moment, he was blinking the water out of his eyes, rowing stoically and thinking about how his backpack must be getting soaked. He thought of his mother's Pablo Neruda book, with its pages soggy and the blue ink smudged and running. Then, the next moment, he was suddenly airborne somehow and launched into the dark sea.

He was flung far and deep and was submerged underwater for a moment, unable to process what had just happened. When he resurfaced, he found that it was difficult to tread water with the growing waves, and was overcome with anxiety when he saw that the raft was already dozens of feet away from him. He saw Camilo and Yunel hanging over the edge, looking and calling for him amidst the angry waters.

"Camilo!

Yunel! I'm over here!" Joaquin shouted, as thunder boomed in the distance. They didn't seem to hear him. He felt that rush of blood to his head once again, and heard his heart pounding in his ears. Don't lose me, he thought. Please, I'm too young to die.

He took a deep breath, and began to swim towards them, trying not to think about any sharks that might have been nearby. After a few strokes, he paused and called again.

Thankfully, this time they heard him. "Keep swimming!" Camilo screamed over the wind. They were paddling toward him now, but struggling to gain control of the steering. Joaquin kept swimming even though he could barely see and was fighting for breath.

A large, black wave emerged and engulfed him entirely. He panicked as he was pulled under, saltwater filling his mouth and nose. After a few seconds, he felt his all his thoughts beginning to fade.

Joaquin made one final effort to save himself—he wasn't sure how long he'd been under or how far he was from the surface—but he extended his arm, hoping to get it out of the water. His eyes were closing.

Almost immediately after reaching out, Joaquin felt someone grab onto his hand. He could hear Camilo shouting at Yunel as he was pulled up from the sea. The two men on the raft each grasped one of his shoulders and pulled him back on board. The raft rocked wildly for a moment, but they did not capsize. Yunel patted Joaquin's back as he coughed profusely for a few moments and regained consciousness.

Then, the three sat back down and did not say a word. They each picked up an oar, and had no choice but to hunker down and try to hold on, keep moving forward, and stay on course.

It was morning again, and the horizon to the east began to glow as the sun rose. The storm was over, and Camilo had declared about an hour before that they were almost to the Florida coast. Joaquin looked at his friends: Yunel was sleeping, sitting straight up. Camilo was still up front, rowing and pausing every now and then to check his compass. His face looked gray and grim in this lighting, and there were dark circles underneath his eyes. Joaquin knew he probably looked similar—they were all exhausted, famished, and shaken from the night before. When Yunel woke up, Joaquin knew it was his turn to nap, and he

settled into an uneasy, dreamless sleep right after scanning the sea for any boats nearby.

"Wake up!" Yunel shouted, shaking Joaquin by the shoulders. Startled, he opened his eyes. Camilo and Yunel were standing up in the raft, looking alarmed.

"What's going on?" He asked.

"That's the US," Yunel said quickly, pointing ahead. Joaquin couldn't believe his eyes—it was only about 500 feet away. "But look," he gestured. A medium-sized white boat was rushing toward them from behind, coming so close that he could read the words "U.S. COAST GUARD" written on the hull. They heard a siren go off, and could make someone out shouting at them in rapid English through a megaphone.

"Jump off and swim!!!" Camilo yelled, and all three jumped overboard, diving headfirst.

Underwater for that brief second, Joaquin could still hear the sirens. He went numb just thinking about being captured and repatriated back to Cuba, after everything they had gone through to get this far.

When he came up, he was facing the land. He started swimming, flailing his arms, and kicking his legs. He imagined himself as a machine— he picked up his speed and did not even look back to see where his friends where, nor to see that the Coast Guard was beginning to close in on them.

He could hear the man with the megaphone still barking at them, and realized how close they were coming. He finally turned for a split second, and saw that Camilo and Yunel were only a few strokes behind him, and that the Coast Guards were now on a bright orange raft only trailing by a few yards, rushing towards them.

Joaquin kept kicking and stroking until he was sure he was close enough for his feet to reach the ocean's floor. He started wading through the water, with the waves sloshing around his shoulders.

Soon, his torso was out of the water, then his knees, and then he was sprinting up the sand. Camilo and Yunel followed, and the three of them ran as fast as they could up the beach and did not stop running for several more minutes.

The Cubans entered a neighborhood just as the

sun was rising, illuminating everything in sight with its golden rays. The sky was vivid blue and clear, and before collapsing on the front lawn of a random house, Joaquin noticed that the green mass dancing above them in the breeze was a mango tree. He was wheezing and staring up at the sky, adrenaline still rushing through his body. Once he could collect his thoughts, he thought of his mother and how she was probably outside the little cement house in Vedado at this time, sitting under that mango tree like she did before work every morning. His eyes welled with tears, and a smile spread on his face.

He looked at his friends, who felt like his family more than ever now. They were still lying flat on the perfectly manicured, green grass. After a few seconds, Yunel got up on his knees and began praying.

Camilo caught his breath and sat up, too.

"We made it."

About the Author:

Taylor Lovullo is a sophomore at The George Washington University in Washington, D.C. with a major in Spanish & Latin American Languages, Literature, & Cultures. Taylor has always been interested in learning about the Spanish-speaking world, especially Cuba. She grew up in Southern California and also enjoys reading, studying other languages, and traveling.

HEARTWOOD

by Maryetta Ackenbom

Andy leaned back in his comfortable lawn chair. "Do you remember?" He turned to Sue, sitting beside him. "We were only 15, but already deeply in love. We would wander through that little woods in the park..."

She stretched and reached for his hand. "Yes, my love, of course I remember. We would get lost in the little woods, happily lost, and we'd find a place to sit, and..."

"And we'd kiss. First kisses for both of us."

The sound of water from the small waterfall Andy had built in their back yard echoed the long-ago kisses they shared.

"Andy," she said, "How did we lose so much time before we joined our hands and our hearts and our bodies in marriage?"

"We were only fifteen, Sue, and our parents tried to keep us apart. And not only because we were only fifteen."

"Those were glorious days, walking in the woods, but then there were the bad, lonely days when they forced us to separate."

"They tried, didn't they? And for a while they succeeded."

"Oh, Andy, I remember the day you carved a heart with our initials together in the sweet old elm tree. 'AM loves SR.' I was so thrilled."

"Then that brat of a sister of yours found the tree and our love initials."

"And my folks grounded me for a month. You were released from detention after two weeks. Now I call that sex discrimination."

"But after two weeks I could at least pass by your house and see you through your bedroom window."

"And I would wave at you and throw kisses. But they wouldn't let us date for another whole year."

"And the first thing we did when we were allowed to see each other again was to go to the elm tree and run our fingers over the carving."

"The sap had already hardened in the tree's bark. That's when we knew for sure our love would last."

"Then you moved away. I was so sad." She sighed. "Every day I'd go to the elm tree and trace the heart, and then our initials."

"And then you'd write me the most beautiful letters."

"Until my mom found out."

"Why would they keep us from writing, Sue? You were just perfecting your poetry, right?"

"And you perfected your artistry, which you began by carving up the poor tree."

They both sighed and closed their eyes.

Some time later, they pulled themselves out of the lawn chairs and walked slowly through the green spring grass into the house, leaning on each other.

Together they fixed their usual light supper, tea and crackers, and maybe a piece of fruit. Together they sat at their small kitchen table.

"How long was it before we saw each other again, Sue?"

"Don't you remember? It was a couple of years, and you made some money delivering papers and used it to come see me."

"Oh yes, and you weren't home. I almost cried, a big seventeen-year-old baby. Then I guessed where you might be."

"And you found me, seated under the old elm tree."

"I was so surprised to see how the heart outline and the initials had widened. But we kissed. And kissed some more."

"Yes, we did." She smiled at him. "I came almost every day to the tree, and I noticed the carving growing larger. And my heart grew with love as I remembered our kisses." She raised her eyebrows. "Do you want to see the evening news?"

"No, dear, I want to kiss you again."

"We have never stopped kissing. Our parents accepted that we were not going to part, and they let us enroll in the same college."

"Sue, do remember learning anything in college?"

"Mostly, I remember strolling around the campus, our arms around each other. Our friends used to call us the Siamese twins."

"I think the old elm tree put a spell on us. I never thought about any other girl. Oh, I admit I liked looking at some of them..."

Sue drew back and lightly punched his shoulder. "Do you want me to confess to my countless affairs?"

"I know you were in love with Rock Hudson."

"Ahem. Weren't you?"

"That didn't get either of us very far, did it?"

They chuckled, drew each other up from their kitchen chairs, and settled again on the living room couch. The green and white print on the couch matched a couple of armchairs, and green drapes were pulled aside to let in the darkening evening. In front of them a coffee table, carved from natural wood and covered with a thickness of plate glass, shone from frequent dusting.

Sue smoothed her hand over the glass, tracing the symbols below it. "I'm so glad we could get this, Andy. It's a symbol for us."

"How many times..." He put his hand over hers on the glass. "How many times did we go back to the elm tree? Every time, it was like getting married again."

"And when we got married, in the old Methodist church, we went to visit the tree before we even went to the reception. And whenever we visited the tree after that, we noticed that the carving seemed a little wider, more distinct."

"Sue, we've traveled all over, and we've lived in different places, but we've always come back to our old home town and the elm tree heart. I'm so glad we retired here."

"We had to come back, Andy. When my brother wrote us that they were cutting down the woods where our elm tree grew, we had to come back and save it."

"And we sure fought with that construction company. I wonder if anyone has ever loved a tree like we loved the elm tree."

"And we only gave up when they showed us the old tree was dying, anyway. I cried so hard!"

"But Sue, we didn't give up. We won! They made us the offer, and we accepted, reluctantly, but we knew there was no alternative."

"We watched them cut down the tree, and I cried all the time. I think you did, too."

Andy put his arm around her shoulder. "I admit it. But then the company representatives took us to their workshop, where we saw their people carve down into the heartwood of the elm tree, and they sanded it and varnished it..."

"And ever since then we've had the tree with its heart in front of us, always reminding us of our young love."

Sue ran her hand over the glass again, over the outline of the carving, now after so many years much smoother and wider than ever. Andy rested his hand over hers.

About the Author:

Maryetta Ackenbom has published several short stories online, and has just published her second novel, "Hope Abides," available on amazon.com. She lives and writes in Merida, Yucatan, Mexico, a warm city with warm, welcoming people.

SCHADENFREUDE

by Jack Coey

The sun was going down when Jessica appeared at Father Brendan's office door, and after being motioned in, in a hissing whisper, told him what happened. Father Brendan recoiled from hearing it; not because he didn't believe it, but more, it was a problem he didn't want. He reassured Jessica he would speak with the named perpetrator, and after she left, rethought the problem, and because of the sensitivity of it, decided to speak with Becket, the choir director. Becket came to Father Brendan's office doorway with trepidation at the unusualness of the summons. Father Brendan asked if he'd noticed any odd occurrence in the choir. Becket put his fingers to his lips, and looked at the ceiling for several moments, before he said,

"Perhaps. There was this moment, yesterday it was, when Jessica jumped in her seat like a Jack-in-the-Box, and I passed it off as a bit of choreography, nothing more."

"Yes, well, she claims Edgar put his hand on her knee."

"Oh, dear!"

"Oh, dear, indeed."

Becket took refuge in the ceiling.

"Awfully good baritone, Edgar," he said.

"We can't have any bad opinion of the church; attendance is waning as it is," said Father Brendan.

"I never knew Edgar to have predilections that way," said Becket.

"What's his status?"

"Bachelor as far as I know," said Becket coming down from the ceiling.

"Perhaps we or I should speak with him?"

"Let sleeping dogs lie, I say."

"Yes, but what if Jessica tells her tale in the community?"

"I've got it! I'll institute a new policy of separation of the genders. Men on one side and women on the other. That should solve it."

"Well done, Becket! Thank-you for your help with this."

That ended the commotion in the choir until the next time which came during an after-service coffee hour when Jessica let out a blood-curling scream from the corner of the room, and a red-faced Edgar made a hasty retreat down the hall. Father Brendan and Becket hustled Jessica to Father Brendan's office and closed the door until it was pounded on by three or four women of the congregation. It was just as well, as it was plain that Jessica wasn't going to speak with any man. The women huddled with Jessica and whispered. Olivia Proctor rose up, and said,

"If you gentlemen would kindly leave the room?"

"I beg your pardon? This is my office," said a perturbed Father Brendan.

"You want to help Jessica or not?" snapped Agnes Williams.

Father Brendan and Becket looked at each other. After a beat, Becket jerked his head toward the door.

"I'll be back in fifteen minutes," said Father Brendan.

The women wouldn't tell the men what went wrong. Father Brendan tried to exert his authority as minister of the church, but the women wouldn't yield. Father Brendan and Becket sat in silence.

"What say we talk to Edgar?" suggested Becket.

Father Brendan thought about that.

"Do you think he'd tell us?" asked Father Brendan.

"Don't know really. He's a bit of an oddball," said Becket.

"You can't recall anything peculiar?"

"Well, come to think on it, and I recall seeing him looking at Patrice."

"He's a funny looking fellow, wouldn't you say?"

"Yes, his long cylinder like nose, and thin torso gives him a rather scarecrow like look."

"Poor fellow probably doesn't do well with the women, I would guess."

"One afternoon I overheard him describing probability theory to Matilda Owens."

Father Brendan put his hand to his chin.

"Oh Good Gracious! That sounds dreadful."

"Okay so he's not Hugh Hefner."

"I think we should give him an opportunity to give his side of the story since the women don't want us to know what happened from their point of view," said Father Brendan.

"Yes. I would say that seems fair enough."

After the Tuesday afternoon choir practice, Father Brendan and Becket waited in Father Brendan's office for Edgar. There was a soft knock at the door. Father Brendan acknowledged the knock and there stood Edgar. He wore a vest two sizes too big that looked like a sail. He glided into the office and took a chair without being offered one. He didn't look at either man.

"Edgar, do you know why you're here?" asked Father Brendan.

"It's not what you think."

"What isn't what we think?"

"What you think it is, is not what it is, but only what Jessica wants you to think it is."

"Why would Jessica want us to think it is, when what she wants us to think it is, isn't true?"

"Dunno."

"Tell us your side of the story."

"I didn't initiate anything."

Father Brendan and Becket looked at Edgar.

"How did your hand end up on her knee?"

"She put it there."

Father Brendan and Becket looked at each other.

"Edgar that's a very serious charge. You're sure that's what happened?"

"I would never touch Jessica on my own. Now, Patrice is another story."

"So your story is that Jessica put your hand on her knee?"

"Yes."

"What happened during the coffee hour?" asked Becket.

"She bumped her rear-end into me like a boat docking."

Father Brendan and Becket looked at each other.

"Edgar you understand the seriousness of what you're saying?" said Father Brendan.

"The truth is always serious. That's why people avoid it."

"I want you to tell me you understand the seriousness of what you're saying."

"Of course I understand. I only look stupid."

Father Brendan felt pain at Edgar's honesty.

"Edgar did you ever think that Jessica might like you?" asked Becket.

"I don't think that's our concern at this point," interjected Father Brendan, "Edgar is there anything else you want to tell us?"

Both Edgar and Becket looked at the ceiling.

"Well, there is one thing…"

Father Brendan and Becket leaned forward in their chairs.

"I think I should get the second verse solo on Faith of Our Fathers."

Becket watched Edgar and Jessica during the next practice, and Edgar acted oblivious, and he saw Jessica look at Edgar several times not without some feeling in her eyes. Becket directed the choir long enough to know to be careful about forming any opinion: the feeling could come from the music or from what she was looking at. But she kept looking at him, there was no mistaking it; then he realized why: his nose.

First chance he got, Becket went to Father Brendan's office. He was on the phone. When he hung up, he said,

"What a nuisance fund raising is!"

Becket slid forward in his chair.

"I've got a clue about that Edgar business," he said.

"Really?"

"Yes, if you watch Jessica, you can discern what's on her mind."

"Really?"

"Penis envy."

"What?"

"Penis envy."

"What in God's Name are you talking about?"

"Penis envy."

"Good Gracious, man, how can she see his penis?"

"You obviously don't understand Freud."

Father Brendan annoyedly stared at Becket. He extended his arms on either side of him.

"Pray, enlighten me, then."

"I don't or Freud don't literally mean his penis. She's fixated on his nose."

Father Brendan flushed red.

"His nose?"

"She looks at his nose and has erotic thoughts."

Father Brendan's mouth was open and speechless; his chest was heaving like he couldn't get air.

"How about this? Come to a choir practice, and watch how Jessica looks at Edgar, and see if you don't see what I see."

Father Brendan with What A Friend We Have in Jesus in his ears came into the basement and sat in a folding chair. There were two and a half rows of men on one side, and two rows of women on the other, looking out at Becket who appeared to be in some kind of reverie. He waved his arms, and swayed his torso back and forth, looking up with his eyes closed. Father Brendan found and focused on Jessica who was looking down at her hymnal. He watched her through Rock of Ages and into This Little Light of Mine, and sure enough, she looked sideways at Edgar's nose with a small smile on her face like she enjoyed what she was thinking, but didn't want anyone else to know. He watched long enough to believe it was diabolical. Flustered, Father Brendan got up and left.

Jessica joined the congregation looking for copulation. The choir was even better because she had to interact with men. She was in her late twenties, skinny, with dirty, stringy blond hair, flat chested, with glasses. She lived with her aunt in a small, run-down house out past the sand and gravel pit. She worked as an accountant for a landscaping business, and at one time, was seen around with Edwin Lancaster who was arrested at a rest stop for lewd activities. That's when Jessica came to the church. Her aunt was known to hold séances, and worked as a greeter at Wal-Mart. Jessica was confused about what she was feeling; she enjoyed looking at Edgar's nose, but didn't know why. She wanted to believe that Edgar desired her enough to put his hand on her knee.

Father Brendan sat behind his big, oak desk and brooded over how to help Jessica; he believed she was possessed by evil spirits. This wasn't the first time he had sex problems between members of his congregation, and it annoyed the hell out of him, because it seemed he was doomed to deal with it over and over. He considered talking with Becket about it, but knew what he would say,

"Have her see a psychiatrist."

He thought psychiatrists made patients feel comfortable with their malady rather than change their behavior for redemption. So, having eliminated all other options, he decided to talk to Jessica.

About the Author:

Jack Coey lives in Keene, NH.

Jessica, with half her face obscured by her dirty blond hair, stood in Father Brendan's doorway. He signaled her in, and she hesitated. He waited. When she was seated, he began to talk to her about how he felt used by her when she complained about unwanted behavior, but didn't co-operate with him when he tried to make things better. Father Brendan unexpectedly heard his voice rising. He stopped talking and Jessica calmly smiled at him. Anger shot through him.

"Jessica toying with peoples' emotions is mean," he told her. She slightly nodded; smiling. Father Brendan waited several beats before he said,

"That's all I have to say." She stood up and walked out of his office, and he had several uncharitable thoughts.

Jessica's attendance became erratic before she stopped coming all together. Becket asked after her several times, but no one seemed to know. Becket was surprised when he suggested he and Father Brendan make a visit to her house, and Father Brendan was lukewarm about the idea. One member of the congregation said he saw her in the supermarket with a six-pack under her arm. Then there was the emergency with Maureen Sullivan being taken to the hospital with chest pains. Father Brendan took the city bus to the hospital, and was waiting in a hallway when a gurney wheeled by with Jessica's bloody and bruised face above a sheet. He smiled, and later that night, prayed for forgiveness.

ANXIETY, TIME, AND BEING PRESENT IN THE MOMENT

by Wally Swist

Time presses upon us in innumerable ways. Proust wrote, "When a man is asleep, he has in a circle round him the chain of the hours, the sequence of the years, the order of the heavenly bodies." Not only can time weigh heavily on our psyche but it may also appear to control us in ways which seem even beyond its measure, as William James wrote, "All my life I have been struck by the accuracy with which I will wake at the same exact minute night after night and morning after morning." Alan Burdick recently provides insight into the psychological aspect of time in a New Yorker article, offering the elucidation that "most likely it's the work of the circadian clocks, which, embedded in the DNA of my every cell, regulate my physiology over a twenty-four-hour period. At 4:27 A.M., I'm most aware of being at the service of something; there is a machine in me, or I am a ghost in it."

"Ghosts" and "machines" in congruence with each other can precipitate a kind of horror. Similarly, as in Edgar Alan Poe's short story, "The Tell-Tale Heart," time can, in the very least, produce within us an anxiety, possibly reigning chaos in our daily lives: in our relationships, in our careers, in every waking moment.

However, Burdick points out that in waking up at 4:27 a.m., in an incantatory prose which is resonant, that "as worried as I am in these waking moments, I also find them oddly calming. It's as if in falling asleep I'd fallen into an egg and woken as the yolk, cushioned and aloft on an extended present. It won't last, I know. In the morning, the hours and minutes will reassert themselves and

this seemingly limitless breadth of time will seem unreal and unreachable—the dream of boundless time, dreamed from the confines of an egg carton. But that's a thought for tomorrow. For now, it's now, and the tick of the bedside clock is the muffled beat of a heart."

Burdick has successfully taken the ire out of the illusion that time needs to be the perpetrator of any anxiety whatsoever. The Amherst poet, Robert Francis, who lived very much as did Henry David Thoreau for nearly a half century in a cottage he had built for himself and his wife, Patience, wrote a poem, entitled "Glass." In it he creates a working metaphor for what a poem, or poetry, could actually be, and, in fact, what life could be, if we remove all that it isn't: "If the impossible were not/ And if the glass, only the glass,/ Could be removed, the poem would remain." Essentially, this is what Alan Burdick has accomplished for us in taking time and the illusion of time away from what it really isn't, and that being the ever-present moment that Buddhists have always propounded we live in—each changing moment being what is our eternal now.

There actually is little room for anxiety if we are present for the words of Plato, writing in the fourth century B.C.E, "The instant, this strange nature, is something inserted between motion and rest, and it is in no time at all, but into it and from it what is moved changes to being at rest, and what is at rest to being moved."

Alan Burdick suggests experiencing how time "unfolds in a sentence. Recite a poem or a psalm by heart: your mind strains to recall what you've said and reaches forward to grab what you will say next." Expounding upon a passage from St. Augustine, in The Confessions, written circa 397, Burdick intimates a cogent theory of time—and consciousness, "Vital energy: that's the essence of Augustine, and of you, too, right now, as you absorb these words, strive to remember, and wonder what comes next. 'Time is nothing other than tension,' Augustine wrote, 'and I would be very surprised if it is not tension of consciousness itself.'"

References

Burdick, Alan, "The Secret Life of Time," The New Yorker, December 19-26, 2016, 68-72.

Burdick, Alan, Why Time Flies: Mostly a Scientific Investigation, Simon & Schuster, 2017.

Francis, Robert, The Collected Poems of Robert Francis, University of Massachusetts Press, 1976.

About the Author:

Wally Swist's books include Huang Po and the Dimensions of Love (Southern Illinois University Press, 2012), The Daodejing: A New Interpretation, with David Breeden and Steven Schroeder (Lamar University Literary Press, 2015), Candling the Eggs (Shanti Arts, LLC, 2017), The Map of Eternity (Shanti Arts, LLC, 2018), and Singing for Nothing: Selected Nonfiction as Literary Memoir (The Operating System, 2018).

His poems and prose have appeared in The American Book Review, Anchor: Where Spirituality and Social Justice Meet, Appalachia Journal, Arts: The Arts in Theological and Religious Studies, Commonweal, North American Review Rattle, and The Woven Tale Press.

ANXIETY & SYNCHRONICITY: LIVING IN THE REAL WORLD
by Wally Swist

The concept of synchronicity was initially posited by the psychoanalyst C. G. Jung as being an incident in our lives that reveals itself as a significant, or consequential, coincidence which apparently has no causal relationship to one another yet seems to be, in fact, directly related. The psychic healer and medical intuitive, Caroline Myss, claims that synchronicity is prevalent in our daily lives. Some writers, for instance, experience typing the same word as it is being spoken as they may hear it when they have the radio on while working. You think of your best friend in fifth grade while shopping at the mall, and when you turn your head, arms full of wrapped gifts, there she is, smiling, having stopped right in front of you.

What if you organize your life to such a degree that all is laid out the night before— as ritual? What if you are having Sunday breakfast before going to the mall, the day after a snowstorm? If there was an anxiety meter, you wouldn't be registering any. You have just finished reading your daily affirmation in Words to Live By by Eknath Easwaran (Ish-war-an), a spiritual teacher who founded the Blue Mountain Center of Meditation in Berkeley, California.

Easwaran prefaces his thought for the day by using a quote from literature, or from a spiritual text, such as The Upanishads, from which he was an expert interpreter. What if the quote was from William Wordsworth, from his Ecclesiastical sonnet, "Inside King's College Chapel, Cambridge," which reads: "Give all thou canst; high Heaven rejects the lore/ Of nicely-calculated less

or more?" What if Easwaran's last paragraph of the guidance for the day reads, "But the spiritual approach is very simple. Whatever you give—it may be a check to a worthy cause, it may be clothes to a person who is cold, it may be food to the hungry, it may be medical help to the sick— do it without thinking of getting anything in return. Do it as a service to God, not reluctantly, but with joy."

Then what if the plowman who is clearing a part of the iced-over driveway, where your car is parked, knocks on your door? It could be he is just the person who plows your driveway. It could even be a neighbor who you have known for many years. It could be all or any of those people rolled into one. He is angry because he phoned you earlier but you were in the shower, and you didn't hear the phone ring. He is angry because of many reasons. He had to wait several hours to borrow the plow truck, he has been salting the driveway since early morning, he is tired, and he is cold—all of the above.

Standing outside with him beside your car, which you are about to move, the weight of his anxiety snaps his otherwise taciturn nature and normal good intentions, and he says, "We need to live in the real world. If I am offending you, I can't help it. I am not sensitive [with the ellipsis filling the air with 'like you']," his eyes burning directly into you.

Well, here it is: your opportunity to accept this moment of synchronicity in either accepting a challenge to engage in a verbal exchange you immediately know you will rue, even by only

193

defending yourself, or by just uttering one inconsiderate word. However, you can, indeed, offer him "not reluctantly, but with joy" by giving "all thou canst." Your intuition is ringing like a bell: there is nothing you can do to assuage him or the situation. Your inner voice is exclaiming, "Let go of his insinuation that you don't live in the real world. Just let go. Let go of being right. Let go of being wrong."

Driving over to the mall in the winter rain, tapping lightly on the hood of the car, you feel a sense of peace. No amount of preparation could have prepared you for just being in the moment, being present, being in harmony with a moment of synchronicity in your life in which your anxiety wasn't a determining or detrimental factor. As Easwaran intimates: doing something "without thinking of getting anything in return" is veritable joy enough to fully grasp "High heaven" rejecting "the lore/ Of nicely-calculated less or more."

You don't even really feel a need to share your new secret with anyone that you feel you are, at this instant, truly, living in the real world.

References

Easwaran, Eknath, Words to Live By: A Daily Guide to Leading an Exceptional Life, Tomales, CA: Nilgiri Press/The Blue Mountain Center of Meditation, 2005.

Wordsworth, William, The Collected Poems of William Wordsworth, Ware, U.K.: Wordsworth Editions, Ltd., 1998.

NIGHTTIME LANDSCAPES: A MEMORY OF IRIDESCENT GREEN
by A. M. Palmer

The porch was elegant and functional. It extended from the front door to the yard in a delicate way that discouraged lounging and accented the sprawling length of the house. This was the time of American middle class prosperity, the postwar era, and such features truly spoke to the context of a home and to its character. Constructed at the height of midcentury modern design, the ranch house next door was similar to ours in many ways; the floorplan, the lush but small front yard, and the overall décor of modest prosperity. I remember it well. Just beyond the concrete slab—that minimal but elegant porch—was an outcropping of ivy that thrived year round and undulated like a sea of sprouting tentacles. At night, when the accent light was on, iridescent green flooded the leaves, giving them a glow that reminded me of a dream, an atmosphere that felt just as promising as it did unpleasant and menacing. This is my memory of the neighbors' front yard. Looking back, it speaks, not only to childhood imagination but to my curiosity about darkness and the landscapes of night.

On Halloween, costumed trick or treaters would approach with caution, clad in plastic costumes from the drugstore, flashlights in-hand, ever mindful of the older couple who would approach them from the cold, concrete slab, administering small candy bars along with a hint of suspicion. Who were these children? Did they emerge from the surrounding homes anticipating a handout? Who were the neighbors? At night, in the restrained suburban atmosphere, the cordial tones of daylight disappeared into darkness.

Children from other areas, less familiar to the neighbors, were hurried away until the following year. The flood lights were a caution as much as an invitation. In similar fashion, Christmas guests would approach the house quietly, always hidden in shadows of iridescent green, bearing gifts and speaking in slightly hushed tones. These were the festivities I remember from childhood.

As an adult, mysterious hues and colorful illuminations of night remain intriguing to me, in the neon expressions of Las Vegas, the bar scene of downtown Los Angeles, and the sprawling cityscapes of Manhattan. All such environments remind me of the peaceful yet haunting presence of my neighbors' yard. Perhaps the effect would have been lessened had they chosen a less obvious color, like blue, or even purple. Fortunately, the symbolism of nature was indispensable to them. And what about this color and its undeniable Impact?

Green. On one of my nighttime journeys to a bookstore, I came upon a memorable work by Kassia St. Clair, The Secret Lives of Color. "Verdigris, absinthe, emerald, Kelly green, Scheele's green, terre verte, avocado, celadon," she lists the various shades in a wonderful narrative. From the artist's pallet to the medicinal and culinary aspects of the color, St. Clair tells us the story of green. Looking back, I find that emerald perhaps best describes my childhood recollection of the hue, as it was made to glow and hint at the nether realms of suburbia. Also, I remember that my neighbors' use of green made it feel quite spontaneous and free, although it remained malleable to the eye of landscape designers. But there is one final connection I found between the color and my memory of night, the one that took place at the end of my mother's life.

Just prior to my mother's death in a nursing home, after a two month battle with a rampant infection, I was reminded of green.

One night, as I looked at old photographs, I found an image of her on vacation in the Midwest, a trip taken during the 1950s. It was a candid black and white picture that captured her as she examined her own camera, one of those ancient devices that required the viewer to glance through a lens mounted

on top. I remember it, because, although caught forever in shades of gray, her dress was avocado green, a favorite of hers that she described to me when I was a child. Those images—the ephemeral life of greenery, the glow of the house next door, and the strange gray tones of illness and demise—all merge into a picture of my childhood, a landscape of night and a memory of iridescent green.

About the Author:

Allison is a municipal park ranger, writer and copyeditor living in San Diego, California. She is currently the editor of Footprints, the publication of the Japanese American Historical Society of San Diego. Allison is also the founder and director of the Palmer Memorial Humanities Library.

BABY BROTHER
by Kat Kiefer-Newman

I had a brother. But I never *had* a brother.

He died before I was born and if he hadn't, I might not be here. His burial was my conception; we are permanently linked, Little Eddie and me. He is frozen as a copper boot-shaped bank, a pair of white leather baby shoes, a small stack of congratulations cards, a handful of photographs. It's a sparse collection. The photos are perhaps the saddest memorial. Two show my father holding my brother, one my mother, the rest him learning to sit up on blankets around the house and yard. Fifteen pictures. Taken on a borrowed camera.

"I always regretted not buying a camera sooner," my mother told me once. "People I knew just didn't own cameras back then. And getting the film developed was a chore. Later, we had Fotomats. That made things easier, but Fotomats weren't really around until after you were born. Oh, and it cost so dear." She shook her head and smiled in a way that suggested the cost was more than money, although I didn't understand what she was getting at. I'm not sure I do now.

My mother bought a camera as soon as she learned she was pregnant with me. There are many, too many, leather-bound albums of my first five years. Little black and white squares of funny faces (I learned early to mug for the camera), drooling chin, food smeared on my face (and in my hair), weird hats (so many of them). Later, there's me in a flowered Easter dress with crisp white gloves and a straw hat; in pajamas under a Christmas tree; standing next to my first bike; dressed for the Colorado Springs Centennial Celebration in a pioneer costume; playing tea party with my stuffed animals; birthday parties, Halloweens, school pictures. When parents have their first child, they over-do the picture taking. Looking through those many albums, one might mistakenly think I was a first child and not the fourth and last. On film I was always "on"; my first five years I was watched over, dressed-up and adorned. I was a doll, A picture-perfect Gerber baby girl. Every giggle, every pout, every lift of my eyebrow. My oldest sister, Eva, had the knack of leaning into photos with me; Maryellen, the middle sister, often looks resentful at having to be there. To the outside it appeared I was the most beloved, the goldenest golden child ever.

But Little Eddie, the true golden child, didn't live long enough for more than fifteen photos. Those fifteen photos were carefully tucked away in their own child-sized album. It didn't live in the hall linen cabinet with the other albums and scrapbooks. It stayed in my mother's stocking drawer, under mounds of perfectly ironed, yellowing, hand-tatted handkerchiefs—all of them kept like lost dreams.

When my father got his orders to go overseas with the USO, my mother was worried. Not because he would be traveling, although that could be perilous. He might have been sent to play in Korea, or in the Philippines—places where civil unrest matched that happening in the States. But he might also have gone to Japan, or Australia—neither of which was so actively tumultuous. Regardless, after living in Hawaii for a couple of years—joyfully, contentedly—my father got his orders to go on tour.

My mother was worried because she was pregnant again.

"I never seemed to be able to birth the babies I'd planned on," she told me when I was about eleven or so. She held my chin and squeezed a little. "It was always you surprises." Her smile said the surprises were happy things, but her eyes carried faraway shadows.

She came from a big family and thought she'd have a big family of her own. She said she never even realized there was any other kind of family, except large, to have. Had she been able to do this, I might have been the last of six or seven; or they might have stopped with Eddie.

And here she was after five pregnancies, with only two living children, pregnant again and about to be alone. Eva was finishing first grade, Maryellen was a toddler, and the new baby would be born while my father was overseas. It wasn't that she expected help with the children. He wasn't the sort of father who changed diapers or made meals. In 1962, dads didn't do that kind of thing. But servicemen's paychecks could sometimes be delayed when they were overseas, and how would she cover the bills?

She called my Grandmother, who said, "You'll bring those girls home and have your baby here, with your family."

"I can't do that. Eva has school. And it would be such bother for ya'll."

"Eva can go to school in Moultrie just as well as anywhere else. Besides, you'd be helping me out. Your daddy would be appalled that his house was sitting empty."

Mother knew that this was likely true.

Moultrie is in the Southern Rivers area of Georgia. Once, this was a dense forest. But by 1900, industry had milled most of the old timber. It's the seat of Colquitt County, Georgia, which has, since the end of the lumber industry, been one of the most prolific agricultural producers in the state. My granddaddy, Charlie Rainey Milligan, was not a farmer, but he did come from a farming family, as my grandmother did. Granddaddy was the eleventh of twelve children, and his father died when he was three. The family struggled so much that when he finished eighth grade he dropped out of

school to go work for his older brother. There, he learned construction, and helped to build many of the important buildings in town, including private homes for the social elites.

When I was building my family tree on a genealogy website, my Aunt Theo told me, "Daddy bought and rebuilt the rental house he and Mother raised us in." Official records hold that this happened sometime in 1935 when he and my grandmother purchased or obtained (finalized) the deed on their rental house. Over the next many years, until his death, he would redesign, expand, and alter both the footprint and the function of the formerly two-bedroom cottage, creating a patchwork four-bedroom home with a den. When he died, my grandmother, then forty-eight, a widower with a thirteen-year-old daughter still at home, had to figure out a new life for herself and it ended up away from that house and away from Moultrie.

It was September when my mother arrived with her rounded belly and two little girls. They barely had time to unpack because Edward "Eddie" George Kiefer, Jr. was born on October 25th, 1963—twenty-four days after his cousin, Theodosia Burr, named for my Aunt Theo. Both births were quickly overshadowed by the assassination of President John F. Kennedy on November 22 in Dallas, Texas. Maybe because of this, or perhaps because of Eddie's short life, the two cousins never got to meet. Aunt Theo told me that she'd meant to come for the birth of Little Eddie, but Sarasota was almost five hours away and she was busy with her own newborn.

Years later she told me, "I never saw him until the funeral." Her introduction to my brother was him dressed in a tiny suit and laid out in one of the smallest coffins anyone had ever seen.

But that was later. In that October, Eddie was still a much-anticipated handful. His face rosy, his eyes clear blue. He wasn't fussy, even when they first brought him home. Mother said he was a dreamy baby, quietly watching the shadows play along the ceiling near his crib. He lay for hours listening to the birds call from outside the bay window at the front of the house. Life was settling in for my mother and her three children in her old childhood home.

Eva said she came home one day while Mother and Grandmother were changing Eddie. At eight years old, Eva had never seen a naked boy. That's not so unusual for the time or the lives my family lived; my mother was circumspect about personal privacy and matters of the body. Eva saw Eddie and squealed, pointing at the baby's tiny penis. She danced around sing-songing, "I see Eddie's pee-pee."

Little Eddie, the center of attention, promptly peed on his big sister. Eva laughed hilariously and Mother joined in. Grandmother, in the meantime, folded her arms in a decided absence of amusement. She may have even clucked her tongue before leaving the room to get towels and PineSol to clean up the mess.

Despite that joyful moment, my mother remembered feeling trapped in that house with its dark, wood-paneled walls and closed-in center kitchen. The layout was ramshackle, one room branching off another without pattern. The narrow, wood-planked stairs that led to a loft bedroom were cacophonous when Eva ran up and down them each day. Sometimes, my mother told me, after Eva was at school, Maryellen and Eddie taking naps, the quiet in the house pressed on her, pressed into her skin, and she wondered if she'd ever not feel the weight of it.

When my father's tour ended, he gathered up my mother, sisters, and brother and moved to an apartment near the Air Force Base in Novato, California. Their home was surrounded by wobbly, gopher pocked lawns and hilly mounds that hid skunk dens, and it backed up on woods where coastal oaks held their own against the predominant pine and redwood.

Eva was in third grade. Maryellen was a sturdy, curious three-year-old. Some days, Mother dropped Maryellen and Eddie off with the babysitter so she could run errands and have a little break. Three children were wearing her out. But she told me once that she was happy there. Father gigged many nights in nearby Sausalito and San Francisco. He was now a sergeant in the USAF. They weren't struggling as much to make ends meet, which meant they weren't fighting as much about money. But underneath the battle over money was a different battle, one that in

1964 was beginning in many working- and middle-class homes. My mother wanted to work again. She'd left the military when she was pregnant with Eva. She'd loved the service and had hoped to have a career, working her way up to officer. My father, though, wanted his wife at home making eggs and sausage for breakfast, keeping the house clean, caring for the children, and having a hot dinner on the table when he got home at night.

Mother detested housework and was a terrible cook. She loved her children, of course. We never had any doubt that she did. But she would rather read historical novels or romance fiction than get on the floor and play with blocks or dolls. Having a job to get dressed for, earning a paycheck— these were the things my mother wanted most for herself. Even though she wasn't working at a paying job, she volunteered with different non-commissioned officers' wives' club charities and committees, and this also caused fighting between my parents.

In Northern California, though, caring for a school-aged child, a toddler, and a newborn was full-time work. Still, she secretly spent hours poring over college catalogs and looking through newspaper want ads.

Decades later, she'd put it this way: "I was just so distracted, thinking about what I wanted to do, to be, and I wasn't paying enough attention to the details."

It was the end of August and Eva came home with sniffles. Soon enough, Maryellen caught them. Shortly after that, Eddie came down with what seemed like a more virulent case. Eva's runny nose eventually stopped and Maryellen's coughing petered out.

Eddie didn't get better.

Mother called the base hospital and got an afternoon appointment with the elderly pediatrician who'd seen Eva, Maryellen, and Eddie for all their shots, their cuts and scrapes, since they'd been in Northern California.

He listened to Eddie's lungs, pinched Eddies chubby knees and cheeks, tested the baby's reflexes. He looked into Eddie's snot-crusted nostrils and then down his red-raw throat. The doctor said,

"He'll be fine, Mrs. Kiefer. You just keep taking great care of him, as I know you are, and he'll be right as rain soon enough."

She asked if they should have some tests done.

"No, no. None of that is necessary," he assured her. "He's just got a nasty bug. No need to get worked up. You make sure he has enough to drink, cool baths when he starts to complain. It'll break soon enough. Fevers always do."

She worried, but trusted the doctor. That nasty bug didn't go away, though. Eddie developed bloody stool and diarrhea, cramping and abdominal pain, then vomiting. She called the base hospital in a panic and got him in with a rotating civilian doctor. That man, fresh out of medical school, immediately called for lab work.

My mother was always reluctant to discuss what happened next. I can imagine it, though. Years later I had a scare with my older daughter, which cast my mother's experience with my brother into stark relief. The details are also in question, as my sisters and aunt have different variations of the story. This is my version, pieced together from things my mother had said over the years.

I believe that my mother brought Eddie back to the doctor when those test results came in. She held him in the center of the silver examination table. One pale hand patted listlessly against the metal, making it ring.

"It looks like Eddie has pediatric small-bowel volvulus," the doctor said. He explained that this is when the intestine loops around on itself and knots up, resulting in acute obstruction of the bowels. His face grave, he said, "It's treatable when caught early enough."

In my brother's case it was too late. He now had gangrene in the intestines. My mother told me once that the doctor's voice had been kind but he was also very blunt, which she appreciated. He said, "Now, we need to make Eddie comfortable."

What did that young doctor with the kind voice do next? Maybe his face bent into a sympathetic mask, his hands, useless, pushed deep into the pockets of his lab coat. It could be that the light glanced off his stethoscope as it swung a little back and forth, like a metronome, or perhaps a pulse. Back and forth, in time with the military

clock on the drab grey walls. The air in the room would have stopped moving. As for my mother— always so collected, so calm— did she feel her breath stop? Did she wonder if she would ever breathe again?

I've only seen my mother cry once. It was during a trip back to Georgia, when I was twenty-two. This was 1987 and we'd just gotten off the plane in Atlanta. It was the middle of July, the air heavy with the summer rain. A man from Ronald McDonald House had a sign: Ruth Ann Kiefer. My mother didn't rush, she hung back, almost afraid to approach him. But I rushed to him. "How's Beth?" I said. And my mother asked, "How's Eva?"

Mother knew. Of course she knew that we needed to be there, to care for my sister, now.

Beth was my niece, my sister's daughter. She had terminal leukemia. She was only two and a half at the time.

The man took my mother's hand and she flinched a little but wouldn't look away. He said, "I'm afraid Beth passed away while ya'll were in the air. Miss Eva is waiting at the hospital for you and Miss Katherine." He drove us there so we could be with my sister and say our goodbyes to my niece.

But it wasn't there that Mother cried. It was later that night. I woke up in a strange bed at Ronald McDonald House. I was screaming from a nightmare that faded almost immediately. My mother came to me and held me and we cried together.

Maybe she cried there in the doctor's office with her baby boy. Maybe she pulled Eddie's fingers loose from the edge of the shiny table. No one spoke. Mother would have become embarrassed by the awkward pause. She'd count the dots on the doctor's tie, how many times he blinked. She'd count the ticks the wall clock made. The flash of light that reflected off his stethoscope might have mesmerized or hypnotized her. Whose turn was it to speak? All those years of etiquette training and comportment classes, useless now.

No. She wouldn't have cried.

Little Eddie likely whimpered. That broke the spell. My mother straightened her cuffs, hitched

Eddie up onto her hip and asked, "May I take my son home now, please?"

She wouldn't wait for the doctor to answer. She would gather up the blanket and the diaper bag, and walk away from the doctor, the hospital, the horrific news. I'm sure she kissed her baby's sweaty hair and wiped his forehead. She laid him down on the passenger seat and tucked blankets around him to keep him from rolling about. Then she drove home, wondering what she would say to my father and sisters.

At the house, she sat in the car, Eddie dozing beside her on the bench seat. "Dear Lord," she began. She couldn't finish. "That was the last time I ever prayed," she told me.

"Not ever again? Not once?" I asked.

"Why? I realized looking over at that sweaty little boy, my little boy, who was dying and had been dying and no one even tried to save him. I looked at him and realized there just couldn't be a God. No god would do such a horrible thing."

Eddie died on September 17th, 1964. My mother had his casket flown back to Georgia. The Milligan family had cemetery plots and Mother insisted that Eddie be buried in hers. When I asked why, because it meant she couldn't ever visit him, she said, "It's more important that he be home. I needed to take Baby Brother home."

The service was in the same church where Mother and Father had been married. My Granddaddy had done construction on the altar and the pulpit sometime in the '40s. His hands had touched so much of the chapel, making it truly a family homecoming for the little boy.

"And there were Easter lilies everywhere. Wreaths, tall vases, bowls full," my mother recalled. "Easter lilies are so beautiful, so lush. But I can't stand the sight or smell of them now. To me, they're death flowers."

My Aunt told me that after the funeral my family took the bus down to Sarasota to visit briefly. The weather was warm, but everyone came down with another flu. Then they all climbed onto a return Greyhound and made the trip back to Northern California. Mother said it was the longest bus ride of her life, trying to take care of my father and my two sisters, all while worrying about yet another flu and what might happen next. She was almost too busy caring for her little family to feel the sadness, the loneliness—almost. She was also queasy, unable to keep any food down, but she kept that to herself. She always took care of herself, rarely asking for help.

Back at Hamilton Air Force Base, Mother told me she had everyone checked out by the doctors, just in case. As expected, with lots of rest and water, Father, Eva, and Maryellen were soon better. But Mother wasn't. She decided she needed some tests done and went in to see her own doctor. She probably didn't even tell my father. Not yet. Not until she knew what was wrong.

Tests always take forever. Waiting for results is a kind of special hell. Instead of getting her results over the phone, the doctor insisted she come back into the office.

Father drove the car to work, as usual, so she took a bus. Her heart seemed to lock somewhere up in her chest as she rode along, the town passing outside the window. Underneath her calf leather gloves with the tiny pearl buttons carefully closed, her palms slicked with sweat. She was escorted into the office and sat, feet forward, knees tightly aligned over them, skirt smoothed, handbag on her lap, hands folded on top of that. She was a straight line, waiting for what would come next.

He cleared his throat. Then said, "Mrs. Kiefer, congratulations are in order. You're going to have a baby."

Once again the air stopped moving. My mother wondered if it was the giant clock on the wall or her pulse thrump-thrumping in the back of her skull. "I can't possibly be expecting. I just buried my baby boy."

The doctor put on his stern face and said, "Not only is it possible, but it's happening. And you're going to start eating again and stop trying to climb into that coffin after your son. You have two little girls at home who need you and another baby on the way."

She blinked at his forwardness. She told me she didn't much care for his tone. Just like that she said it: "I didn't much care for his tone."

"He'd just said you were pregnant and you didn't much care for his tone?"

She laughed. "Well, I suppose that does sound ridiculous. But he was scolding me so. 'You will go home and take care of yourself, young lady.' He said that." She smiled at the memory. "And I was so mad that I got up and did just that. In fact, I did better than that. I quit smoking, drinking. I took calcium and other vitamins. And I ate everything in sight. Oooh, but I got fat. And you were a fat little baby when you were born."

But my Aunt Theo tells it a little differently. She says my mother knew she was pregnant when they buried Eddie. She clearly had morning sickness during that visit to Sarasota. Eva confirms that everyone was throwing up on the long bus ride back to Northern California.

My daughter, Geneveive, once said that she thinks both of these stories could be true. "Grandma was so good at compartmentalizing. She wasn't ready to be pregnant, most likely, and so waited to be pregnant."

Gen asked me what I thought. "Which version do you believe?"

I shook my head and said, "I believe it doesn't matter which way it happened." She hugged me and left the room. My mother buried her son. What else can you say about that? That's the end of a story, not the beginning of one.

One of the last times Mother and I talked about Eddie's death, she admitted that all she really wanted to do was stay there in Georgia with him. Maybe it hadn't been the stern, fatherly doctor who told her she couldn't climb into the coffin with Eddie. Maybe it was something she thought all on her own.

I said, "So I saved your life?"

And she said, "You made it so I had to keep living." Then she changed the subject.

They aren't the same.

About the Author:

Kat Kiefer-Newman is a writer in the dusty dairy valley of San Jacinto, California. When she's not writing, she teaches myth and mythic themes at California State University, San Bernardino. She is a graduate of the University of California, Riverside, Low Residency Palm Desert and holds an MFA from this program; she is also a graduate of the Pacifica Graduate Institute, and holds an MA and a PhD from this institution.

DEAL BETWEEN FRIENDS

by Desiree Jung

I open the drawer to find part of myself: shoes from another time, green knee-length boots, amidst books. The objects scare me. Remembering petrifies me – the passage of time haunting. I cannot control my feelings. Before any resistance, the past arrives into the present. I remember when my father gave me all the books from the Vaga-Lume collection. It was a Birthday Gift. With tremendous anxiety, a mixture of excitement and fear, I wanted to read them all at once. Obviously, I couldn't; the stack of books representing what already at that age, no more than ten years old, overflowed in me: the complexity of human emotions, the tragedy of such material. My child tried to control time obsessively. Under such young skin, frustration grew with the impossibility of holding time in one's hands, the lived minutes not returning. This rhythm, worth saying, lasting a lifetime. Or just a second. Today, again, time surprises me with its presence, embodied in the old boots and books. Looking me sideways, as though asking: are you still afraid of me?

I smile at the question, for the shoes aren't even that important. But, considering my hesitation, I recognize I have harvested certain traumas, among them the emotional fear of finding old smells and memories. In short, a generalized paralysis for knowing that, soon after such encounter, emptiness may surge, along with the experience of what is impermanent. Avoiding such constitutive lack of daily life is even worse, I know. Within these gaps are born the necessary and structuring silences. Those one only encounters after strong emotional events, the death of

something important, be it real or symbolic, for example. The end of anything brings quietude and a certain interior lament. A wait, god knows for what. On the other hand, a greater opportunity to reset one's subjective gaze.

Starting with anything: the unexpected visit of a hummingbird in a cold autumn morning, imperceptible before, searching for a sweet summer taste. The trees, the seasons, the ongoing conversations in the markets. And of course, the ghosts. Because in the middle of the road there is always a shoe, a book, or even a rock, as Carlos Drummond de Andrade used to say. These, filled with joy, pain and sadness – a coming and going of emotions and hurting; because there is always a bit of them. Memories, bits of unrealized dreams, expectations, disappointments, revived in the present and making us who we are.

I am all that. I am also saudade, of mother specially. Of her loving and affectionate way. And that, throughout her life, thought me what today I cultivate in myself. To believe in what you can't see. To have faith. In dreams, even if they don't realize the way you imagine, but are in themselves a life force. For that reason, I won't excuse myself before I put my old boots and reread the teen book of old times. Take a walk around my past. Meet my mother once more, holding me in her lap. See in that child's eyes a bit of myself but also my niece. Become emotional with this mystery without being ashamed by my tears. Walk freely, cradled by every arm that has touched me with love. Will do. Throw the seeds. So that in the daily harvest, I can find the necessary affection, come sad or happy days. In this agreement that I and you, time, have signed – lovers until the end.

ACORDO ENTRE AMIGOS

de Desiree Jung

Abro a gaveta e encontro um pedaço de mim: sapatos de uma outra época, cano alto verde, misturados entre alguns livros. Os objetos me assustam. Recordar petrifica. A passagem do tempo atormenta. Não consigo controlar os sentimentos. Antes que possa resistir, o passado está de volta ao presente. Lembro-me quando ganhei do meu pai todos os livros da coleção Vaga-Lume. Presente de aniversário. Numa tremenda ansiedade, mistura de excitamento e temor, quis ler tudo ao mesmo tempo. Não consegui; a pilha de livros representando o que já naquela idade, não mais que dez anos, transbordava: a complexidade das emoções humanas, a tragédia deste material. Obsessiva, minha criança buscava controlar o tempo. Na pele tão jovem, se frustrava com tamanha impossibilidade: segurar a vida entre as mãos, os minutos vividos e sem retorno. Esta dinâmica, vale dizer, a durar por toda uma vida. Ou apenas um segundo. Hoje, de novo, o tempo a me surpreender com a sua presença, encorpado nos velhos sapatos e livros. Me olhando de soslaio, como quem pergunta: ainda tens medo de mim?

Sorrio. Os sapatos nem são assim tão importantes. Mas considerando a minha hesitação, compreendo que adquiri certos traumas, entre eles o receio emocional de reencontrar algo antigo, rememorar cheiros e lembranças. Enfim, uma paralisia generalizada por saber que logo depois pode chegar um vazio, uma experiência do que é inconstante. Evitar estas faltas participantes do cotidiano é ainda pior, eu sei, pois elas constituem um silêncio necessário e estruturante. E que só se conhece depois de alguma experiência emocional forte, a morte de

qualquer coisa importante, seja ela real ou simbólica – o fim de um período da vida. Isso traz uma quietude, um certo lamento interior. Uma espera, sabe-se lá por que. Por outro lado, uma grande oportunidade: refazer a vida, o olhar subjetivo.

A partir de qualquer coisa: a visita inesperada de um beija flor numa manhã fria de outono, antes imperceptível, em busca de um sugo doce do verão, por exemplo. As árvores, as estações, as conversas soltas nos mercados. E claro, os fantasmas. Porque no meio do caminho há sempre um sapato, um livro, ou mesmo uma pedra, como já dizia Drummond. Estes que são repletos de alegrias, dores e tristezas – num entra e sai de emoções e mágoas; porque há sempre um pouco delas. As memórias, os pedaços de desejos não realizados, as expectativas não vividas, revividas no presente, fazem de nós quem somos.

Sou tudo isso. E também saudade, de mãe principalmente. Do seu jeito doce e carinhoso. E que, ao longo da vida, me ensinou o que hoje cultivo em mim. Acreditar no que não se pode ver. Ter fé. Os sonhos, mesmo que não se realizem como se imagina, mas que movimentam a vida. Por isso te peço licença mas vou vestir meus velhos sapatos e reler o livro da coleção infantil. Dar uma volta pelo passado. Reencontrar minha mãe me segurando no colo. Ver nos olhos daquela criança que fui um pouco de mim, mas também da minha sobrinha. Me emocionar com o mistério disto tudo sem ter vergonha das minhas lágrimas. Andar livre, embalada por todas as mãos que um dia me acariciaram e tocaram com carinho. Farei isto. Lançarei estas sementes. Para que na colheita cotidiana seja capaz de encontrar os afetos necessários, venham dias felizes ou tristes. Neste acordo que eu e você, tempo, traçamos, amantes até o fim.

About the Author:

Desirée Jung has published translations, poetry and short stories in North American magazines and others around the world. Among them are Exile, Modern Poetry in Translation, The Antigonish Review, Belleville Park Pages. Her book of short stories, Desejos Submersos, is published by Chiado Editora, in Portugal. She has received a film degree at the Vancouver Film School, as well as an MFA in Creative Writing and a PhD in Comparative Literature from the University of British Columbia. Her website is www.desireejung.com

THE FIRST TELEVISION ON THE BLOCK
by Anita Gorman

It was 1950 in Queens. On the street where the Andersons lived, they were not the only Swedish immigrants; the Carlsons lived next door. The rest of the block was comprised of what the Andersons and Carlsons would call outsiders or just people who were different, or foreigners.

Mr. Anderson worked in a factory in Brooklyn. He did not think of himself as an innovator or a revolutionary, but for some reason he decided that he wanted to buy a television set. Mrs. Anderson was skeptical. "What do we want that for? We're perfectly fine the way we are right now, with the radio in the kitchen."

Their two children, Greta and Stig, were all in favor of the television. At their school, Public School 102, also known as P.S. 102, a few kids already had television sets in their houses, and Greta and Stig were beginning to feel inferior. "We want it!" they shouted together, and their mother was overruled, though, if truth be told, Mrs. Anderson secretly wanted a television set. She wanted to impress her neighbors, the O'Briens, the Pulaskis, the Torrentinos, and all the other foreigners on their street. As for the Andersons, they had been thoroughly Americanized, by removing an "s" from their names. In the old country they would have been Andersson, the son of Anders, not the son of Ander, if you, dear reader, are following. So the Andersons really thought of themselves as Americans and the others as immigrants, even though they themselves were immigrants.

They lived in Elmhurst, which sounded better than it looked. There were elm trees in those days, but before long they would be destroyed by the infamous Dutch Elm Disease. Still, even in the best of times, there weren't that many elms, but there were the usual city noises and some cars and a general ugliness to their surroundings that they tried hard not to notice.

Mr. Anderson knew about a store in Maspeth that sold Stromberg-Carlson television sets. He liked the name, Stromberg-Carlson. It was so obviously Swedish and could not be anything else. So the family, Mr. and Mrs. Anderson and Greta and Stig, walked to the bus stop on Grand Avenue and rode to Maspeth. They did not have a car. A car was deemed unnecessary in New York City, but Greta and Stig knew that a car would be really helpful if they ever wanted to go to interesting places on Long Island or beyond the borders of the Bronx.

They got off the bus and walked to the store. Unfortunately, from Mr. and Mrs. Anderson's point of view, the store was owned by someone named Prokopf, from somewhere in eastern Europe. Not Swedish, obviously, but the store sold Stromberg-Carlson, and that's what the Andersons, at least the senior Andersons, wanted.

By the time they were finished being swept away by Mr. Prokopf's sales pitch, the Andersons had bought the fanciest television set in the store. But it was not just a television. No, this twelve-inch television screen was housed inside of a stupendously large wooden cabinet. Nor did it live there alone. On the lower right hand side there was a little door that when opened revealed a 45 rpm turntable. That meant, of course, that the Andersons would have to start purchasing 45 rpm recordings at an alarming rate. But that was not all:

the large wooden cabinet also housed an AM radio and an FM radio. Mr. and Mrs. Anderson were dazzled by the fact that one cabinet could hold four astounding ways to be entertained; what they failed to realize was that they could be entertained by only one medium at a time.

Mrs. Anderson was a baseball fan, so she wanted to use the AM radio. Mr. Anderson thought he was more cultured than most, so he wanted to use the FM radio. Greta wanted to play the 45 rpm recordings and was determined to buy whatever was popular that day and that hour. Little Stig just wanted to watch Captain Video or maybe even a test pattern, those funny screens that the networks showed during the hours when they weren't broadcasting. Just imagine: there were many hours in the day when the networks, and there were just three of them, were not even broadcasting!

So the Andersons were faced with a dilemma: who was to watch or listen or in any way use the new four-in-one Stromberg-Carlson behemoth that now stood in the corner of their living room?

As it turned out, that was the least of their worries. The most of their worries involved the neighbors on their street, the ones who did not have televisions. The foreigners didn't care about AM radio (they had that) or FM radio (what was that?) or 45 rpm recordings (huh?), but they knew they wanted to watch television and so, one by one, or two by two, they started to fill up the Andersons' living room, sometimes with lame excuses, sometimes with blatant excuses, and sometimes with no excuses at all. And Mr. Anderson, who was a polite man to strangers, if not to his immediate family, always graciously allowed the Irish and the Poles and the Italians to sit in his living room and watch what he eventually decided was not, in fact, worth watching.

Eventually, the neighbors drifted away. They, too, had decided that there was not much worth watching. Mrs. Anderson retreated to the kitchen, where she could listen to a Brooklyn Dodgers game on the radio or even, on Saturday afternoons, to the Metropolitan Opera. Greta decided that she liked books better than television, so she spent a lot of time in her room reading the classics that her mother bought her at Macy's or the

contraband Nancy Drew mysteries that no one approved of but everyone loved. Mr. Anderson insisted on watching the news, and he usually watched the news alone. When the news was not on, which was most of the time, he spent his leisure hours working on Stig's model railroad setup in the basement, convincing himself that he was doing it for his son and not for himself, but he was really doing it for himself.

In the end, little Stig was the only one who spent hours watching television: Howdy Doody, Captain Video, Captain Kangaroo, Buck Rogers. In spite of all that, he grew up to be a responsible adult and earned a doctorate in economics.

About the Author:

Anita G. Gorman grew up in Queens and is aging in northeast Ohio. Her scholarly work has appeared in such publications as Clues: A Journal of Detection; FOLLY; Mythlore; Dime Novel Roundup; the Swedish-American Historical Quarterly, and eight volumes of the Dictionary of Literary Biography. "Where Are You, O High-School Friends?" was published in Unfinished Chapters (2015) and "Finding Bill" in Finding Mr. Right (2016). Her short stories have appeared in Gilbert, Down in the Dirt, Dual Coast, Jitter Press, Red Fez, Speculative Grammarian, Scarlet Leaf Review, and Knee-Jerk. Her one-act play, Astrid; Or, My Swedish Mama, will be produced by the Hopewell Theatre in Youngstown, Ohio in 2018.

HUMBOLDT

by Thomas Larsen

"Get the gate for me will ya, pardner?"

He's been calling everyone "pardner" for a week now in clear violation of the code. I work the twisted length of wire.

"Other way," he tells me.

"What the hell do we need a gate for anyway?"

"Looks like your finger's bleeding."

I yank the loop off the post. The gate drops on my foot like it always does.

We are on our way to do laundry. We decided on Saturday as laundry day thinking other things would come along to occupy our Sundays through Fridays. This has not been the case. Great gaps of time to kill have reduced us to the mundane, throwing rocks across the river, watching the goats and chickens. Mostly we smoke dope and sleep.

But laundry has gotten away from Steve, which accounts for the duffel bags and his overall appearance. Most Saturdays I launder alone, a practice the locals find as amusing as my daily dip in the icy Matol. In the land of lax hygiene I stick out like a finely groomed thumb.

The thing is, Steve really likes it here. Everyone seems to like it here. I don't know what I was expecting, but counting down to laundry day doesn't ring a bell. I'm all for getting back to the land, just don't get it all over me. For a time I thought that filthy jeans and black socks were Humboldt de rigueur. Then I realized the natives weren't wearing socks.

"Here take this will ya?" Steve hands me one of his bags in exchange for mine, the contents barely rounding the bottom. Past the garden, weed choked and wilting, cultivated in a cocaine frenzy then left to the deer when the Quaaludes came. Skirting the cluster of abandoned trucks and school buses, tiptoeing by the guy who lives in the tree stump, on through the last stand of live oaks and out into open country. A scene as idyllic as Steve swore it would be. Idyllic. The very word taking shape like a row of Greek columns. I can dig it. Skies so blue you lose your balance, grassy hills folding into each other, scattered horses, so right on.

"Oh what a beautiful moooor-ning," Steve's Goulet is right on the money. It's a schtick that gets him stitches only I'm not laughing.

"What's on your mind pard?" he gives me a nudge.

"Pard? What the fuck is pard?"

"Derived from pardner. A rural southwestern colloquialism indicating partnership in, or symbiotic -"

"Give it a break."

"What? ... Pard?"

"Or anything derived thereof."

"Whatever you say p-uh-"

Around the bull nose base of Karen's hill, tent flaps open to the breeze, silhouette so still you wonder what she's doing. I worry about Karen, though not enough to keep from sneaking up there every other night. I fear that she will kill me in my sleep for no reason other than she's bat-shit batty and heavily armed. Maybe part of the attraction, bored shitless and horny as I am. At the crest of the hill we stop to watch a pair of turkey hawks soar on the thermals. We're thinking about what we look like, long-haired and berry brown, eyes all squinty against the sun.

Steve pulls a roach from the cigarette pack in his pocket.

"Rains coming," he cups his hands and fires it up. "I can smell it in the wind."

"Blow me clown."

Near the flatbed bridge we see dust clouds to the north. A car, or more likely an amalgam of parts cobbled together and bearing makeshift living quarters. These hills abound with vehicular aberrations unseen since the Oakie days. Makes and models unto themselves, as much a part of the White Thorn milieu as baby butts and brown teeth. Breaking out of the far trees in a flash of sunlight, yellow jeep with a dog in back and a real looker at the wheel. The type that strikes a cord of longing, blow dried blonde, and fresh as a daisy, clearly not of this place.

"What have we here?" Steve drops his duffel bag and shades his eyes. A rind of dirt runs from wrist to elbow.

"She must be lost," is all I can think.

"Maybe she came to a fork in the road and just took it."

"Someone should warn her."

"Leave it to me. "

The jeep stops at the lip of the bridge. The dog jumps out, circles once then jumps back in when blondie doesn't budge. Sits slouched behind the wheel scanning the hills behind high priced shades.

"Howdy ma'am," Steve gives her his goofiest grin. "What can we do for you this fine morning?"

"Johnny Cash? Is that you?" she rakes her hair straight back so it falls over her face, a move that makes my heart melt.

"The name's Steve. This here's my pardner, Tim," a rare reference to my first name.

"Steve and Tim. How homespun."

"Right purty dog you got there."

She looks to me. "He's kidding, right?"

"He better be," I say, more to him.

She slides sideways out of the jeep and strides over the flatbed, the last few in a slow sashay that's pretty much out of our league. Standing too close as we downright ache for her. Our needy concave faces reflected in her shades, Steve looking less than human in his laundry togs, myself, so much taller and neat as a pin.

"Do me a favor boys, watch Romeo and the jeep while I go buy a horse."

"Give us ride into town and you got it," I strike the standard deal.

"Sorry, I'm going west. You know, into the sunset?"

"To the road then."

"Play your cards right, cowboy," she turns and heads up the trail, butt cheeks churning for as long as we care to watch. Until she's just a tiny speck veering left and straight up the hill to John's cabin. Not a cabin so much as a carport chained to pine trees and draped in blue plastic, the building material of choice in these parts. Untold acres of it lashed to rooftops and duck taped to shanties, forever not blending in. John of the horses and flamenco guitar, big guy from Yonkers, all I know about John. Watching until we can no longer see her, just the patch of blue where we know her to be.

"Mmmmmmmmmmmdoggies!" Steve says before I can stop him.

"Steve … Steven," I step around to face him. "Lose the gomer routine OK? You're from Pittsburgh. You wouldn't know shitkicker if you stepped in it, remember?"

"Sure thing Tim," he says in his normal voice.

" 'preciate it," to ease the blow.

"I thought I had it down pretty good."

"Too good. It's like hanging out with an imbecile."

"I meant it as an inside joke."

"Too cagey. The cagey starts to fray the nerves."

"For years from now, to get a laugh."

"Also a sort of leering quality to it. Unbecoming."

"But good, though."

"Too cagey. It wasn't working."

"I gotta tell you it feels right. A million miles from home you can be anyone."

"No you can't."

"It's the fu-manchu isn't it?" he gives the ends a twirl.

"No. The fanchu-manchu is another thing entirely"

"Hey Tim, it's 1975. Loosen up a bit."

"One affectation too many, since you brought it up."

We turn our eyes to the hillside. Two figures, one less tiny, move at an angle to the top and over. I picture them coming down the other side, passed the nasty dead thing, over the water line that runs to Karen's, through scrub pines to a small unfenced clearing where his John's horses gather for no apparent reason.

"You really want her, don't you Tim?"

"Are you kidding? The first girl I've seen in weeks without head lice?"

"How will you stand it after she's gone?"

"That was my first thought."

"You know what I say don't you?" Steve folds his arms across his chest.

"What do you say?"

"That's one fine looking woman. Jaysus!"

"I got no problem shooting you, you know."

Steve smiles and slaps me on the back. "Hey! That's more like it, p-uh-."

We gather our bags and start across the flat-bed, White Thorn creek a-gurgle below us. The yellow jeep gleams like something perfect.

"Ican see it in your eyes, Tim. What you wouldn't give."

"To sleep in clean sheets."

"What we came to get away from."

"Take a shower, watch TV."

"Mere creature comforts, friend. While she's taking a shower and watching TV you're out here living history. Something you can tell your grandkids about."

"Right. The summer I shit behind a tree."

"The last of the badlands. It's crude, I grant you, but so out of touch."

"And the good points?"

Steve shrugs his eyebrows as if the good points are obvious. As if living in a lean-to and shooting smack is a noble rite of passage, as if killing and eating campsite mascots is to be expected, as if helicopter surveillance is a really a good thing.

"When will you ever get a chance to do this again?" he says in all seriousness.

A dozen comebacks come to mind but I hold my tongue. What we're doing, essentially nothing, speaks for itself. Oddly, the moment passes into an interlude so elementally perfect, I swear I can hear the sun shine. The essence of the north coast goes straight to our heads. Stillness, deep and seductive, light and color like no other place, the shadow of a hawk rippling over, the buzz of a fly right out of Steinbeck.

Steve tosses our bags in the back of the jeep and slips in behind the wheel.

"This thing about women and horses," he checks himself in the side mirror. "It's not natural you know."

"Why is that? Men like horses too."

"Not if they don't have to. With women it's genetic."

"Stereotype?" I settle in beside him.

"Exactly. The thing we use to explain away the truth."

"I thought that was reefer."

"Which reminds me," he slips another roach from his pocket, the local blend, ungodly stuff. Here in Humboldt it's not the quantity of drugs, it's the quality. Reefer so potent you can't work a pencil, lines as pure as the driven snow. It's the main reason nothing gets done around here. That and the quantity.

Over Steve's shoulder I see another dust cloud approaching. Tom and Laura's panel truck, by the sound of it, rods knocking as it clears the trees, sheathed in blue plastic and shingled in cedar. Tom's bulbous head lolls behind the wheel, a gaggle of limbs flail in the back, Laura and the triplets, Moe, Larry and Curly. They pull up behind us. Tom grins his half-wit grin and leans on the horn.

"Clampett's at twelve o'clock," I give Steve a nudge. "You better move this thing."

"Me? I haven't driven in months."

"OK, move."

"No wait, I can do it," he reaches for the key then changes his mind.

"Come on, before he comes over here."

"OK," he turns the key and the jeep jumps to life. "Let's see, first gear?"
"Straight up, Just do it, will you?"

He eases the clutch and there's a sudden lurch followed by a thump and a string of blood curdling yelps.

Romeo!

Off like a shot but running funny, the echo of yelps curdling as he lists to the right. Turning to a moan when his front legs crumple, low and mournful like he knows what's coming. Eyes rolled back, tongue flaccid in the dirt, dead before we even get there. The image sears into memory, our end of the deal gone horribly wrong. Confirming what we've always suspected. If there's a way to fuck up we will find it. The dog dead for a minute now, soon to be two and so on. Steve and I kneel on either side, the sun shines, the creek gurgles, but it's all so different now. No way to fix it, over in the blink of an eye. We have done what we came all this way to do.

"Oh Christ, we've killed it."

"Steve, it was an accident."

"Jesus, oh Jesus, what do we do?"

Larry and Curly come up from behind, mouths agape and eyes bulging. Worse yet, a distant scream heads our way.

"Is he dead?" Larry wants to know.

"Did you kill him?" snot-nose Curly, more to the point.

"He's dead all right," Tom says for the record.

"They killed him, OK" Laura sets it straight.

It came out later that Romeo was seven. Prime of life and the picture of health right up to moment we killed him. If we hadn't, the girl, the dog, the and possibly a horse may have passed a happy decade together. Of course if we hadn't, Steve might have remembered to set the emergency brake. For Romeo and the yellow jeep, any road not taken could have only been longer.

About the Author:

Thomas Larsen has been writing fiction for 25 years and his work has appeared in Newsday, Best American Mystery Stories, Raritan, Philadelphia Stories Magazine and the LA Review. His novels, FLAWED and INTO THE FIRE are available through Amazon.

DOGS, HOGS, AND SIGNS

by Bill Vernon

The motorcyclist turning onto Bakers Road ahead of us had the 1960s Hell's Angels' look, but that impression didn't occur to me then anymore than did the fact I'd never seen a motorcycle on the hill before. I was too caught up in memories. This was a homecoming of sorts after a dozen years' absence.

We were at the foot of the hill on which my father's family had lived. Before coming, I'd studied a satellite image that lost the contours of the hill and Bakers Road. It didn't show that the bricks on the road surface were planted sideways so a long rectangular edge of each jutted out to improve traction for the engines that clawed uphill on its back. Climb the road on foot, and you had to lean so far forward into the hill that your hands touched the bricks ahead like a knuckle-walking ape. In my days there, folks willingly bowed to the hill's demands, and as I turned off onto it, Bakers Road seemed unchanged.

But this now was decades later from my childhood. Within a few yards off the state route at the base, I lost sight of New Straitsville and entered the wild countryside. "This is as close to a wilderness as you'll find in Ohio, the foothills of the Appalachian Mountains," I told my wife and younger brother. He was wallowing with me in nostalgia, remembering. At once, he and I saw that this wasn't the same as our memories. The WWI veteran's house on the right was gone, replaced by a house trailer. I imagined the owner I'd known, a gassing victim who coughed a lot and wiped his mouth and nose with a splotched handkerchief. Above that site the pit on the right was so grown up with trees and brush we couldn't see

its bottom, which I knew was over 100 feet straight down. Another trailer replaced the house that had been higher up on the left.

Around the sharp curve and seemingly straight up from there, we eagerly looked to our right and encountered a shock: a bulldozed yard. Our father's parents' house was erased, along with the iron stanchions and the wrist-thick grapevines that had lined a sidewalk. Also gone was the three-hole outhouse in back. The retaining wall was gone. So was the well for drinking water and the fruit cellar. Both had been scooped out of the hillside and lined with bricks. The garage was gone too.

Amazed, I stopped in the street and stared. Shocked! Part of my past was missing. Part of myself obliterated.

On the second tier of leveled ground, above where the house and retaining wall had been, Aunt Bette's big trailer was still there, squatting on concrete blocks, but its rusty, dirt-laden carcass suggested her demise—she'd been dead at least eleven years already. God knew who lived there now.

No one, I told myself, noticing the knee-high grass hiding the path that led from the road to the wood steps before the trailer door. The trailer's abandonment and continued survival, however, reminded me of the sentimental hand's-off-the-homestead practice of my father's family. For four decades they'd not touched the house itself after my grandmother's passing and so let time have its way with the structure. Every year it stood it leaned farther and farther downhill, slumping with gravity toward the pit. I noticed the ongoing process of decay whenever I passed this way, which was seldom.

Seldom because my family was distant from my father's people. He had chosen to move us away from them. I didn't even know some of his brothers and sisters. They all of course knew why he'd moved us. They understood the area's poverty and lack of opportunity to provide for his growing family. He had not only his wife and himself but also four children to feed. His side of the family knew that he couldn't find a profitable enough job in the hills. But Grandma Vernon, nee Dishon, misspelled from Dushong when her folks immigrated into the US from Canada, she wanted her boys home, in her house, where they belonged.

So my father's family resented our moving away, and my mother resented their attitude because my father took his boys to see Grandma and the others every holiday despite the three-hour road trip between their place and our home. Attitudes and assumptions built a wall between us and the Vernons.

Facing the emptiness of the place where a lot of my past had occurred, I wondered what remained here for my brother and me? Uphill from the trailer and everywhere we looked, there were trees. The Wayne National Forest. It was older now, full grown, almost a climax forest, not the way it had been when we, as children, visited the place 5 to 10 weekends a year. While visiting Grandma, my brother and I thoroughly searched the woods uphill, downhill, and sideways. We had the freedom to roam. Climbed into and out of the craters, that is the sinkholes that pockmark the hill, by grasping the honeysuckle vines cloaking the earth. When I received a .20-guage Mossberg, 3-shot, bolt action shotgun on my 12th birthday, I spent my next two winter visits there, tromping around, hunting rabbits. Then my father died and our visits ceased. The emotional warfare between my mother and Dad's mother separated us boys from Grandma and the others. She died when I was with the military in the Far East, unable to attend her funeral.

John said, "Let's keep going and see the rest of it."

In gloomy silence I drove us on uphill and noticed that the road was somewhat changed as well.

Tarred in big and small patches, it was still so narrow that cars approaching head on had to edge off road to pass. Within a hundred yards, a cleared place on the right hosted another trailer and a mean looking, growling dog chained to a stake between the trailer and road. The same thing within a hundred yards on the left. A bit farther, at the site of Binx's old house—I mean a rotund, jovial, hard drinking, tobacco-spitting man in blue denim bib-overalls—the fenced yard, his baying hound, his house and garage, the pines that shaded his house were all missing. In their place? A clearing with the ubiquitous trailer, dog, motorcycle, and pickup.

These details finally sank in, along with a perception of yellow no-trespassing, red printed Beware-of-Dog signs at each trailer, and the encroaching forest otherwise pressing in against the road. I felt uneasy. We were really isolated. I recalled the motorcyclist who'd turned off ahead of us onto Bakers Road. Clearly, the people living in these trailers didn't want intruders. I rehearsed what to say if questioned. I wondered what to do if threatened. My car held people I needed to protect. I shook my head: trailers, dogs, hogs, and signs.

I drove on because I wanted to see Uncle Buster's old house at road's end. Before his purchase of it, my mother's sister Mary and her husband John, a native Straitsville resident, had owned it. By visiting them, my mother had met my father. There'd been a dance hall near the crossroads down at the center of town, where the younger crowd gathered every Friday and Saturday evening to shake a leg. Before television, this was, when the movie theater and dance hall were popular gathering sites. Aunt Mary and John brought my mother to the dances and passed my father's house on the way. I'd heard the story many times, how they'd walked this road to reach the dance, talking, huffing and puffing there and back. My parents falling in love.

We crested the hilltop to find the house on the left totally collapsed. No surprise there. It had been falling in during my childhood. Ahead, though, Buster's house, fields, and corral were totally gone. Another trailer stood in its place, attached to an open acre that looked as if it might have been mowed. A man, maybe the one I'd seen riding up Bakers Road earlier, a red bandanna on his head, was leaning with one hand on the motorcycle seat, shading his eyes with the other, watching us. Absurdly perhaps, I sensed hostility and suspicion in his stance. Therefore, instead of driving to the circular space at road's end near the man, I reversed onto a gravel area by the collapsed house, turned back onto the road, and headed downhill toward safer ground.

Like an exclamation declaring a decisive end to our attempted return to the past, the bottom of the hill showcased a large new sign. Apparently an ATV campground existed on the backside of the hill. Surprised by it as well, I investigated. The place was not just roughly hewn out of the woods. It had modern cabins with air conditioning and an online presence. A modern business taking advantage of the federally mandated ATV trails for motorized traffic. The website for the campground says that accessible from it are "over 300 miles of trails with 75 designated for ATV/OHM's." It was a final intrusion that dispelled my outdated vision. It emphasized this unpleasant truth: times had indeed changed.

My brother and I were unhappy, and our rapid flight from the hill was ironically irritating. Those trailers and dogs we'd seen, the motorcycles and pickups stationed along Bakers Road had meant only one thing to me: drugs. Newspapers and television often reported Meth labs, opioid sales, and marijuana-growing operations in this area. The Piketon, Ohio massacre/execution of eight family members involved similar living arrangements just 78 miles away. I'd assumed that such activities were occurring on my hill. They were certainly occurring on other hills nearby. I'd abruptly turned around and fled the hill because of these suspicions.

I was also aware of being guilty of an outsider's stereotyping despite this personal irony: the people living in those trailers on my hill could very well be relatives. Cousins. Descendants of my father's family, who'd been a rather secretive group. The older generation I knew included moonshiners and bootleggers, an occupation similar to the drug trafficking I suspected now. The site of my father's still was an abandoned coal-mining tunnel whose entrance was hidden in brush east of Binx's house more than halfway up

Bakers Road. That was where the revenuers caught my father and took him to jail. These considerations made me feel guilty.

I bowed to the truth of Mr. Wolfe, you can't go home again. And Mr. Heraclitus, "No man ever steps in the same river twice, for it's not the same river and he's not the same man." My hill would never be the way it once was, nor would I. Nothing could ever restore the land beneath the Wayne National Forest to its primeval state nor bring back my youth.

I wondered, however, if I might restore my common sense and cautious trust of strangers. What if, instead of fleeing, I'd driven on up to road's end and greeted the man at the motorcycle? We might have introduced ourselves and shaken hands. I might have found out that he was one of Uncle Buster's adopted sons. Good possibilities. Establishing contact with the people living on the hill might be worth another visit.

But not as a wide-eyed innocent. Not on another spur-of-the-moment drive up my hill. I was already planning, applying logic. Someone had told me an aunt was still living in town or nearby, my father's youngest sister. I'd met her only once, 25 years ago at a funeral, though I'd never met her husband or children. If I could find and meet her again, maybe she could tell me about the residents on Baker's Hill. She might even become my Sacagawea driving up Bakers Road to meet them. My interpreter and guide through the unknown present.

About the Author:

Bill Vernon served in the United States Marine Corps, studied English literature, then taught it. Writing is his therapy, along with exercising outdoors and doing international folk dances. Five Star Mysteries published his novel OLD TOWN, and his poems, stories and nonfiction have appeared in a variety of magazines and anthologies.

THE LOSS OF HER

by Kimberly McElreath

That Wednesday started with a pink pig pancake pajama party. In Kindergarten, getting a new weekly letter means a lot. It's another step toward being a member in the secret society known as...readers. With big, innocent eyes, the little ones come to school every day and just wait to be given the next piece of the puzzle.

I never realized how comforting it can be to live in a world of innocence. As an adult, finally having the security of being taken care of, and not having to worry about feeling safe and secure, opened up the world of innocence that I longed to visit. The few months since my wedding allowed me to wallow in self-indulgence and just be content. I felt settled. The constant chaos of my life was gone, and the society shaped stigma of normal seemed to have come at last.

The phone call only lasted a few minutes, and the next half hour was a blur of collecting my belongings, making arrangements for my students, and getting home to Georgia. The lack of emotion and automated planning of a flight and packing my clothes made this event feel like any other trip home from Seattle. I could not allow myself to step outside of the routine and let fear seep in. I just had to get there.

The flight seemed longer than usual. As I gazed at the people around me, I could not help but wonder who else just found out that their own new found innocence was only a mirage? The landing mirrored my bouncing emotions from the past twelve hours. Collecting my baggage was an annoyance, and having to wait for someone to pick me up was irritating. However, I realized that this

was happening to me, not them. Everyone orbiting around the situation did not make this happen. They are being affected. I cannot place blame and condemnation on someone for being stuck in traffic. Finally, being in the car and knowing that I was on my way to her settled my nerves. All I had to do was get there.

I did not expect him to be there when I stepped off the elevator. He has the same right as I do. Maybe even more since he is the first born. He should be there. If this is true, then, why are my ears flattening and my fur starting to stand on end? Why am I truing to guard territory that I voluntarily resigned?

A hug seemed to be the right thing to do. I stepped forward and put my arms around him. I missed the expected greeting and proverbial questioning about my flight. The explanation of the stroke changed to hearing one word that had not anticipated. Terminal. A word that carries that much weight and meaning should sound so much more sophisticated. Over the next couple of hours, I found myself using the word as a descriptor of the situation as casually as I would tell someone that the day was chilly. Terminal. The finite understanding of that word would not come to me until hours later after the biopsy and the meetings with the doctors who just shook their heads with pity. Pity for whom? Pity for me for losing the innocence that I just discovered was so precious to me? Pity for him who had never taken care of himself much less someone who was now needing more than the curing cup of soup? Pity for her who remained hopeful that surgery would happen, and she would be fine?

The understanding of the depth of the word came when a nurse touched my arm and preceded to explain to me the different choices I had with choosing an in-home care service. Hospice was a foreign word to me. In-home care? How could I allow someone to come into our world of denial and unacceptance? We were always taught to cover and shield ourselves from onlookers and meddlers, but it was up to me to betray the pact and sign away the independence and self-righteousness of someone who knew no other way of life.

As I sat in the ICU room that night watching the blinking lights and listening to the octaves of beeping machines, I pulled my pink pajama clad knees up to my chest. I wrapped my arms tightly around myself and wished that I could have tasted at least one pancake.

About the Author:

Kimberly McElreath, originally from Georgia, is a music educator in the Seattle area of Washington state. She received her Bachelors of Arts degree in Music Education from Piedmont College in Demorest, Georgia and her Masters of Education degree in School Administration from Central Washington University in Ellensburg, Washington. When not teaching and directing choirs, Kimberly enjoys spending time with her friends and family. Being a novice writer, she looks forward to continuing to explore her voice and style.

STRANGERS

by Jeff Bakkensen

No one ever came to the motel without being seen a long way off. From one side was all flat with nothing growing more than thigh high, from the other more of the same until the mountains with the canyon carrying the road that used to be the interstate. By the time the shimmering dot became a green sedan that steamed and disgorged two full-grown men into the afternoon still, Nephi and Sam were already waiting on the pavement in front of the main office.

"Looks like you're overheating," said Nephi.

The men's undershirts were soaked through. They wore tennis shoes and matching blue work pants. The taller man had a perfectly round bald head, the shorter, a crew cut.

"This one says it's the radiator." Taller pointed to shorter. "We haven't seen a gas station in who knows how long."

Nephi gave Sam a key and sent him to get antifreeze, the blue bottle, from one of the empty guestrooms that lay in a row to one side of the main office. They all watched him disappear through the doorway. When he was gone, the shorter man turned back to the car and, wrapping the bottom of his shirt around his hand, popped the hood. He stepped back and waved steam out of his face.

"See I told you we'd find some help out here if we just kept looking," said his partner. "I'm Ray. This is Donny. Something tells me you don't get many guests."

"We don't actually rent the rooms," said Nephi.

No one said anything else until Sam came back with the antifreeze and some rags, and handed them to Nephi, who handed them to Ray, who passed them on to Donny. Donny flapped the rags over the engine and turned back to face the boys.

"Gotta let it cool first," he said.

"Speaking of, don't suppose y'all would have some water? Or maybe pop?" asked Ray.

Sam went into the main office and came back with two plastic cups of water.

"Now when the car gets overheated," said Ray, "Donny here tells me that you gotta run the heater to try to move the hot air out of that engine. So we've been running that thing with the windows down for the last twenty miles or so. Nearly heated me to death." He plucked at his shirt with two fingers and held it away from his chest.

He sipped his water and made a show of looking around. The parking lot was empty and the pavement cracked. Some of the rooms had tape across the windows. On the roof above the office doorway stood an oversized fiberglass chieftain with his hand raised in greeting and the words Smilin' Injun splashed across his headdress. A camper was parked in the grass at the far edge of the parking lot.

"Y'all don't got real Injuns, do you?"

Sam smiled.

"We'll be out of your hair soon as the engine cools down and Donny can see what needs to be done. He's a real whiz with cars. Me, I don't know a darn thing. By the way, where are your folks? Y'all aren't out here alone, are you?"

Nephi said, "It's just our dad, but he's away on business. He should be back any day now."

Ray whistled and looked to Donny, who shrugged as if to say, That's life, partner.

"We have a two-way radio if you need to call for help," said Nephi.

"No, no. Not necessary. We'll just let Donny work his magic."

They couldn't all stand around and watch the car cool, so Nephi and Sam left the men and walked around to the vegetable garden out back. As they turned the corner of the motel, Nephi's hand went down to the giant key ring that hung from his belt. He turned back and locked the office doors.

"We always lock the doors," said Nephi. "Keep the animals out."

"Can't be too careful," said Ray.

The garden was about a half-acre laid in uneven rows of beans, peas, onions, and squash. Along one side was a chainlink fence trellised with to-matoes. Nephi got two plastic shopping bags from a shed at the back of the office and gave one to Sam. They started in on opposite sides of a row of snap peas.

"You remember what we say about strangers?" said Nephi. "I was thirsty and you gave me drink."

Sam nodded.

"But no more than that, right? Don't let them inside or go anywhere alone with them. If something doesn't feel right, call for me right away. Treat them well and they'll be on their way."

They got to the end of the row and swung around to the next one, then started back the other way.

"You don't think Dad might have sent them? To keep an eye on us or something?"

Nephi gave him a look over the peas.

"They don't know Dad and they don't know us."

They were starting on the third row when Ray came around the corner of the motel and went into the shed. He came out with a hoe, holding

the blade at eye level. The boys stopped picking.

"Do you need something?" asked Nephi.

"Look at this here!" said Ray, sweeping the hoe back and forth to indicate the garden. "Going green and off the grid, am I right?" He winked. "Donny said he's looking for some epoxy if you have any. Says there's a hole in the radiator bottom."

Nephi stepped over a row of peas to circle Ray at the edge of the garden. "Just a minute." He took Sam's bag and led Sam and Ray around to the front, leaving them in front of the office while he went into one of the rooms. Sam looked to Ray leaning on the hoe and realized he was already breaking the rules. He backed a few feet down the walkway to put some air between them.

Ray watched him go. "Regular Hole-in-the-Wall you got out here. Not much to do except shoot the shit. You know what that means?"

"No sir."

"It's just a mean way of saying chat. You ever play twenty questions?" Sam shook his head. "I ask a question, and you give me an answer. Has to be truthful, though, that's the rules. And I get twenty of them."

Sam said okay.

"Alright," said Ray. "First question: What's the point of a motel if y'all don't rent rooms?"

Sam shrugged. "We just live here. We used to live in the camper."

"That camper there?"

He pointed to the van at the edge of the lot.

"Is that another question?"

Ray smiled. "Withdrawn. So it's just the two of you. Dad's away on business. And your mom, is she in a place where she can come visit from, or -"

Sam shook his head.

"Hmm." Ray stabbed at the pavement with the hoe handle. "That's tough. My momma raised me. Dad skipped out when I was born. But yours is coming back any day now?"

"Yessir."

"And he's really coming back? Drive up at any minute?"

"What do you mean?" asked Sam.

"Silly question I guess."

Ray cleared his throat and the throat clearing turned into a coughing fit that doubled him over. When it was done, he spat a speckled hunk onto the pavement and spread it around with his shoe.

"You don't have any more?" asked Sam.

Ray looked around until his eyes settled on the Smilin' Injun.

"You ever talk to that old chief?"

Sam shook his head and said no and blushed all at once.

"Thought so."

Nephi came back down the walkway with a bolt-action hunting rifle slung over his shoulder. He set a can of sealant on the ground a few feet from the car.

"Hey there pilgrim," said Ray. "What's the gun for?"

"It'll start getting dark soon. We have coyotes sometimes, snakes. Have to be careful."

"Nephi shot a deer this spring," said Sam. "Good eating."

Donny came around from the far side of the car and picked up the can.

"This'll do," he said. "Supposed to sit overnight though." He looked up and saw Nephi. "What's with the gun?"

"He doesn't want the snakes to get us." said Ray. "Overnight, huh?"

"Supposed to."

"Even with this heat? You'd think the dry - "

"If you want it to hold," said Donny, "it's supposed to sit overnight. I dunno what else you want me to say."

Sam and Nephi listened to chatter on the radio while they made succotash with ham and bread, which the four of them ate under the overhang in front of the office. They were short one folding chair; Nephi stood, the rifle still on his shoulder.

Ray could hardly eat he spent so much time giving praise.

"I never knew a boy could cook before."

"We grew it, too," said Sam.

"You don't say?"

"Just not the corn or the bread. And not the ham."

"Well I love it," said Ray. "Regular Swiss Family Robinson."

The boys looked at each other. Nephi shrugged.

"Where are you trying to go?" asked Sam.

Ray smiled.

"Your brother's all business and you're the curious one, is that right?" He put down his fork. "Well I can tell you, but you boys gotta keep it secret. Guessing y'all don't have a television or anything like that?" Nephi shook his head. "Cell phone? Computer?"

"We're not allowed," said Sam.

"That's too bad," said Ray. "Because the thing is, the two of us are baseball scouts. We're supposed to be up tomorrow to see this kid pitch over at UNM."

He gave Donny a long look.

"We like to watch all the games we can," said Donny, watching himself move peas around his plate. "Too bad about no television."

"But this kid," said Ray. "Oh boy can he pitch. Your dad ever take you to the games over there?"

"No," said Nephi.

"You wouldn't know him then. Name's Wagner. Got a killer fastball. Killer changeup too."

"One of our top prospects," said Donny.

Nephi nodded towards the car. "Your plates say Missouri. Did you drive all the way out here?"

Ray snorted and reached for his water.

"In fact we did. St. Louis Cardinals." He turned to Sam. "You look like you've got an arm on you. Ever play?"

Sam shook his head.

"Ever seen a baseball?" asked Donny, looking up. "You ever been out there at all?" He pointed with his thumb towards the darkness growing behind him.

"Out where?" asked Nephi. "Off the motel?"

Donny nodded.

"Of course we have. We're not idiots. And you're not baseball scouts."

He began to walk around the circle gathering plates.

"Now hold on," said Donny, and reached after him.

Ray put a hand on Donny's shoulder. Nephi took the plates inside.

"The young man's got a right to be skeptical. We're strangers after all. Sam, do you believe us? Are we baseball scouts?"

Sam shrugged.

"Okay. And that's fine. But I'll tell you what, alright? Cards on the table. Honest Injun hope to die." His eyebrows inched up his forehead. "We're baseball scouts."

Sam and Nephi did the dishes in the main office. While Nephi put away the folding chairs, Sam took bedding from the one of the empty rooms and left it at the doorway to the camper. He was just turning to walk back across the parking lot when the door opened and Ray stepped out. He coughed, cleared his throat, and spat.

"Hey Sam," he said. "I was thinking. You'd know to tell someone, right, if you ever needed help?"

"We have the radio," said Sam.

"Right, right. But you could tell a friend, too. You know what I mean?"

"Okay."

"Never think you can't." Ray thrust out his left hand like he was holding a bow, drew back the string with his right hand, and let an arrow fly in a high arc towards the main office. He winked.

"Sleep tight young brave."

"Good night," said Sam.

He crossed the parking lot and followed Nephi

into their room. After they'd locked the door, said their prayers, and turned off the light, Nephi kneeled on Sam's bed and watched the parking lot. From over his shoulder, Sam could just make out the camper, a dull gray against the deeper dark behind it.

"You don't think they're baseball scouts?" asked Sam.

"Not a chance."

"Then what are they?"

"What's the opposite of a baseball scout?"

Nephi stood and walked over to his own bed.

"Hey, where's the radio?"

He turned on the lights. The radio wasn't on the nightstand. It wasn't in the bathroom. Nephi got down on his hands to look beneath the beds and then pulled back his sheets and threw his pillow onto the floor.

"You had it at dinner," said Sam.

Nephi looked out the window. "Wait here."

He took the rifle and went outside. Sam watched him go back and forth over the payment, go into the office and come back.

"I think they took it."

"It wasn't in the office?"

Nephi shook his head.

He took another lap around the room, turned out the light and sat down on his bed.

"Shit!" he said and sulked silently in the darkness.

Sam's bed was beneath the window, and lying down, he could see the Smilin' Injun through the space between the blinds. The truth was that sometimes, just as Sam was falling asleep, the Injun did speak. The Injun told him all about what things were like before the white men came. He had crazy powers like night vision and everlasting life. He could also talk to animals and enter people's dreams, and sometimes he brought messages from Sam's dad, and from his mom, too.

Tonight the Injun told him that he didn't need to worry about the radio. The men hadn't come to the motel by accident. They were messengers, and they had a very important important message just for him.

But why don't you just tell me what it is? asked Sam.

He didn't actually say this out loud. To speak with the Injun you put words in your head and closed your eyes real tight and then kind of pushed the words out, and the Injun could hear them.

I wish, said the Injun, but that's way above my pay grade.

The Injun didn't make any noise when he spoke, either. You just emptied your head and breathed in, and the words would come to you. Sam asked the Injun once whether he ever spoke to Nephi, and the Injun said he'd tried, but Nephi was always too busy to listen.

Sam must have fallen asleep, because some time later he woke to hear someone fumbling with the door. He sat up in bed, leaned against the window. Through the blinds he could see the outline of a figure hunched over in the entryway.

He looked over towards where Nephi's bed was hidden in the darkness.

"Nephi? Are you awake?"

More fumbling as something scraped against the lock.

"Hello?"

The lock clicked and the door inched open.

The lights flicked on. It was Nephi, holding a finger over his lips for quiet.

"Still can't find it," he said.

He leaned his rifle against the wall, turned off the lights, and settled himself back into bed.

Sam closed his eyes, but whenever he was about to fall asleep he got a feeling like he was slipping down a hole beneath his bed. Down, down, with the dust and worms on either side, and then he'd land back in his bed with his whole body tensed. Towards dawn, he woke to find Nephi already dressed, leaning over him, two fingers spreading a gap in the blinds.

"Come on," he said. Sam threw on shorts and a t-shirt and followed him outside.

He stopped in the doorway. The car was gone, and Ray was lying on the pavement, hands folded under his chest like he was trying to unbutton his shirt. Nephi walked up slowly and nudged him with his foot. Then he crouched and put a finger on his neck. He looked up at Sam and shook his head, reached down and touched Ray's face, and Sam realized he was closing his eyes.

Nephi walked back to the doorway and took Sam by the hand and led him on a wide arc around Ray and then across the lot to the camper. He circled the camper and looked through each of the windows before going inside. Sam waited, watching Ray, until Nephi came back out.

"The radio's gone," said Nephi. "He must have driven off while we were sleeping."

"He's dead?"

Nephi shrugged. "We'll have to bury him, you know."

Sam kept his eyes on Ray as he backed up and sat on the camper steps. He was like a regular person, only with the shimmer gone.

Nephi circled the camper again and came back to the parking lot. Then he walked out into the field beyond the lot, beating through the bushes with his rifle. Sam closed his eyes and pushed out his thoughts.

What happened? he asked. I thought you said he was going to tell me something.

I know I know, said the Injun. I took my eyes off the ball. But he was old and under a lot of stress. He's had a very busy week.

What do you mean? asked Sam.

It's complicated, said the Injun. You know nothing lasts forever, right?

Nothing?

Well I guess forever lasts forever. But that's like it's own thing, you know? Like saying red is reddish.

Isn't there anything you can do?

Let me see.

The Injun grunted and strained like he was lifting something heavy and from across the parking lot,

Sam heard a cough. He opened his eyes to see Ray pushing himself up into an Indian style sit. Ray stretched his neck and spat. He scanned the lot until his eyes locked on Sam.

"Hey there!" he said, and waved with both hands. "Any idea where I parked my car?"

Sam raised his finger to his lips for quiet.

"Rusty-ass green thing," said Ray. "Guy named Donny might have it?"

Sam heard Nephi call his name. He stood and took a few steps towards Ray, lowering his voice.

"Donny's gone. He drove away."

"Typical Donny," said Ray. He rested his head on his fist. "Which way did he go?"

Nephi was coming back out of the bushes, his rifle raised up and ready to shoot. Sam pointed in the opposite direction, towards the mountains.

"You sure?" asked Ray.

Sam nodded.

"Much obliged."

Ray stood and took off at a jog towards the highway. Nephi tracked him through the rifle sight, then lowered the rifle and watched him go. He turned to Sam.

"He just stood up," said Sam. "I dunno."

They climbed to the top of the camper, Nephi going first and pulling Sam up after him. They watched Ray pass through the low brush that lay around the hotel offramp and then keep going down the highway. A ways down the road, a shining dot became a truck that slowed for Ray, then stopped to let him in. The boys lay down on the camper roof and watched while the truck came closer and finally went past. And as it passed, they could make out a face inside the cab, eyes wide and one hand raised in greeting.

About the Author:

Jeff Bakkensen lives in Boston. Recent work has appeared in A-Minor Magazine, Oblong Magazine, Smokelong Quarterly, and The Antigonish Review.

HURRICANE MOON
by Tony Whedon

The town where we had rented our cottage that summer when I was thireen, called Port Clyde, sat at the end of a long peninsula that jutted into the Atlantic. It had a sardine cannery, a lighthouse, a long rocky beach covered with mussels and kelp, and a view when the fog cleared of islands spread out far as you could see along the coast. A kitchen wall map showed Port Clyde, circled in red, and islands -- Hooper's Island, Teal's Island and, farther out, miles in the ocean, Monhegan and Matinicus. That first week, the fog never cleared, but I imagined in detail the color and shape of those islands: they were spruce colored with high bluffs and shaggy inlets, inhabited by occasional fishermen and grazing sheep.

Our next door neighbors were the Hawkins. My parents had rented our cottage through Jack Hawkins' brother back on Long Island. Jack was away on an archaeological dig of Indian mounds in Canada, leaving his wife Jane in charge of Phillip and Alice.

I first saw thirteen year-old Alice on the dock extending out from our cottage, a tall girl standing with her little brother. I watched as they dangled their lines into the water, then I came up on the dock. Alice invited me to fish with them, and I held the pole she handed me a few minutes. I waited for a tug while sunlight sifted through the fog. I was aware of the tide rising beneath the dock pilings.

I said, "So what d'you do around here?"

"We come up every summer, Phillip, mother and I, that is when we aren't visiting my Gram's in England," Alice said and Phillip nodded his head vigorously -- his cheeks jiggled as his head shook, and he made a sort of sputtering sound.

"I'm getting too old for this. I'm tired of the parties my parents ceaselessly drag us to."

She was wearing a long checkered dress which made her seem taller, even slimmer than she was. She had greenish-brown eyes and olive skin. Her brother, equally dark but fat, reeled in a fish – it flopped and squirmed on the dock, a round spiny creature with quarter-sized eyes. He tried kicking it off the dock, and it puffed even larger as he bent down to grab it, then it flipped around and with a splash shot into the cove.

At least this is how I remember Alice as my imagination has romanced her over the years. How elusive she was, always disappearing and reappearing, representing both the end of something and the start of something new and exciting. I saw her a number of brief times the next few days: in Port Clyde's bait & tackle store with her mother Jane (She was taller than her blonde, sweater-girl mom, and between the two of them, Alice seemed the most serious, the most prim). I saw her along the bridal path that ran the length of the peninsula (riding a brindled pony) and later that week on the beach. I was glad she wasn't with her brother.

She said, "I've got to go back home. Phillip's made me promise to take him into town."

"I'll go along with you," I said. "We can ride our bikes."

"Phillip doesn't know how to ride a bike. I'll see you back here later. Of course I'd like you to come into town. But this brother of mine. . , " and then she left me on the stoop where I surveyed the cove and the sailboats tacking out to the bay.

That afternoon, I trudged up the beach and heard Phillip's voice in the cottage. Alice was below the dock picking mussels – in the silence I heard the hard shells hitting the bucket. When she turned toward the cove and back at me there was a coolness in her stare — a coolness that penetrated me to the core.

After dinner, I saw her stride through the high grass between our cottages, her hair pulled back so you could see the brown of her neck. While my mother cleaned up after the meal, my seven-year-old sister, Delerie, danced by herself to the "Nut-Cracker Suite" on the radio. My father hid behind the Bangor paper -- the headlines must have had something about a hurricane named "Alice" moving up the coast -- and my mother sketched in her pad.

I remember Alice slipping in the screen door and then my little beagle dog barking and my sister swirling onto the porch, bumping into Alice.

"What's that you've got on?" Alice said, referring to the dirty pink tutu my sister wore.

Delerie squealed and rushed out of the room and turned up the radio in the kitchen. Small-craft advisories were posted from Nantucket along the Maine coast: the hurricane would go out to sea, hummed the announcer's voice. A moment later Alice and I walked down to the beach. We pulled up kelp from the rocks to find periwinkles and starfish and clam-holes that pissed into our faces: farther down the beach, in shallow water, we found green sea-urchins round as pincushions.

The rising tide forced us farther up the beach, and we sat in a crevice of a big rock and looked across the cove toward an island rising out of the fog. Alice said, "This is our last vacation here. . . I'm sorry I won't be coming back. But, you wouldn't care about that. My father's teaching in England next year when he comes back from his dig. Actually, he's English. That makes me half-British."

She looked at me and added, "You know, probably I'll be happier in England than here."

Well, that might be true, I said, but I'd miss her next summer if I returned to Maine.

"You hardly know me. How can you miss me if you don't know me? I don't know anything about you. Like what does your father do?"

Before I could answer, Alice said: "Mine's an archaeologist. I plan to be one, too, when and if I grow up."

Next day she invited me to have lunch.

Alice's mother served us chowder. After lunch Alice and Phillip and their mother drove into Port Clyde and I went back to our cottage and sat on the porch listening to the radio with my mother and father. The storm-watch had upgraded to a gale-warning, already I could see low clouds rolling in, and by the time I heard Alice and her mother and brother return, the wind tossed rough waves against the lower beach. After a while Alice came outside and stood on her own porch in a rain slicker, her cheeks in full color. She shouted across to me: "Have you ever been in a nor'easter? This is my first time. Philip's out of his mind. Mother's going to a church dance in Tenants' harbor. Isn't that irresponsible? She wants to invite your mother and father along."

Whether my parents were going or not, I didn't care. My father and I were never close -- now that I was older I'd grown apart from my mother who was more involved in her artwork than she was with my sister and me. Since I could remember, my family had been ruled my father's fear of financial failure. That hadn't stopped him from quitting his paying job to set up a ceramics business with my mother. While he chose to work at home for the same reason my mother did, I couldn't imagine that twelve hours a day nailing together trivets, cheese trays and coffee tables didn't drive him crazy. And he was crazy -- I told Alice – from the beer he drank and from the glaze and lacquer fumes -- you could smell all that on his breath.

Our first two days in Port Clyde, I told her, he'd quit drinking but he was more miserable, if that was possible, than he'd been. He'd bought a ten-foot dingy fn town and was stripping the chipped paint, calking and repainting — a gift, he claimed, to me — but abstaining made him even more surly (and borderline abusive) toward Delerie and me . I couldn't trust my father; him not drinking encouraged his nastiness, besides, last night he'd drunk again and I found him on the porch, slumped in a stupor in a deck chair, mumbling my mother's name. I told Alice all this in one breath, half-expecting she'd pity me.

But she was in her own world. "I don't see Jack much at all," she said, referring to her own father. We'd gone down to the dock and were fishing in the low tide pools. "But he's big on presents – once he brought back a pair of polar bear claws from Baffin Island for Phillip."

My memory of that afternoon is of a spattering rain and the sun coming out and disappearing behind the clouds. Past the dock the beach expanded as the tide went out to reveal mud pocked by clam-diggers' holes. Out in the bay a lobster boat appeared, breasting the waves, and was quickly smudged out by the rain.

"Phillip's having his nap," she said as we left the dock and walked down the shingle. "He's my problem while Da's gone. Mother is negligent." After a moment, she added, "I'm worried about Phillip. He's very dense and is flunking everything in school. Actually, I'm his tutor while our Da's away," she said.

We continued down the beach and came on a ramshackle dock that went out so far it was lashed by waves. The dock pilings were ringed by barnacles and starfish. Alice leaned down and pealed one starfish off.

"I'm a terrible tease my father says," she said. "If I don't watch it I'll have boys all over me. My father doesn't actually know if I like boys. If I miss him. Or if Phillip misses him. He's never around to know."

We climbed some stairs to the splintery dock. The wind began to blow the bay into whitecaps, I heard the ocean waves striking rocks down at the lighthouse.

We returned to Alice's cottage – our parents were gone, my sister with them, and Phillip was rocking back and forth in the hammock. Darkness spread across the beach. The gale came up quickly and the sky turned oily black. We went inside Alice's cottage and she put Phillip to sleep for the night. Then she brought out a SCRABBLE board, and we

shuffled the letters around as the wind howled and the night closed around us.

I don't know how long we sat together on the couch, maybe an hour. The lights flickered and finally went out, and Alice lit an oil lamp.

"My mother's a neurotic," she said. "That's what she calls herself. The doctor gives her Milltowns, and with one glass of wine she's floating. My parents get into an argument, she packs her bags, but she never goes anywhere. Once my father had an affair. I read one of his girlfriend's letters. I never thought of my father that way. But I didn't feel sorry for my mum. Normal's not my father. Mum's the same story, a different breed my father says." She told me about England: "We lived in the country. I had a nanny who took me for long chatty walks. If you came to visit you could stay with us. I'd take you to Buckminister Palace. I'd introduce you to The Queen."

She looked down at the SCRABBLE board.

"Once my father lived for six months on the tundra with Eskimos," she said. "He collected artifacts for the Museum of Natural History. It was dark all winter. He was quite homesick." She leaned toward me. "You know what I'd like? I'd love to live here the rest of my life. I'd never get married, I'd have a houseful of extraordinary animals."

I glanced helplessly down at the SCRABBLE board and said that in some ways, our families were alike.

"Not at all," she said flatly and turned to me with a changed expression. "My mother's afraid of everything."

She got up and looked out the window at the coming storm. "And I'm not afraid of anything," she said, her voice quite frightening. I watched her move from the window. She began arranging books and tea-cozies, retrieving her brother's toys and depositing them in a pile by the stairs: suddenly I saw Alice as an eccentric older woman, she'd mapped out the life before, nothing came to her by accident while everything happened to me by chance.

The fact was my father's drinking and philandering and my own difficulties — I was a runt and had been bullied by bigger boys on our suburban block— had brought me to a place, many children feel at in early adolescence. Did Alice know and would she care? Of course, eventually that night our talk did turn to sex. Alice led me to her mother's darkened bedroom where she kept a "love-manual" in her dresser. We sat on the bed and leafed through the book, stopping at the graphic drawings of sex acts and then Alice asked if I'd ever "made out" with a girl, and I said I had but it was nothing. She laughed and kissed me and as I met her mouth with mine delight swept through me.

But now the storm was on us, it burst through the maples outside the cottage with a racket of splitting timbers and a child screaming and another bellowing wind gust that shook the cottage. Out in the yard, the trunk of a fallen tree was visible in the dim lamp light shining from the bedroom window. It had fallen through the porch, smashing the screen.

Back upstairs, sheet-lightning flickered against Alice and her brother hunched against the backboard, their arms flung around each other.

"It's all going to be lovely, Phillip, just wait and see," she said. "Mommy'll be back. And so will Daddy. I'm sure he's got all sorts of nice presents for you."

A moment or two more of quiet was followed by another violent wind gust, then doors slamming, and our parents, and my sister -- crying, too – as they entered the cottage.

Next morning a north-west gale blew down between the islands. I woke to a buzzing chainsaw. Two men were cutting up the big maple that had been blown down last night. Alice's mother and my parents watched the men saw up the maple. I looked for Alice who'd gone to the lighthouse and wouldn't be home till after lunch. I walked down the point to the lighthouse and saw her on a rock facing the Atlantic.

"Isn't it wild?" she said.

Beyond the rocks the ocean tumbled. A line of

laundry strung from the lighthouse flapped in the spray. Phillip was crouched in the weeds, watching his sister.

"Phillip, go home," Alice said.

"I won't," he said.

The wind rose. Gulls flew upward in the spray: the blue spittle of Alice's cigarette blew downwind. She'd come here to smoke and didn't want Phillip to see her.

"Promise me, little brother," she said, "You'll turn around and go home. When you get there you'll tell Mother I've gone into town -- with him."

I was that HIM, I realized, no more than a happenstance.

"I'll go back with Phillip," I said.

"No you won't," Alice said.

Out of the grass Phillip dragged a pail of stuff he'd picked up on his way to the lighthouse -- a soggy Field Guide to the Birds, shells, worn stones and tangled fishing tackle. He dumped it all at Alice's feet.

"I don't want this," she said. "It's all junk."

"And I don't want to go home. CAN'T go home," Phillip said. His eyes got wide, his cheeks jiggled emphatically. He began untangling the fishing line. Alice helped him, carefully, methodically, and I thought of their father, collecting arrowheads in Canada.

Finally Phillip wandered home -- we watched him on the beach path till he was no more than a yellow slicker.

That night I saw Alice's shadow against the shade in her room. I had gone for a walk along the water and stopped where the beach met the lawn between our houses. As she stood there smoking, the light pouring onto the shade, I wondered if I'd not already lost whatever I had held of her -- not her affection but my delight in her. Next day her mother got a telegram from Jack who was to be returning from Canada. They made quick arrangements to leave for Portland the next day, and

Alice and I walked to town and drank cherry-cokes at a marble-topped drugstore counter. Later, we stood at the wharf and watched men stacking crates of sardines at the cannery. On our way back to the cottages, two teenagers were making out in a convertible near the cove. We watched them for the longest while, not saying anything, and I should've felt terribly sad, but I didn't. Maybe for Alice our days together meant nothing — maybe a short entry in her journal. For me, they marked the end of something I wouldn't fully understand until years later.

About the Author:

Tony Whedon is the author of "A Language Dark Enough: Essays on Exile" from Midlist Pres and forthcoming from Green Writers Press "Drunk in the Woods," a nonfiction collection. He also published four poetry collections. His poetry, critical essays and creative nonfiction have appeared in Agni, American Poetry Review, Harpers, Salmagundi, Shenandoah, ThreePenny Review and more than a hundred other magazines. In the past ten years three of his essays have been listed as "notable" in the Best American Essays.

LOOKS OF HAPPINESS

by Frannie Gilbertson

Do you ever look at someone and think, "Wow, I am so lucky that I have you"? You catch yourself staring at them, watching the way their lips form into a smile or the way their eyes shine beneath the brightness of the sun. You look at them and you just have to sit and admire their existence because you cannot fathom how someone so beautiful and so unbelievably kind could exist in a world that is often full of ugliness and hate. I do that. All the time, but with one specific person.

Before I get into those gory details, I want to start from the beginning. About two months ago, I was online, minding my own business, looking at and liking various videos when I got an inbox message from someone I didn't know. I'd never gotten a direct message from a stranger before, and the whole thing kind of freaked me out a bit, but something was also telling me that this stranger was not someone to be afraid of. Of course, I was questioning myself and wondering why in the hell I was responding, but I did. The message was just a thank you for liking a video that said stranger had posted, harmless enough. Later that night, I learned that my new direct message friend was a guy named Josh.

Of course by the time I finished talking to him that evening, it was really late and I was falling asleep. I asked if I could talk to him again tomorrow because, well, I enjoyed talking to him. He seemed nice and harmless, two traits that I have confirmed to be true now. He told me that of course we could and wished me a good night before we signed off and went to bed. The next day I talked to him again, and all that next night, too. That night turned into another day, which turned

into another night, and another, and another, and another. Days became weeks, weeks became months, and during those months we got closer and I learned two things: we were completely opposite people, but had a lot of the same interests. He likes cold weather, I like hot weather. He likes math, I think math is the language of the devil. He's really tall, and I'm really short. He's soft spoken, and I'm a little on the loud side. But despite our opposites, we have things in common, too. We have the same favorite band, the same nerdy tendencies, we procrastinate like hell, and, my favorite: we're crazy about each other.

Two months went by of sweet messages, late night phone calls, and math tutoring sessions that usually turned into "you're so cute" and "I like you" fights. Josh became my new best friend and my new something else, but like all possible new relationships, I had seeds of doubt planted into my mind. I'd find myself sitting behind my phone questioning if what he was saying to me was really true. Did he really like me? Was he talking to more than one girl like this? When was it going to end because surely this was too good to last for very long. Guys like him didn't exist in real life. They were fairytales. They were characters in the novels I read and wrote about. No man was that good. They never had been before. I kept thinking back to all my past relationships, remembering how badly they'd ended and how hurt they'd left me. I'd been played, used, and lied to before so I knew what it felt like. I knew how pretty a guy could make his words sound because I'd heard them before. I didn't want that to happen to me again because by now my heart was invested, and if it ended now I was going to be hurt again. Badly.

But that's the thing about Josh. He stayed. He stayed despite my worries and my fears. He'd talk with me on the phone about it, no matter what it was. No matter what insane thought I had in my head, he had a way of making it disappear. He had a way of making me feel like my insecurities and my concerns were not the ramblings of a crazy girl, but just that of a girl who'd been hurt one too many times and was always going to have the scars to prove it. The evidence was there on the table for us both to see, and he didn't mind.

As time drew on, we found ourselves talking about meeting. Talking about what we'd do the first time we saw each other in person. Pictures are one thing, but you can't hug a picture. You can't kiss a picture. A picture is a picture. It's a copy, and a copy is nothing compared to the real thing. That's what we wanted. We wanted the real thing, and that's what we were determined to get. So, with enough preparation and 11:11 wishes, we got our real thing on September 23, 2017. I got my first real date and it was one of the best days I'd ever had.

He bought me lunch, and we completed our long-awaited dream of walking through Target together. He bought me flowers, a movie I'd been wanting on DVD for a while, and my favorite pastry: cupcakes. He never let my hand go and stole kisses from me. Many kisses that I had no problem stealing back throughout the day. We went to the water gardens and walked around downtown. There were many other things we did, but I want to pause for a moment and refer back to my first paragraph because it was on this date that I had to stop and admire Josh for what was probably too long.

The water gardens in downtown Fort Worth are one of the best places to go to on a date because who doesn't want to sit and listen to the sound of water fountains for a few hours? It's calming, watching the water seep out of the stone walls and tumble down into the pools below. There were two groups taking their Quince pictures there and I remember Josh and I comparing the colors and the dresses of the two parties. I preferred the first group because of the pale pink color of the girl's dress. It was big and looked so wonderful on her. I was watching everyone around us and trying not to blush at the sweet things Josh was telling me. He'd tell me how beautiful I was or how much he liked me. I think my favorite was him poking my cheek and asking if I was real and if we were really together. I'd laugh and he continue to stare at me like I was some type of artwork that rivaled something of Claude Monet's.

I know that I am no masterpiece. My face is not blemish-free, my thighs are full of stretchmarks, and sometimes I let anxiety and depression overrule logic. I've done things I am not proud of, and I let my head get the best of me. I can be a conceited brat, and I can be an insecure baby. I'm not perfect, not even close, but none of that matters to him. It doesn't matter because he sees the good in me. He sees the things I can't see and probably never will. I know this not because he's told me so many times, but because it was reflected in his eyes that day. I saw the admiration glowing within the crystal blue irises. I saw the care brightly shinning like the gleam of the sun sitting on the Caribbean Sea. He looked at me like Jay Gatsby looked at Daisy Buchanan. Like I was the only girl that mattered in that moment because to him, I was. I could feel it and that feeling is one that I will always remember.

I looked back at him the same way, of course, but my expressions aren't in my eyes. They are in my lips. My words are what I use to express my feelings towards him, but Josh? Josh uses his eyes. I can always see his emotions in his eyes. They change color, you know. They go from blue, to green, to gray, to silver. They are little tiny windows into a heart that I know is big enough for the both of us. I think I have a pretty good heart too, but not like his. His is much more lovely.

Josh is who I find myself shaking my head to and laughing at for no apparent reason because he just makes me so incredibly happy. I'm always happy when I talk to him. I make him happy, too. I know because I saw it at the Fort Worth water gardens. There are just some people in this world who make you so happy and you have no real explanation as to why. They just do. You find yourself smiling for no reason and it doesn't matter because you know you're lucky. You're lucky to find someone that brings you that much joy. I know I am.

About the Author:

Frannie Gilbertson is an aspiring author who enjoys writing fiction and poetry with an occasional dabble in non-fiction such as "Looks of Happiness". Her love for writing began at a young age, but never fully blossomed until high school when she completed her first full-length novel as a freshman. When she is not writing, she can be found reading, eating, or sleeping.

CAPTURE HILL No. 49

by Allen Long

My brother Danny and I grew up in Arlington, Virginia, in the Sixties and Seventies. Although this was a period of significant social turmoil because of the civil rights movement, the Vietnam War protests, and the women's liberation crusade—my heart goes out to all of these causes—this was also a time of great economic prosperity, and one might think white kids of well-educated parents in a prosperous suburb of D.C. within walking distance of top-rated schools had it made.

Home, Bittersweet, Home

Danny and I were physically abused by our parents. In 1962, the summer I was almost six, my mother invited a woman friend from our church over for lunch. Mrs. Cunningham brought along her son Webster, a red-haired boy slightly younger than me who was infamous for leaving a wide swath of destruction in his wake. My mother warned me ahead of time, "If Webster harms anything in this house, I'm holding you personally responsible, and your father will blister your bottom."

This was no idle threat. The first time my father spanked me with a store-bought paddle, he hit me so hard the paddle snapped in half. After that, he fashioned a thick oak paddle. He would strike our bottoms about a dozen times with nearly all of his strength.

Needless to say, when Webster arrived, I watched him with a keen eye. He wore a white cowboy hat with red piping, and he carried a large metal toy six shooter. He ran through our house, his gun nearly gouging divots in a dozen walls and pieces of furniture. With heroic efforts, I protected our house and furnishings—until I had to use the bathroom. I peed as fast as I could, but when I returned to the living room, Webster had set his pistol on my father's prized stereo, the one inside the gorgeous mahogany cabinet he polished daily. Just then, my mother and Mrs. Cunningham entered the room and saw Webster, me, and his metal gun on the hi-fi. My mother's eyes filled with fury. Of course, I pleaded my case, but it was clear I was paddle fodder.

That evening when my father arrived, he burst into my room with a roar. When I wasn't in plain sight, he knew I was hiding in my closet. He reached in and jerked me out by the arm, which I was afraid would come out of its socket. Then the second part of the punishment ritual began. My father grabbed me by the back of the head and ground my forehead into his while he stared into my eyes with utter hatred and growled. This might have broken some kids' wills—Danny had a particularly hard time with the head grind—but I knew my father was insane with anger and hatred at that moment, and I returned his gaze with hatred of my own. As my father dragged me to the bathroom, my mother said, "Take off his pajamas so it will hurt more."

My father complied, then bent me over his knee and spanked the bejesus out of me. The blows were unbelievably painful and I was afraid he'd break my arm or fingers if I tried to shield my bottom. He struck me two dozen times.

Why did our parents treat us so cruelly? I believe, at some level, our father is insane, probably because he was abused by his mentally ill mother and inherited her affliction, although he's led a highly functional and successful life. He recently turned ninety. When I was home for a visit, he got into an argument with our mother. After she marched stiff-backed into the kitchen to cook dinner, he pointed at her, showed me a familiar look of insane hatred, and gleefully gestured strangling her. Danny and I can't imagine why our mother encouraged our father to beat us.

Luckily, when our mother wasn't directing our father to thrash us, she was attentive, loving, and kind, and Danny and I pretended her alter-ego didn't exist.

But this wasn't the only darkness we experienced at home. We had an evil teenage baby sitter named Ryann who locked us in the basement as soon as our parents left the house. Then she'd raid the refrigerator and gab on the phone for hours with her girlfriends. She'd let us out just before our parents returned home. Every time Danny and I reported these events to our parents, they shook their heads and said, "Wow, that's quite a story. I'm sure Ryann would never do anything like that."

Once, when Ryann locked us in the basement, Danny and I pretended that Danny had fallen down the basement stairs and was seriously injured. When Ryann opened the door to check on us, we charged her and pushed past, but not before she kneed Danny and drove his head into the metal strike plate in the doorframe. Danny's scalp bled so profusely Ryann had to put his head under the bathtub faucet to wash away the blood. When my parents came home, Ryann told them we'd badly misbehaved.

As soon as Ryann left, we told them what happened and showed them the bloody knot on Danny's head. They dismissed this as some kind of cheap trick, and our father beat the daylights out of us.

Even the homes of our relatives weren't necessarily safe. Once, when we visited a nearby elderly aunt and uncle, our tall and gruff-voiced uncle said to Danny, "Come down the hallway with me and let's look out the window."

Danny got up from where he sat in the living room with my aunt, our mother, and me and followed our uncle down the musty apartment corridor. When they arrived at the window, our uncle said, "Want to feel my pocket knife?"

"Sure," Danny said.

Our uncle indicated the knife was in his right pocket and it was okay for Danny to reach in. Danny did so but found only a hole.

"Keep going, you're almost there," our uncle said.

Danny located the knife, but it was surprisingly soft.

"This knife feels funny," Danny said.

"It's okay," our uncle said. "Squeeze it."

Danny obliged but suddenly realized something was wrong. He fled to the living room. Like many of Danny's darker memories, this one ends abruptly, the dénouement blocked out.

Danny recently told me he had horrific nightmares as a kid. So did I. In one of my worst ones, terrifying monsters march up the basement stairs with booming footsteps while the eerie music from Perry Mason plays. I run to our kitchen to make sure the basement door's locked. Sometimes I secure the door just as the monsters reach the top of the steps, and sometimes the monsters burst through just as I arrive. I'd wake, screaming in terror.

In the Sixties, there was a horror story going around about a boy who cries out whenever his parents open the basement door. Assuming their son's a neurotic coward, his parents tie him to a chair, open the basement door, and leave him there shrieking while they go out to dinner. When they return home, the house is silent. They're pleased their "cure" has worked—until they discover their son has been ripped to shreds by whatever evil creature lurks in the basement.

In another nightmare, I'm hiding from my father at the back of my bedroom closet. Suddenly, I realize there's something in there with me, an invisible monster called the Nozzer that buzzes like hair clippers and crawls all over my helpless body while I try unsuccessfully to cry out.

In real life, when our parents were angry with Danny and me, they sometimes drove us to the barber shop and ordered the barber to cut off all of our hair to humiliate us. Enter the Nozzer.

I recall two other recurring nightmares. In one, an invisible angry ghost plucks me out of bed at night and shakes me like a rag doll while I levitate above my bed. In the other, an evil circus strongman grabs me in the hallway at night while I'm trying to reach the bathroom and bounces me repeatedly off the ceiling in terrifying slow motion, as if time has slowed and I'm caught there forever.

Despite the darkness that enshrouded our home, Danny and I still managed to have many bright childhood moments. Our many pleasures included listening to the Beatles and other rock 'n' roll, Saturday morning cartoons, comic books, baseball cards, watching Star Trek, Batman, James Bond, The Man from U.N.C.L.E., and Voyage to the Bottom of the Sea on TV and playing with the associated toys. Other favorite TV shows included The Twilight Zone, The Outer Limits, and The Alfred Hitchcock Hour. Swimming, hanging out with friends, watching Universal Studio monster movies, and reading Famous Monsters magazine provided other successful diversions from our dark predicament. We also loved the psychedelic colors, posters, black lights, incense, peace symbols, and lava lamps that pervaded the Sixties. Using the same vivid imaginations that drove our play, we pretended our parents were normal and our dreams were sweet.

The Old Neighborhood

Our neighborhood offered many interesting diversions, such as Mr. Schmidt, who slicked his hair back and bore a thrilling and uncanny resemblance to Lon Chaney Jr.'s Phantom of the Opera. Also, the sidewalks and streets were filled with kids piloting bikes, trikes, red wagons, and groups of children engaged in games, such as whiffle ball and kick the can. On summer evenings, the adults smoked, laughed, and conversed in the driveway of our next door neighbors. Overall, it was a pleasant place, but it also exhibited darker aspects.

On an evening that was sweltering hot and we didn't yet have air conditioning, I tried to cool my room by opening the windows. In the middle of the night, I woke to the sounds of a woman or teenage girl screaming and a siren fast approaching. Through the window screen, I saw several figures huddled farther down the block, illuminated by the flashing lights of a police car.

The next morning, I asked my mother what had happened. She said she guessed Mr. and Mrs. Callahan had gotten into another loud argument and someone had called the police. As soon as I finished breakfast, I headed straight for where I'd seen the police cruiser.

Chuck, our neighborhood bully who lived next door to the wife beater and his family, stood at my destination.

"What happened last night?" I asked. "Did old man Callahan beat up his wife again?"

Chuck shook his head. "Surprisingly not," he said. "Mr. Phillips across the street started whaling on his daughter Vanessa, and she ran out of the house and stood here screaming until the police came. He cut her up badly. Look."

Chuck pointed to a bloody bone on the sidewalk swarming with ants.

I stared in horrified fascination, imagining Mr. Phillips chasing Vanessa around their small cottage with a butcher's cleaver.

Many years later, I realized Chuck had placed a beef bone on the sidewalk and waited patiently for a sucker like me to come along asking questions.

It Takes a Village

Like our neighborhood, our community was an interesting and generally benign place; however, it, too, offered up several dark experiences. A few months after the beef bone incident, my mother took me to the dentist. She remained in the waiting room while a dental hygienist led me into an exam room and helped me into the dental chair. I was just there for a cleaning and exam, so I relaxed and checked out the unfamiliar equipment. A few minutes later, the dentist came in, a tall man with thinning hair and a serious expression.

"Hi, I'm doctor Jerkens," he said. "I'm just finishing up with another patient. Then I'll have a look at your teeth. In the meantime, would you do me a great favor?"

"Yes, sir," I said. "What is it?"

He reached into the top of a closet and pulled out the largest hypodermic needle I'd ever seen. It looked like it was meant for a horse. "If you'd be kind enough to hold this for me," he said, "I'd really appreciate it."

He placed the syringe in my already-trembling hands and stepped out of the room. When he returned in five minutes, I was a quivering blob of protoplasm, and he eyed me with cruel satisfaction.

Bastard!

My father's favorite sports were surfing, cliff diving, and toboggan racing, which he watched on the Wide World of Sports on Sunday afternoons after a weekend of yard work and home maintenance and repair. My father was so athletically disinclined in high school that the administration looked the other way when he substituted chorus for his required physical education classes.

As one might imagine, when I developed an interest in baseball around the age of six, my father wasn't in a good position to teach me about the game, even if he'd wanted to, so my mother enrolled me in a baseball clinic at our local YMCA, which I greatly enjoyed. Soon after, my brother Danny and I attended a Saturday program for kids there.

Danny and I ended up in separate groups, which were led by counselors who were in their late teens and early twenties. My counselor's name was Butch, and he was a stocky, muscular guy with blue beard shadow and slightly insane brown eyes. At first, I liked him because he was handsome and made up thrilling games. His favorite was Capture Hill #49. He advised us kids in a helpful manner as we built a gigantic, multi-story

fort out of all the folding tables and chairs owned by the YMCA, a considerable number. Then everyone but Butch climbed inside the fort.

"Okay," he said. "Here're the rules. You're in a fort on Hill #49. I'm trying to capture it. I'm going to throw this ball at the fort. If I hit you, you have to come out and be my prisoner of war. If you want to desert, you have to run to the safe zone behind me. While you're running, you're fair game. If I hit you, you're also my prisoner. The game ends when the fort is empty. Understand?"

We assented.

Butch wound up and hurled the red rubber ball, which was a little smaller than a basketball and inflated to the max.

BOOM! Suddenly, two chairs blew away from the fort and a table collapsed. Butch quickly recovered the ball and fired it into the "hole" he'd created. A boy screamed as the ball smashed into his face. BOOM! The hole widened, and two boys made a break for it. One sprinted and slid into the safe zone, but the other kid took a ball to the chest and went down, coughing and crying. BOOM! The game continued. A few kids made it to safety, but the rest of us were injured by flying chairs, falling tables, or the ball. Although I knew Capture Hill #49 was wrong because some kids got really hurt and upset, this was the most exciting game I'd ever played! Compared to the beatings Danny and I received at home, this was a restful night's sleep.

However, at least one set of parents complained to the YMCA's director. She didn't fire Butch, but she banned Capture Hill #49. On the following Saturday, the YMCA was short a counselor, so Danny's group and mine were combined under Butch, who was bored and angry that his creative genius had been stymied. He spun a three-foot long orange rubber snake around a beefy hand and glared at us.

"Okay," he said. "I've made up another really cool game, but first I want to know which of you little ankle-biters ratted me out."

He stared at each of us in turn until his gaze fell upon a slight kid named Henderson who had twitchy brown eyes and a pulsing blue vein on his forehead.

"I think it was you, Henderson," Butch said. "You're a nervous little freak and always on the verge of tears."

"No, I—," Henderson said, just before Butch snapped the snake at his stomach. Henderson screamed and dropped to the floor, crying. We were in a remote corner of the gym, and the floor was deep with dust bunnies. Henderson coughed violently.

Danny leaned over to help Henderson up, and Butch wielded the snake and inflicted a large welt on Danny's back where his T-shirt rode up.

"You leave my brother alone!" I shouted. I went down with a snake flick to my right side.

"Enough!" Butch yelled. "Everybody up and at attention!"

We did as we were told.

We stood there for five minutes until the crying subsided.

"Okay, that's more like it," Butch said. "We're going outside now—I've thought of a game even better than Capture Hill #49. I hope nobody's afraid of falling out of trees."

As we filed toward the door that led outside, Danny and I glanced at each other and formed a plan. We slackened our pace until we were at the end of the line. Once Butch and most of the other kids were outside, we slowly backtracked and exited the other side of the gym as if we were headed for the bathrooms. Once we were in the main part of the YMCA, we ran out the front door to a phone booth on the grounds and used our snack money to call our mom and ask her to come get us.

She arrived a few minutes later. Luckily, when she saw our welts and dusty clothes, she believed our story, and we never returned to the YMCA.

School Daze

The final dimension to our young lives was school. Often, it was fun and rewarding. However, at other times, it could be strange and dangerous. For example, I liked my first grade teacher, but one day she was out ill, and we had a substitute teacher who said, "You know, I have friends who

are parents with a small son. Whenever he misbehaves, they dip his penis in alcohol."

I have no idea what inspired her to make such an inappropriate statement, but it worried me for years. I figured if our parents could subject us to severe beatings, what was to stop them from sexually abusing us?

My second grade teacher was grandmotherly but odd. At naptime, she told us all the molecules of the universe were pressing down on our eyes and we needed to shut them for protection. Once, when she escorted us to our table in the lunch room, she tilted her head at me and told our sixth-grade table monitor in a voice I wasn't supposed to hear, "Keep an eye on this one. I think he's trouble." To this day, I have no memory of misbehaving in her class.

My third-grade teacher was nice, but my fourth-grade teacher constantly screamed at us and often fled our classroom in tears and sought refuge in the teachers' lounge for long periods of time. Sometimes we were left unattended, and sometimes a kindly teacher would come to our classroom and urge us to please be on our best behavior with Mrs. Carter. As far as I remember, we were good kids and tried our best, but Mrs. Carter succumbed to a nervous breakdown several months before the school year ended. We had a substitute teacher for the remainder of the year, and we got along with her fine.

On the first day of Mrs. Scarsdale's fifth-grade class, she said, "Children, I've made a list of all the students in this class who were also in Mrs. Carter's class last year. I'm giving you fair warning. If your name's on this list and I see any misbehavior, I'm going to get even with you for causing my poor friend to have a nervous breakdown."

I can't speak for my classmates, but Mrs. Scarsdale certainly got her revenge on me. I already had one strike against me because I'd been in Mrs. Carter's class. Second, I made friends with an unhappy and unruly boy named Randy whom Mrs. Scarsdale strongly disliked. Third, Randy and I both developed crushes on a beautiful girl in our class named Anna, and Mrs. Scarsdale deeply disapproved. Fourth, I was a bit of a class clown, such as the time she told us we needed to master our fear of long division, and I said, or else your fear will master you. At the time, I had no idea why I took on this role, but, looking back, I realize I felt driven to lead the battle against Mrs. Scarsdale because she was full of anger and hatred like my parents and had threatened us on the first day of class. Striking out at Mrs. Scarsdale was much safer for me than attacking my abusive parents.

Every six weeks, Mrs. Scarsdale sent a report card home saying that my behavior was unacceptable, and each time my father gave me a severe spanking. I soon reformed, shutting up in class and focusing on my studies. Still, the negative report cards and beatings continued for the rest of the school year.

That year, we were the "smart" fifth-grade class, and the top six brightest students left class every day to attend a four-hour seminar for gifted kids. I yearned to be accepted into the program. For one thing, the seminar participants carried around books I wanted to read, such as Ernest Hemingway's The Old Man and the Sea. Second, the program would allow me to escape Mrs. Scarsdale's evil reign for half of every day. And my ambition wasn't far-fetched—at some point, I'd been told that I was next in line for the seminar program, provided a space opened up.

One day, long after I'd reformed my class behavior, Mrs. Scarsdale announced that one of the seminar kids named Billy Taylor was moving to Houston, and his slot in the program would be filled by a student named Frank Benson. She looked at me with triumph as she made this announcement.

Later, Mrs. Scarsdale cornered me, her steely eyes floating eerily behind the thick lenses of her glasses, and said, "I told you I'd get even."

When I attended the first day of class in sixth grade, I discovered Mrs. Scarsdale's final act of vengeance: she'd placed me in the "dumb" class.

Luckily, my sixth grade teacher recognized I was bright and skilled at language arts; she encouraged me to write a short story every week instead of completing the standard spelling, grammar, and punctuation assignments.

Seventh grade was the year school became dangerous. Our health / physical education teacher

was Mr. Barrett, a burly Jamaican who'd played professional football until a knee injury permanently benched him. He wore a large gold watch that might have been a Rolex, dressed in expensive sports warm-up clothes, carried a thick roll of cash in his jacket pocket, and brooked no nonsense.

One day in health class, he told us, "I'm going down to the office. This room better remain totally silent, or there'll be hell to pay."

I focused on reading the relevant chapter in our health book, but a kid named Mark Freeman launched into an imitation of Mr. Barrett threatening us. Several classmates laughed. Then Mr. Barrett exploded into the room and grabbed Mark by the collar and jerked him to his feet.

"I told you there'd be hell to pay!" he shouted. "Get into the push-up position!"

Mark complied, still grinning slightly because he was muscular and figured punishment push-ups were no big deal.

Mr. Barret closed the door, lifted the pool-cue shaped pointer off the blackboard chalk holder, and savagely beat Mark's butt and legs. Mark started to scream, but Mr. Barrett said, "You scream, boy, and I'll beat you within an inch of your life."

We watched in horrified fascination as Mr. Barrett hit Mark a dozen times with vicious blows. The next week, our health unit ended, and we became a P.E. class again. In the showers after a game of flag football, we observed the angry red welts on Mark's bottom and legs.

"You tell your parents?" a classmate said.

Mark looked around, terrified. "Are you out of your fucking mind?" he said.

Many other kids met Mark's fate, and Mr. Barrett was universally hated by his students. When Mr. Barrett decided he'd established complete dominion over us, he made a habit of leaving his roll of cash on his office desk to demonstrate we were too frightened to take it. However, one day someone stole it, and a furious Mr. Barrett was unable to weed out the culprit.

When we had seventh grade PE class, we shared the sports fields and locker room with Mr.

Maple's eighth grade PE class. There was a not-too-bright runty blonde wise-ass kid in that class that Mr. Maple and his students called Roach. One day, just for fun, Mr. Maple convinced Roach's classmates to hold him down while he sprayed Roach with an entire can of an insecticide called No-Roach. Unlike Mark Freeman, Roach complained to his parents, who made an outraged call to our principal, and Mr. Maple was put on probation and suspended without pay for a week.

Finally, when I played on our high school's junior varsity football team, we had a three-hundred pound foul-tempered coach who wore cleats and leapt into the air and landed on the feet of my classmates whenever they made mistakes in practice. Luckily, he never observed any of mine. Like Mr. Barrett's beatings, no one ever reported this physical abuse.

So that's the type of child abuse that was permissible back then in the Arlington County school system, supposedly one of the finest in the United States.

The Board of Education

Sometimes us Arlingtonian kids of the Sixties and Seventies enjoyed small victories over our adult oppressors, but most of the time the adults won, hands-down. However, we did secure one larger-scale victory, and, oddly enough, and it was precipitated by Roach.

During his senior year, he dated a short and pretty redhead named Amy Weaver. One day during lunch hour, Roach and Amy kissed while they sat on a grassy hill near the high school's main entrance. Well, one thing led to another, and suddenly there was a flash of a condom wrapper in the bright sunlight, and the two young lovers were doing the horizontal mambo.

Almost instantly, a crowd of surprised but delighted students formed a dense circle around the base of the hill and shouted, "Go!" with each manly thrust. As our cheers reached a frantic climax, Mr. Wharton, our school's vice-principal, who spanked kids' bare bottoms with a giant oak paddle known as The Board of Education, sprinted out of the school, yelling for us to clear a path so he could separate the young lovers. But we crushed forward, and he did not pass.

About the Author:

Allen Long is the author of Less than Human: A Memoir (Black Rose Writing, 2016). His memoirs have appeared or are forthcoming in Broad Street, Copperfield Review, Eunoia Review, Hawaii Pacific Review, Scholars & Rogues, Stepping Stones, and Verdad. An assistant editor at Narrative Magazine since 2007, Allen lives with his wife near San Francisco.

I HAVE COME HOME

by Antonio Wong

"It is time to wake up. Today is the biggest day and you do not want to miss it," my grandfather said. As I slowly move away from my bed, I see the sun peering across my room and casting its long yellow bright light in the red concrete wall. To me, the overlapping colors looks like a bright orange dinner plate, yet with ominous cracks. Why today? Why does of all day has to come? I can hear my grandparents scurrying around the house and covering the hallways with the smell of incense, yet I stood frozen in my room, hoping that today can pass by quickly.

"What are you standing around there for?" my grandfather asked, "We need to make for time and get there early."

He was fully dressed in his white button-down shirt and gray pant as he usually does. He used to be an energetic kind fellow and had bright joyful brown eyes, before old age had caught up to him. Now all I saw were wrinkly lines running through his forehead and white spots of hair appearing on both side of his head and those two dull black beady eyes filled with disdain.

I look around my room one more time, trying to capture multiple pictures of my room before I leave. In one corner, the large wooden closet stood still on its four hind legs and always served as my safe spot when playing hide-and-seek. Inside were scribbles of drawing whenever I waited out for my captors. On another corner sat the basket of robotic warriors and Power Ranger figurines which I hope that someday would save me

from my "monsters." However, this was a dilemma which neither safe zone nor imaginary superheroes can help me escape from. As soon as I got to the front door, a dark blue luggage bag stood there with its long plastic arm sticking up and waiting to whisk me away to unknown places. I said begrudgingly to myself, "You can do this. Today is the day that you will be leaving China for America."

I had always thought that I would stay in Guangzhou, China for the rest of my life. My grandparents and I lived in a five-story gray apartment in the middle of the ever-growing city. At the time, I was seven years old, and have finished preschool and preparing to enter 1st grade in the coming month. During school break, I would always go to my uncle's girlfriend's house and play Super Nintendo with her brother. Every Chinese New Year, I would get dozens of red envelopes, almost the size of my palm, with 10s, 20s, and occasionally 100s yuan, waiting to be uncovered. I though this perpetual cycle would never break until the day of the departure.

As my luggage was loaded into the car, I see students, clad in their colored school pants and jackets with a red scarf wrapped around their neck, cheerfully walking away from school with others and discussing their greatest moment of their day. Out of that stampeding crowd, I spot a familiar face; my best friend and classmate, H, who I was supposed to begin the new school year with. I tried to catch up to him, yet my grandfather tightly held on to me. My mind started flooding with emotions and thought, like the turbulent flow of traffic running through the streets with horns blaring and drivers shouting to others to get out of their way.

As I took in more of the scenery around me, I felt the urge to rush back into the house and locked myself in my closet, waiting for my superheroes to protect me from my pending doom. "Time to get into the car," my grandfather exclaimed. His gentle, yet hoarse voice snapped me back from my illusionary moment of escape, cutting off any sliver of hopes of staying.

As I sat in the car, past conversations with H reiterated in my head. I could still hear it as if it was just yesterday.

He asked, "Why are you going to America?"

"I am going to America because I am going to live with my parents."

"Aren't they (my grandparents) your parents? Why are they not here in Guangzhou?"

His last two questions have baffled me which I had never thought about. I had neither met my parents, nor even remember any feature of them. I had never heard from my grandfather speak about my parents in America, nor did any of my relatives had spoken about them once. Were they ashamed of them? Did my parents do something wrong? Why did they leave me with my grandparent? There were so many question that came to mind on that day.

I asked my grandfather, "How does my parents look like?"

He paused for a moment before responding, "I do not know. You will have to see them for yourself when you get there."

"Why did my parents went to America without me?

"I said I do not know. Can you please not ask too many questions? I am driving." He said with a hint of anger in his breath.

Even when I stopped asking him question about my parents, I can see him holding tightly onto the steering wheel and felt that the car was accelerated even more. Even so, his actions were foreign to me as I have never seen him like this before.

During a time when I was practicing my Chinese calligraphy, I would always lose my patience. My lines were not straight, some looks crooked or jagged. Instead of putting effort, I turned to television. My grandfather saw this and took the remote from my hand.

"Why are you not finishing up your calligraphy?"

"It is too hard. My hands would always shake and when I stopped my shaking hand with the other, both of my hands suddenly draw the line away from the character."

"You need to keep practicing. No television until you were done. How about I hold on to your hand while you were writing?"

He stood behind me with his right hand holding on to my right. I grabbed on to the brush and he started leading my hand with his own. As we wrote the characters five times, suddenly my grandpa told me to not stop writing and released his hand from mine. I began to write the characters five more time without him, each time the characters become more smoothly straightened than before. My grandfather may be a stern man, but he would never tell me to stop doing the right things.

As we moved further away from my former home in the city, the car began to shake back and forth. Outside, the road had become a wide lane of rocky terrain. On both side of the road, rice and green vegetation pads would stretch as far as there is no end. The buildings would be as low as one or two-story high. Most of the people who would wander the field would be elderlies and children, while the adults were nowhere to be seen. It is as if almost adults were taken somewhere far away and the elderlies and children had to fend for themselves to keep their living.

Once we got to the airport, I thought that this was the place where the adults went away and leave their family and children behind. We waited by the entrance, thinking that my grandfather had changed his mind and decided to take me home. However, a young woman, who might be in her late 20's, came up to my grandfather. They talked for a moment and it seemed as if my grandfather handed the woman a thick white envelope.

My grandfather ushered me to him, "Make sure you follow this woman no matter what. Do not take your eyes off her for one second."

When I saw the departure gate, it looked like an arched upper half of the mouth, waiting for me to be swallow inside. As I get closer to the gates, my feet had gotten weaker and my lower abdomen began hurting as if dozens of needles had stabbed me from the inside. I began to tuck away from my grandfather's hand, getting as far away from the gate, but my grandfather would not let go. I gave one final forceful pull and ran toward the entrance. As my grandfather caught up to me, he gave me a scornful look, his eyebrow pointing down towards the ground.

He harshly asked, "What are you doing? The airplane is going to leave soon."

Words were barely coming out of my mouth as tears continuously flowing out of my eyes and flooding into my mouth. I wanted to say something but it was just too difficult.

With my head facing towards the ground, I asked, "Will I ever come back home?"

My grandfather responded, "You are going home. Your parents are your home. However, you will not be coming back to Guangzhou for a long time. You need to finish your study in America and once you are older, you can come visit at any time."

His reassurances did little to comfort my confusions and fears. As I stood there for what seemed hours, I had regained my composure and began to follow the woman through the gates, I took one last look at my grandfather before he disappears behind the wall. As the airplane took off, I look out the window to see the large green pastures stretching out toward the mountain and random tiny gray spots, which looked like stacks of hardened clay.

As the airplane began to descend into the Guangzhou Airport, I peered out the window and saw that the tiny gray spots have grown to overtake the green pasture field by nearly a half. The former dull grey buildings have been replaced by glass high-rises and taller conjoining apartments.

The airports had turned from a rectangular shaped into a glass dome that has arms wrapping around the newly developed asphalt roads and highway. It has been eighteen years since the day I had departed from Guangzhou. Many progress has been made to turn Guangzhou from a small town into a metropolitan city. Most of the green vegetation fields has been turned into public parks, and roadways.

My mind began to flutter back and forth, thinking of ways to say to my grandfather as I get closer to seeing him. As I walked out of the arrival gate, my uncle and his girlfriend-turned-wife waved to me to go toward the very end of the line.

I asked them, "Hi Uncle and Auntie, it has been so long. How have you been? And where is grandpa? I though he is coming to meet me at the gate.

My uncle responded, "He is not feeling very well these past few days. His leg was getting weak and he cannot stand or walk for long distance, but you will definitely see him in the new house."

I did not know if this might his excuse as a repercussion of my parent's relationship with my grandfather or symptoms of old age. Even till today, the enmity between my grandfather and my father were still there, but they had started talking with each other for a while and try to not to bring up the past for the sake of mending their relationship.

As my uncle and aunt-in-law drove me around Guangzhou, I can still see my former apartment and school. They have become quite dilapidated and inhabitable. Windows were either cracked or shattered. The buildings were closed off due to runoff and invasive plant growth. Not only that, as I get closer, the smell of feces and wastes becomes pungent and repulsive. As soon as the car pulls into a gated region where it enclosed several eight-story bright yellow apartments and grass-enclosed square, the sun's ray can be seen reflecting off the side of the building like it is welcoming any visitor, both foreign and domestic.

While I take the elevator toward the top floor, I am overwhelmed by a surge of uneasiness, waiting to see him. My uncle assures me to not be nervous, yet I am sweating profusely in the cold air. The elevator finally made it to our stop. I was the first to step out and waited for my uncle to lead the way. As he knocked on the door, I can hear faint sounds of grunts and cheers, each fighting for dominance. As the door opened, my grandmother was the first who rushed quickly to greet me and check out my well-being before anyone else can get their turn. As I hastily evade my grandmother's sticky hands, I see my grandfather standing under the bright blue light. For that moment, my grandfather seemed to remain the same as when we parted ways. I cannot seem to remember what to say, but the first phrase that I said to him on that day was "I have come home."

Antonio Wong graduated from SUNY Stony Brook University with a B.E. in Biomedical Engineering. As unusual as it is, he considers himself as an outlier in the writing community. He currently resides in New York and studying in medical school. When he is not studying, he likes to volunteer in hospital and participates in outreach programs. He hopes to soon write literary piece pertaining to his interpersonal experience in the medical field.

About the Author:

Antonio Wong graduated from SUNY Stony Brook University with a B.E. in Biomedical Engineering. As unusual as it is, he considers himself as an outlier in the writing community. He currently resides in New York and studying in medical school. When he is not studying, he likes to volunteer in hospital and participates in outreach programs. He hopes to soon write literary piece pertaining to his interpersonal experience in the medical field.

HALF OF SOMETHING

by John Ballantine Jr.

The glass is half full, even though it is emptying fast. Life seeps out of the body as we wake to another day with the sun rising.

The water station, with plastic cups lined up in neat rows, cannot possible quench my thirst as I trod my way up First Avenue after sixteen miles and the slight Queensborough Bridge incline that broke the unsuspecting—water cups are thrown randomly to the side. The Willis Avenue Bridge, with its diagonal grating, will trip up some as we stumble into the Bronx hot, tired, and ready to turn toward Manhattan and Central Park. My fifth or sixth NYC Marathon with spectators of every shape, language, and color cheering us on—Hare Krishna, black fist raised, and gay pride—my feet keep moving as thighs lift slowly and my back clenches. The knees will not give out for a couple more years and many miles. I stumble with thirty thousand victorious runners with hands raised under the banner at 26.2 miles with legs cramping. I eat my banana in the November sun and cold rain next to Tavern on the Green.

Our glass is half full even with the Boston Marathon bombs, the World Trade Center planes, and the cut off-heads that ISIS tweets across our consciousness. I see the outstretched hands with water cup, orange slice, and the smiles shouting, "Keep on going." I touch the small hand of the black boy running with me through the sprinkler who says I am just a step behind his dad, the fireman running with one plastic leg. A soldier back from Iraq. "Keep going, you can catch him." Never, I think.

Half of something is better than nothing. Half of life is better than disappointment on the final day

because, even then, the white orchid bends its head. The smiles lining the streets astonish me still. "You want it all but you cannot have it. Take what you get, hold it tight, and keep breathing deep." I trace the steps of the man with one leg and one prosthetic limb just ahead of me. A life half lived, half full lifts my head in the Bronx as I push my revived body toward Central Park and the cheers of Manhattan onlookers.

Why, you ask, did you not drop your head, not see the horrible rapes of Boko Haram or the trafficking across Asia? Did you not hear the screams of Idi Amin's dead or the drunk, confused stares of your mother, unable to tell what was true and what was not? The vodka in her hand, the rape on the ocean liner as it made its way to Hitler's brown shirts ready to exterminate civilizations in the name of what?

Did you not hear Wagner picking up the pace with the killings—know that Genghis Kahn conquered almost all the world, or wonder why gods of every name sent the locust to scratch the sores of plague-weakened people? Did you not see the horribleness of living here?

Still you climb the mountain, look at the stars, see beauty, love, and kindness. I cannot kill the naïve spirit, crush your illusion, or stir the meanness in your soul. I cannot break you, yet.

No, you dropped me on my head time and time again, cut my fingers, and pierced the veil of civility. You piled bodies decaying in trenches buried nearby. Still I hear the violin mimicking a melody of morning bird songs, a jig, a dirge. I know the call of doves, the warm touch next to me—dog, wife, and even my mother with uneven hand.

My glass is half full. I know the world is not always good. That meanness and greed prevail and that the kindness of strangers cannot be expected. Still, turning my eye to the light started with the first cry, with the ray of sunlight, the miracle of being. Believing, seeing, and feeling the half-full glass, the spring of each day, and the song you cannot hear. It started so early, before the silver spoon, with the first smack of love on my bottom, the pabulum that fed me, and the first smile that lit my mother's eyes.

This is how I will walk to my grave with a song reverberating like a symphony of turning leaves, a glass brimming to the rim.

You did not lead me astray—though you tried. Shock, disappointment, alienation with dropping head and loneliness late at night with one light burning. Broken heart too. I stood with no breath and did not turn. The darkness opened to deeper notes of love—the saxophone calling, the howl of the wolf, and my imagination that rides on the crescent of the moon with the creatures of the night wind.

Maybe if the black star sucks in all—crushing even consciousness of our steps along the path, maybe then the mass of the universe will smash hope and destroy all the light around me. But that black hole holds the weight of being—all history, knowledge, and even the nightmares of universes crashing in cannot negate my being, not blacken the yellow petals of each flower. No, the place where there is nothing, where all is infinite, where the heaviness in my hand, that black hole is how I see the half-full glass. The water nourishes me still, the glass is still half full even as I drink.

Hope cannot be crushed in me, even as the ashes are scattered, the voice goes, and all consciousness is gone. Hope, love, and faith in the half-full glass stays. I wake to it each day, and I will carry it out. My hope strikes back, I turn from the blackness that you say surrounds me. I hear symphonies yet unwritten, and I touch the lips of undeclared love. I dream of fountains nourishing me—good and bad—leading me to new pathways. I fill the empty vessels. The glass is half full in the blink of an eye. I just imagined it and it is so.

You wonder why the devil never, ever wins—even as you twist the truth to the ground—that is because the flowers spring from the ashes, and my smile laughs with the half-full glass in front of me.

About the Author:

A professor at Brandeis International Business School, John Ballantine took his Bachelor's degree in English at Harvard, with an M.A. from the University of Chicago and a Ph.D. in Economics from NYU Stern. He has published economic commentary in Salon and the Boston Globe. His literary work has appeared in Crack the Spine, Existere, Forge, Lime Hawk, Penmen Review, Ragazine, Rubbertop Review, Saint Ann's Review, Santa Fe Literary Review, Slippery Elm, and SNReview. He writes to understand the world we walk in and to ouch our complicated lives.

FAREWELL

by George Freek

FAREWELL (After Tu Fu)

Now we have to part.
You go in one direction,
I go in the other.
Will we be drunk together,
ever again? Last night,
walking beside the lake,
we sang ballads to the moon,
nearly until dawn,
answered by a lonely loon.
Today, we share headaches.
We can't know what direction
our lives will take.
I'll return to my home.
You'll remain in my mind,
but you're also on your own.
When I finish this poem,
once again, I'll also be alone,
listening to the waves lap
against the shore, quietly
eating away the stones.

AUTUMN NIGHT (After TU FU)

The day ticks to its conclusion,
a clock without a face,
a symbol of my confusion.
Far into the night,
I look at the moon and stars.
I watch them fade from sight.
They glow like lanterns,
but they don't last.
They show me no path.
A sparrow searches for worms
in the cold autumn grass.
It seems futile, as leaves
fall with infinite peace.
They fall in brown and red.
They fall because they are dead.

THE SHELTERING SKY (After Su Tung Po)

The sky is like a table
I am hiding under,
a table made of glass.
Clouds drift through its cracks.
Night arrives and the day
is lost. A star flickers.
It's what we're made of.
But it sees nothing.
It knows no desires.
Soon it will burn to ashes.
It does what it was
meant to do. It rises.
It flickers, then it dies.
I was only meant,
it seems, to wonder why.

About the Author:

George Freek is a poet/playwright living in Belvidere, IL. His poetry has recently appeared in 'West Trade Review'; 'Off Course Literary Review'; 'The Ottawa Arts Review'; Limestone Journal'; and 'The Sentinel Literature Quarterly'. His plays are published by Playscripts, Inc.; Lazy Bee Scripts; and Off The Wall Plays.

INVITATION
by Gloria Monaghan

Invitation

The road is waiting for you to walk

into the open air
into the slightly grey day
with the sliver of sun just over the clouds
orange and unpredictable

we are in God's way

each of us golden
and waiting

where does it come from
this amazing day with the low clouds
the fallen small oval yellow leaves
wet on the path to your home

the invitation is waiting for you to come out
and explore the early frost on the green grass
encompassing a deeper green than even you

never thought of

something fell away
and it is time now for you to leave your desk.

Meditation One

*"Let us suppose, then, that we are dreaming, and
that all these particulars--namely, the opening of
the eyes, the motion of the head, the forth-
putting of the hands--are merely illusions; and
even that we really possess neither an entire body
nor hands such as we see".*

Descartes

I am letting sadness seep in

to the corners of my brittle body.

I wake to adolescent children talking

and fall in the air.

A praying mantis came into the living room

and stared at my daughter and myself

huge soft eyes; so kind

what to do about that?

It was teaching me about stillness.

It was a hard lesson.

I can't let go of summer.

Provincetown

The light in Provincetown is fading. It is very grey.
My favorite color that moves from light to shallow darkness.
You have shown me lightness in fallow, you have shown me humility.
At the restaurant, with barely perceptual move you went to the back of the line.
You showed me grace.

The light darkens and I like it better.
You are not afraid, of verb tense, or tragedy.
You read mystics, children, and lunatics.
You have your palm read and you read others. It is all the same this reading.

But what astonishes me more than any of these things is your steady and careful walk
to the boat in the pouring rain,
your thin coat and careful paper fingers, your delicate blue eyes.
You walk on the plank to the fast ferry, only it is a slow walk and the rain is falling all around you.
And you persist like a plover, like a willful bird ready for the morning.
Practical, bewitching and exquisite.

Meditation Two

I lost a thread of myself
in a Bill Evans song-
no matter the title
you get the picture.

Slow unraveling of smoke
decimated
like the smattering cigar ash.

When someone holds your hand,
try and remember it,
not like the rain,

try to remember how easy and casual the whole thing was.
Don't assume it will happen again,
and just shrug off the connection

feel the lines of the person's hand
the slow energy of their hair
between the nape of the neck and the collar bone
the small isolated brown dot just below the hairline

take in where they place their hands
the weight of the hand on your hip.
Don't try and imagine how your hands feel on them

notice where the hair from the scalp ends
and the neck recedes into slow movement
like a song
that leaves you transparent and lost

the road forgotten
the flowers you saw only yesterday, now are brown

there is still that feeling.

About the Author:

Gloria Monaghan is a Professor of Humanities at Wentworth Institute in Boston. She is a published author and poet. She has two books of poetry, Flawed (Finishing Line Press, 2011) and The Garden (Flutter Press 2015). She has published in Blue Max Review, Slope, Adelaide, Aurorean, and 2River among others. She currently live south of Boston.

OUT IN THE DISTANCE
by Holly Day

Spring

ice melts in noisy rivulets
resumes descent on muddy river banks

poking its greasy snout out of the water
a bullhead lumbers out of torpor, floats to the surface

frightens newly-hatched crawfish and water striders
small sand crabs hiding in the silt

When You Want Me Least

You, who are so different, can't be
expected to agree on anything
with me. I just need you to hold me long enough
to understand what is written on the small tag attached
to my toe, and then you can go.

There are streamers and iridescent ribbons
for you to reflect on
while you sit here with me, in the dark
a newspaper with your name written in black felt pen
over the original headlines
memories of what we could have had
if you had only become the president, or the Pope.

The real memories
are still here, somewhere, as well as
the rest of my heart. You
can wrap them all to go
if you want to forget.

Out in the Distance

The ground welcomes me, even though
I'm still alive, even now
I am just another something
that sends out roots wherever the dirt
is soft enough to receive me. I can feel the flowers
growing under my skin
can feel them struggling to break free
to sing out under the sun.

You can put your own roots out, too
spread out over the soft grass with me,
shake loose your skin
let the earth in. Eventually, we might
grow as high as trees, thick trunks and limbs
twisting around one another in a frozen embrace
blooming in a garden

of our own making.

Outside My Room

I can hear your hand on the door
your fingers sensing my room
on a time-learned path
shadows no longer as if I'm asleep
brazen, you're here anyway

I hear your feet dragging down
the hallway, hear the jagged
intake of your breath, even now
hollow fingers brush my hair back
all the thing I'm screaming to forget.

Y

The beast inside me is screaming free the
dead thing inside you is still dead
either way, I can't go home

under the light of early sun
violet streaks across the sky
what the hell am I doing

About the Author:

Holly Day has taught writing classes at the Loft Literary Center in Minneapolis, Minnesota, since 2000. Her poetry has recently appeared in Tampa Review, SLAB, and Gargoyle, and her published books include Walking Twin Cities, Music Theory for Dummies, and Ugly Girl.

MY GRETEL

by John O'Connor

My Gretel

My sister never called me Hansel
but she knew I would lead her to trouble.
The hollyhocks looked at us mischievously

from the frost wall garden and we stole out
in the twilight to escape a mother trying
to convince us she was ours,

with her rituals of blood and stale bread,
large bosomed matriarch standing
over us like a mysterious mountain range

you wouldn't enter unless life
depended on it. We made our way down
the leafy paths trying to find a place

where we would not feel lost.
My sister looked up to me, always,
as if my hair were on fire and I would

try to put her at ease though I had no idea
where we were going. Here, eat this,
I would say to her and she would put

the brown morel in her mouth
and chew in slow motion. Along the stream
bank were little snake holes

where you could see tiny dots of light
that might have been eyes of some kind.
Don't look. Keep going. Shoes and socks wet,

cupped hands around the candle flame.
Somewhere along the way I lost her.
I grew older alongside someone

who sang the wrong melody and couldn't repeat
our secret phrase. I pretended to be fooled,
gave her room to breathe her aerosol of mold,

allowing her walks alone, never again to hold
her hand. This world is a lonely garden
and no one can say the names of what

grows there. That's why Latin died.
There are garlands along the path,
cottages built with what is left of our

memories. The strangers that pass us
on the road may be our cousins, our
siblings. We don't know. The markers

are gone. We ate them long ago for breakfast,
their earthy taste still lingering, their musty
scent hanging in the air.

Etude

Every time I tune this thing I hear the A string
telling me there's a long way to go, a line that repeats
and repeats, the way my mother's fingers went up
and down the keyboard making the same mistakes
as if they were written on the staff. A cow stands
in the middle of a narrow winding road that makes
itself out of a long summer of unseen trampling beasts,
laying down the fall before the winter.
Everyone knows the snow is coming
and everyone wants to take that path up the hill
where the sky begins, where the muddy earth
starts over. It's a monotonous and singular melody
until your realize it's the timing that has control,
that the flute is sad and the clarinet wants her mother.

In Your Garden

The air does not listen to the water even when the sky
writes down instructions on how to make syntax out of wind.
Are you following me? I think not, your body stooped over
your tiny box plants in your garden, the sun disappearing
behind the new condominium rising over your shoulder.
We thought this was our beginning, leaves flying upward
from hickory and birch that have lived so long without us.
Your mother died while you were on the other side
of the ocean. You had always felt that far away. Sometimes
our waters seem to widen between us. That's why we have
our arms, so slender, so sore, so longing to hold something.
Stay with me one more day. Then tomorrow, do the same.

About the Author:

John Paul O'Connor's poems have appeared in numerous literary journals, including St Ann's Review, Hanging Loose, Sycamore Review, Silk Road and Indiana Review. His work has been nominated twice for a Pushcart Prize and he won the Violet Reed Haas Prize for Poetry in 2015. His book of poems, Half the Truth, is available from Snake Nation Press.

Erosion

From our plane we can see what the storms
have done to the coastline, that the houses
will fall into the sea. What a brilliant day
now that the clouds are gone and you turn
your attention to me. You stayed inside
for days watching those boys in their tennis
whites, the volleys long, the wind still
in London, while up from the gulf
came gales and torrents and I sat
at my desk and wrote little bits of trash
the wind blew away. And all the while
our country grew smaller, withering
at its edges. I know how you love the sea,
especially in mist and a little fog.
And I love the mountains. No, we don't
really own a plane, but I forget that
when I'm looking at aerial photos.
They say so much about a nation
and its people. You have to back up
for perspective as if you lived in the sky
or on the other side of the Milky Way.

How Light Is Made From Darkness

Do you recognize a gray day
when you are living a gray life
or even a gray year, the color
of which you worked so hard to mix?
A stomach can grow flabby

just as a mouth becomes less gabby
and you can retreat further
into your inner ear where the snare
and the whistle play the march
you have been trudging in order to avoid

any direct light, keeping the sun
away from your delicate new skin.
The summer drifts in with its heavy
cloud and rhythmic rains, its dark
green tangle, its out of control

uncertainty, its emerald froth,
its drenched touch, its encroaching
growth, its vines, its transcendental
moths, its repetitive hysteria,
its rising water, sinking heat,

its accusing path of ferns, its muffled
thunder and smeared lightning,
its botched patterns, its insane
language, its gross insubordination,
its sour mouth, its cheap delusions

and sunken mirages, its dry humor
that no one gets, not the echo
of the forest nor the dumb animals,
its rank composted air, its ludicrous
logic, and you, your gray turning blue,

painted over half your torso, while you catch
clouds in bottles and line your shelves
with jars of chalky earth. Do you recognize
these or have you forgotten like the rest
of us and wiped your memory clean?

253

MY FAVORITE NIECE
by Patrick Mahoney

Any form of writing exposes the soul, exposes the heart exposes the essence of what and who we, as humans, are. Particularly so with poetry...words become passion, emotion, and breathe life into the printed page. Poetry, to me, is what a blank is to an artist, what a roll of film is to a movie director. Poetry is...me. And who am I? I am one who has a lifelong love affair with poetry. I'm an American living in England. I'm a dad, a teacher, a husband, a son. I'm a poet.

MY **HEART IS NOW A TATTERED WEB**

Love is a many splendor thing
Until you fall in love
The trap that's set is one of joy
Til the jaws close very tight
The poets marvel at the grace
And beauty love entails
But hardly ever is the saga told
Of a love that has gone sour
I know now how Lucifer felt
As He tumbled from the Gates of Heaven
A trip from Paradise to eternal damnation
Will harden the softest heart
As it has mine in this hour of darkness

The feeling of the desolate,
The darkness, and the cold
Will always bear a deep, deep scar
In this broken heart of mine
The passion that I once enjoyed
And bathed in for a moment
Is lost in that abhorrent passage
Where all past loves do go
My heart is spent on what I had
And will never be the same
And just as Lucifer I will dream
Of breathing life again

MY FAVORITE NIECE

A little girl you are to me
A little girl you'll stay
You'll always have your way with me
An uncle never strays

We play around with all your dolls
And have alot of fun
But soon the dolls will fade away
And the braids will tumble down

But when that happens, you and I
Will still remain the same
We'll laugh, we'll play
But not with dolls
You are a woman now

THE BASEMENT OR THE ATTIC

The line is long and never-ending
As it winds throughout the sky
Across the clouds that hide the sun
And stars that never shine
The melting pot of human forms
Blend in with one another
There is no color to define
One person from another
Each face is drawn and hollow-looking
Like a dried out piece of fruit
There is no shoving or pushing here
In this line of forgotten souls
For what awaits at the end for them
No one can change it now
For some the wait will reap a dream
That life has tuned for them
For others it will mean regret
The guilt will be upon them
And they can be assured of that
Their destiny has found them
The line draws closer to The Gate
That has but two small doors
And standing there in majesty
Is The Creator, One and All
The souls of men from yesteryear
Proceed through either door
Not randomly, you understand, for they have cast their mold
That sends them either up the stairs
Or to The Basement down below
The carpet that adorns the floor which leads into The Basement
Is worn from heavy feet of men
About to leave their souls
The stairway leading to The Top
Is like that of a virgin
Because the line is leaning left
To the door that does lead downward
Our judgment day is coming soon, the mold has just been cast
Which door will we be walking through...
The Basement or The Attic?

MY HEART IS NOW A TATTERED WEB

Love is a many splendor thing
Until you fall in love
The trap that's set is one of joy
Til the jaws close very tight
The poets marvel at the grace
And beauty love entails
But hardly ever is the saga told
Of a love that has gone sour
I know now how Lucifer felt
As He tumbled from the Gates of Heaven
A trip from Paradise to eternal damnation
Will harden the softest heart
As it has mine in this hour of darkness

The feeling of the desolate,
The darkness, and the cold
Will always bear a deep, deep scar
In this broken heart of mine
The passion that I once enjoyed
And bathed in for a moment
Is lost in that abhorrent passage
Where all past loves do go
My heart is spent on what I had
And will never be the same
And just as Lucifer I will dream
Of breathing life again

255

ON THE MATTER OF THE END OF THE WORLD

AS THE HEAVENS MUST DISCOVER

Somewhere in this universe
There lives a mortal man
And also in this universe
There is a promised land
The mortal man is in his cage
And waits to be released
The Promised Land was always free
For it was not in danger
The mortal man dreams of the day
His prison is collapsed
The Promised Land is here to stay
As long as man is not
The mortal man is thinking why
His sentence is so long
And the Promised Land is still in shock
For the cousin it had lost
The mortal man is ignorant
Of what he really did
The Promised Land is jubilant
That it is not now dead
The mortal man remembers why
His punishment was harsh
And the Promised Land begins to weep
Its enemy has been found
The mortal man awakes his brain
To start his way to home
The Promised Land just melts away
The conquest has begun
The mortal man repels his cage
And he is now the master
The Promised Land is swept away
To join its ghostly cousin
The mortal man just walks away
Another Eden to discover

The heavens rage in ceaseless furies
As the holocaust begins
The Earth revolts from its quiet sleep
It now has been awakened
The sky becomes a slurring field
Of smoke and dust and ruin
And all the world screams out in pain
Armageddon has returned

In Heaven God begins the task
Of taking in the sinless
Of making sure His loyal ones
Will live as He has promised

In Hell the Devil laughs with glee
And curses God the Father
For Satan now is paying back
His former friend and founder

On Earth the people raise their eyes
And beg for His forgiveness
But begging will not save their souls
And they bow their heads in shame

The angels of the Lord set out
For the final test of power
To seek domain and Holy Rites
That are all but now forgotten

The demons of the Underworld
Prepare for their new Kingdom
By feasting on the rotting souls
Of Hell's unnoticed prisoners

With a final blast from Gideon's Trumpet
The battle lines are drawn
And Heaven and Hell unite in terror
As the lands turn into dust
The Devil snaps the World in two
And starts His way to Heaven
As all the Angels of the Lord
Announce: "It's Armageddon"

TO THAW

by Annelise Mozzoni

Kenmore Electric Dryer

Room steeped in blue,
her and I,
folding cotton waves.

Standing in a swallow of light,
she pulls sheets out
like taffy
from dryer teeth.

She strokes my cheek,
with toasted thread,
wanting me to catch the sheets' last breath.

To Thaw

In spring
we shakeout
like seasoned linens.

Work fast,
to clean our once newlywed nest,
and beat the retreating frost.

When finished,
we bathe citrus in gin,
and join the sweet potato vines on the porch,
to toast the clean baseboards and weeded garden.

But our tongues have yet to thaw.
Wintered problems plated between us,
you haven't paused to notice,
I let them sit,
and crystallize in the newborn sun.

About the Author:

Annelise Mozzoni grew up in Rogers, Arkansas. She studies English with a concentration in creative writing at the University of Arkansas. In between class and slinging pizzas at a local pizza shop, she finds time to write. Her influences include Lisel Mueller, and her home deep in the Ozarks.

DAY AT THE BEACH
by Debbie Richard

Luminescence

Exuding brilliance, you step into a room
as an actor steps onto a stage,
heads turn, instantly drawn to your smile,
the tilt of your head, the graceful
way you carry yourself –
an illumination of something deeper,
a mirror into your soul, the evidence
of the abode of something divine.

Day at the Beach

Multicolored chute soaring o'er the waves,
Wind directed, yet anchored.
Children frolic along the shore
With sand buckets and shovels,
Knightly castles under construction.

The wind shifts, and we nearly kiss the crest,
A sudden stir, and we're drawn up again,
Free as a waterfowl –
All cares and worries lost,
In the froth, beneath our parasail.

To My Mother

I went to the sea
And the waves, sensing your presence,
Hurled against me.
I floated in the current
And reached for your hand
As I'd done so many times before.
I caught your gentle fingertips,
No – it was only a small piece of debris,
Soft, brown with short tentacles,
Churned up by the changing tide.
I looked skyward,
Felt the warmth on my face,
And knew you were there, somewhere.
I walked along the shore,
And picked up a shell, holding it to my ear,
To hear its message.
Instead of the ocean's roar,
I heard your whisper, *I miss you too.*
But, perhaps it was just the wind...

About the Author:

Debbie Richard is listed in the Directory of Poets & Writers as both a poet and creative nonfiction writer. Her poems have appeared in Halcyon, Torrid Literature Journal, WestWard Quarterly and others. "Resiliency," a chapbook of poetry, was published in 2012 by Finishing Line Press. "Hills of Home," a memoir about growing up in Appalachia, in the hills of West Virginia, was released in 2014 by eLectio Publishing. Visit her website at www.debbierichard.com

PURPLE DAWN
by Edward Bonner

WAVES OF MAGIC

I fell in love with a girl
Her name I shall not tell
Everyday I dreamt our hearts would collide
Watching the sun go down
in the mid summer's eve
I see her eyes aching inside

Irresistible waves of magic
Outpouring energy to the sky
Holding me close to her breast
Where our love shall never be denied

BETWEEN ETERNITIES

If I wrote you a letter asking
how much I mean to you
Will you answer
For
Our eternal torch is burning
An everlasting love revealed
A relentless yearning
Of few secrets concealed
Yet
Your eyes are hidden by a veil
With a luminous mist
Circling
A prevalent glow of amber
That will always exist
Then
I fall into a trance of your perfumed scent
Between eternities
Filling my heart content
Through my extremities

YOUR RAPTURED WAYS

I am the one that was made of fun
Slow at wits and eaten to bits

The one who would dream of the sun
Where your life would become undone

Then one day you filled my heart with kerosene
Where I learned how people can be mean

Unspeakable regards of a human life
Your raptured ways were a dreadful plight

Don't ask don't tell for the pain I endured
In written words they are finally secured

THE SPIRIT WEEPS

Last night I watched myself sleep
Looking out I see
Your judgment is how the spirit weeps

People that fabricate are fools
Who corrupt and break the rules

Where beauty and pleasure seldom fail
Truth and reconciliation will always prevail

MY HEART IS NOW A TATTERED WEB

Love is a many splendor thing

Until you fall in love

The trap that's set is one of joy

Til the jaws close very tight

The poets marvel at the grace

And beauty love entails

But hardly ever is the saga told

Of a love that has gone sour

I know now how Lucifer felt

As He tumbled from the Gates of Heaven

A trip from Paradise to eternal damnation

Will harden the softest heart

As it has mine in this hour of darkness

The feeling of the desolate,

The darkness, and the cold

Will always bear a deep, deep scar

In this broken heart of mine

The passion that I once enjoyed

And bathed in for a moment

Is lost in that abhorrent passage

Where all past loves do go

My heart is spent on what I had

And will never be the same

And just as Lucifer I will dream

Of breathing life again.

About the Author:

Edward Bonner grew up in a small mill town in Pittsburgh Pennsylvania. Hazelwood, Pa. A very rough neighborhood. Raised by his mother and grandparents until he was 13 years old. That's when his mother remarried. He then moved to a suburb south of Pittsburgh. Growing up, he probably got into trouble like most kids. An avid outdoorsman. 5th degree black belt / 36 years in Shotokan karate. Author of "One Kiss" Just One Kiss. A collection of love poems and more. Author of Through The Eyes Of A Lost Boy. A collection of poetry about "Love, Loss, Trauma, Pain and Healing." A journey of life through writing.

AMERICANS ON HOLIDAY
by Donovan James

Stomping atop cobble stone streets,
Capturing a filament of existence,
in a photograph,
Americans meander down
Thin and weathered
Cities like tattered scarfs,
Rivulets connect spats
Of old colony architecture,
Past dens emanating a musk
Of fried cheese,
The dim hum of tortilla's smacking
Against stone,

Exuberant cathedrals drenched
In vibrant colors,
Lively merchant booths house
Plump women politely offering
Hand carved pottery,
And the ancient masks
Of Spanish gods.

Kids whizz past, the melody
Of laughter floating
Past wanderlust crows,
Careening upwards,
While statuesque old men
Perch upon canes,
Locals curiously observe
The odd sight of three
American men traveling,
Alone, out of season,
We flicker from one immediate interest

To another,
We are boys again,
Dancing along,
The broken arrow
Of time.

The earth breathes,
Thick white fumes from soil,
Humid dew stirs
Americans from an ethanol steeped
Slumber, the automobile whirs
Into gear, flings Americans down hills
Alongside wild horses roaming thick
Swaths of jungle, bubbling over
Cresting hills to a hazy horizon.

Grumpy chickens bark arguments
Over imposing tourists,
Oblivious hogs munch grass,
While mangy dogs cope,
With past lives
Of abuse,
Timidly rubbing noses,
Near tourists,
For food.

Voluptuous waitresses effuse
Kindness, caress well intentioned
Broken English,
And bestow decadent meals
Of hearty grains, stewy beans,
And succulent fish to sop up
A heathenesque mix of tequila and beer.

Americans on holiday,
Stumble down streets at dusk
Where the moon and night's kiss
Reveals a hidden caste;
The present's incarnation of
A hundred thousand years of thankless sacrifice,
Young women rearing children,
Birthing the seeds of every civilization,
Hoping to weather the storms of ideology,
The cacophonic winds of misogyny,
Sisyphean attempts to nurture,
A better world
Into being.

While men idle in alleyway stoops,
Warm beer pooling in bellies,
Hazy minds reside
In the stubborn canyons of tradition,
Charging privilege and wanton
Ecological destruction,
To future generations.

Endless bottles of beer quell
Existential angst, flickering
Thoughts of imperialism--
Reagan and the Sandinistas--
The lives of locals distilled
Into textbook paragraphs,
Making tourism a question of ethics;

We glimpse only slivers
Of the lives of others,
Random collisions where we confirm biases
Of kindness or cynicism,
Where we either,
Strengthen the stubbornness of
grand assumptions,
Or rekindle that youthful mantra of humility:
We are certain of so very little,
All of us,

A tender fillet of vulnerability,
A fleeting cascade of strangers,
Where the spark of connection bursts
Over a joke,
A smile,
All space between us,
Perceptions and grievances,
Gone.

About the Author:

Donovan James is an artist, philosopher, and writer who lives in Portland, OR. His work has appeared in Vox Poetica, The Chaffey Review, Commonline Journal, and Curious Apes. He's also the author of the poetry collection "Saudade."

Hopeless Romantic

Dating without alcohol reveals
The Buddha nature of affection,
I drank to enliven
Tepid conversations,
Defibrillate a connection,
A time machine to the moments
Under the jurisdiction of lust,
The season of
Skin upon skin,
Fingers tracing lips, sucking
Her scent from fingertips,
Thrusts encapsulate base desires,

While immature sexual proclivities,
Dance,
In a carnal garden of lust,
Fueled by whiskey sours, ciders,
And joints whose journey from
Grass to flame to ash,
Spread damp thighs,
And fuel
Long nights,
Insatiable thrusts,
Until,
Morning light creeps across carpet,
Warms unprotected toes, her
Stretch elicits a long moan,
And she flings her arm over my chest.

I want to be alone.

Over coffee we discuss
Nothing.
Runny eggs swim around a plate,
Mashed against undercooked hash
Browns, I give her a ride
Home, wondering
If it will always be like this,
A theft,
Of lust from false affection,

We will always
Just take what we can get?
Stealing orgasms from strangers,
The elusive shadow of intimacy,
Haunting,
Through glimpses of past loves,
Flickering,
Across consciousness,
An echo from a fairy tale,
Another life,
A lie.

GHOSTS

by Richard Dinges

Ghosts

When young, I viewed
the outside world
in a black and white
box, veiled by a thin\
dusting of snow, voices
a static blend spoken
in simple sentences,
that winded out
when I slept, my
thoughts and memories
echoed by ghosts
that haunted scenes,
then vanished,
my only clue
that something more
paralleled this world
in two dimensions.

Dementia

Each spoken word
vibrates life, expresses
breath, ends in wind,
a mild breeze.
I watched my mother's
lips move, tremble
on form, attempt
to connect something
that lost itself
in the brief space
between us, empty
air. I nodded,
responded, smiled,
and she smiled too,
a nuance we forgot,
lost and found again,
a punctuation mark
at the end.

July

Yet to be born,
rapt in this clammy
hot stink, we hurl
through July from
one cold dark door
to another. Only
hope considers
it unlocked,
sun and open air
no place to pause.
Earth bakes a pair
of thighs that cling.
Unable to breathe,
we wade through
summer's thick ooze.

Flow

Nothing fuller than wind's
moment passes through
trees. Leaves whispers,
dry rasps against guttered
swoons. Birds awaken
from fitful sleep on one
leg, wings tucked around
frail bones light enough
to lift far above
my pale aspirations.
Breath steady, monotonous,
forgotten yet ever there,
I pause to listen
to my own hopeful gasp.

Hovering

Far too quiet,
we hover between
what passes for day
in this part of the world.
A brilliance blinds
between horizons.
Just before darkness
descends, we remember
how many stars
this broader understanding
contains. A fiery
expanse we cannot
grasp, we look up,
gaze in childlike wonder.

About the Author:

Richard Dinges has an MA in literary studies from University of Iowa, and he manages information security risk at an insurance company. Willow Review, Slant, Miller's Pond, Chantarelle's Notebook, and California Quarterly most recently accepted his poems for their publications.

GAZES

by Tomas Sanchez Hidalgo

Gazes

A refrigerator slides down the street,
moved by the wind.
Its owner chases it.
"I'm a doctor!", "I'm a doctor!",
she will have to say,
this woman, some time later,
in a courtroom.
Mrs. Toolson is eight months pregnant:
she cannot hinder the very sophisticated,
and shiny,
kitchen appliance on wheels,
nor can the employees of the funeral parlor
(nor the people leaving the costume party).
"I'm a doctor!", "I'm a doctor!",
she will repeat, some time later,
in a courtroom.
Neither can Mr. Cooper,
at the wheel of his lawnmower,
nor the soccer playing sons
of Mr. and Mrs. Liverpool
(mathematicians, these:
a subtle metaliterary premonition:
two Venn diagrams overlap
in the story we are dealing with:
sinister NGO and illegal cornea transplant).
"I'm a doctor!", "I'm a doctor!",
in a courtroom.
The shiny kitchen appliance on wheels
starts rolling uphill
after reaching the bottom,

and finally disappears into the mist;
it later reappears after impact:
some mods with their forty-mirror Lambrettas
with a figurine hanging
inside the windshield
(it's the Queen of England, waving).
"I'm a doctor!", "I'm a doctor!".
The gazes of some women
(dressed as punks),
"They look like upside down brooms",
the doctor will have to say,
in a courtroom,
emanate curiosity, also caution;
now faced with the open fridge, fear;
now everyone, arranged in a semi-circle,
was behind them.
"I'm a doctor!", "I'm a doctor!",
she will repeat, barefoot,
in a courtroom.

Human Society: Low Cost

15

Big Brother society,
did you really believe
that the business could be relaunched?
Toss them, God, a circus
(and a love for the poor old maids?):
fame replaces prestige,
the idea the proposal,
the clever the intelligent
and scandal the fruits of labor.
There is no more "adolescence",
as most adults don't have the maturity
that adulthood used to require.
Today one has to be "progressive".
In the media,
talking heads with internal conflicts,
about their sexual conditions,
follow the rules of "freedom of expression"
(and modesty is as archaic
as a handwritten letter).
The forecast is rain all day.
They should have consulted it.
Be careful.

My arsenal of excuses is closed,
I am going to stop making myself suffer:
now, right now,
I concentrate on those so many infinite gasps;
those remote twilights, exorbitant instants
(with the arrival of drugs,
new Baudelaires appeared,
writing in the corners of time).
I also bring together
so many journeys without a compass,
with those girls,
all of those girls,
and with my Mediterraneans
on this side of desire
(have the clouds covered them?):
to build, finally, at the zenith, Utopia,
comparable to the cosmos
and with the color of your eyes.

About the Author:

TS Hidalgo holds a BBA (Universidad Autónoma de Madrid), a MBA (IE Business School), a MA in Creative Writing (Hotel Kafka) and a Certificate in Management and the Arts (New York University). His works have been published in magazines in the USA, Canada, Chile, Argentina, UK, Germany, Spain, South Africa, Botswana, Nigeria, India and Australia, and he has been the winner of prizes like the Criaturas feroces (Editorial Destino) in short story and a finalist at Festival Eñe in the novel category. He has currently developed his career in finance and stock-market.

WHEN I DREAM WELL
by David Matthews

When I Dream Well

Her head held as if she were posing
now for Renoir, yesterday Rodin,
her face I know
from when I dream well
chance encounters on grand boulevards
where peacocks admire themselves
in windows of shops
and brilliant reflecting pools
while memory fades into nostalgia
as what might be
is passed on
to what might have been
for us to lose
or love
in the passing on of what ever was.

Work Week Eve

When Sunday night is reduced to no more
than Monday morning eve,
and the false hope of Friday night
exposed for the desperate gambit that it is,
I do not know quite what to say
or make of the man
who can eyeball the coming work week
without reaching for the revolver
or medication.
Meditation is not sufficient
to a task that screams
for electroshock.
Hook me up, mama,
Give me some juice.

Beautiful Soul

They say he walked into the room
as if from an unfinished book
by a nineteenth-century Russian
with a taste for roulette
and women with a past.

They say he was the kind
to let others think what they would
and do what they might with it.
If that came with a price,
he bore it well,
a kind of vengeance
exacted on a world
never so much hostile as indifferent.

How much of yourself
must you give away?
How much can you afford to owe?
Can anyone tell the worth
of a beautiful soul?

Does There Stand One?

does there stand one
who in her pause
considering a photograph,
a temple on
a rocky hill, say, Greece,
contemplates an old film
by Bergman
a quest
for faith and love
through a silence
that speaks
with eloquence
and ruin

if there were such a one
her heart might beat
as this heart might,
her voice speak
with reticence
and grace
her eyes embrace
erotic mountains
and forge soliloquies
of fog

Blood in the Air

there is blood in the air
fever in the sky
rage runs wild
in rivers
and along boulevards
there is commotion
in my mind

the tombstone investor
is in on a growth industry
more death than an inkwell
might hold and spill
out on this world
that reels out of control

so much of everything is loss
we need an abacus
of entropy —
to calculate the cost

I see people caught up
in all this confusion
and pain
I hear them say,
nothing is the same
I have to wonder
if it ever was

About the Author:

David Matthews is a native of the South Carolina Midlands, resident of Portland, Oregon, poet, runner, and unaffiliated intellectual. He draws on diverse traditions to fashion poems that at their best convey a sense of something akin to what the Romantics referred to as the sublime and the Surrealists termed the marvelous. "Matthews heaves his heart against the bulwarks, sets his siege engines of verse a-going into the fathomless ludicrous nonsensical void."—Wade Dinius

CONSIDERED OVER
by Victoria Randall

PSYCHO AND SOMATIC

red artillery aims to inflame injury
white walls raise to slay diseases
too diffuse to destroy
an air light feeling first
that later weighs all the water down
burdening one pound per bead
of morbid sweat
its stench brings birds
circling and singing of evening meals
comprised of the motionless laying,
looking lively to us
but rotting resolve
for carrion fowl were thought as songbirds
and death rattle as long-lost chatter
the bodies swelled
cysts in imagination
the only trace being neon streams
of chemicals in acronym machines
they attempted flight
but succeeded falling

CONSIDERED OVER

tragedy is an earthquake, or a bomb
the explosion's excitement passes away
our calamity considered over in the quiet
but the shockwave shunt caught us off guard
we burned again in the wall after the pillar
flood after fire, strong enough to hit
deep in the gut and beneath the belt
the next mourning could sweep us away

About the Author:

Victoria Randall is a student at Palm Beach Atlantic University. She will graduate with her Bachelor's in Psychology this May. Victoria has a passion for both psychology and creativity. She seeks to devote her career towards blending the two, especially through reading and creative writing, for the enrichment and empowerment of her community. Some other works Victoria has written will appear in the upcoming publication of Sigma Tau Delta's Rectangle.

JAMES AND THE GODFLESH
by Robert Beveridge

James and the Godflesh

He bit into the truffle, felt
the hot coppery gush
between his teeth. Only for a moment
did he pause to consider
the usual solidity of truffles,
the absence, most times,
of the distorted sound of guitar
across a winter plain.

O-Ring

The scent of allspice
and Chinese cinnamon
on your fingers.
You had run them across
your breasts the night before
and the sweetness stuck
only to come off against my tongue

The Surrealists Were Obsessed with the Eye

I'm not as observant as I once was.
Where once I would have seen
a glorious flock
of souls, clamoring
on their way to Hell,

now it's just a bunch of Canadian geese
in the middle of the road.

Yet still
I can see you, Laura,
and I see
hundreds of birds
singing praises to you
I see
verses of poets long dead
written in your name
I see
trees with our initials
buried deep in their roots

I can see you everywhere.

About the Author:
Robert Beveridge makes noise (xterminal.bandcamp.com) and writes poetry just outside Cleveland, OH. Recent/upcoming appearances in Wildflower Muse, Noble/Gas Qtrly, and The Ibis Head Review, among others.

MISTAKE
by Thom Young

Mistake

mistake
mistake
like bluebirds
quiet
ad singing
the regret song
it sounds
alive
it sounds forgotten
but I know what she did
even the angels
do
and nobody cries on the outside
anymore
tears stay warm
they stay safe
they hurt a little more
there
inside holding
tiger eyes

Sad

a pretty sad
gentle rain on Tuesday
nights, a ghost in the hall,
broken shard promises, and loving
again without love.
can you hear her now?
quiet wings
tucked in the past
she could have been a dream
she could have been orange
skies
above
me.

Devil

life is often strange
the used
car lot
with the pocket protector
dead salesman
greasy
and nicotine
teeth
like sodden trench
warfare
in France
circa 1916
he's got the deal
of a lifetime
if you're
willing to go down
under the desk
in the refurnished
office.

About the Author:

Thom Young is a writer from Texas. His last poetry collection A Little Black Dress Called Madness hit #1 Poetry in Germany. Hi is a 2016 Pushcart Prize nominee and his work appears in over a hundred literary journals including International Journal of Poetry, Poetry Quarterly, 3am magazine, Word Riot, Thirty West, and many more.

MAKING IMAGES
by Martin Altman

Making Images

By the painter's brush
An image is born as picture before it's born as speech,
But in a cloud of pictures,
The infant wails until the fog lifts, and
The crowd speaks to him through a veil of sounds, and
The image of speech inhabits him.

But if every object must be made into an image, then
The eye is the river to the dark sea on which
Visions are exchanged for speech.

And though there's still coherence
When a mother gives the breast, and
The back hand, too,
An icon is demolished;
If the image of the woman is the mother of the man,
How many shards does he become?

Night Vision

Luminous lamp turned off,
And there's night;
Though darkness is, and has seen its face
In God's face for an eternity,
Before the lamp switched on;
And His mind and all things contain
The gene for darkness, and
Flowers bloom under the forest canopy.
If He at one with darkness conceives of light,
Then darkness must retreat behind every rock,
Until the sun has set.
We're made of the dust of shattered rock
And the dark beneath it,
Our home and resting place.

Fragile as fog

Egg when penetrated
Sperm when absorbed
Die in the act of unifying;
Their consummation
Forms a self that could not be conceived,
But conceived, can't conceive itself.

Rain, dew, frost contains the self,
Day-break's gray-blue light, not mind,
Inhabited by images others have conceived,
Ghosts wandering in our consciousness;
And yet we think we own them,
The pseudonyms inside us.

Self is ephemera in air,
Not just image and shadow,
But shadow's shadow, reflecting, refracting,
So if the bare scintillation of light
Stands between face and mask,
The fleeting being stays anchored
to a fleeting hope.

Progeny

And darkness was ingrained,

And He brooded on the empty sky,

And the egg cracked,

Then two embers, Dream and Nightmare,
Cognates coalescing around the broken egg
Celebrate their origin and go their separate ways.
A trace is on their face or DNA.

There's no air in dream or nightmare,

But one is out of her mind,
So holding the breath is ecstasy.
The other is too much inside it,
So taking a breath is ecstasy.

An ember in a womb of ice fears the ice will melt,
An ember in a womb of light fears it will drown in light.

Darkness seeks the Mother who
Stirs the pot of hellish flames.
The Father's great red eye
Observes it all.

About the Author:

I was born and raised in The Bronx, graduated from Lehman College (CUNY) with a B.A. in English, and worked in New York City's Garment District for 40 years. Since 2010 I have lived with my wife Joyce in Chicago. I was Featured Reader at The Café and at TallGrass Writers Guild in Chicago. I have been published in Outrider Press, Red Ochre, Blue Minaret, Aethlon: Journal of Sport, Light: A Journal of Photography, Penwood Review, and an LGBT magazine Off the Rocks. Being a stutterer from childhood, a major concern of my poetry is speaking and hearing, breathing and cessation, connection and isolation, and silence.

RAPTURE OF FUNK

by Lenny Lewis

Two nights before Fredia
was due back
from elective castration
I carried her one-eyed
black dog down the stairs.
Both of us soaked
in his urine.
It was all he could do
to stand up. Tottering
in circles. Too weak to lift.
Urine simply leaked.

He ate cat feces
from the litter box.
A taste
I was loathe to acquire.

We'd shared days
of summer joy.
Skylarking from one
concert in a park
to another.
Fond memories.
Good memories gone.
Blackie nearly so.

As I held him
on the sidewalk
out of my half-wit
delirium appeared
a scarlet harlot.
It had to be
a mad fantasy
for us both.

Drop dead gorgeous.
Curves for days.
Snow White loveliness
Beauty queen on night street.
Down low. On the rebound?

Oh the impediments
to love.
Bed bugs and dog urine.

It was beyond
the rapture of funk.
I burned her
with my eyes
before she smelled us.

Instant whiplash.
Between fear
and
"I can do that"
on her face.

"Honey, no we can't"

Come early October
Blackie's spirit will visit me.
As for the lady in red
we have what was
and
what might have been.

About the Author:
Lenny is a jack of all trades. Frequently to be found working as a carney. South in the winter. Coney Island in summer.

WALKING
by Patrick Hurley

letters and numbers converge
then dissolve into pure sound

suddenly visible in the pavement
a repeated pattern of circles

late sounds come to us
approaching dissonance beautifully

eyes burn and water—
the airborne miasma

each cold breath a knife blade
and here a crystal jar of

cobalt ink lying at the edge
of the pavement

did it fall from the poor
calligrapher's worn pocket?

will he now trace letters in sand
or on the surface of moving water?

litter thickens and loud
voices speak of commerce

insistent percussion sends
ripples through the sky

fragments leavings detritus

vision of subsequent and antecedent layers
is sometimes accounted madness
hearing sounds that exist beyond
the confines of time cannot be tolerated

there is permanence and there is
the mutability of the superficial
the pavement is wet but
the warmth of the sun will dry it

colors are approaching their
actual hues once again
blue teachings crackle
in the still air

along the path lays
a rusted flute
pick it up

strange mathematics in
what appears to be a
northern village

structures are painted
in bright primary colors
the birds too have been
painted—the crow's
bitter caw is now
a rich white sound

figures in a circle—animals
remade by strange mutation

in the landscape
green's sweetness
is leaving

first simple sounds
tapping on heat-fused glass
blowing through a
corroded cylinder

now paths are streaked
with sour yellow
and salty red

winding up a music box
found amongst the carcasses

a tape found in the ruins—
play it forwards
play it backwards
perhaps a sequence will emerge

somewhere a voice
counts to five

somewhere mallets
strike metal wires

the circle will start to spin
and the monsters that comprise it
will rotate in the opposite direction
movement within movement

this path south
is downhill

refuse increases
along the descent

colored fragments of parchment
blow in the wind

seeking only addition
someone is immune
to the magic of subtraction

plus's cross is just the
intersection of two
perpendicular minuses

the warm air is sour
competing frequencies
charge the ambient air

fresh tree stumps dot
the former landscape

walking on bleached bones
walking on shells
walking on fragments

lead paint chips
frame broken windows

corroded fan blades
turn slowly

security cameras'
forlorn wires dangle

no spells
no sacraments
no algorithms

stocky humanoids
scale crumbling ruins

they feed on the
flesh of the weaker ones

About the Author:

Patrick Hurley was born in an unimportant midwestern American city in 1969. After wasting several years in graduate school, he published a book on Thomas Pynchon and taught writing and literature at a few colleges in Saint Louis, Missouri. He is now a full-time bartender and poet, currently obsessed with a long poetry collection in progress called Walking. He lives and works in Saint Louis.

ON VIEWING THE CORPSE OF MY MOTHER-IN-LAW
by Nolo Segundo

How could this –thing, have been her?
Lying shriveled and small on the bed
As those who loved (and feared) her
Gathered in the bereft hospital room
To let their shock and grief melt and
Mold itself into its own atmosphere.
Her body seemed never to have been
Real, never to have been a woman,
Never to have been young once, and
Surely never to have been a mother…..

And if it had been a body once, housing
A small dragon who could lash out fire
Solely with her harsh and brutal tongue,
Keeping those who loved her at bay and
The rest of us wary, aware of her power,
Her terrible gift for shrinking one's soul,
Then where did she go when her mouth
Froze open as the last breath of a long,
Life left quietly, without fuss or rancor?

Still, though imperfect as you or I, she
Was loved, and mourned and honored.
If God only housed saints, think how
Terribly lonely He would be…..

About the Author:

Nolo spent years teaching in the Far East, including as an ESL instructor in Cambodia before the time of the killing fields, and later in Taiwan and Japan. He wrote poetry, 2 children's stories and an unpublished novel and then stopped writing altogether for some reason; and for an equally obscure reason he began writing poetry and essays again after a 30 year hiatus.

WHEN YOU WERE BORN
by Colin Dodds

When You Were Born
for Miriam Bridget Dodds

Warm weeks,
fat men with chests out
bob down the street like sails full of wind

Digitized fetal heartbeats
mingle with cicada-chitter
and dry leaves across concrete

Marking time in fluids, there were clear warnings
day-long classes and dreams

My landlady peeks from her door
to see the blood moon in eclipse
Inside, my wife struggles near the end
of her nine months

Passing a night in a B-52 bomber
the whole horizon erupts, and the pilot says
"They're making room for a baby"

Busy, tired, travelling, poor—distance
is the rain, the surface of the contract I sign,
crossing my fingers like that means anything

The temple crumbles as the infant escapes
past the distorted corpses of her co-adventurers
through cobwebs and familiar perils
with a golden artifact of untold value

Nature steps from her accustomed highwaysides
window boxes and green-scummed piers
in civilized September
her voice rattling my pores

somewhere on her person
-
It arrives unsurprising as autumn
in the soupy air of an Indian summer
right about when we stopped calling it that

It sends me spinning, rushing
baffled among car-service dispatchers
in the last September we had such men

A lot at once
A greeting card and trench warfare
and it's all one thing

Terror and love mingle, fuse
in the bloodgleam
congealed into hair, shaven for surgery
but just a patch, then skin open and closed all at once
eyes shaped by ten thousand generations
of looking away and looking again

No more delay no distance or affectation
I catch sight of my own face, the one
that doesn't care about the music or food I eat
what I think of the state of civilization
and whether I'm ecstatic
or in endless, ash-black agony

The great chain of weeping catches
and draws the scenery along

That's the one who shakes her head
at the wondrous dreams of meaning dreamt
not disappointed but amazed at the dreaming

The first few weeks, her tiny hands attack her
through an unknown territory to sleep
the blue vein of dreams visible under her cirrus hair

That's the one who continues after I disappear

Awash in mercy and emergency
the minds of mother and father attack them regularly
murmuring urgent assurances

It is easier to soothe
an infant than our own minds

And one afternoon, pondering an invitation,
we speak of our newborn daughter's wedding
and weep because having thought of it, it's occurred
and our lives already come and gone

Somewhere, an archaeologist packs mud
on our last standing complaint

For my tiny daughter, hunger
and lamp fascination are undivided
within a single unbounded question
and a single unbounded knowing

Together, we listen to the shortwave static
of the November radiator
and I hum the things I don't want to explain
that she blessedly couldn't understand if I tried

Tiny bright eyes relay all the majestic world
back to an administrative office in heaven
across distances spanned in a stanza
or never spanned at all

She turns bagels into giggles
and squawks like a happy parrot
toothless mouth full of light

Doing nothing much, she informs me:
We are not here for anything
We are here, and everything is for that

Cardiopolis

Floating through the world
dispensing permission
unknowingly

Cranes raise houses, office boxes
bivouacs for a war not yet agreed upon

Buildings like the stock exchange
blossom in the snow

At midday in midtown
towers pose for their ruin

The city from any distance at all—
its surges, precipices, idiosyncratic ridges
repetitions and anomalies

like an EKG in three dimensions
like the shape of a life

The more you look at it
the harder it becomes to even ask
which parts matter

About the Author:

Colin Dodds is a writer from Massachusetts. His novels include WATERSHED and The Last Bad Job, which the late Norman Mailer praised as showing "something that very few writers have; a species of inner talent that owes very little to other people." His work, appearing in more than three hundred publications, has been nominated for the Pushcart Prize and the Best of the Net Anthology. The poet and songwriter David Berman (Silver Jews, Actual Air) said of Dodds' poetry: "These are very good poems. For moments I could even feel the old feelings when I read them." His book-length poem That Happy Captive was named a finalist in both the Trio House Press Louise Bogan Award and the 42 Miles Press Poetry Award, and his screenplay, Refreshment, was named a semi-finalist in the American Zoetrope Contest. Colin lives in Brooklyn, New York, with his wife and daughter. You can find more of his work at thecolindodds.com.

PURGE
by Matt Barker

Purge

Recently,

I have been guilty

of leaving
the paper

blank

a writer

is only
as good
as the ink

that makes it
onto the paper

I am scared

I might have

lost it.....

Deposit

the day is drowning
unable to endure
the unflinching trickle of time

writers never die
effortlessly evading extinction
inevitable immortality implied in ink
molded by the momentary mindset

it will come

      don't take it

            too seriously............

About the Author:

Matt Barker is a 24 year old poet from Boston. Active in the Boston poetry scene, "Deposit" and "Purge" are his debut published poems. His passion for poetry is rivaled only by his love for corgis.

CLARITY

by Irene Mitchell

Premonition

Fallen grapes eaten beneath the vines' enclosure.
All those annoying twists and tangles.

Wiser not to dwell on complexity
but feast on regenerative imagination.
A drop of water on the lilypad
alerts me to possibilities in the field.

What enthralling methods I shall devise
 to keep the spider from the shoe
 and the bee from supping with me
when viands are on the table.

Clarity

Open, world, in all your disguises —

though there is no easy way from the earth to the stars. Hark
back to the dream and dream in praise of optimism. Wait!
It's coming now, like a comet which has been longing
to show off its brimming head. Petition the sky for a favorable glimpse,
and wipe any tears of joy with a natural detergent.
All the centuries passing by, and she abides in this one.
A gift not to be taken lightly, especially when eyesight
is still so keen and the looming azure and adelade-yellow
asperitas clouds are right before her.

Ease

Thanks for a load off my mind! So easy to be receptive,
especially when magnolia is in its first phase of bloom
on a purposeful day, emitting perfumes for everyone's
benefit and pleasure.

On the hillside, elemental forms are heard murmuring.
A lizard in natural surroundings is a kindred species,
its prissy coat and slick gait.

I have been given a rare taste of contentment infused
with energy because a sweet May breeze – more like
a trade wind – has engendered the prettiest bird calls,
the pretty birds in chorus calling.

Tranquil noon has passed. Evening presents with a rash
of yellow irises primping here and there through the mead's
tall grasses.

A finger pressing on the neck's trigger point relaxes
the melancholy aches which usually accompany
my interpretation of the hours.
Now all is fine as fine can be.

Fierce

How does vivid pain suddenly disappear so that the wonder
becomes that the invasion ever took place at all. Yet
the memory of it lingers as potent as the original pain which,
having disappeared, allows a relief as boundless
as asperitas clouds dipping down like mounds of ice cream
overturned from their cones, cool and distant but part
of the expanse.

With pain gone, such lightness of body slightly mitigates the mind
still embroiled in dark meanderings, hard
to simplify.

That is the meaning of asperitas: uneven, rough, difficult, fierce.

Earth's Porcelain Clearing

No throes, only gladness for now, for now
there is a porcelain clearing on fragile Earth
which widens to a wild complexity
having many angles but none sharp,
a sheen but no finish.

Everyone to table. It is laid for lunch —
wine, bread, nuts, cheese in its wrap,
a knife, a jug in shadow upon a slab.

I am painting how art lays bare
old and new, sublime in color and compaction.

I am underscoring how the porcelain center's
fixative guards against smudging, grounds the whole
like a lunch eaten, envied, enjoyed,
made much of.

To the depiction of bread and cheese, I will add
an egg,
for I am the constructor of this plate
and will make it beautiful.

About the Author:

Irene Mitchell is the author of Equal Parts Sun and Shade: An Almanac of Precarious Days (Aldrich Press, 2017), Minding the Spectrum's Business (FutureCycle Press, 2015), A Study of Extremes in Six Suites (Cherry Grove Collections, 2012), and Sea Wind on the White Pillow (Axes Mundi Press, 2009). Formerly Poetry Editor of Hudson River Art Journal, Mitchell has served as poetry contest juror, and facilitator of poetry workshops. She is known for her collaborations with visual artists and composers.

AMBITION
by Abigail Van Kirk

Ambition

Scrape coffee grounds from under nails for the altar.

Lift up tatters of atriums and ventricles,
two each for disheartened ones,
beside other meager
bruised-fruit offerings.

Peaches in sick-sweet rottenness,
downing their pits and kulning
with this throat.

Swallow salt off my brow
for a semblance of thanks.

Suburbia

Hole-punched stars peer through black construction paper,
insistent wind prying its way through cracked open sliding glass doors.

I am half-here, half-not, have not the ability to let you go.
Minutes before, in dusk, geese squawked their cacophony.

A mockery, they and humans can fly and yet
how can I find my way to you, if you don't want me?

Aubade for Autumn

Kiss me on the mouth
the way you found me–

pollen dust
over last days of summer
when mountains are in west aphelion
to golden sunup.
Slinking with forest sylphs
in hushes like half-turned leaf shuddering,
choking on the haze of summer's last rebellion,
wildfire on plains to have its say before the turn.

Kiss me on the mouth like the drizzle of afternoon,
the last of my mother's garden silhouetted on the
blinds in honeyed light.

About the Author:

Abigail Van Kirk is a student at Western State Colorado University and often adventures along the Western slope of the Rockies. Her work has been published by The Haiku Journal, the Manifest West anthology, Caravel Literary Arts Magazine, and elsewhere.

GONE GIRL
by Lana Bella

AMPHIBIOUS HORSE

ENWREATHED

Now she knew it has been winter
soaking long stretches of rivers
and fields. Moving hands into
pockets thick of tweed, skin felt
the hollows flaked softly what
snow patterns made, enwreathed
to the islands of her bone-bed.
Parched lungs dry with scratched
in gin, she pitched whistles to
the stings of a drizzly sun frantic
to sink, loose-limbed, the tinct
of some quiet wild thing. Turning
a brown pair of Moccasins over
the raw braille of grass, she borne
lilts angling like fatwood worn
to stumps, slivering the slippery
slope of the hills from which
her flesh on this land-locked life
bruised long in the light of winter.

Eased by the confluent still and
dun feathered shroud, she gentled
down the hunt of a sandpiper's
call, haloing the island with steps
turning haste. The sea gave
back to shore of an amphibious
horse, hitching ride on the flesh of
her at the burden of swift marrow.
Sidestepped over the shivering
down of its torn wings, hand traced
lattice strip reaching for wisps
of neigh in the silt, she put ear to
air to horse to the bones inside
holding the stiff giving of its chest.
Softly, she wrung out the equine sea
from her moan until the last drop,
croaked and hurt as some wayward
shift abraded in rocks, setting
to carcass great darlings of sadness,
seeing to magpies calling high on
the dead trees.

GONE GIRL

I come home always to my leaving
packing its bags, with goodbyes
feeding perished things to stay alive.
Missing me a hundred perfect times,
I am cast by entropy given arms to
faces as big as Rafflesia*, fast as
perennial discontent. Almost dark
and slanting, I shout but do not hear
me, pulse Gauloises smoke inside
the evening viseing cold, as trumpet
notes pull long my winter's black.
Hair in updos, I sip the old tea cup
watering my ordinary lips, like some
destroyed reaching sea in which
my reverie hisses out this gone girl's
name.

*Rafflesia: The rare flower is the world's largest bloom
is the Rafflesia arnoldii, found in the rainforests of Indo-
nesia, and it can grow to be 3 feet across and weigh up
to 15 pounds.

I WALKED MY SHADOW

Dark arched the deep dish of my hands,
down a shadow of far where new arms
flexed as stems. Silvering up the lane,
I walked my shadow into town, bent
to its river walking my December legs.
Casting eyes to the breeze, more lonely
than two should be, I took us by older
skies shaking in the dirt, a phantom to
the fond. Now as an old woman back in
her stilled land, I hooked under skin
struggling free the familiar dark fists,
and how their small bones hollowed like
a bouquet of forks, willing my body to
f
   l
     O
       w
         e
           r.

BLACK WATER

Nocturnes sieved neatly
far a narrow throat, snared,
carbonated by all that iron
and hard. Even standing
still, the dead slow-soaked
through so down the jaw
ached, with the inured held
up between storm and dry.
Now, gravel tumbled from
timber over walls, trussing
corpses beneath the water
black, stirring into an hour
so exact as to pool heavy
and wet repleting the dead
of trees. Narrow sneer of
moon rose and went away,
freeing a manic thrashing of
elements lapsed under sand
and murk, nightly lullabied.

About the Author:

A four-time Pushcart Prize, five-time Best of the
Net, & Bettering American Poetry nominee,
Lana Bella is an author of three chapbooks,
Under My Dark (Crisis Chronicles Press, 2016),
Adagio (Finishing Line Press, 2016), and Dear
Suki: Letters (Platypus 2412 Mini Chapbook
Series, 2016), has had poetry and fiction
featured with over 400 journals, Acentos
Review, Comstock Review, EVENT, Ilanot
Review, Notre Dame Review, Rock & Sling &
The Lampeter Review, among others, and work
to appear in Aeolian Harp Anthology, Volume 3.
Lana resides in the US and the coastal town of
Nha Trang, Vietnam, where she is a mom of
two far-too-clever-frolicsome imps.

I HESITATED
by Mark Prebilic

I hesitated.

Not out of spite
Not out of anger
Not out of unhappiness

My will lacked fervor.

Now I'm staring back
    Glaring at the opportunity missed
    Disgust overtaking rational thought.

The past echoes of our future
Have been muffled by the crashing waves.
Where once stood a mighty redwood
Now sits a mountain nymph
Preparing for its exit.

If we approach it sanguinely
Apologetically
Invitingly
Will it then hesitate?
Will our attempts to cajole it,
to pamper it,
to entice it,
prove fruitful?
Or will it,
    with suspicions swelling,
    with solitude beckoning,
    with survival imploring,
Take the risk of solitude as the harbinger of peace.

Take the offered promise of wholeness
      through a dissection of the soul;
A sated appetite
      fed only by the one hand.

I've sat along the creek's edge.
Watched the water's rising;
Reacted not.
Hesitated.
And now those waters rush over me
Inundate the ground beneath me
Uproot the sycamores that once danced before the bane.

Will I get to higher ground?
Will I survive the tempest?
Will I escape this self-inflicted certitude?

I've peered into the face of the storm
Been tossed by its fierceness
Been terrified by its ferocity
And yet awed by its single-mindedness.

How did I get to this station?
How did I miss the forecast?
How was I unknowingly overtaken?

Perhaps the answers won't come easily
      or ever
Perhaps the mystery that we investigate
Will remain unsolved
And carry us from this life
To the next.

SHHH...

Last time we talked
I shivered.
Swishing shoals of shimmering sand awash in the tide.
Quieted I was by the sound.
Ne'er ending, rather undulating.
I drifted then,
aimlessly seeking a shore;
ceasing short.
Battered back before the bane -
Bandied and banished.
Sunlight swoons in the sepulcher;
Then vanishes.

About the Author:

Mark Prebilic is a database expert by trade with a penchant for creativity on the side. He writes both poetry and fiction. He is also a university-trained musician. Mark lives in Reston, Virginia. He has three grown children in addition to three still-growing grandchildren.

SEXPECTATIONS
by Kathy Coman

Sexpectations

i can't help but to think
about what tomorrow will bring
after i tasted the sweetness of your kiss
that paralyzed my heart

what have you done to me

that has me longing for days that have yet
to come

a broken promise

is what happened after our souls became one
with no intention of yours waiting around for love
to know your name because my body was
your only target

Tucked Away

there are feelings
i have yet to discover
and
i don't know if
i want to know them

Do Not Own Me

you do not own me

you do not have the rights
to my body that was created
to house the precious soul
that holds the magic to my
existence

you do not own me

you do not have the rights
to my heart that holds the
precious treasure of my love
that i give out only to those
who are deserving

you do not own me

you do not have the rights
to my mind that possesses
the depths of my existence
from the time i was created
to the moment i met you

you do not own me

everything i am belongs to me
until you have proven yourself
worthy to carry my gift
only then will i share it with
you

About the Author:

Kathy Coman has received a Bachelors of Art in English from the University of Toledo as well as taken graduate level courses in creative writing. Past publishing credentials include: A&U Magazine, Carty's Poetry Journal, Blinking Cursor Literary Magazine, and others.

FROM HERE TO THERE
by Roger Singer

FROM HERE TO THERE

He wore a loud tie. Checkered
shirt and black high top sneakers.
Thoughts tumbled from him like leaves;
fast tracks combined with solid sounds.

He mumbles a prayer, though not looking
heavenward. At midnight he howls at the moon,
caring nothing for those nearby. Town dogs return
his call to arms, signaling paths of safe
passage past alleys and unfamiliar corners.

Rivers not far away crested the banks.
Dark waters surged with excitement, drawing
crowds like carnival days. A few moments of
interest and then he moves on to something else.

THE UNEXPECTED

A blue sky yielded to layers of
Ivory clouds. Flat and useless the
Heavy air absorbed sounds; the pleasure
Of the afternoon was washed away.
Newspapers lost their crispness. Words
fainted between people due to
dullness in the air. Birds halted flights,
retreating to thin curtains of shade.
There is a memory of times like this.
The experience fails to prepare us for the
next day or night when weather fails to charm.

STEADFAST

He leans back
against a brick wall
on a three legged chair
playing the harmonica.
Angels pause at the sound.
Traffic passes unnoticed.
The sound is gold in his mind.
He thinks of words despite
detractions.
There is an overpass of thin
weaving clouds.
The sun warms his hands.
Pigeons rustle their wings
with feathered cymbals
blessing his sound
His eyes are closed. He
dreams of visions, familiar
and sad.
It's how he escapes without
leaving.

About the Author:

Dr. Roger G. Singer has been in private practice for 38 years in upstate New York. He has four children, Abigail, Caleb, Andrew and Philip and five grandchildren. Dr. Singer has served on multiple committees for the American Chiropractic Association, lecturing at colleges in the United States, Canada and Australia, and has authored over fifty articles for his profession and served as a medical technician during the Vietnam era.

Dr. Singer has had over 890 poems published on the internet, magazines and in books and is a Pushcart Award Nominee. Some of the magazines that have accepted his poems for publication are: Westward Quarterly, Jerry Jazz, SP Quill, Avocet, Underground Voices, Outlaw Poetry, Literary Fever, Dance of my Hands, Language & Culture, The Stray Branch, Tipton Poetry Journal and Indigo Rising.

AT THE BREWERY DOWNTOWN
by Hannah Kludy

Martyr has six definitions on Dictionary.com

Fire never looked so sinister to me, a moth in North America. We speak of martyrs as though they are brave for dying when living is the real bitch. How does one look into the light and not want to come closer? It is warm and sensual, like the tingle of antennae spreading what they think is perfect sense. Or on the radio, for instance, where I hear this is revenge for a Latin lifestyle. Latin, as in the scriptures, like the basis for the western romance languages we speak. Nolite te bastardes. Nolite te bastardes. The martyrs are dead now, but I am still drawn to the fires burning on the lawn of some college or another. There once was a man who saved almost six hundred children from the Holocaust. Years later, when he was an old man they all came together and surprised him. I hope he's dead now, and I am sure all the survivors do too. He has already lived too long.

The Emperor of Ice Cream

When his friend died my husband broke
a table.

The funeral was open casket
and the gunshot wound
made his face look like the mortician
made without ever seeing
a person.

I didn't know what to say.
he died and I never cried.
He was seventeen.
Let be be the finale of seem.

When I die, I want everyone to drink.
When I die
I want to be walked
into my own funeral
like a marionette.

At the Brewery Downtown

We are in a new town trying new things.
The restaurant I am at is expensive
so I am thinking about the time I was in DC.
All the lawyers in the world came
and ordered drinks which meant that my mojito
was late and I was snappy.
This expensive place has great martinis
but I am somehow less happy here
 though I am not entirely alone.

We order fried pickles because they are cheap
and we decide to get frozen pizzas on the way home.
He picks Jacks and I don't say anything but I think
I would rather die than eat Jacks pizza once more in my life.
That's what poor people eat.
That, and pasta with melted American cheese.
When I smell it cooking, I want to scream.

About the Author:

Hannah Kludy is an MFA candidate at Creighton University. She earned her BA in Creative Writing and Publishing at Northwest Missouri State University. Her work has been published in the North-west Missourian and Medium Weight Forks, Surcarnochee Review, Red Mud Review, Broad Magazine, Unlikely Stories, The Progenitor, Drunken Monkeys, Five on the Fifth, Adanna Literary Journal, Windmill, and The Bitchin' Kitsch. She has also been published, and won the fiction prize in, Cardinal Sins Journal.

Shandy

The gin and tonic tastes like the pine-and-citrus cleaner that coats
the wooden floors of my favorite bar.
 I took my best friend there last week and she played ski ball
and an overly long game of pool. I wondered why beer tastes better
in a glass than in a bottle. She finished hers and asked me and I said
I don't know, it just does.
My dad said summer shandy was invented because some brewer had
almost run out of beer when a huge crowd showed up and he mixed
what he had left with lemonade but my dad was drunk when he said so,
so I don't know.
The shandy makes me want to skinny-dip in a lake, but I'm afraid
of water that isn't clear and shallow.
I want to see the bottom. I never see the bottom.

THREE POEMS
by Tamara Williams

Pain, there are many women who carries your labor.

Here are their stories.

Cheers to the woman in Black with no strings attached.

Your soreness goes where ever you do.

You lose yourself in everybody of water and tree banks seem to release songs of truth every time you walk by.

Do you listen?

Every time it rings I breathe. I used to be closed off to success but by holding on to grief I climbed into myself just in time to make the sea cry.

Hating wasn't allowed anymore. I told you that winter didn't breathe, and you didn't believe me.

Wanting, earning, warnings.

All the signs how could I have missed them?

Lying on my back I heard the moon cry, do you forgive me? Granted was a new life.

It was as if I never left.

\# \# \#

The way skin touches your nose

I only knew lovers who laughter somehow managed to match their lies.

You mourn women, just like your father and his father before.

I had been a seed of uncompressed doubt that sat in the back of your mind,

too eager to come up whenever you thought you need something.

I never thought anything would pass expect the wisdom in my lines in my hand.

They tell the future, don't they?

I hold your tongue- gripping the only form of reality I thought I would never know.

You bleed sips.

Running through forests

I can go nowhere but I up.

I can go nowhere but through

I can go nowhere but you.

\# \# \#

Sometimes I rage war on myself.

Bring death to unfit corners. Leave peace in the hands of strangers.

Neglect my wounds to bring others happiness.

Be anything but earth.

There is blood on my hands.

Sticky, wet, moist.

Pressed up on against the surface it does not heal.

I keep telling myself the wounds won't lick themselves and how can then when my arms are so heavy?

I hold them up as a sign I surrender. Both a sin and a curse, I watch the moon dance in my pain. Rejoice in my burn.

Lie in my agony.

If I could win the game I would. I don't doubt love like I use to. I just doubt the questions behind it.

The movement behind the screen. The emptiness behind the man.

The planets seem to move gently

as if they aren't hearts.

As if they aren't heavy.

But I can see them next to the moon.

So distant.

So far.

Almost as if they are nonexistent.

Almost as if they are me.

About the Author:

Tamara Williams is a NYC native and received her MFA from Mills College. She believes in writing from the heart space.

2nd FLATTEST STATE
by Noah Slowik

Rabble-rousers

Night traffic performing cautious deeds;
good people awaited sacred sins
while diligent ones are sound asleep,
unnecessary suffering begins.

Shadow-wanderers seeking starlight
could never resist earthly desires;
undeterred by countless warning signs,
liable for action that transpires.

Travelers travelling nowhere soon,
unknowingly destined for danger.
privileged, lost without a clue,
innocent; trouble is no stranger.

To the Freshman Lit Major

Feel these words jump off the page
and build a home in your cranium
like a loud, rolling whisper
from a vast, abandoned mountain range.

Great art isn't really about Bilbo or Prufrock,
it's about her, you, him, not me.
Take your time exploring Middle-earth,
you'll have plenty still for visions and revisions.

Whatever you do, don't trust anyone;
especially not me, this poem.
The best advice I ever got
was that all my professors are wrong.

The only person who is right is you,
as long as your reading is true.

2nd Flattest State

Illinois: 2nd flattest state.
Thoroughly unremarkable

tourists might assume.
Wind gusts shake plains.

The land of Rolling Meadows
and Highland Park.

Parallel to the ocean blue;
a microcosm, nonetheless.

Cloud bubbles, huge
ivory buffalo.

Hypnotized by
prairies industrialized.

Proud of zilch,
except corn.

Opposite of boring
you dimwitted idiot.

Don't never forget
the 2nd flattest state.

About the Author:

Noah Slowik is an undergrad at Lewis University in Romeoville, IL double majoring in English and Secondary Education. He has never been published before. At Lewis, he is an assistant poetry, fiction, and creative nonfiction editor for the school's international literary journal, Jet Fuel Review. He maintains a music blog titled "Between Rock and an Indie Place," and is also a tutor for the Writing Center and a reporter for the school newspaper, The Flyer.

THINGS IN A GAP
by Eduardo Escalante

Again Google, Mo Gawdat lines on happiness

Lemons or magnet for us?
Rational smells with an old story:
What part of my glass would I drink?
Would I be a different actor?
On the edge,
Still, I prefer: Step back step forward to growth
Probably some steps back — settling for good enough.
A few pauses, breathe, reflect, and then the step
And wait for a sudden illumination, not an equation
Or remain happy eating my orange and should not
Invest in failing or loosing. I should

Lemons or magnets or smiles for us?
petals smell with an old story:
What part of my glass would I drink?
Would I flow like a different actor?
Plato still in a shadow
On the edge,
A few pauses, breathe, reflect, and then a touch
Right left back forward up down
Probably some touch back — settling for good enough.
Wait for a sudden land, tree, wave, woman, not an equation
Or remain happy eating my orange and should not
Invest in failing or loosing or crumbling. I should not.

Something To Consider

Beauty, rare word,
name of hunger.
You want the fruit intact
nothing, pure look,
the skin tastes like desire,
and the desire, to what?

You wait for hunger,
breeze enclosed,
craving waits
the caress
of the eye.

Stubborn outline
the body –the fruit–
aroma or paraphrase

or desire, voracity
of the eye that, blind, looking at you,
see who you are

The beauty that does not hold anything,
 lives on air ...

as one in loving

Human Fatigue

1. close into symbols

The city looked full
artery of Santiago choked with cars
a tatted man
was standing in front of a tree
Affirmed to a symbol
in this street
there was no crosswalk
his body jumped
It seemed 3d drawing
We can leave we can look
the tattoo is the sign because he jumps

2. the boy with the gun

The morning opened obscure
The sun had eye closed
I walked for different streets
An old lady looked at me from her window
When the church
men with revolvers assaulting a car
One looked at my head
he was fourteen years old
And with a bullet touched my shoes
While a bus passed

3. winter city

Poor looks poor
Shoes too big
He did have a hat
He lacked affection in his arm
He scratched his head again and again
The city is always indulgent

4. being in the city

it is like swimming in the swamp
it does not walk away
The pain is there
suffering seems a fate
tighter tighter tighter
against an endless swirl of human wind.
the whole world comes to spectacle,
arrive all private woe and
we see the public farce.
Samples of oligarchy even if they are plastic
too much people fill their hearts and lungs with
ashes
It is difficult to be a part
of a policy signed and sealed.

About the Author:

Eduardo Escalante is a writer and researcher living in Valparaíso, Chile; he publishes regularly in Hispanic Reviews (Signum Nous, Ariadna, Nagari, Espacio Luke, Lakuma Pusaki, among others); and reviews in English (StlylusLit, Writer Resits, Spillwords, Slamchop and in Gramma Poetry).

LOVELY DREAMS
by Mitchel Montagna

For Ann, 1953-1970

There's darkness ahead, with reels of grief.
But on Christmas Eve nobody could know.
They gathered in church to voice their belief
in tones as serene as the falling snow.

Ann's brother served me the ping pong ball
as she drove off wearing her silver gown.
Soon a carload of fools, drunks one and all
sped recklessly into the college town.

David's parents were worried but I didn't care.
After the holiday we walked into class.
All eyes focused on him in his chair
like an oddball caught in a looking glass.

The photo of Ann on the Tribune's front page
showed a bashful smile and long-lashed eyes.
And an innocence that would never age
nor understand a world that could brutalize.

Now we are old men, David and me
having long ago gone our separate ways.
Is he dogged by ghosts of his family?
Does he hear their prayers on winter days?

Rainbows and Moonbeams

A thousand
mirrors, always brown
eyes: dull, disturbing,
constant,
pitiless.

Something inside you breathing
wrong, you think
you're a hero they
care for.
Dashing into a sunset
of burning rainbows.

You say goodbye to
window panes
polished metals
clear rain puddles.
All of you have
the same brown eyes, your
faces change like
moonbeams.

Lovely Dreams

I cannot sleep
because I fall
into a dream
as beautiful

as summer fields,
the aqua skies
and streams are clear,
the sun is high

above the hills
that line the plains,
a breeze rolls down
as sweet as rain.

The petals spark
like polished jade,
the sunset blinks
and stirs the shade.

We see the light
is fading there
while whistling winds
blow through our hair

so that we laugh
and wail and seethe,
we're sure the air
is ours to breathe.

I'm driving through
a dimming dome,
with air enough
for me alone,

the moon comes up,
the breeze turns cool
through lovely dreams
of lonely fools.

Catskill Ghost

Think I'll go back to the Catskills
by its canyons and its streams.
Let the land undo my weariness
and soothe my troubling dreams.

A nice girl used to wait there
beneath the summer skies.
The sun put diamonds in her hair
and brightened her blue eyes.

We slipped inside the forest shade
to seek what lovers do.
The leaves assumed a fiery glow
as twilight drifted through.

If I get there before autumn
I'm sure my faith will last.
Her light will shimmer through me
like a spirit from our past.

About the Author:

Mitchel Montagna is a corporate communications writer for a large professional services firm. He has also been a special education teacher and radio news reporter. Publications include White Liquor Journal, Naturewriting, The Penwood Review, Scarlet Leaf Review, In Between Hangovers, and Amarillo Bay. He is married and lives in New Jersey.

DOG DAYS by Ian Smith

Dog Days

Overheard in the early stages of these beige days,
my last challenge, trekking the desert
far from a ruinous prime when oases always shimmered,
two women walking laps refer to a dog named Smooth
reminding me of our cat dubbed thus as a kitten
for his velvet pelt that shone, catching the sun,
later regarded by our gang as an operator
who (yes, I know he's an animal, but so like us)
tried to open doors with paws, who emailed
from adoptive careers, kind former neighbors
tolerant of his overacting in videos sent
when my time came to exit paradise for east of small,
dismantled to a room where I hear my slow breathing.
A theme plied in art, this sudden arrival shocks.

Reassured by Smooth's new quarters, I reply,
Furry nice, if not downright perfect: playing along
with fond recall trusting his head won't swell,
prevent him squeezing through confined spaces
to our old trails, their spoors to my heart.

On the canal path from town, a usual threshold of loss,
adventures morphed into dreams, I see a terrier,
distant, skittering my way where I sometimes sit,
solitary, on a bench watching cyclists, joggers.
I expect its owner carrying a leash but I'm alone
with what I now see as a rabbit approaching fast,
not a terrier, more terror-stricken, like me
by the notion of appalling decline.

This happens in seconds before I realize it's a hare,
fugitive over gravel, not on the verge, so I stop
before it veers to the softer grass, slows down,
adjacent, eyeballing me as though I'm the one lost,
endangered, heading in the wrong direction
recalling a Cambridgeshire field, wind in my jacket,
flints and hares abundant, time's triumph distant,
thinking now of Auden's years running like rabbits.

Those Monumental Men

Alpine Austria, WW2 exhausted by carnage
almost over, Europe a dangerous smouldering ruin,
two of them hold lamps aloft, squeeze through a gap
in dynamited rubble blocking an old salt mine adit
where, in a chamber, on cardboard, musty air cool,
lies The Adoration of the Mystic Lamb by Van Eyck.
On her panel, the Virgin, radiant in rich purple,
reads a book waiting for her rescue from vulgarians.
In the lamplight her crown of flowers flickers.
They search deeper, discover the Madonna of Bruges,
once commandeered by another upstart, Napoleon,
needing only a soft cloth to be revealed again,
also, several Vermeers, scenes of calm moments,
some of millions of works salvaged from Nazi looters.
Art restorers, professors, wearing army uniforms,
track that artist manqué Hitler's greedy grabs,
true war heroes, some killed, glorious intelligence
knowing right should triumph over wrong,
like those who create our masterpieces.

To the Island

We all know the scene from clichéd dramas.
Returning emigrants, time-short, kiss the ground,
penitents, the place left become sanctified,
a disproportionate rite of guileless hearts
bruised by vicissitude, by abeyance.

The aircraft sways above winter waves.
I peer down at a lone tufted rock,
sea-swirled, caressed in isolation, stranded
unchanged while centuries of lives pass.
My old heart strains, islands on the horizon.

Skirting dun pools on this bereft expanse of beach,
distant voices stilled, I muse for nanoseconds
over dampening my knees in homage.
The rain batters across, scumbling our bay,
a cold wind blasting my heart's caverns.

The sun a blessing when I ran, touched
the far sandstone rock-shelf's faded graffiti
then back to laughter in the ruined long ago,
shines in memory, or habit, or love,
as I scuttle to my rough-hewn encampment.

About the Author:

Ian C Smith's work has appeared in , Antipodes, Australian Book Review, Australian Poetry Journal, Critical Survey Poetry Salzburg Review, The Stony Thursday Book, & Two-Thirds North. His seventh book is wonder sadness madness joy, Ginninderra (Port Adelaide). He lives in the Gippsland Lakes area of Victoria, Australia.

LEAPING WITH YOUR LEGS LOCKED by Don McLeod

Excerpt from the full-length poetry book (Leaping With Your Legs Locked)

Leaping With Your Legs Locked
       (section 4)

the retarded boy down the street
said hey I want to be somebody
I knew what he meant

but I didn't know
what to say
it's why I play poker
but only with strangers
whiling away the hours
in cautious relaxation
watching the little numbers
flip by
waiting for royalty
to bestow me
with riches and a chance
to be somebody
my friend likes her doctor
because he hugs her
can't recall that
ever happening to me
I get so many ideas
for things I could do
without accreditation
body language advisor
for up-scale businesses
personal zen coach
for the NFL
sell blank autograph cards

through the mail
write a self-help guide

for aging strippers
own an all-night bookstore
which specializes in haiku
and literary journals
that nobody buys
be an ambassador of movement
to explain the U.S. to aliens

maybe I'll get a slice of land
raise peanuts
and bamboo
sketch nude models
maybe-sell condoms
and Dodger dogs
drink some whiskey
and be somebody
all over again

things I truly regret
not telling mom and dad
I loved them
or getting them a gravestone
things I don't regret
but probably should
not answering the phone
liking living alone
not walking the dog
watching Butt slammers 10

the porno tape
letting my insurance run out
doing that waitress in 72

without getting her name
calling my ex
a crazy screaming
psycho bitch
after she hit m
for touching her
cassette tape
and taking acid
on the day I pitched
in a championship
college baseball game-
that's about it
except for buying
that TV memory course
I forget where it is
and those last three shots
of Goldschlager
the night I fell
on my head
on the bricks
and then called a cab
from my own house
to go back for my car
at a bar
I'd been driven
home from
yeah that's about it

time's flying by
on my Salvador Dali

exploding pocket watch
calendar page

I thought it was
still Saturday
but now I see it's Sunday
maybe that's why
I didn't get any mail
things to do today
return 123 back phone calls

send cat calendar
to Japan
wash the dog
spray the termites
in my bedroom door
or better yet
meditate them
into someone else's house
pay back taxes
get a part-time girlfriend
seek partial enlightenment
and nirvana if time
cleaning cat box
and make a dental appointment
then go to instant university

and for $39 learn how to
clear up my clutter
do Qi Gong
go to 2-day film school
finishing reading
How to Drive Your Woman Wild in Bed
all between
6:30 and 9:00 p.m.
on the same day
remember our values
come from writers
not politicians
so be careful
what you read
hurry up

give that wedding gift
to the soon-to-be divorced couple
but have faith
in what you can't figure out
make me stop
spouting slogans
if I don't know
what they mean
don't take me serious

make me humorous
the laughing Buddha burps
and sticks
his finger in his belly
I pop a breath mint
think about tenure
and buying a pipe
the wind blows
and the brittle branch breaks
but the weeping willow
just bends and sways
and now a nonsense parable
maybe
a young monk wanders for years
in search of the wise old master
at last he finds him
sitting by a wide river
next to a wooden boat
the young man says
I've been searching for years
what is the meaning of life
but the old master just sits
staring out in silence
so the young monk
cuts off his right arm
and gives it to the old man
there he says
now you must know I'm sincere
and again he asks the master
what is the meaning of life
the old man picks up the arm
and hits the young monk
over the head with it
then he gets into the boat
and using the arm as a paddle
he rows to the other side
the young monk gets
his answer
and the old master
gets where he is going
it's the going

I was getting at and I think
I got an answer
this is the last page
and by not planing
to put anything in
I've left nothing out
not even the kitchen sink
a mind made up
is a terrible thing
to waste a mime
you need a silencer

      old man
      in the cafe
      crumbling crackers
or
      tom cat
      eating a Cardinal
      others keep on singing

and so it goes
like pincher-bound lobsters
in a holding tank
we too feel restrained
and know not why
every day is a good day
eat your rice
wash your bowl

LATE AT NIGHT
by Daniel Senser

Late at Night

The clock is drunk and I'm too sober
To sit and listen to it unwind.
Each tick and tock of its time pours over
Like a wino spilling over the sides.
The rain is insane and so is my lover.
Sweet nothings soon become sweet somethings
In her rapacious mind.
Sex is a literal act, she says.
Like dying. The trick is to do it for another.
Love is wounded lust carrying a white flag.
Now every word I hear her speak sounds like "surrender."
She sleeps beside me now, her memory transmuting dreams.
I'll stay up all night and sprint my will against time,
Chase my lover's dreams, blind, as I lie beside her.

Night Adieus

Languid night. I am sitting on a dirty couch
in my back yard, listening to the whirl of the air conditioner
as it motors cool air into the house.
The soft spell of this machine is broken by another—
the clicking of a side door opening on its hinges next door.
Four people exit: quiet, unintelligible phantoms
lit by an orange lamp in chiaroscuro.
Out first comes a woman, her silvery wisp of hair
moving gently like fog over her sharp, lean face,
Her spectacles reflecting the orange light like jellyfish.
In her gentle British accent, she is saying her goodbyes
to three men in shadow, cheek kisses for all.
"Pleasure, gentlemen! I will call you from France!"
The three men go back inside, and she gets into her car.
I can hear it gently rumble as it drifts off into the night.

Lunatic Song

The moon is a coiled spring
Who's made mastery of madness.
My tongue is like a moon
Orbiting a thought
Lighting the night with crazed soliloquy.
The moon up there has nothing to say.
He has said everything already.
If one listens, one can hear its echo
In the strange somnambulent singing
Of the star-gazing lunatics
Wandering these tangled streets.
With every phrase, the coil of the moon
Gets tighter. We sing its praises
And, bashful, it won't surrender.
As I gaze, I mark a tear running
Down its face. Falling from its chin,
It becomes: a star.

For My Niece, Blakely Thomas

You fill my heart with sweet song and laughter
And kick up the old dust in my world-weary soul.
With all the spunk and pluck of a seasoned master
You reach out your hand and bid me take hold.
Together we dance the dance of the young and the old
And all that binds them together
(it is, after all, the whole world,
Or so I'm told).
Though my feet tread heavy
On the long and lonely road of my life,
They now step lightly in this dance of ours.
With gentle urgency, they serve as a guide
For your own. Where this music takes us,
No one can know. But you can be sure
That when the drum stops kicking,
And the fiddler plays his final chord,
I'll dance with you again. You just say the word.

To Write a Poem

To bury one's self in tormenting silence
To withstand the evil eye of solitude
And the dragon's fire of Not Knowing,
To peer like a suicidal man into the mind's abyss
And then jump, remaining always conscious
Of something not yet there. To lose sight
Of all dreams and nullify all prayers,
To kindle fire in the back of your throat,
To have one's neck wrung with the vice-like
Grip of a muse's hands,
To die a thousand times inside each phrase,
To sprint headlong towards an oncoming train
And know that for every death your soul achieves
A thousand times over it will be saved.

About the Author:

Daniel Senser has been writing for about twelve years, primarily as a poet. His writings have appeared in California Quarterly, Poetry Quarterly, Haiku Journal, and Jewish Currents, among other journals. He published a book of poetry about two and a half years ago entitled, "Chasing Crows." Daniel graduated from the University of Cincinnati with a BA in English in 2014.

SELF TALK
by Emily Butler

Self Talk

Looks like somebody forgot to take their Dylar this morning.

Did you wake up on the wrong side of the tracks?

Got a bad case of the un-days? The end times?

Don't you dare rhyme. You're very clever.

How's that working out for you?

Quit playing with your words already and eat them.

About the Author:

Emily F. Butler is a high school librarian by day, stand-up comedian and musician by night. Their work has appeared in Halfway Down the Stairs, Moonglasses, Eunoia Review, This Zine Will Change Your Life, and Bone Parade. They live in western Massachusetts and write book reviews for School Library Journal. You can follow them on Twitter @EBetcetera.

Modern Sins

To check Facebook in the middle of a bright, insect-filled field
is a kind of blasphemy .

Is challenge a core component of religion?

If so, I may have created an adequate faith:

> Resist the sins of technology (jealousy, hubris) and reality
> will set you free.

This is not unlike advice I was once given
which encouraged me to focus on concrete
images.

Concrete as in tangible
 ("concrete" is more "concrete" than "tangible" is "tangible"
because of concrete's material connotation)

not as in a mixture of cement, water, sand, stone.

The challenge of attention. The split self of addiction.
I can't hear the birds over my words.

Just now! God played a joke on me.

So distracted by jerking off my mind, I did not see the fuzzy caterpillar crawling up my leg and when I
finally noticed, I flicked it with my pen, startled.

Humans are comically cowardly giants.

Just when I am too busy to notice the world, the caterpillar crawls up to remind me that nature is
frightening even when it isn't.

I'd rather stay in the artificial place
we have created.

The place where we pretend we aren't prey.

(S)LAUGHTER by Henry Reneau

(S)laughter

Silent as something dark to sparkle from. The slight degrees
where the truth goes missing. When we exit
with or without intention
one ruthless tradition
of social ruination for another. The antidote's
unmentioned nod to poison, to auto-erotic
asphyxiation. The way a car free-bases gasoline
refined from the bones of doomsday dinosaurs. Accelerating
toward extinction. Is a madman's laughter as old as
humanity itself.

The imperial age of the 21st century: Their crack high, like kissing
Jesus, seeking omnipotence by way of drone strikes. The means
to scapegoat the disavowed killer: Lee Harvey Oswald
manipulated into an air-conditioned office turned bunker, in Nevada.

Even before it happened, everything we always believed
could happen—the way Amerikkka strangles herself—would happen.
When avoiding the truth we usually knew, but never talked about—
did happen. Something feral, like the way to get people talking, is to
let them fill in the silence.

About the Author:

henry 7. reneau, jr. writes words in fire to wake the world ablaze: free verse that breaks a rule every day, illuminated by his affinity for disobedience, a phoenix-flux of red & gold immolation that blazes from his heart, like a chambered bullet exploded through change is gonna come to implement the fire next time. He is the author of the poetry collection, freedomland blues (Transcendent Zero Press) and the e-chapbook, physiography of the fittest (Kind of a Hurricane Press), now available from their respective publishers. Additionally, he has self-published a chapbook entitled 13hirteen Levels of Resistance, and is currently working on a book of connected short stories. His work was nominated for the Pushcart Prize by LAROLA.

winged diamond with ruby lips

every child has a story, something quantum measureless
& full of light. the crystal-blue river of imagination
that flows into a child's searching hands, giving shape to

the circle of mystery that answers each question
with a question. a something from nothing mile of wire
that makes a screen door, an introspection turning inward.

the one,
an unfiltered narrative seemingly guileless,
illuminating his imaginary friend, his evidence of companionship

unseen. & the other,
the x-factored ever-changing chameleon face: what's going on
in her mind? is it the same as what she's saying?

the one,
his digging, a hole symbolic of unearthing the origins of magic &
happily-ever-after, the way the ceramic smoothness of a coffee cup

warms the soul. & the other,
manipulative as the shrill falseness of plastic, but her
fascinating neon face, like a wolf carving out the flock for food.

the one,
his ever searching for refuge from abuse, a gazelle,
checking the exits for fight or flee, at the first whiff of predator.

& the other,
watching what mommy & daddy's hands do, as opposed to,
listening to the roundabout obfuscation to her question,

every child,

inhabiting the mystery that is becoming: a scatter of
priceless gems across black velvet, as clock-beautiful as creation.

TONI MORGAN
A LOVER OF WORDS

Toni came home to Oregon from a summer as an exchange student in Denmark knowing two things: she loved history, and she loved traveling and meeting new people. Her parents collected early-American antiques. By their measure, anything over 75 years of age qualified. The house of Toni's host family in Denmark was 400-years-old, and the church where her host-father preached was 800-years-old. She saw where battles had been fought and where Danes had lived ten centuries before she was born. It was a revelation. Her writing career began with that trip, keeping the editor of her hometown paper apprised of all she saw. A former NYT editor, he convinced her that she should continue writing. Although a west-coaster by birth, marriage, and preference, Toni has lived in many places, including nearly four years in Japan. That rich experience led her to write Echoes from a Falling Bridge, Harvest the Wind, and Lotus Blossom Unfurling.

ALM: Tell us a bit about yourself, about Toni Morgan – something that we will not find in the official author's bio?

TM: I've always loved words, especially big ones, even when I didn't know what they meant. When I was nine or ten, I famously asked my father if he was a communist or a pedestrian. He answered that he was a communist and kept his flag in the closet. That, of course, sailed right over my head.

Growing up, we moved a lot—from Alaska, where I was born, to Washington and then on to Oregon, where we moved several times, always further into the country. We finally ended up in Hawaii, of all places, where I met and married my husband, a career Marine. His career took us to many places, from coast to coast—I've lost track of the number of cross-country trips we made. One time, in 1973, when my husband came back from his second Vietnam tour, 30 days out of the jungle and still half-feral, with four kids and two dogs, we left Oregon, headed to North Carolina. By the time we got to Eugene, Oregon, I was ready to get out of the car and join a commune.

The most memorable place we lived was Japan. The first six months we lived there, I felt like I was living in a National Geographic special. Everything was so different, the architecture, the farms—like miniatures the traffic—ask me about driving on the wrong side of the road—but especially the people. But the longer we were there (nearly four years) the more I grew to realize that except for coloring, we were the same. We had the same concerns for our children, for our future, the same desires, needs, worries. And what a wonderful and broadening opportunity for my children. The youngest was seven when we arrived, and the older boys were in their early teens. They've never forgotten that experience and the friendships we all made. My one regret: my husband's secretary, like Nobuko in Echoes from a Falling Bridge, grew up in California, was sent to Japan by her parents to learn the culture of her ancestors, and was trapped there by the war. Also like Nobuko, she ended up staying. I wish I'd asked her more questions about that experience. In 1939, by the way, there were over 50,000 young Japanese-Americans in Japan, sent there by their parents for the same reason.

As well as all the wonderful times and memories I have experienced, I've also had some rough times. Our first child died as an infant from a heart defect that would now be detected and repaired before he was born Another son, diagnosed with affective schizoid disorder, committed suicide at twenty-two. I learned following the death of our first child, that one day I would smile again, even laugh, but that was a really rough period. Some have told me that I should have written through that period. Perhaps they were right, but for years I couldn't go to that quite place I wrote from, and avoided it at all costs. Others have suggested writing a memoir. Well, I already know what happened with that story —I was there. For me, writing is about finding out

TONI MORGAN

ECHOES
from a falling bridge
A NOVEL

TONI MORGAN

HARVEST
the wind
A NOVEL

TONI MORGAN

LOTUS
blossom unfurling
A NOVEL

what's going to happen. But as every writer knows, every experience, good or bad, eventually finds its way into the writing.

ALM: Do you remember what was your first story (article, essay, or poem) about and when did you write it?

TM: I remember it very well. I was sixteen. As writers, we are told to write what we know. At sixteen, I didn't know much about much. I had never flown and never had a boyfriend, so naturally I wrote a story about a romance between an airline stewardess (which is what flight attendants were called back then) and a pilot, and sent it off to the old Saturday Evening Post, dreaming of fame to come. You can't imagine how I felt when I received a very nice, hand-written rejection letter, telling me my story showed promise and I should keep writing. The words were nice, but it was a rejection (the first of many) and I was crushed.

I sort of gave up on fiction after that, and stuck with school essays and then, non-fiction articles about banking, until after I retired and went back to my first love.

ALM: Why do you write a prose? What motivates you to sit down and write? Have you ever thought of writing poetry?

TM: Everyone has natural talents, but too often we dismiss them as 'too easy.' In this culture, we're taught that to be valued, a thing needs to be hard—like math. My natural talent was in writing and in art. As a kid, I was always writing a story or a poem or doing art projects. Even so, I didn't value that natural ability. When my high school art teacher wanted me to apply for an art scholarship, I wasn't interested. The editor of our local paper, a former NY Times editor, told me I should pursue a career in writing. Nope. I majored in history.

A few years back, there was an article in The Guardian about a Noble Prize judge who said that grants and fellowships were ruining Western literature. I Facebook with lots of writers and follow others on Twitter. Everyone was outraged by his remarks—he just wants young writers to suffer for their art, people (mostly young writers, I suspect) said. I didn't have the same takeaway. I thought he meant people needed to live and have life-experiences before they could write about them. I had a rather boring childhood myself. My parents loved me. I had tolerable siblings whom I mostly ignored. As a teenager, I was an exchange student to Denmark one summer, which sparked my interest in history. But that's about the only exciting thing I'd done. Some people have very different childhoods, maybe they were abused or lived in poverty, and maybe some are more reflective than I was. They can distill their experiences and write with authenticity at an early age. I couldn't.

It wasn't until I was in my sixties and had retired from banking that I took up writing seriously. And the more I wrote, the more compelled I felt to write. I have a friend, a writer who was a finalist for a National Book Award, who claims a writer is someone who feels guilty when they aren't writing. So maybe that's the answer to your question about what motivates me to sit down and write. I feel guilty when I'm not writing. Plus, maybe a little escapism: when the writing is going well, it's like a movie in my head.

As to writing poetry, my grandmother once said that poetry is condensed prose, so yes, I've tried my hand at poetry. I'm not sure I'm all that good at it, though. Too wordy.

ALM: You wrote six novels before publishing your first book. How does it feel writing and not sharing with readers? Did you ever think that your writings will never be published?

TM: I think I always felt they would be published someday, but at times I thought it might be posthumously. But it didn't really matter. I've always written to please myself, to answer the question of what comes next. I love my characters, even the villains, and want to know what happens to them.

ALM: What is the title of your latest novel and what inspired it?

TM: Currently, I'm finishing Lotus Blossom Unfurling. It features the characters introduced in Echoes From a Falling Bridge and Harvest the Wind. Both of those novels are set during WWII and then have a gap, picking up forty or fifty years later. I kept wondering what happened in between, how did they cope after the war? Nobuko ended up staying in Japan, but how did she get along, what happened to her? How were Keiko and her family treated when they returned to Portland after the war? What about Virginia Franconi? Did she marry John Sato? Were they happy?

ALM: How long did it take you to write your latest novel and how fast do you write (how many words daily)?

TM: My latest novel is certainly taking less time to write than my first novel—part of the reason is that I know the characters so well. But also, I think, I'm a better writer. I revised my first novel,

"Write about what you love...

A writer writes. A writer feels guilty when not writing. The difference between an unpublished good writer and a published one is persistence.

Born in Alaska, raised in Oregon, where she studied history at Portland State University, and married in Hawaii, Toni Morgan has lived all over the United States, from California to Washington, D.C., and the world, from Denmark to Japan. She now makes her home in southwestern Idaho. She is the author of six novels: TWO-HEARTED CROSSING, PATRIMONY, ECHOES FROM A FALLING BRIDGE, HARVEST THE WIND, LOTUS BLOSSOM UNFURLING, and QUEENIE'S PLACE. Toni's articles and short stories have been published in various newspapers, literary magazines, and other publications. To learn more about Toni, visit her website.http://authortonimorgan.com

Patrimony, at least twenty times. For one thing, I was going to write it and Two-Hearted Crossing as one novel—which would have made it about 700 pages long! An editor convinced me it should be two novels. Patrimony takes place in 1969-70, and Two-Hearted is set in 2000-2001, so I wrote Patrimony first. I'd complete a draft and then put it in a drawer. I wrote another novel, Queenie's Place, before writing Two-Hearted Crossing. Then I'd go back to Patrimony. Over the years, as I became a better writer, I'd workshop it with other writers. I started it in 2002 and it was published in 2017, so that kind of tells you how long that one took. Lotus Blossom Unfurling—about nine months. So, big difference.

ALM: Do you have any unusual writing habits?

TM: I don't think so. I sit wherever and write on a laptop.

ALM: Is writing the only form of artistic expression that you utilize, or there is more to Toni Morgan than just writing?

TM: As I said earlier, my 'natural talents' have always been writing and art, which for me has lately taken the form of painting. I think writing is painting a story with words, while painting is telling a story with color. In my opinion, there are five steps in the creative process, whether it's writing a story or essay, painting a picture, designing a product, or starting a business. First comes the idea. Second is gathering your materials, doing your research. Third is laying it out—darkest darks/lightest lights, just tell the story, build the prototype, write the business plan, etc. Fourth is going back over and making corrections. Fifth and final is putting in the highlights, adding the bells and whistles.

ALM: Authors and books that have influenced your writings?

TM: At the risk of sounding cliché, Ernest Hemingway, of course. Also, Arthur Golden (Memoirs of a Geisha) and David Gutterson (Snow Falling on Cedars). Tony Doerr's All the Light We Cannot See blew me away. I'm a huge admirer of Edward Gaines. Also, Molly Gloss, who writes science fiction as well as western fiction—for her, setting is another character. The thing all of these writers have in common, as well as many more writers I haven't mentioned, is story. They are great storytellers.

ALM: What are you working on right now? Anything new cooking in Toni's kitchen?

TM: Oh, I have all sorts of ideas. A sequel to Patrimony and Two-Hearted Crossing. Another one to Queenie's Place which I intend to call Charlotte's Place. I've also been noodling about a series of 'cozy' mysteries featuring an eccentric old lady who cruises—cruising is cheaper than a nursing home, has a doctor aboard, features great food, fascinating places and all sorts of new and unusual characters coming and going. I'm thinking a river cruise and Budapest as my first site. I might need to do a little more research, no?

ALM: Did you ever think about the profile of your readers? What do you think – who reads Toni Morgan?

TM: This probably sounds very egotistical, but no. I've always written to please myself, about things, places and characters that interest me, searching for 'what happens next,' and 'what if.'

ALM: Do you have any advice for new writers/authors?

TM: Here is what I once told my granddaughter's tenth-grade class about a writing career: A writer writes. A writer feels guilty when not writing. The difference between an unpublished good writer and a published one is persistence. If you want to become a writer, read a lot, practice your craft whenever you can, and most of all, follow your passions and your interests. And live.

ALM: What is the best advice you have ever heard?

TM: Write about what you love.

ALM: How many books you read annually and what are you reading now? What is your favorite literary genre?

TM: When I'm actively writing, I don't have much time for fiction. I'm usually too busy researching. When I do read fiction, I like all sorts of genres—historical fiction, mysteries by Louise Penny, Jacqueline Winspear and Elizabeth George. I enjoy light reading, like Major Pettigrew's Last Stand. One of my favorite novels was Kate Atkinson's Life After Life. Mainly because I thought she must have had so much fun writing it, continually changing the story trajectory with some serendipitous event. It was a tour de force by a great writer.

ALM: What do you deem the most relevant about your novels? What is the most important to be remembered by readers?

TM: I think I'm drawn to the underside of things. It's not that I don't appreciate the beauty of a tapestry, I do. But I always want to turn it over, too, examine the back, see the way the threads go, see what made it. I want to know both sides, understand why people say and do the things they say and do, listen to the words beneath the words. It's all about story.

ALM: Thank you Toni. Looking forward reading your new books. Good luck.

agon:

Partisan Arguments as Collective Utterance (1) Enthymemes as Philosophy, Poetry, and Political Discourse

By Wally Swist

agon

by Judith Goldman, Brooklyn, NY

Paperback: 230 pages

Publisher: The Operating System; 1 edition (April 10, 2017)

Language: English

ISBN-10: 0986050598
ISBN-13: 978-0986050596

Product Dimensions: 6.5 x 0.5 x 6.5 inches

Iconic volumes of poetry that offer themselves as examples of protest literature are rare. This reviewer recalls writing about Diane Di-Prima's Revolutionary Letters (City Lights, 1971) and espousing the book as the poetical anarchist classic that it is. Judith Goldman's agon furthers even DiPrima's accomplishment. Goldman, who earned a Ph.D. in English and comparative literature from Columbia University in 2007, is Assistant Professor of English at the University of Buffalo. She had co-edited the annual journal, War and Peace, with the late Leslie Scalapino. Just a mention of Leslie Scalapino's name immediately evokes Langue Poetry. Although Goldman's poetry may be classified as such, it goes well beyond such a concept. Writing a review of a previous book, DeathStar/rico-chet (O Books, 2006), by Goldman, poet Joyelle McSweeney christens Goldman's poetry as one of "a conceptual or formal framework that brings attentive pressure to bear on grimly mundane content; the other rejects conventional frameworks and concocts a parallel system of language at once as violent, arbitrary, and paradoxically prophetic of a fait accompli as a highlight reel of daily carnage on the evening news."

With agon, whose origin is from the Greek and ostensibly can be thought of to mean struggle, but whose root is also in agony, and based in tragedy, classically pitting an antagonist against a protagonist, Goldman creates a hybrid text which blends philosophy, poetry, and political thought that includes an index of such progressive minds as Belgian political theorist and post-Marxist critic Chatel Mouffe and the French philosopher, renowned for his combining of phenomenological description with hermeneutics, Jean Paul Gustave

Ricoeur. In Goldman's own words, this book is "a potential inventory of current agon. But failing this, pointing instead to a possible contemporary mutated extenuation of dissensus in current economic, political, and social formations in near-foreclosure by the hyper-militarization of hegemonic power; its near-immediate symbolic and other cooptation through social media and digital capitalism; its near-unpredictability given attenuations of agency, the complicities required for bare attrition survival."

However, any discussion of Goldmans agon would be inchoate if it did not mention either hapology or enthymemes. About half of agon is composed of Goldman's textual barcodes which serve as a hapological poetry. The barcodes stand to serve a multipurpose aesthetic norm: as art texts themselves using a superficial hackneyed layering and as poetic semiotics deconstructing ideas, idioms, and memes in contemporary 21st-century society. The definition of haplology is the elimination of a syllable when two consecutive and/or identical similar syllables are juxtaposed. The word originates from the Greek of haploos, meaning simple, and logos, or speech. The phenomenological concept was identified in the 20th-century by American philologist Maurice Bloomfield. Expansively speaking, Goldman's inventive use of hapology within her poetical bar code form is not a dissimilar aesthetic experience of viewing a painting by conceptual contemporary artist Sol LeWitt. Both Goldman and LeWitt guide our vision quite uniquely to see, as well as possibly comprehend, what we haven't seen before—although what we, as readers and viewers, realize is that the reality we are now aware of is, and was, ever-present.

With respect to enthymemes, Goldman best defines them in her own inimitable language: "Enthymemes are locations of enculturation: to say speech is encoded is to call out the enthymeme. Yet an enthymeme solicits inference that draws on its audience's resources in terms of what it already recognizes and what it may be spurred to imagine . . . supplying a proof's givens even when the given must be fabricated (as given)." Essentially, what Goldman so brilliantly creates in agon is an imaginatively clever interactive text in which the aesthetic accomplished is of a social order in which her audience or readership

is made more aware of its own implication in current societal norms than ever quite realizing before, often with their own new self-awareness providing a keen wince from within—through what is a "fabricated (as given)" form of Goldman's invention. Quoting Professor Henry Farrell on page 67 seems apt here, "The enthymeme, for better or worse, offers a provisional interpretative frame, a caption, that, lends temporary stability to an otherwise unstable and ambiguous complex of appearances."

In other words, Goldman rather resiliently turns language in agon inside out for us so that we might see and participate in the struggle in which comes at us from all sides especially in Donald Trump's solipsistic and authoritarian view of America that has poisoned the culture. What might best illustrate what Goldman achieves are the last two lines from "Two birds the one watching and passive, the other enjoying its activity:" "He was fracking me/ What goes in may come out."

Goldman furthers, followed by a quote from Thomas de Quincey's "Rhetoric" (1828), that: "Enthymemes are prevalent in speech. (How tiresome it would be if they weren't.)" A significant part of the DeQuincey reads "an enthymeme was understood to be a syllogism of which one proposition is suppressed . . . But what possible relation had that to rhetoric?" Of which Goldman, nearly in dialogue with DeQuincey, writes "Utterance "naturally" surrounds itself with enthymemic implicature. It may be that speech must presuppose more than it says, that everything said is an enthymeme."

Goldman then summons Valentin Voloshinov's "Disclosure in Life and Discourse in Art ("Concerning Sociological Poetics") (1927), in which he proclaims, "Every utterance in the business of life is an objective and social enthymeme. It is something like a "password" known only to those who belong to the some social purview . . . "

Perhaps an example of such a "password" or at least an enthymemic poetical trope presented by Goldman shortly after her quoting Voloshinov may possibly illustrate Goldman's noir newsreel vision in which verisimilitude is never spared in what is a largely tarnished cultural portrayal.

"the scholarly study of candy-tampering legends. He collected newspaper
reports
razor blades, needles, or broken glass in and distributing the candy
that Children copy or act out stories they overhear, adding pins to or
died after eating a cyanide-laced package of Pixy Stix. A subsequent police
investigation eventually determined that the poisoned candy had been
planted in his trick-or-treat pile by the boy's father,
Due to their fears, parents and communities restricted trick-or-treating and
Developed alternative "safe" events
also promoted the sale of individually wrapped, brand-name candies and
discouraged people from giving homemade treats to children."

In what is one of the more lyrically imbued philosophical passages in agon, one in which might have been admired by German poet-philosopher Novalis, Goldman lends an attribute which the composer John Cage found endearing as it is powerful: "The peculiarity of the enthymeme's silence. There is a gap in the enthymeme, but there is no gap, as if reinforces the common sense of common sense, the obvious and its obviousness . . . What is not said is leveraged on and leverages a reality principle. To pass over in silence is not to negate but to make good on. Here, then, is a silence that is not subordinated to speech, but needed by it: it is the source of speech's power . . . The omitted may be included by exclusion, but its status is that of constitutive interior, not constitutive exterior."

Goldman cites American philosopher and gender theorist Judith Butler in her book The Psychic Life of Power (Stanford, 1997) in that she "returns to the notion of the subject's 'passionate attachment to subjection.'" She also quotes Butler clarion call in that it "arrives severally and in implicit and unspoken ways." Of which Goldman posits: " . . . it is enthymemic. To be addressed by enthymemes is to be called to reproduce and supplement the symbolic order in all its imaginary probability, to practice social belonging, literacy, emplacement. Enthymemes meet our readiness to .

know. We attach deeply to such implication, it claims us."

What truly "claim us" is Goldman's definition of text itself: "It is both the "collapse [of] 'context' into 'text,' and the essential incompleteness of the context the text that dissolve and resolve discourse into a network of enthymemic prompts." What better working indictment of Trump's version, or inversion, of "fake news" other than Goldman's inflection regarding text. However, it is also those individuals who believe that "fake news" is, indeed, fake, which not so much invokes compassion as it does a self-righteous, and perhaps uncalled for, anger. Goldman, in quoting postmodern rhetorician Michael McGee, offers "text construction is now something done more by the consumers than by the producers of discourse." If so, then we are provided insight into an Orwellian version of Trumpian skullduggery.

This brings us to the topic of censorship, of which Goldman mentions the work of Pierre Bourdieu in his book, Language and Symbolic Power (Harvard, 1993), in that Bourdieu defines "euphemization" as the general condition of public speech. To this Goldman replies, "Bourdieu's discussion of censorship involves less emphasis on repression per se than on the productivity of constraint, and the way that social context, position, and relation become legible in euphemized utterance. In a racist society discursively organized around the denial of racism, most speech is marked by the tension of avoiding describing social reality and social processes as racist and, above all, by a taboo on white self-presentation as racist, much of which depends on altogether evading direct mention of race and racism." We just saw a stark example of this in President Barack Obama's eight years in office—in which he distinguished the role of the presidency with eloquence and grace—also in which the American media did very little, if any, reporting about the openly hostile and racist demagoguery and rhetoric of the Republican Party.

Here, again, Goldman offers us an incisive exegesis of American society, "Euphemization bound up with symbolic violence: complicit misrecognition-recognition relies not just on a naturalized social order or the unquestioned desirability of the stakes on offer; but on the soft hypocrisy of public discourse in every field; circumlocution through which power leverages its production and reproduction: language as mystifying displacement, conversion, currency exchange."

Goldman declaims that "citational literature comes into being through iteration." She also eloquently echoes Amiri Baraka's deceptively simple yet elegant phrase, "Speech is the effective form of culture . . . Speech, the way one describes the natural proposition of being alive, is much more crucial than even most artists realize" ("Expressive Language," 1963), in that Goldman gives credence to "citational poetics" as an adequate weapon and as a political act: "the weaponized citationality that citational literature deploys—is necessarily bound up with how the citational work functions as textual speech act."

These "speech acts" which "function [as] citational poetics" of Judith Goldman are as profound as they are inventive, as significant examples of erudition as they are exhibitions of genuine aesthetics, and as insightful and visionary as they are keys in providing us a sense of who we are both individually and as a society and where we might be stalling and how we possibly can move onward with some modicum of self-awareness and human dignity. agon is a valuable and exciting work of poetics and philosophy. The book also is a prime example of the hybrid mix and meld of genres which is the signature of Lynne DeSilva-Johnson's Brooklyn-based press, The Operating System. Goldman and DeSilva-Johnson were brought together through the publication of this book in an aesthetic and intellectual fusion which is what makes literature such as this even more remarkable and so immensely relevant and unusually exhilarating.

Instructions Within:
The Poetry of Necessity

Book review by Wally Swist

Instructions Within
by Ashraf Fayadh

translated by Mona Kareem, with Mona Saki and Jonathan Wright;

Edited by Ammiel Alcalay, Pierre Joris, and Lynne DeSilva-Johnson;

Brooklyn, NY: The Operating System, 2016,

297pp., paperback, $28.00.

The Turkish poet, Nazim Hikmet (1902-1963), is known for his courageous book of lyrical poems written in prison, Things I Didn't Know I Love. The outstanding translation of these poems in English by Montlu Konuk and Randy Blasing was published by Persea Books in 1986. If anyone is missing out on reading literature that is life-affirming, read Hikmet's poems in this book. They are a tribute to the human spirit.

Another, and more recent testimony to humanity is Ashraf Fayadh's Instructions Within. The book shared the 2017 Oxfam Novib/PEN Award for Freedom of Expression, along with Malini Subramaniam. Fayadh is of Palestinian heritage and is an artist and a poet but lives in Saudi Arabia. Subramaniam is freelance journalist living in India who has made a name for herself by reporting the atrocities in the Maoist-infested Bastar area in Chhattisgarh state.

Fayadh was affiliated with the British-Arabian arts league, Edge of Arabia. He also was active in curating art exhibits in Saudi Arabia. In 2013, he was detained by religious police after a soccer game and charged with apostasy. It is believed he was apprehended because Fayadh had been circulating a video of a man being publicly lashed. He was sentenced to death. However, in February 2016 Fayadh's sentence was overturned and an eight-year prison term and eight hundred lashes, along with his publicly repenting for his apostasy, were imposed on him. He was also charged with having promoted atheism by his having published the poems contained in Instructions Within, as well as in his texts, and in conversations he held in a coffee shop in Ab-ha.Middle East researcher for Human Rights Watch, Adam Coogle, portrayed Fayadh's death sentence as Saudi Arabia's "complete intolerance of anyone who may not share government-mandated religious, political and social views." German PEN which is also associated with PEN International, made Fayadh an Honorary Member. The Berlin International Literature Festival published an appeal to support Fayadh with a Worldwide Reading on January 14, 2016. As of the writing of this review, Fayadh is still imprisoned.

Although the poems included in Instructions Within were not written in prison they constitute a poetry written to stand up to oppression. They are powerful lyrical poems that also double as trenchant political literature denouncing an oppressor. Publisher Lynne DeSilva-Johnson's design of the book enhances the reading experience of Fayadh's poetry. It is not only published in Arabic with face en face English translations, it also published as a book in Arabic would be, with the text reading right to left. So, the book appears to be published in reverse, with the reader beginning at what, in the English-speaking world, would be the rear, or end, and then moving toward the beginning, or what we might commonly think as the front. To read Fayadh's work in the same format as it would be issued in Arabic brings the Anglicized reader closer to his cultural roots. With this incisive insight in the book's design, we, as readers see more clearly into Fayadh's Arabic heritage and are able to hear the pliancy in his lyrical voice.

To read Fayadh's poetry knowing he is in prison and that he either is having to or had to endure eight hundred lashes for his being framed by the authoritarian Saudi government's harsh stance on political opposition, provides a background of a combination of compassion and unease. We don't read American poetry in the same way. American poetry often differs just by its reflection of an entitled society. There is no entitlement whatsoever in the poetry of Fayadh. Instead, there is a kind of purity in it. Take these "Prayers of Longing," written to a lover, perhaps, as an example of how Fayadh condenses the largesse of emotion into the force of a poetry of necessity:

"with a leaf of thorns
I comb my hair . . . gathering the curls,
the way you would gather me in your arms."

"they said a siege was canceled
and that your worn-out hands
are no longer embraced with shackles,
and that I might meet you."

How Fayadh steers clear of sentimentality and straddles the line between overt feeling and leans toward the stark beauty of the image and what is resourceful in the force of language is admirable. Who could imagine both "curls" and "shackles" in the same poem and through their prudent juxtaposition bring "I might meet you" to a whole new level of human experience. We are embraced and crushed, at once, in Fayadh's poetry.

Perhaps the Saudi State discerned a trace of apostasy in this next poem, appearing on page 132, which challenges false beliefs and exalts freedom of thinking. The simplicity of Fayadh's poems is deceptive. Few poets of any country in the world can write so directly but instill within their verses a reserved lyrical resonance. "Night" is truly a haunting poem in that also exhibits Fayadh's unique sensibility of Puer, or "the eternal boy." We are entranced and charmed, concomitantly.

Night,
you are inexperienced with time
lacking raindrops
that could wash away the remains of the past
and free you of chastily
and of a heart that can love and play
asserting your abandonment
of a flaccid religion, a fraud revelation,
and of faith in gods
who had lost their pride.

In the following poem, and in just six lines, Fayadh manages to combine metaphor and symbolism in such a way that the reader is also made aware of not only a mystical message but also that of a political one. There is an accented aridity that is almost desert-like in the poem in which the soul also springs to life in the darkness of the night. If there ever was a poem regarding not only an individual dark night but also that of an entire nation or society, this is it.

"This body needs showers of soul water,
clouds to make rain with,
words of longing,
and degrees recognized in exile
to practice all the love rituals
that could overthrow the regime of Night."

The title poem for the collection appears to be contained in the following poem, "God is Ours!" There are several turns of phrase and meaning in the poem, and in it is a kind of hall of mirrors. As Emily Dickinson writes in "Tell all the truth but tell it slant" (1263, R. W. Franklin Edition, Cambridge: Harvard University Press, 1999), Fayadh impresses a veracity upon the reader, presupposing or not, and he quite figuratively hands the reader a literary construction which employs an acute lens, actually several of them, in which he creates a poem as a kind of holograph. He also seems to be giving guidance in how not to be apprehended by the religious secret police.

"God is ours!
He made us out of mud
and for every illness he made a cure;
for the healthy he brought sickness
and for the joyful he made tears!
Wrap yourself with songs
and don't get directly exposed to longing.

"your chances to be cured are slim
so follow the written instructions on the back of
the mirror
and keep your picture away and out of
reach!"

Even in poems in which Fayadh fashions images with utter clarity he imbues his poetry with a mystical element in which there is an accompanying uncanny political echo. "Logic" is such a poem. How he shifts "an old door" with wind in the trees and "a dancing school" is not only aesthetically accomplished but also entwined within the use of these tropes is a message of admonishment, of pause, and of exhilaration, as well as one of a wary discernment and acceptance.

"The old door applauds the wind
for its dancing performance with the trees.
The old door has no hands
And the trees were not trained at a dancing
school.
The wind is an invisible creature,
even when its dancing with the trees."

The poem also evokes a similar lyrical symbolism that prevails in the poetry of Cesar Vallejo, the Peruvian poet, whom Thomas Merton referred to as "the greatest universal poet since Dante." In what is perhaps one of the finest poems in Instructions Within, Fayadh offers a testament to the human spirit, at once downtrodden but unvanquished, Sisyphean but resurgent, impossibly hindered at times but perennially luminous as a sky filled with shooting stars.

"the star shepherds find it strange
that I exploit time
throwing future intoxications
behind my steps.
The clubs went on watching my worries
trying to avoid the slaps which no longer miss
the way to my face—
my destiny—to intersect
with all these suspicious fantasies
between cloud, thunder,
and astronomical objects in exile . . .
I claim to have mastered
the act of raining on sand grains
in order to make a memorial for mankind."

Few poets of any nation come close to creating "a memorial for mankind." However, Fayadh does. Not unlike Hikmet, his nondenominational late Turkish poetical cousin, and not dissimilar to Peruvian symbolist Vallejo, Fayadh offers us a resonant poetry of courage and even faith—certainly courage to take on Saudi political and religious norms and definitely faith in his resilient representation of human spirit which issues like a fountain through the dross of the human condition. Fayadh's poetry is especially significant to read in lieu of the authoritarian leanings and wildly unpredictable wiles of the Trump administration. Like Hikmet and Vallejo, Fayadh is an international poet of importance. Reading poetry that matters is consequential. Reading poetry that is necessary can be as illuminating as it is revelatory in providing new perspective in our lives—one of social value, spiritual courage, and inestimable moral worth.

"on the walls . . . you enjoy reading
until the time comes for you to read a lusty body

. . .

. . .

no voice is stronger
no voice is stronger . . . than the voice of people
but you cannot hear anything
moments ago the sound barrier was hit
so at least you don't have to worry about the
mosquitoes anymore"

In 1939, Nobuko Ito, a young Japanese-American woman, travels from her home in California to Japan, where she is to learn the culture of her ancestors. Tensions grow between the two countries. Soon her country and the country she has grown to love are at war. The next four years are brutal, both for those who go to fight (Hirotaka Katsuragawa, a young art student, Masato Abi, the son of local merchants, Toshio Hara, a farmer turned soldier), and those who remain behind (Nobuko, Yoko Yoshida, who manages the local pottery factory while her husband is fighting the war, and the women and children of Nishimi). In 1997, these characters are in their twilight years. Nobuko is a widow. Yoko is reduced to dusting and serving tea in the factory she once ran. Toshio has gone mad. Hirotaka has become the sensei, honored teacher. While the pottery factory is the heart of the village, Hirotaka is its soul. When a murder is committed, the motive is found buried beneath the rubble of a bridge destroyed in New Guinea, fifty-five years earlier. The noise of its fall still echoes.

Toni came home to Oregon from a summer as an exchange student in Denmark knowing two things: she loved history, and she loved traveling and meeting new people. Her parents collected early-American antiques. By their measure, anything over 75 years of age qualified. The house of Toni's host family in Denmark was 400-years-old, and the church where her host-father preached was 800-years-old. She saw where battles had been fought and where Danes had lived ten centuries before she was born. It was a revelation. Her writing career began with that trip, keeping the editor of her hometown paper apprised of all she saw. A former NYT editor, he convinced her that she should continue writing. Although a west-coaster by birth, marriage, and preference, Toni has lived in many places, including nearly four years in Japan. That rich experience led her to write Echoes from a Falling Bridge, Harvest the Wind, and Lotus Blossom Unfurling.

(http://authortonimorgan.com)

ECHOES FROM A FALLING BRIDGE

A novel
By Toni Morgan

Paperback: 304 pages

Publisher: Adelaide Books (January 2018)

Language: English

ISBN-13: 978-0-9996451-2-3

ISBN-10: 0-9996451-2-9

Product Dimensions: 6 x 0.8 x 9 inches

Price: $22.30

Achingly raw and beautifully written, coming-of-age tales, set in the picturesque Cape Cod and Boston area. The insights into growing up of a boy, looking for positive, masculine, role models, chronicled through ten sequential short stories. They begin when the main character, Ryan, is very young, and end when he has just entered manhood. The author delves into the personalities of his characters bringing them to life through dialogues, internal monologues, and emotional responses, rather than actions. An utterly charming and thoughtful meditation on the transition of a protagonist from youth to adulthood.

Jonathan Maniscalco has taught English to ESL learners in Japan, Spain, and New York City. A Massachusetts native, he is a graduate of Boston University and a stringer for The New England Review of Books. Ten Stories to Manhood is his first published book.'

TEN STORIES TO MANHOOD

By Jonathan Maniscalco

Paperback: 160 pages

Publisher: Adelaide Books (January 2018)

Language: English

ISBN-10: 0-9996451-3-7

ISBN-13: 978-0-9996451-3-0

Product Dimensions: 6 x 0.8 x 9 inches

Price: $19.60

Cinderblock Houses is a fascinating, powerful collection of eight short stories. The most common theme throughout is that of young girls and women in the rural south trying to make sense of the world around them. It builds a picture of the multitude of social and emotional challenges women face and the many ways they learn how to rise above them. Each story is deeply tied to place, the South, and the collection spans topics of mental illness, ambition, death and hope.

Krista Creel received her undergraduate degree in creative writing from the University of Memphis and her graduate degree in journalism. She has had short stories and poems published by the Universities of Pennsylvania, Chicago, Johnson & Wales, South Arkansas and Memphis, as well as other independent literary magazines. She lives in rural West Tennessee with her family.

CINDERBLOCK HOUSES

By Krista Creel

Paperback: 190 pages

Publisher: Adelaide Books (January 2018)

Language: English

ISBN-10: 0-9996451-4-5

ISBN-13: 978-0-9996451-4-7

Product Dimensions: 6 x 0.8 x 9 inches

"Dr. Dean had a spectacular view of Mount Monadnock, and he milked his cows late in the morning, and late at night, and after his body was found stuffed down a well, it was thought he had information about the lights that someone didn't want him to share with The Department of Justice. People saw lights from the mountain beginning in the summer of 1916, and it was feared there were German spies signaling boats in the ocean sixty miles away about troop movements from Fort Devens. The Department of Justice sent agents to Peter-borough, NH in April of 1918 to investigate the lights under The Espionage Act of 1917. On the morning of August 14, 1918 Dr. Dean's body was found in a well at the same time his good friend showed up with a black eye."

Jack Coey lives in Keene, NH.

THE DEATH OF DR. DEAN

By Jack Coey

Paperback: 160 pages

Publisher: Adelaide Books (January 2018)

Language: English

ISBN-10: 0-9996451-5-3

ISBN-13: 978-0-9996451-5-4

Product Dimensions: 6 x 0.8 x 9 inches

ACEITAMOS SUBMISSÓES
Convite a todos os autores independentes: Vamos tornar esta revista um sucesso!

Looking for contributors and guest editors.

A Adelaide Magazine é uma publicação internacional independente publicada trimestralmente em inglês e português, de momento, à procura de submissões.

We are accepting fiction, nonfiction, poetry, book reviews, interviews, event announcements, artwork and photography.

Pretendemos publicar ficção, não-ficção e poesia excepcionais assim como promover os escritores que publicamos, ajudando os autores novos e emergentes a atingir uma audiência literária mais vasta. Na Adelaide Magazine, os autores podem promover o seu livro de modo grátis, listando o seu livro na página dedicada a Novos Títulos, submeter uma entrevista e uma crítica literária, e ainda oferecer os seus serviços de escrita, edição, design e tradução assim como outros serviços na área da edição, gratuitamente, na secção de Anúncios Classificados.

Check our submission guidelines at:

http://adelaidemagazine.org/submit.html

Esta é uma revista literária de autores independentes para autores independentes! Seja parte do nosso sucesso! Seja um dos editores convidados desta edição!

In our magazine you can promote your book for free, list your book on the new titles page, submit an interview or book review, and place an ad for free on our classifieds page, offering your writing, editing, design, translation, or other publishing services. You can be a guest editor for the issue!

Check out our website and don't be shy to send us your work. This is a literary magazine by indie authors for indie authors!

http://adelaidemagazine.org

www.ingramcontent.com/pod-product-compliance
Lightning Source LLC
Chambersburg PA
CBHW080719020726
47502CB00009B/2471

* 9 7 8 0 9 9 9 9 6 4 5 1 6 1 *